[
BLACK
EXPRESSION
]

BLACK EXPRESSION

Essays by and About Black Americans
in the Creative Arts

Edited by

ADDISON GAYLE, JR.

City College of the University

of New York

Weybright and Talley • New York

"Negro Folk Expression" by Sterling A. Brown. Copyright © 1950 by *Phylon*. Reprinted by permission of the editor.

"American Negro Folklore" by J. Mason Brewer. Copyright © 1945 by *Phylon*. Reprinted by permission of the editor.

Introduction to *The Book of Negro Folklore*. Reprinted by permission of Dodd, Mead, and Co., Inc., from *The Book of Negro Folklore* by Langston Hughes and Arna Bontemps. Copyright © 1958 by Langston Hughes and Arna Bontemps.

"Of the Sorrow Songs" reprinted from *The Souls of Black Folk* by W. E. B. DuBois, by permission of Fawcett Publications, Inc.

"The Forerunners" from *To Make A Poet Black* by J. Saunders Redding. Copyright © 1939 by The University of North Carolina Press. Reprinted by permission of the author.

"Negro Poets, Then and Now" by Arna Bontemps. Copyright © 1950 by *Phylon*. Reprinted by permission of the editor.

"New Poets" by Margaret Walker. Copyright © 1950 by *Phylon*. Reprinted by permission of the editor.

"The Future of Negro Poetry: A Challenge for Critics" by James A. Emanuel. Copyright © 1969 by James A. Emanuel.

"Who Speaks Negro?" by Sarah Webster Fabio. Copyright © 1966 by *Negro Digest*. Reprinted by permission.

"The So-called Western Avant-garde Drama" by Ed Bullins. Copyright © 1967 by *Liberator*. Reprinted by permission.

Five essays were written expressly for BLACK EXPRESSION. They are: "The Future of Negro Poetry: A Challenge for Critics," by James A. Emanuel; "Black Poetry," by Dudley Randall; "Black Theater," by Toni Cade; "Ralph Ellison: A Critical Study," by Barbara Christian; and "The Man Who Cried I Am: A Critique," by David Henderson.

[*Preface*]

ALTHOUGH THE NEGRO novelist has made a breakthrough of sorts into the long barricaded halls of the universities, the Negro critic remains outside, much like Shelley's nightingale, singing to cheer his own sweet solitude. As writers of fiction, Richard Wright, James Baldwin, and Ralph Ellison are studied in more college classrooms today than any Negro writers heretofore; and yet, each of them has written competent criticism—a fact unknown to those who appreciate their creative efforts.

If, then, Wright, Baldwin, and Ellison are neglected as critics, the censure is much more severe in the case of such competent, professional critics as Alain Locke, Stanley Braithwaite, and Saunders Redding, to name but a few. Not only have these critics contributed to the understanding of Negro literature, but they have also contributed those ideas without which, to paraphrase Matthew Arnold, no creative epoch is possible. Yet, in the America of today, renowned, as one critic has remarked, for its great criticism, Negro critics have died the death of public and academic anonymity.

One may advance several reasons for the academic neglect of the Negro critic, yet three stand out with more prominence than the others. First and foremost is the incontestable fact that Negro literature has never been considered an integral part of American literature. Second, and an outgrowth of the first, is the consensus among Americans, black and white, that whites are more capable of rendering objective, unbiased opinions about Negro literature than Negroes. (This idea pertains to every facet of Negro life. Books and magazine articles abound with self-appointed experts on the

Negro—the majority of such experts being white.) And third, the persistence of the myth, in colleges and universities, that Negro critics lack the sensitivity and perception necessary for literary criticism.

In 1940 Richard Wright's *Native Son* was hailed as "A great American Novel." In 1952 Ralph Ellison was awarded the National Book Award for *Invisible Man*. Gwendolyn Brooks won the coveted Pulitzer Prize for Poetry in 1950, and in 1956 James Baldwin was hailed as the "greatest American essayist since Ralph Waldo Emerson." Despite these accomplishments, however, Negro literature remains an unwanted and unacknowledged appendage to the vast body of American literature.

In part, this results from the effective use of the term "protest literature" which is bestowed upon any work by a Negro author. It is as if white critics were capable, en masse, of undergoing the experiences of a John Howard Griffin, of viewing the Negro world from within, thereby drawing the conclusion that anyone relegated to permanence in such a world cannot help but scream, yell, and shout.

However true this may be, in much of Negro literature, the shout of racial protest is missing. In much of the poetry written by Phillis Wheatley during slavery, under conditions which necessitated protest, neither shout, yell, nor scream was heard. And in many contemporary Negro novels, the search for racial protest is unrewarded. Where is Baldwin's protest against the racial situation to be found, for example, in *Giovanni's Room?* Or in Willard Motley's *Knock On Any Door*, or *We Fished All Night?* Or in the novels of Frank Yerby, novels made conspicuous by their total neglect of Negro life experiences? Evidence of such protest is hard to come by; for to argue that the condition under which the Negro lives mandates a literature of protest is one thing; to argue that the Negro author will obey such dictates is another.

However, the most important reason for the inferior status of Negro literature stems from the social mores deeply imbedded in the American psyche. A nation incapable of recognizing Negroes as other than inferior beings—hewers of wood and drawers of water—has been unable to transcend the myths used to buttress the arguments of slaveholders and modern-day segregationists. Even so gifted a writer and liberal thinker as Norman Mailer can today be found parroting the most popular of such myths: ". . . the Negro . . . could rarely afford the sophisticated inhibitions of civilization, and so he kept for his survival, the art of the

primitive . . . he subsisted for his Saturday night kicks, relinquish-
ing the pleasures of the mind for the more obligatory pleasures of
the body."

Such concepts have led to certain corollaries: Negroes are
unlikely to produce important literature, or to undergo the kinds
of experiences, universal in character, which form the basis of
competent literature. For if one views the Negro through the sociological microscope, his inferiority mandates that his progeny
too will be inferior. The old myths, therefore, remain. Black is
inferior, of a poorer quality than white; black people as a result
are different beings, existing in narrow worlds, enclosed by petty
experiences—experiences unrelated to the national character.

Viewed in the light of such deeply ingrained concepts, Negro
literature is simplistic, immature, and unimportant. A distinguished
editor of numerous anthologies remarked caustically, when asked
why no Negro writers were represented in his latest work: "I never
thought about it." Neither, it seems, have other anthologists, for
anthologies today are noticeable by their omission of selections by
Negro writers. Well might Robert Bone lament: "For it is a fact
that Negro poets are virtually unknown among the teachers of
American literature. Their poems appear but rarely in the textbooks and the anthologies; and their voices are seldom heard in
the high schools or the college classrooms."

An outgrowth of the concept of the inferiority of Negro literature is the widely held belief that Negroes are incapable of objectively criticizing efforts by other Negroes. Such a task, therefore,
can best be performed by whites. Thus a major publishing company, seeking an editor for a collection of Negro writings, settled
upon a white man who had little or no previous literary experience.
Again, the most publicized study of Negro literature remains
Robert Bone's *The Negro Novel in America,* whereas Saunders
Redding's equally perceptive *To Make a Poet Black* and Hugh
Gloster's *Negro Voices In American Fiction* have long been out of
print, with no new editions in sight.

But Negro critics have seldom been partial to their brother
writers. Indeed, some of their polemics are reminiscent of the days
of John Dryden and Thomas Shadwell, of Alexander Pope and
Lewis Theobold. For example: neither Baldwin nor Ellison has
been reticent in attacking *Native Son.* John Killen's attacks on
Invisible Man have been vehement, and no more scathing an attack
has been made on any literary work than that by Saunders Redding
on *Another Country.* Far, then, from being partial, Negro critics

have assaulted the works of other Negroes with a vengeance that makes Samuel Johnson's critique of the works of Thomas Gray judicious by comparison.

However, the oft-stated argument that Negroes lack the sensitivity and perception indispensable to the critical appraisal of literature is of far more import than the preceding ones, if for no other reason than that such arguments are vigorously set forth by members of the academic community. In an article, "American Negro Poetry: On the Stage and in the Schools," critic Robert Bone is the Danton of the literary establishment. Bone writes of two Negro critics, Pearl Thomas and Carolyn Reese: Miss Thomas ". . . is . . . a birthright critic, miraculously schooled in Negro literature by virtue of her race alone." And Miss Reese ". . . cannot deal with Negro poetry because at bottom, she has failed to acquire the necessary skills."

Bone's argument is that these critics approach literature from a sensitive and perceptive vantage point, sharpened primarily by their racial experiences, which to Bone are inadequate. What is demanded is a knowledge of the critical tools sanctioned by the academic establishment. Writes Bone: "For the poet . . . teaches us to recognize our murderous and self-destructive feelings and to master them through form." Ralph Ellison has said something of the same: "Since fiction is always a collaboration between writer and reader . . . if a moral or perception is needed, let them [the readers] supply their own. For me, of course, the narrative is the meaning."

Through form, through the aesthetic presentation of the work of art, the writer communicates with the reader, allowing the latter to share aesthetically the varied nuances of the writer's experience. Form thus becomes a *deus ex machina*, a mechanical construction leading to "a heightened appreciation and awareness of life." Another way of stating the same argument is that form is the most important element in a literary work, while content is only ancillary, a necessary appendage, yet useless as a monitor or approximator of life. Literature is, then, reduced to mere artifact, timeless symbols of enduring beauty, much like the artifacts of Yeats' "Byzantium," appealing to man's natural propensity for beauty, and thus, to paraphrase John Keats, truth. In the final analysis, art is a luxury, the sole prerogative of the aristocracy—a new aristocracy, born of the academies—to be judged and evaluated upon those canons established by the aristocracy whose needs it serves.

The Misses Thomas and Reese, like Negro critics in the main—
and there are exceptions—begin from an entirely different concept
of the function of Negro literature. They are one with critics from
Aristotle to Tolstoy who have demanded that literature, above all
else, be moral; and with Samuel Johnson, they would argue that
the academic critics "seem to think we are placed here to watch
the growth of the planets, or the motion of the stars . . . what we
[have] to learn [is] to do good and avoid evil."

This emphasis upon a moral literature may appear medieval
to many in the context of the amoral atmosphere of the twentieth
century. For the Negro, however, and for the Negro writer, the
emphasis upon morality, a clamor for men to do justice and avoid
evil, has been the hallmark of his struggle in America, and his
most fervent pleas to his country have been couched in moral
terms. None of America's minorities believes more in the American
creed; none has staked more upon the Constitution; none has de-
pended more upon man's natural instincts for justice and tolerance;
and none has shouted with more patience, with more passion, with
more eloquence—white man, listen! The Negro has been concerned
with the problem of life, in a physical and moral sense, in a society in which Negro life has been the most expendable commodity.
Such a concern is a moral one, for "the question how to live is
itself a moral idea."

In this context, the Negro critic approaches the work of art
from a moral perspective, believing with Matthew Arnold that "It
is important to hold fast to this; that poetry is at bottom a criticism
of life; that the greatness of a poet lies in his powerful and beautiful application of ideas to life—to the question: How to live."

This is not to imply that the Negro critic eschews aesthetics.
All realize, of course, that aesthetics are a necessary requirement
of art. Most are opposed to the naive, unmeaningful, critical formu-
las vouchsafed by the academic community. Criticism which at-
taches importance to the investigation of the contortions of lines,
the hidden meanings of punctuation marks, the ambidextrous usage
of words may be of value to the "New Aristocracy," yet completely
worthless to men and women seeking an affirmation of life in positive terms.

Again, criticism based upon the search for metaphysical
themes: Who am I? What is my identity? What is my relationship
to the universe, to God, to the existential other? is of no value to
a Negro community daily confronted by the horrors of the urban
ghetto, the threat to sanity and life in the rural areas of the South,

and the continual hostility of the overwhelming majority of its fellow citizens.

Though convinced of the importance of aesthetics—a point which has never been seriously contested—Negro critics are wary of theories applicable only to a nonexistent golden age. Believing with Robert Lehan that "the writer is the last remaining hope for the modern world . . . ," the Negro critic has demanded that the writer concentrate on life, that life, despairing, laughing, hoping, and dying, in the ghettoes of this country. To be sure, the Negro critic has used his Negroness as a vantage point, a point which enables him, unless he has been quite lucky indeed, to view the American scene from a moral perspective. In so doing, his insights and perceptions have been sharpened to deal morally with that material which is, or which should be, the preoccupation of the Negro writer. And what Gwendolyn Brooks said with regard to the Negro poet is applicable to the Negro critic: "Every poet has some-thing to say. Simply because he is a Negro, he cannot escape hav-ing something important to say."

Here, too, Robert Bone's statement is applicable: "By virtue of his deeper insight, he, the Negro writer, can exorcise the demons that threaten his people from within." But it is equally true that he can exorcise those demons which, today, rend the American society. For the Negro writer is America's conscience; and the Negro critic must be the conscience of them both.

This role of the Negro critic as moral adjudicator has never been more necessary than at present. And no period of Negro literature has demanded that the Negro critic exercise his critical sensitivity and perception for more moral reasons. For today, a dialogue persists in the community of Negro writers which threatens the moral foundation upon which Negro literature has, in the main, been predicated.

Alain Locke planted the seeds of the dialogue in 1925 in his introduction to *The New Negro*. Wrote Professor Locke: ". . . it is the Negro problem rather than the Negro that is known and mooted in the general mind. We turn therefore . . . to the elements of truest social portraiture, and discover in the artistic self ex-pression of the Negro today a new figure on the national canvas. . . . In these pages . . . we have . . . commented upon self expression and the forces of determination. So far as he is culturally articu-late, we shall let the Negro speak for himself."

The idea that the Negro should speak for himself was not new. Though much of early Negro literature was marred by propaganda, still Frederick Douglass, W. E. B. DuBois, James Weldon Johnson, and Langston Hughes spoke from that deep wellspring of Negro experience which represented the extent of Negro culture of that time. What was new, however, was Locke's insistence that the time had come for Negro writers to turn from moralizing, from attempts to force their just cause upon the conscience of the nation. Because attempts to make white men listen had aborted, the New Negro was admonished to forego such attempts and to turn inward to self expression.

To do so, however, called for a new kind of literature, and a new Negro to write that literature. Albert Barnes characterized both the literature and its creator: "The later Negro has made us feel the majesty of nature, the ineffable peace of the wood and the great open spaces. He has shown us that the event of our everyday American life contains for him a poetry, rhythm, and charm which we ourselves had never discovered. . . . His insights into realities have been given to us in vivid images loaded with poignancy and passion. His message has been lyrical, rhythmic, colorful. In short, the elements of beauty, he has controlled to the ends of art." And perhaps Stanley Braithwaite stated the argument more succinctly: "Negro poetic expression hovers for the moment, pardonably perhaps, over the race question, but its highest allegiance is to poetry. . . ."

This philosophy has been stated anew by Negro writers today. Ralph Ellison has written: "If *Invisible Man* is 'free from the ideological penalties suffered by Negroes in this country' it is because I tried to the best of my ability to transform these elements into art." And, demands Ellison, "I can only ask that my fiction be judged as art; if it fails, it fails aesthetically." James Baldwin, theoretically at least, was certain of the saving grace of art: For the only concern of the artist was "to recreate out of the disorder of life that order which is art."

Not until 1940 were these arguments, first set forth by the proponents of the Negro Renaissance, effectively challenged. The challenge came from Mississippi-born Richard Wright who, as artist and critic, transformed a monologue into a dialogue by presenting, dramatically, forcefully, and persuasively, the other argument. Wright argued, in essence, that conditions in America had not changed to the degree that the Negro could desert the race question, engage in an art for art's sake endeavor, or wander free in the sunny utopia of abstraction in an attempt to desert the harsh reality of being black in the twentieth century. "The grind-

ing process of history," wrote Wright in 1945, "had forged iron in
the Negro's heart [and therefore] we heard a new and strange cry
from another Negro." And this cry came from the pen of Claude
McKay, the *enfant terrible* of the Negro Renaissance, in bitter,
vehement protest, in the militant poem, "If We Must Die."

Though certainly not antagonistic to artistic principles, Wright
realized that an era of oppression was not one in which "art could
be the only consideration." Negroes capable of ignoring the brutal,
inhuman treatment of other Negroes were, according to Wright,
Negroes "who recorded the feelings of a Negro reacting not as a
Negro."

So central a part does this thesis play in Wright's critical
theory that he returns to it in 1956: ". . . the fact of seperation
from his native land has now sunk home into the Negro's heart;
the Negro loves his land, but that land rejects him. . . . Here we
can witness the emergence of a new type of Personality." That
personality was George Moses Horton who: ". . . was an emotionally trapped man; he lived in a culture of which he was not really
a part; he was a split man believing and feeling something which
he could not live; . . . Horton's cry for freedom was destined to
become the lament, was to roll down the decades swelling, augmenting itself, becoming a vast reservoir of bitterness and infrequent hope."

But Richard Wright died in 1960, and no other Negro writer
of his stature has arisen to enjoin the dialogue, presented today by
the new proponents of a Negro Renaissance. The New Negroes of
the 1960's apropos of their namesakes of the 1930's have, according to Herbert Hill, ". . . made the creative act their first consideration. . . . As the Negro writer moves beyond anger, he develops a
new concern for the writer's craft, for literary discipline and control and seeks an involvement in the larger world of art and
ideology."

The Negro critic remains, then, to present the other argument.
He must, like Richard Wright, take an active part in the dialogue,
not as a Lycurgus dispensing arbitrary laws and rules, nor as a
Polonius brandishing answers and solutions, but instead as an engaged participant, fully respectful of both sides of the dialogue.
His criticism must be guided by a temperament which allows him
to explicate the work of art in terms of its contribution to the
alleviation of those problems which have confronted humanity for
too long a time. This entails a sensitive and perceptive awareness
which can only, in part, be conditioned by the academic establish-

ment. Robert Bone's cry of despair, therefore: "But you really must know Ezra Pound, Hart Crane, and Charles Olson if you hope to understand Melvin Tolson, Robert Hayden, and LeRoi Jones," is presumptuous; for the understanding of such poets depends equally upon a critical perspective conditioned by the many-faceted experiences of the Negro in the turbulent American society.

On this point, the Negro critic and the university will remain at odds. If the day ever arrives when Negro literature is accepted as an integral part of American literature, the Negro critic will still remain invisible. For his is the predominant voice in American criticism which calls upon the Negro writer to dedicate himself to the proposition that literature is a moral force for change as well as an aesthetic creation. In so doing, he risks not only continued invisibility, but denigrating charges that he does not know enough, coupled with insistent attacks upon his credentials as a critic.

This cannot be helped. Though the moral argument has little relevance in America at present, still the Negro critic must demand that the Negro writer articulate the grievances of the Negro in moral terms; for the time is far distant when the Negro writer can cry out in sweet delirium with John Keats:

> *Away! Away! for I will fly to thee*
> *Not charioted by Bacchus and his pards*
> *But on the viewless wings of Poesy. . . .*

Addison Gayle, Jr.

[*Contents*]

Preface   vii

ON FOLK CULTURE:
Negro Folk Expression, Sterling A. Brown   3
American Negro Folk Literature, Arthur Huff Fauset   14
American Negro Folklore, J. Mason Brewer   19
Introduction to The Book of Negro Folklore, Arna Bontemps   29
Of the Sorrow Songs, W. E. B. DuBois   37
The Negro Spirituals, Alain Locke   47

ON POETRY:
The Forerunners, J. Saunders Redding   59
Negro Poets and Their Poetry, Wallace Thurman   70
Negro Poets, Then and Now, Arna Bontemps   82
New Poets, Margaret Walker   89
The Future of Negro Poetry: A Challenge for Critics,
    James A. Emanuel   100
Black Poetry, Dudley Randall   109
Who Speaks Negro?, Sarah Webster Fabio   115

ON DRAMA:
The Drama of Negro Life, Alain Locke   123
The Drama of Negro Life, Montgomery Gregory   128
Black Theater, Toni Cade   134
The So-called Western Avant-garde Drama, Ed Bullins   143

Towards Our Theater: A Definitive Act,
    K. William Kgositsile   146
The Negro Theatre and the Harlem Community,
    Loften Mitchell   148
The Gift of Laughter, Jessie Fauset   159

ON FICTION:
The Negro in American Literature,
    William Stanley Braithwaite   169
The Negro in American Fiction, Benjamin Griffin Brawley   182
The Myth of a "Negro Literature," LeRoi Jones   190
The Literature of the Negro in the United States,
    Richard Wright   198
American Negro Literature, J. Saunders Redding   229
The Literature of Harlem, Ernest Kaiser   239
Race and the Negro Writer, Hugh M. Gloster   255
The Negro Artist and the Racial Mountain, Langston Hughes   258
Towards a Black Aesthetic, Hoyt W. Fuller   263
Into the Mainstream and Oblivion, Julian Mayfield   271
A Blueprint for Negro Authors, Nick Aaron Ford   276
Perhaps Not So Soon One Morning, Addison Gayle, Jr.   280
The Negro Writer: Pitfalls and Compensations,
    William Gardner Smith   288
The Dark and Haunted Tower of Richard Wright,
    Nathan A. Scott, Jr.   296
Richard Wright's Blues, Ralph Ellison   311
Many Thousands Gone, James Baldwin   325
Notes on a Native Son, Eldridge Cleaver   339
The Alienation of James Baldwin, John Henrik Clarke   350
Ralph Ellison: A Critical Study, Barbara Christian   353
The Man Who Cried I Am: A Critique, David Henderson   365

Suggested Readings   373
Index   381
About the Author   395

For my mother

"*Literature is of great value to any people as a preserver of manners and customs—religious, political and social. It
is a record of growth and development
from generation to generation. No one
will do this for us; we must ourselves
develop the men and women who will
faithfully portray the inmost thoughts
and feelings of the Negro with all the
fire and romance which lie dormant in
our history. . . .*"

PAULINE E. HOPKINS

$$\begin{bmatrix} \text{ON FOLK} \\ \text{CULTURE} \end{bmatrix}$$

STERLING A. BROWN
Negro Folk Expression *

FOR A LONG time Uncle Remus and his Brer Rabbit tales stood for
the Negro folk and their lore. One thing made clear by the resurrection of Uncle Remus in Walt Disney's *Song of the South* is the
degree to which he belonged to white people rather than to the
Negro folk. A striking contrast to the favored house servant is such
a folk character as Huddie Ledbetter, better known as Leadbelly,
whose knowingness is stark rather than soft, and whose audience
(certainly in his formative years) was his own kind of people, not
the white quality. The bitter brew that Leadbelly concocted in the
levee camps and jooks and prisons differs from the sugary potions
that Remus and the other "uncles" dispensed. Both Uncle Remus
and Leadbelly portray sides of the Negro folk, but to round out the
portraiture Bessie Smith, Josh White, the Gospel Singing Two Keys,
and such big old liars as those heard by E. C. L. Adams in the
Congaree swamps and by Zora Neale Hurston in Central Florida
are also needed. In any consideration of American Negro folk expression it is important to realize that even before Joel Chandler
Harris revealed the antics of Brer Rabbit to America, John Henry
was swinging his hammer in the Big Bend Tunnel on the C. & O.
Road.

There is rich material on hand for a revaluation of the Negro
folk. Out of penitentiaries in the deep South, John and Alan Lomax
have brought the musical memories of singers with such names as
Iron Head, Clear Rock, and Lightning. From what is more truly
folk culture these men and others like John Hammond, Willis

* This is the first section of Mr. Brown's essay on Negro lore. The concluding
portion will appear in a forthcoming issue of *Phylon*.

James, and John Work have brought hidden singers and songs. The
Library of Congress Archives of Folk Music are crammed with
solid stuff; the large recording companies are following the lead of
small companies like Disc, Folkways and Circle in issuing albums of
Negro folk music. Ten years after her tragic death in the Delta,
Bessie Smith has been honored in a Town Hall Concert (even now I
can hear her surprised cry: "Lord, Lord, Lord!"). And in Carnegie
Hall Big Bill has sung blues from the sharecropping country, and
Josh White has sung both mellow-blues and sardonic mockery, and
Blind Sonny Terry has blown on his wild harmonica the joys of the
fox hunt, of a high-balling train, and the wailing fear of a lost
wanderer in a southern swamp. Folk singers of the spirituals, unknown yesterday, have their names placarded now; Harlemites pass
around the name of Mahalia Jackson as they used to do that of
Mamie Smith; and in the Harlem dance-halls where jazz bands
"cut" each other on Saturday nights, spiritual singers battle each
other on Sundays to cheering crowds. This commercializing will
affect the genuineness of the stuff, but it is getting a hearing for folk
material. And an audience for the authentic is growing.

All of this is part of the generally awakened interest in American folk culture, indicated by the diligence and popularity of collectors, anthologists, musicologists, and interpreters. Before its demise
the WPA Federal Projects laid in a fine backlog of American folk-
stuff and World War II, of course, quickened interest in the American past. Though the furore may have something of the faddish
about it, American folklore stands to gain more from enthusiasm
and careful study than from the earlier disdain and neglect. The
Negro creators of an important segment of American folklore
should no longer be subjected to the condescension of the "oh so
quaint," "so folksy," school. Looking on Negro lore as exotic *curi-
osa* becomes almost impossible if the body of available material is
thoughtfully considered. Outmoded now are those collectors who
could or would find only ingratiating aunties and uncles, most of
whose lore consisted in telling how good their white folks were.

With the discarding of the old simplifications, the study of the
Negro folk becomes complicated. The field of folklore in general is
known to be a battle area, and the Negro front is one of the hottest
sectors. One sharply contested point is the problem of definition of
the folk; another that of origins. Allies are known to have fallen out
and skirmished behind the lines over such minor matters as identifying John Hardy with John Henry. But this is not a battle piece. In
general the vexed problems of origin are left for others, more com-

petent in that area; strict delimitation of the concepts "folk," "folk literature" and "folk music" are not the purpose here. This essay aims instead to tell what the "folk Negro" (as most students understand the term) * has expressed in story and proverb and song. It is well known that folk culture among Negroes is breaking up. Some of the material (in discussing the blues, for instance) has been transplanted in the cities, but, though inexactly folk, it is used because its roots drew first sustenance from the folk culture.

Folk tales and aphorisms

Collectors, both scholarly and amateur, have long paid tribute to the richness of Negro folk expression. Enthusiasts like Roark Bradford and Zora Hurston overpraise Negro folk speech at the expense of the speech of white Americans. According to Bradford, "The most ignorant Negro can get more said with a half-dozen words than the average United States Senator can say in a two-hour speech." † But folk should be compared with folk; and considering the speech of white America to be barren and bleak does injustice to a large part of American folklore, to the gusto of the tall tale, for instance. The folk Negro's imaginativeness and pith can easily be recognized; they stand in no need of dubious comparisons.

In Africa the telling of tales is a time honored custom. The slaves brought the custom with them to the New World. According to the latest scholarship of Melville Herskovits, the body of tales they brought has been retained in relatively undisturbed fashion.‡ These tales were not dangerous; they were a way to ease the time; they could entertain the master class, especially the children. So they were not weeded out as were many of the practices of sorcery, or discouraged as were the tribal languages. In the African cycles the heroes were the jackal or fox, the hare, the tortoise, and the spider. The last, a sort of hairy tarantula, is little used in the lore of the southern Negro, but is hero of the Anansi tales of Jamaica. The African fox, more like our jackal, has become the American fox; the African hare, "Cunnie Rabbit," really a chevrotain, water deer-

---

* That is, as a rural people, living in a kind of isolation, without easy contact with the outside world. Sometimes they are cut off from progress geographically (especially the sea-islanders or swamp dwellers or the people on back-county plantations). But even rural Negroes with better communication and transportation facilities are socially isolated by segregation and lack of educational and economic advantages. Unlettered, folk Negroes have a local culture transmitted orally rather than by the printed page.

† Roark Bradford, *Ol' Man Adam an' His Chillun* (New York, 1928), p. xiv.

‡ Melville Herskovits, *The Myth of the Negro Past* (New York, 1941), p. 275.

let, or gazelle, has become the American rabbit with the word cunnie Englished into cunning, and the African tortoise has become the
American dry-land turtle or terrapin. In America, Brer Terrapin is
a hero second only to Brer Rabbit whom he bests occasionally. Of
the hero's victims the African hyena has become the American wolf,
and the American fox and bear have joined the losing side. African
animals—lions, leopards, tigers, and monkeys—are still in the cast
of characters.

Close parallels to American Negro tales have been found extensively in Africa and the Caribbeans. Nevertheless, folklorists are
wary of finding Africa the place of ultimate origin of all of the tales.
Many of the basic plots are of great age and spread. Oddly enough,
the three stories that Joel Chandler Harris considered unquestionably African, namely: "How the Rabbit Makes a Riding-horse of
the Fox," "Why the Alligator's Back Is Rough," and "The Tar
Baby Story," have close European counterparts, dating back
hundreds of years. "The Tar Baby Story" has been traced to India
through a study of nearly three hundred versions. According to
Stith Thompson, it reached the Negroes and Indians of America
by several paths, the main one being "from India to Africa, where it
is a favorite and where it received some characteristic modifications
before being taken by slaves to America." * In the Congo version a
jackal is stuck to a tortoise covered with beeswax; among the
Pueblo Indians a coyote catches a rabbit with a gum-covered
wooden image.

To indicate the problems facing source-hunters, one of the most
popular European stories might be considered here. In the Reynard
cycle, and reappearing in Grimm's *Fairy Tales*, is the plot of the fox
who played godfather in order to sneak away and eat food that he
and the bear have stored in common. Asked the name of his god-
children (for he leaves three times) he answers Well Begun, Half
Done and Done. Several collectors found the story in South Carolina, with Brer Rabbit cheating Brer Wolf, and the children variously named: "Fus' Beginnin'," "Half-Way" and "Scrapin' de
Bottom," or "Buh Start-um," "Buh Half-um" and "Buh Done-Um."
Easy attribution to American slaveowners, however, comes up sharp
against the numerous African versions in one of which the rabbit
fools his working partner, the antelope, with non-existent children
named Uncompleted One, Half-completed One, and Completed One.

All of this illustrates the underlying unity of Old World cul-

* Stith Thompson, *The Folk Tale* (New York, 1947), pp. 225 ff.

ture. Africa, then, is not the starting place of all the favorite Negro
tales, but was a way-station where they had an extended stop-over.
The long association with Asiatic Moslems in East Africa and the
penetration of European powers into West Africa beginning with
the slave trade affected the native tradition of tale telling. According
to Stith Thompson, "The African finds enjoyment in nearly every
kind of European folktale. He may do some queer things with them
and change them around so that little more than a skeleton of the
original remains and so that it takes the expert eye to discover that
they are not actually native. On the other hand he may take the tale
over completely with all its foreign trappings." Nevertheless
Thompson believes that "the great majority of their [African] tales
have certainly had their origin on the soil of central or southern
Africa." * Regardless of original source, whether in Europe or Africa, American Negro fables have been so modified with new beasts
and local color added, different themes, and different experiences,
that an almost new, certainly a quite different thing results. Such is
the way of written literature where authors took "their own where
they found it," and such is even more the way of folktales.

"Den Br' Hoss, an' Br' Jack-ass, an' Br' Cow an' all dem,
crowd close roun' Br' Dog, for dem was like yard-chillen, dey is
peaceable an' sort o' scary. An' all de creeters what stan' up for Br'
Gator scatter out wide away from dere, for dem was woods-chillen,
rovin' an' wild." † Thus, according to a South Carolina tale, started
the big row in the world between the tame and the wild creatures
that is never going to stop.

This illustrates the process. The basic incident, the war between
domestic and wild animals, is widely used in folktales, from the
Orient to the Reynard cycle. But the details, the "entrimmins,"
according to Uncle Remus, the phrases "yard chillen," and "woods
chillen," and the naming of their traits, give the flavor of the low
country, where Samuel Stoney and Gertrude Shelby heard the above
yarn.

Public recognition of the wealth of American Negro stories
came in the late eighties with the appearance of Joel Chandler
Harris's Uncle Remus Tales. A few animal tales had seen print
earlier, but Harris was the first to give a substantial number. Soon
he was besieged with correspondents who told him new tales or
variants that they had heard from Negroes. Harris deserves the

* *Ibid.*, pp. 284–286.
† Samuel Gaillard Stoney and Gertrude Mathews Shelby, *Black Genesis* (New
York, 1930), p. 21.

credit of a pioneer. He insisted that he gave the tales "uncooked," but there is too much evidence of his alterations to accept his word. The tales are not genuine folktales, in the sense of by the folk for the folk, for they are told by an old Uncle to entertain Young Marster. In line with literary trends of the time, Harris made them more sentimental and genteel and less racy than the folk tell them; he gives much about Negro life and character, valuable for purposes of local color but likely to be taken for granted by the folk; and he uses the devices of a skillful short story writer. Simpler and starker tales, with fewer alterations, have been taken from their native habitat by collectors such as C. C. Jones, Jr. (a contemporary of Harris), Ambrose Gonzales, Elsie Clews Parsons, Guy Johnson, and A. W. Eddins. Negro collectors are few and far between; Charles W. Chesnutt fashioned skillful short stories out of folk beliefs in *The Conjure Woman* (1889); and Thomas Talley, pioneer folk-collector, Arthur Huff Fauset, Zora Neale Hurston and J. Mason Brewer have published collections. Stella Brewer Brooks has written the best study of Joel Chandler Harris as folklorist. But educated Negroes by and large have not been greatly interested. From Harris's day to the present, collectors, being of different race or class or both, have been viewed by the folk with natural distrust.

Nevertheless, a considerable number of tales has been recorded. Many are animal tales; of these all are not strictly fables, which convey an ostensible moral, though some are. Whereas the more efficient Fox, crafty and cruel, hypocritical and scheming, amused the European peasantry, the American Negro slave took Brer Rabbit for hero. The harmless scary creature he invested with a second nature, and made him a practical joker with a streak of cruelty, a daring hunter of devilment, a braggart, a pert wit, a glutton, a lady's man, a wily trickster, knowing most of the answers, and retaining of his true characteristics only his speed on the getaway. Animals noted for greater strength and ferocity are his meat. Brer Fox has degenerated from crafty Reynard into something of a fool, though still a worthy opponent, but Brer Wolf and Brer Bear are numskulls. Commentators have long considered these tales of cunning overcoming strength, of the weakling out-smarting the bully, as a compensatory mechanism, a kind of oblique revenge, the wish fulfillment of an ironic people who could see few ways out of oppression.* It might be pointed out that none of the hero-animals in

* For a very suggestive essay on this point, F. Bernard Wolfe, "Uncle Remus and the Malevolent Rabbit," in *Commentary*, July, 1949 (Vol. 8, No. 1), 31–41.

Africa are quite so helpless as the American rabbit. It is unlikely that the slaves did not see pertinence to their own experiences in these tales. Outsmarting was one of the few devices left them. So they made heroes out of the physically powerless who by good sense and quick wit overcame animals of brute strength who were not right bright. "You ain't got no cause to be bigger in de body, but you sho' is got cause to be bigger in de brain."

With his pardonable fondness for the creature, Joel Chandler Harris placed Brer Rabbit in the limelight. He is less focused on in other collections, though still the star performer. The theme of weakness overcoming strength through cunning remains uppermost. Brer Squirrel escapes from Brer Fox by reminding him to say grace; when the fox closes his eyes, the squirrel is treetop high. Brer Goat foils Brer Wolf, never trusting him from that day to this. Brer Rooster outeats Brer Elephant: "it ain't de man wid de bigges' belly what kin eat de longest." Animals and birds of everyday observation swell the company: the officious yard dog, the fierce bulldog, the hound, another fall-guy for the rabbit; the horse, the mule, the jackass, the bull, the stupid ox; the deer, the raccoon, possum and squirrel; the frog, the crawfish, and many kinds of snakes; the turkey buzzard, the partridge, the blue-jay, the marsh-hen; the mosquito, the hornet, the gnat.

Many tales drive home a point about mankind based on the animals' observed traits. The gnat, riding the bull's horn, says: "I gwine now. Ain't you glad you don't have to tote me puntop yo' horn no more?" The bull answers: "I never know when you come, and I ain't gonna miss you when you gone." The possum tells the raccoon that he can't fight because he is ticklish and has to laugh when in the clutch of his enemy, but the raccoon sees through the rationalization. With his belly full, running in the pasture, Brer Mule dreams that his father was a race-horse, but harnessed to a heavy cart and hungry, he recalls that his father was only a jackass. The ox rebukes the axle wheels for groaning; *he* is the one pulling the load, though he refuses to cry out. "Some men holler if briar scratch his foot, and some men lock their jaws if a knife is sticking in their heart." *

Ingenious explanations of animal characteristics and behavior occur in many tales. You never see a blue-jay on Friday because that is the day for his weekly trip to hell; the woodpecker's head is

* The quoted lines in the above paragraph are taken from Ambrose E. Gonzales, *With Æsop Along the Black Border* (Columbia [South Carolina]: The State Company, 1924), *passim.*

red because Noah caught him pecking holes in the ark and whipped
his head with a hammer; the possum's tail is bare because, wanting
music on the ark, Ham used the hairs to string a banjo; the alligator's mouth is all out of whack because the dog, God's apprentice
helper, was either careless or cruel while wielding the knife in the
week of creation, making the alligator and dog eternal foes; the
porpoise's tail is set crossways because with his tail straight up and
down the porpoise was too fast, he outsped the sun; Sis Nanny
Goat, self sacrificing, allowed all of the other animals to get their
tails first, hence, "Kind heart give Sis Nanny Goat a short tail"; the
wasp is so shortpatienced because he thinks everybody is laughing
at his tiny stomach (he can't laugh himself because he would "bust
spang in two").

Though performing other functions in the Old World, animal
tales are often considered by American Negroes as "stories for the
young uns." Animal stories were by no means the only stock, even
in slavery. More realistic tales made direct use of unallegorized
human experience. In coastal Georgia the folk still remember the
tale of the Eboes who, hating slavery, marched singing into the tidal
river and were drowned. The name of Ebo's Landing gives historic
color to the tradition. The same folk tell also of the magic hoe that
worked itself, and of the flying Africans who changed into birds and
soared away to their homeland rather than take the overseer's whipping. Modelled on tales in African folklore, in the New World they
take on the quality of dreams of escape.

More widespread in Negro folklore are the tales of the trickster
Jack or John. In slavery days he outwits not only the devil but Ole
Marster, Ole Miss, and the "patterollers." More recently his compet-
itors have been the grasping landlord, the browbeating tough, and
the highhanded sheriff, deputy, and policeman. Sometimes Jack,
like Brer Rabbit, comes to grief himself, but oftener he outsmarts
the opposition or makes his dare and is long gone. Jack schemes to
get out of a whipping or to obtain freedom. Sometimes he is in
cahoots with a sharp witted master to take advantage of gullible
neighbors. Sometimes the repartee is sharp; a master tells that he
dreamt of a heaven set aside for Negroes and found it to be run-
down and generally messed-up; Jack retorts with his dream of white
folk's heaven, all gleaming and glittering, with streets of gold, but
without a solitary person in the place! The tellers aim at comedy,
often richly satiric; the hardships of slavery are casually mentioned
as if taken for granted by teller and audience; but Ole Marster and
Ole Miss and the slaves themselves are ribbed with gusto, with

toughminded humor. Pretentiousness and boasting ride for a fall; sentimentality is pricked; all the characters, white and black, master and slave, come "under the same gourd-vine," all are "made out of meat."

A favorite object of lampooning, familiar in general folklore, was the old maid, the master's sister. One of the fanciful plots has her turning into a squinch owl, her long-drawn wails voicing her yearning for a husband, but other tales satirize her bossiness and silliness in down-to-earth situations. The Irish were also satirized. Comparative newcomers with their own brogues and dirty jobs, the Irish were characterized as big dunces. Here, of course, the American Negro shares an Anglo-Saxon tradition. The "po' buckra," the "poor white trash," the "cracker," came in for contempt and hostility in Negro tales, but the stories about them were not often funny.

Exaggeration in the hearty tradition of American tall talk is pervasive. In Zora Hurston's recording, mosquitoes sing like alligators, eat up the cow and then ring the bell for the calf. The plague of the boll-weevil is graphically symbolized: "Old Man Boll Weevil whipped little Willie Boll Weevil 'cause he couldn't carry two rows at a time." Land is so rich that the next morning after a mule is buried, "he had done sprouted li'l jackasses"; it is so poor that "it took nine partridges to holler Bob White" or needed "ten sacks of fertilizer before a church congregation could raise a tune on it." A snail is sent for a doctor. After seven years his sick wife heard a scuffling at the door and cries out her relief. The snail says, "Don't try to rush me—ah ain't gone yet." He had taken all that time to get to the door. Weather is so hot "till two cakes of ice left the icehouse and went down the streets and fainted." *

Quite common are the "why" stories; jocular explanation of the creation of the world, the position of woman, the origin of the races. One teller informed Zora Hurston: "And dats why de man makes and de woman takes. You men is still braggin' about yo' strength and de women is sitting on de keys [to kitchen, bedroom, and cradle] and lettin' you blow off 'til she git ready to put de bridle on you." But another informant explains why "de sister in black works harder than anybody else in the world. De white man tells de nigger to work and takes and tells his wife." †

Mythological tales explain the origin of the ocean, where the hurricane comes from, why the wind and waters are at war, why the

---

* The quoted lines in the above paragraph are taken from Zora Neale Hurston, *Mules and Men* (Philadelphia, 1935), *passim.*
† *Ibid., passim.*

moon's face is smutty. Others enlarge material from the Bible. Ingenuity is especially exercised on filling in gaps in the creation story.
Up in heaven a newcomer tells of the havoc of the Johnstown flood
to a bored listener who turns out to be Noah. Peter is humanized
more than the other apostles: famished, he brings a huge rock to the
Lord to turn into bread and is nonplussed when he hears the pronouncement: "And upon this rock will I found my church." Religion is treated freely, even irreverently, but not to the degree of
Roark Bradford's *Ol' Man Adam an' His Chillun,* which is synthetic, not genuine folk-stuff.

Tales about the origin of the races leave little room for chauvinism about a chosen people. The slaves knew at first hand that the
black man had a hard road to travel and they tell of the mistakes of
creation with sardonic fatalism. Uncle Remus tells how all men were
once Negroes, "en 'cordin' ter all de counts w'at I years fokes 'uz
gittin' long 'bout ez well in dem days as dey is now." One of Zora
Hurston's informants told her that "God made de world and de
white folks made work." Another said that the Negro outraced the
white man and took the larger of two bundles that God had let down
in the road. But the smaller bundle had a writing-pen and ink in it,
while the larger bundle had a pick and shovel and hoe and plow and
cop-axe in it. "So ever since then de nigger been out in de hot sun,
usin' his tools and de white man been sittin' up figgerin', ought's a
ought, figger's a figger; all for de white man, none for de nigger." *

Irony has been in the stories from the earliest recorded versions, but recent collectors have found it less veiled. Zora Hurston
retells the yarn of the dog's convention where a law was passed not
to run rabbits any more. But Brer Rabbit stayed cautious: "All de
dogs ain't been to no convention and anyhow some of dese fool dogs
ain't got no better sense than to run all over dat law and break it up.
De rabbit didn't go to school much and he didn't learn but three
letters and that trust no mistake. Run every time de bush shake." †
She tells another of the slaves who saved his master's children from
drowning. Old Master sets him free. As he walks off, old master
calls to him: "John, de children love yuh." . . . "John, I love
yuh." . . . "And Missy *like* yuh!" . . . "But 'member, John,
youse a nigger." John kept right on stepping to Canada, answering
his master "every time he called 'im, but he consumed on with his
bag."

The age-old tale of the deceptive bargain gets added point

* Zora Neale Hurston, *Mules and Men* (Philadelphia, 1935), pp. 101–102.
† *Ibid.,* p. 147.

down in the Brazos Bottom. Brer Rabbit, father of a large, hungry family, is share-cropping for Brer Bear who has him in his power. Brer Rabbit is forced to promise Brer Bear everything that grows above the ground. But that year he planted potatoes. The second year, Brer Bear settles for root crops, but Brer Rabbit planted oats. The third year, Brer Bear claimed both tops and roots, leaving Brer Rabbit only the middles. As a fine climax, Brer Rabbit planted corn. Another old tale of the goose that the fox threatened to kill for swimming on "his" lake, now ends with Sis Goose taking her just cause to court. "When dey got dere, de sheriff, he was a fox, and de judge, he was a fox, and de attorneys, dey was foxes, and all de jurymen, dey was foxes, too. An' dey tried ole sis goose, and dey convicted her and dey executed her, and dey picked her bones." *

There is similar edge in numerous jokes about sharecropping and the law. Landlords who "figure with a crooked pencil" are derided. One sharecropper held back a couple of bales from the reckoning. When told, after elaborate figuring, that he had come out even, he expressed his happiness that he could sell his extra bales. The landlord then cursed him to hell and back, telling him that he had to do all that hard figuring over again. When another share-cropper was told that his return was zero after making a bumper crop, he shut up like a clam. The landlord, distrusting his silence, insisted that he tell him what he was thinking. The sharecropper finally said: "I was just thinking, Mister Charlie, that the next time I say 'Giddap' to a mule again, he's gonna be setting on my lap." Yarnspinners weep in mimicry of the landlord who, in the early days of the New Deal, had to give government checks to his tenants, crying: "After all I've done for you, you so ungrateful that you cashed those checks."

Negroes borrow, of course, from the teeming storehouse of American jokes. Jokes about Negroes are of three types. The first includes those told by whites generally to whites (the kind collected by Irvin Cobb, for instance, and the stand-bys for after-dinner speakers, with such black face minstrelsy props as watermelon, chicken, razors, excessive fright, murder of the English language, etc.). Some of these may be found among Negroes who will belittle their own for a laugh as quickly as any other people will, but they are not the most popular. The white man's mark on a Negro joke often does not help it. A second type is told by Negroes to whites to

* A. W. Eddins, "Brazos Bottom Philosophy," *Publications of the Texas Folk Lore Society*, No. II, 1923, edited by J. Frank Dobie. Austin, Texas: Texas Folk-Lore Society, pp. 50–51.

gain a point. Sometimes verging on sarcasm, they use the license of the court fool. Then there are jokes strictly for a Negro audience, what John Dollard calls "part of the arsenal of reprisal against white people." *

Often too, the joke lays bare what the tellers consider a racial weakness and the outsider must not be let into the family secrets, as it were. Sometimes it pleads the racial cause. Jokes ridicule the myth of "separate but equal"; a Negro gets off free in traffic court by telling the judge that he saw whites drive on the green light so he knew the red light was for him. Hat-in-hand Negroes and workers too zealous on the job are satirized. During the war the jokes, or more truly anecdotes, took on a grimmer tone. One folk hero became the soldier who after being badgered on a bus, faced his tormentors and said, "Well, if I am going to die for democracy, I might as well die for some of it down here in Georgia." One repeated line concerned an epitaph: "Here lies a black man killed by a yellow man while fighting to save democracy for the white man." Many of these anecdotes are bitter; some, dealing with sadistic sheriffs and mobs, are gruesome; yet they produce laughter, a sort of laughter out of hell. But they are shared by educated as well as uneducated and though passed along by word of mouth, they take us somewhat afield from the folk.

[ARTHUR HUFF FAUSET
American Negro Folk Literature]

MOST PEOPLE are acquainted with Negro Folk Literature even if they do not recognize it as such. There are few children who have not read the Uncle Remus stories of Joel Chandler Harris, which were based upon the original folk tales of the African slaves. But the great storehouse from which they were gleaned, that treasury of folk lore which the American Negro inherited from his African forefathers, is little known. It rivals in amount as well as in quality that of any people on the face of the globe, and is not confined to stories of the Uncle Remus type, but includes a rich variety of story forms,

* John Dollard, *Caste and Class in Southern Town* (New Haven, 1937), p. 308.

legends, saga cycles, songs, proverbs and fantastic, almost mythical, material.

It simply happens that the one type of Negro story has struck the popular fancy, and becoming better known, blurred out the remaining types. For this result, we are indebted to Joel Chandler Harris, who saw the popular possibilities of the "Brer Rabbit" tales, and with his own flair for literature, adapted them with such remarkable skill and individuality that today they rank with the best known and most highly appreciated works of American literature.

Familiar as he was with his material, and with an instinct for its value—even in his day these tales were fast disappearing among "modern" colored folk—his approach was nevertheless that of the journalist and literary man rather than the folk-lorist. "Written," as has been said, "with no thought of the ethnological bearing which critics were so quick to discern in them, they established themselves at a bound as among the most winsome of folk tales." There is some possibility of their having passed out unnoticed and thus being lost to posterity if he had not done the work which drew attention to them. Yet in spite of the happy providence that produced a Harris, and although his intentions were of the best, we are forced to recognize the harm as well as the good that these stories have done. This query may come as a shock to some, but on further analysis we shall see there is reason for wondering.

In the first place, the Uncle Remus Stories, as the Harris tales have become known, are not folk tales, but adaptations. This fact alone is enough to warrant some hesitancy about placing them in the category of folk lore. To be sure, folk lore was their background, but this can be said of many literary works (Dracula, for example) which we would not think of classifying with folk literature.

The misrepresentation goes further than simply the name, however. The very dialect of the Uncle Remus Stories is questionable, statements to the contrary notwithstanding. Scholars have tried to show that Harris very faithfully recorded the dialect of his time, in its truly intimate expressions, mannerisms and colloquialisms, but it is doubtful whether Negroes generally ever used the language employed in the works of Joel Chandler Harris. Rather, in these works we observe the consciously devised, artistically wrought, patiently carved out expressions of a story writer who knew his art and employed it well. They have too much the flavor of the popular trend of contemporary writing of the Thomas Nelson Page tradition, and though they endeavored to give a faithful portrait of the Negro and did so more successfully than any other of these Southern writers, it cannot be denied that such portraits as they gave were highly romanticized, and gave an interpretation of the Negro seen neither objectively nor realistically.

These stories of Chandler Harris made and still make their most powerful impression and appeal through the character of Uncle Remus himself. But it is in just this projection into the picture of this amiable and winsome ante-bellum personality that contorts the Negro folk tale from its true plane. The American Negro folk tale, borrowed as it most certainly was from Africa, is an animal cycle, recounting the exploits of various members of the animal world of which "Brer Rabbit" was arch-villain or hero, as you please. As in the case of all true folk tales, the story teller himself was inconsequential; he did not figure at all—a talking machine might serve the purpose just as well. As a result the stories take on an impersonal character, more or less lacking in artistic embellishments. The Uncle Remus stories break this tradition, however; instead the story teller plays an important, a too important, rôle. By that very fact, this type of story ceases to be a folk tale; and becomes in reality a product of the imagination of the author. Of course there is such a thing as an intermediate type; there is a place for Hans Andersen, and Brothers Grimm. But Harris, familiar with his material and genuinely loving it, could not be spiritually saturated with it under the circumstances. And this was more a matter of class than race; for human kinships are spiritual after all, but these stories cannot present Negro folk life and feeling seen and felt on its own level. Enough has been said, perhaps, to show, without in any way detracting from the true service and real charm of the Harris stories, that there are enough incongruous elements insinuated into the situation to make it impossible to accept them as a final rendering of American Negro folk lore.

We would not be so much concerned about a "distinction without a difference" if there were actually no difference. Unfortunately the treatment of these stories by Harris resulted in certain developments which are too noteworthy to pass by. The most striking consequence of the fact that Uncle Remus is written all over and interwoven into the stories which bear his name, is that the Harris variety of the Negro folk tale assumes to interpret Negro character instead of simply telling his stories. The result is a composite picture of the ante-bellum Negro that fits exactly into the conception of the type of Negro which so many white people would like to think once existed, or even now exists; whereas in the material in question there is reflected a quite different folk temperament—apart from the question of what is or what isn't *the* Negro temperament. When we find one critic naïvely suggesting that Uncle Remus "makes clear to every thoughtful reader that the system of slavery pernicious as it may appear to us now, took the dusky savage from his haunts in the African jungle and made of him a Christian and a gentleman," we can clearly see that any writing that can be taken as an *apologia* for a social system, or the idealization of the plantation régime, cannot be taken unsuspiciously as the chronicle of a primitive folk lore.

Nevertheless, Harris wrought well from the standpoint of art, and by so doing let the world know that Negroes possessed a rich folk lore. The unquestionable result of this was a keener interest in the Negro and his lore. Just the same, the intrusion of a dominant note of humor, not by any means as general in the material as one would suppose, fell in line with an arbitrary and unfortunately general procedure of regarding anything which bore the Negro trademark as inherently comic and only worth being laughed at. It is not necessary to draw upon sentiment in order to realize the masterful quality of some of the Negro tales: it is simply necessary to read them. Moralism, sober and almost grim, irony, shrewd and frequently subtle, are their fundamental tone and mood—as in the case of their African originals—and the quaint and sentimental humor so popularly prized is oftener than not an overtone merely. But the unfortunate thing about American thought is the habit of classifying first and investigating after. As a result this misrepresentation of the temper and spirit of Negro folk lore has become traditional, and for all we know, permanent.

There is strong need of a scientific collecting of Negro folk lore before the original sources of this material altogether lapse. Sentimental admiration and amateurish praise can never adequately preserve or interpret this precious material. It is precious in two respects—not only for its intrinsic, but for its comparative value. Some of the precious secrets of folk history are in danger of fading out in its gradual disappearance. American folk-lorists are now recognizing this, and systematic scientific investigation has begun under the influence and auspices of the Society for American Folk Lore and such competent ethnologists as Franz Boas, Elsie Clews Parsons, and others.

Simply because we are considering Negro folk lore, we do not say that it is superior to other folk material, nor even that it is as

great as any other folk literature; but we do insist that all folk
material, in order to be appraised justly, must be read and considered in the light of those values which go to make up great folk
literature. Briefly stated, these values are:

1. Lack of the self-conscious element found in ordinary literature.

2. Nearness to nature.

3. Universal appeal.

Search the body of Negro folk literature and you will find these
characteristics dominant. As one writer has well expressed it: "All
nature is alive, anthropomorphized as it were, replete with intelligences; the whispering, tinkling, hissing, booming, muttering,
zooming around him are full of mysterious hints and suggestions."
Out of this primitive intimacy of the mind with nature come those
naïve personifications of the rabbits, foxes and wolves, terrapins
and turtles, buzzards and eagles which make the animal lore of the
world. Many tales ascribed to lands far away find parallels in Negro
stories bearing indubitable traces of African origin; opening out
into the great question of common or separate origin. Fundamentally, as Lang points out, they prove the common ancestry of man,
both with regard to his mental and cultural inheritance. Whichever
way the question is solved, the physical contacts of common origins
or the psychological similarities of common capacity and endowment, it is essentially the same fundamental point in the end—
human kinship and universality. Yet there is much that is distinctively African in animal lore, and of a quality not usually conceded.
The African proverb, in its terseness and pith, the shrewd moral-
isms of the fables, the peculiar whimsicality and turn to the imagination in many of the tales, are notably outstanding. Clive Bell to
the contrary, it is by their intelligence, their profound and abstract
underlying conceptions, that they possess a peculiar touch and originality that is distinctively African. Æsop, it is claimed, was African,
but any folk-lorist knows that the African folk fable of indigenous
growth outmasters Æsop over and over. Africa in a sense is the
home of the fable; the African tales are its classics.

It is interesting, in this connection, to consider the case of the
rabbit, which figures so largely in Negro Folk Lore. It was the
belief of Harris, and still is the belief of many, that the Negro chose
the weak rabbit and glorified him in his stories because this animal
was a prototype of himself during slavery times; according to this
theory, the stronger, more rapacious animals such as wolves, foxes,
etc., represented the white masters. But this cannot be so, for as

Ambrose E. Gonzales aptly points out in his volume entitled *Æsop Along the Black Border*, these stories, or their types at least, came with the Negro from Africa where they had existed for centuries. In the African tales, the hare is the notable figure. Surely, then, the rabbit is none other than the African hare. As a matter of fact, the "Brer Rabbit" character simply confirms the opinion that Negro Folk Lore is a genuine part of world folk literature, for we find the hare one of the animals most frequently encountered in folk lore the world over. In Scottish and Irish Tales he is associated with witches. In the ancient Druidical mysteries the hare was employed in auguries to indicate the outcome of war. Chinese and East Indian stories feature the hare and he is common even in the tales of the American Indian. The Easter "bunny" shows the hare cropping up in a Teutonic atmosphere. So that when all these instances are added to the African and American Negro we may be reasonably safe in assuming that "Brer Rabbit" comes into American lore from the level of true primitive folk material.

The antiquity and authentic folk lore ancestry of the Negro tale make it the proper subject for the scientific folk-lorist rather than the literary amateur. It is the ethnologist, the philologist and the student of primitive psychology that are most needed for its present investigation. Of course no one will deny or begrudge the delightful literary by-products of this material. Negro writers themselves will shortly, no doubt, be developing them as arduously as Chandler Harris, and we hope as successfully, or even more so. But a literary treatment based on a scientific recording will have much fresh material to its hand, and cannot transgress so far from the true ways of the folk spirit and the true lines of our folk art.

$$\left[\quad \begin{array}{c} \text{J. MASON BREWER} \\ \textit{American Negro Folklore} \end{array} \quad \right]$$

OF THE FOUR major fields of American folklore: Indian, Mountain White, Cowboy, and Negro, the latter is one of the most prolific. In song, story, superstition and rhyme, the uneducated Negro has created a vast body of traditional material which has been dominated by his social conditions and economic status under the slave system on one hand, and influenced by his position as the weaker economic group in the present day scheme of American civilization, on the other hand.

The folklore of the American Negro is characterized by work, worship, superstition and fun, the factors which constituted his chief interests during the period of his enslavement. These forces caused him to develop a definite psychology—a fixed way of looking at life—as tragic or comic. The folksongs and superstitions are tragic for the most part, while the bulk of the rhymes and tales are comic in nature.

Most of these folk materials are the American Negroes' inheritance of Old World and African survivals, but a large proportion of them are indigenous. They are not the products of one Period alone—the Slave Period—but of the two subsequent eras in the process of American Negro development as well. While the Slave Period, beginning in 1619 and ending in 1865, furnished the background for the entire framework of Negro folklore, the era of re-adjustment and progress, 1866 to 1917, and the modern epoch, beginning in 1917, have provided additional types of Negro folk inventions.

In the limited scope of this paper, I shall point out the primary forms of Negro folklore which are current in the present era, give evidences of types that are rarely released for general reading but which offer fertile fields and suggest what the future collectors of American Negro folklore may find in this native folklore field—the springs of which have scarcely been tapped.

A rehearsal of the folklore of the slavery period and of the period of re-adjustment is not necessary, except as to show the existence of certain forms which have come over into the present era. Thus, a comprehensive recital will not be given, for time will not permit mention of the innumerable folklore collectors and writers to whom American Negro folklore owes a large debt of gratitude. But suffice it to be said, that there are still valuable materials of the slavery period and re-adjustment period that have not been collected.

It is a sad state of affairs that most of the ex-slaves are dying out and carrying with them a wealth of songs and stories that would have made excellent reading had collectors but busied themselves by getting from these people the homely wisdom and practical philosophy of their naive folk expression so genuinely typical of the folk-spirit of their race.

In addition to the folk materials of the preceding eras are those

of the modern epoch which are strongly flavored by migration, the
First World War and more recently by the depression, unemployment, and the culture of the underworld.

The impersonal relationship existing between the Negro and
his present employer forces him to look after his own resources and
manage his own affairs. Consequently his concept of life is getting
to be the same as that of any other individual living in the same
community and subjected to the same environmental factors. This is
developing in him what is termed "Reality thinking." Life to him is
no longer a show—something to be laughed at, but a series of crises
to be lived through.

The care-free, fanciful, almost childish nature of the folklore of
the old Negro has been lost in the harsh realities of his modern
independence. Therefore it becomes more imperative that the folk
attitudes of the past be captured and recorded.

Let us now glance at the various forms of Negro folklore that
prevail today and note the inviting trails which beckon collectors to
follow.

In the immense variety of patterns we find hangers-on of the
slavery and re-adjustment periods: blues, work songs, superstitions
and proverbs, but there are also new types which potentially offer a
splendid opportunity for exploration and study; among these are
the new style social songs, incidents holding interest by the symbolical lingo, children's rhymes, slave tales, "professor" stories, religious tales, rich-soil tales, of Louisiana, poor-land tales, of Alabama, the court story cycle of tales of the Arkansas Negro, the
Mexican-Negro group of humorous anecdotes, Uncle Mose, the care-
free Negro, recitals of John, the clever Negro, of the Mississippi
delta and narratives of Georgia race-prejudice, ghost stories, etc. A
detailed discussion of these types and illustrations portraying them
will be found in subsequent paragraphs.

The social songs such as:

Last night as I was makin my rounds
I met my woman an' I blowed her down.
Went on home an' I went to bed,
Put my hand cannon right under my head.

typify the kind of songs that will still deserve some consideration
from future collectors. Songs of this type will exist for some time to
come, for wherever there are Negroes, there also will be sorrow
songs and all kinds of laments.

On a trip to the plantation districts, in the vicinity of Baton

Rouge, Louisiana, in July, 1937, a group of Negroes working on a P.W.A. project in one of the suburban towns near Shreveport, Louisiana, boarded the early morning train with me at Shreveport. One of their number had composed the following song and was singing it:

> *If de Government give yuh work, boy*
> *Be sho an' do yo' work good;*
> *Oh! if de Government give yuh work, boy*
> *Be sho' and do yo' work good;*
> *Cause de Government's helpin' po' folks*
> *In evuh neighborhood.*

> *Oh! Unker Sam's flag is painted*
> *Red, white, and blue;*
> *Oh! Unker Sam's flag is painted*
> *Red, white, and blue;*
> *If Unker Sam evuh fail us*
> *What in de worl' we gonna do?*

Although the loss of government aid is substituted here for the usual loss of woman's love, the same tragic strain is inherent in its structure.

World War II has also made a contribution to folklore in the making in the social song area. An itinerant Negro guitar player alighting from a freight train in Memphis, Tennessee, makes his way to one of the corners of the famed Beale Street—traditional home of the blues, and entertains a throng of eager listeners with a patriotic composition of blues genre composed by himself:

> *Oh! the war would soon be over*
> *If Unker Sam would use my plan;*
> *Oh yes, the war would soon be over*
> *If Unker Sam would use my plan;*
> *Jes put me in Hitler's bed room*
> *Wid a razor in my han'.*

The same tragic theme is found here, but in direct contrast to the motive expressed in the preceding song. In the former the writer is expressing his thanks to the Government for saving him from tragic consequences—in the latter the composer is expressing a desire to bring tragedy into the lives of those who would harm the United States.

In the other sector of the tragic materials, superstitions, which

in the Negro's terminology are called "signs," much work remains
to be done, not only in the field of Voodooism, but also in the realm
of popular superstitions similar to those of the following:

> *Ef'n a kettle wid grub in it shakes on yo' stove it's shakin
> somebody out o' you' fam'ly.*
> *Ef'n you brings eggs in de house atter dark, de Sheriff gwine
> be in yo' house fo' de week is up.*

To incidents holding interest by the symbolical lingo the
rhymes of the adult Negro in the modern era bear conformity. Their
rhymes are usually in dialogue form and are frequently influenced
by the underworld. For example:

Two Negroes of the underworld are seated at a table in the
corner of a dive in Ft. Worth, Texas. An officer of the law enters.
The first Negro, whom we will call Cup Grease, and his companion,
whom we will christen Red Horse, exchange the following:

> *Cup Grease: Hello Stranger!*
> *Red Horse: I'll see you in Ranger!*

Whereupon they both get up and leave the beer tavern, one
going in one direction and one in another. The "Hello Stranger"
was a signal that a policeman had entered the door and the response
"I'll see you in Ranger" meant that it is better for us to go separate
ways when we leave this place, but I'll see you at our hang-out
where it's safe. Ranger symbolizes an oil town near Ft. Worth,
where plenty of money and good times prevail. The headquarters of
the gang to which these Negroes belong bears the same ear marks as
Ranger.

Another interesting innovation in the field of American Negro
folklore is that of Negro children's rhymes. The race problem, the
street crier, work in the fields, the living conditions in urban homes,
and invention, all of these have influenced the rhymes of the Negro
child since the latter part of the nineteenth century. One resulting
from a local race problem was given me by Marcus B. Christian, a
Negro poet, who resides in New Orleans. Mr. Christian lived as a
child in Houma, Louisiana, in a French Cajun community. The
Cajun children use to "poke fun" at the Negro children, so, in
answer to the Cajuns' jeers, the Negro children made up the following rhyme:

> *Po' crawfish don't stan' no show,*
> *Blue-bellied Cajuns catch 'im, make gumbo,*

So all aroun' de Cajuns' beds
Don't see nothin' but crawfish heads.

The Negro street crier is fully aware of the effect that rhyme
has on the Negro child, so he, too, advertises his wares in rhyme. In
Houston, Texas, a Negro peddler walks up to a group of children at
play on a sidewalk and in a sing song manner says:

Little boy, little girl, git yo' nickel in yo' han',
An' run an' tell yo' mammy here cum de ribbon cane man.

On a plantation near Montrose, Arkansas, the children of
sharecroppers habitually grew tired of picking cotton during the
latter part of the picking season. They always viewed the appearance of rain clouds as a blessing in disguise—rain meant rest from
the cotton rows. But frequently they were disappointed and the rain
clouds proved to be just a bluff. The children observing that cloudy
skies did not always forecast a heavy rain made up the following
couplet:

Lawd, if you wanna show yo' powah,
Please send a rain—don't send no showah.

In Dallas, Texas, where children are still whipped for the
offenses they commit, a little boy came running into a "shot gun"
house on an alley in North Dallas, squalling out to his mother:

Mama, mama, open de do',
Here come papa wid a forty-fo'.
If you don't open de do' rail quick
Papa gonna whack me wid a stick.

Invention too, has come to mingle itself with folklore and in no
less place than the North. A Negro youth of Kokomo, Indiana, who
is now a Junior at the University of Indiana recalls a rhyme that he
and his playmates made up when he was about the age of six—at
the time when street cars were first introduced into Kokomo. The
youngsters were thrilled with the new method of transportation and
whenever they had a nickel to spare they would take a ride around
the town. A rhyme resulting from their interest in the trolley car
was:

Old Aunt Fannie—black as tar,
Tried to go to heaven in a 'lectric car.
'Lectric car slipped de track,
Thowed Aunt Fannie flat on her back.

One of the most popular folk-tale types of the reconstruction period is the "Professor" story, centering around the uneducated Negro's attempt to teach school with his limited training. One of the best is concerning the would-be professor who applies for a teaching position in a rural school where all of the school trustees are Negroes. When he calls on these gentlemen and makes his wishes known, one of the trustees walks up to him and says: "Uh, Professor, how does yuh teach de Jogerphy? Does yuh teach de flat o' de roun' system?" "Genmens," replies the professor, "hits immaterial to me, ah teach hit either way."

The Negro religious folk-tale is concerned with the absurdities associated with the liberated Negro's attempt to carry out the practice of religious ceremony during the reconstruction period and later. A father, for example, is the only member of his family who has not been converted. This causes his wife and his sixteen children some annoyance. Finally the pastor of the church to which his family belongs suggests that Pink—this was the man's name—go out into the woods nearby his home and pick out a "prayer tree" to which he must go each night and ask God to convert him. So Pink goes out that night, locates him a "prayer tree," gets down on his knees and asks God to convert him. He keeps up this practice for three nights, but on the third night that he goes out to the tree a dead tree limb falls off of the tree and almost hits him. Becoming frightened, he runs home.

Four days pass before he summons up enough courage to return to the tree, but on the fourth night he goes back to the "prayer tree" and says: "Lawd, ah cum out here tonight to have a close-up talk wid yuh 'bout dat tree limb you thowed at me de othah night— you know if you had 'a' hit me dese niggers never would 'a' had no mo' confidence in you."

Then there are the rich-soil tales, of Louisiana, which are supposed to have had their origin among the sons of Negro farmers in the rich-soil districts of that state. These boys gathered at the crossroads' stores on Saturday afternoons, or met at a pasture gate in some cow lane and bragged about the rich quality of the farm lands of their respective fathers.

One would express himself in these terms: "Yeah, mah papa driv a nail in de groun' one night an w'en he woke up de nex' mawnin' dey wuz a crow bar in hits place."

Then another would remark "Yeah, an' mah papa planted a row o' popcorn de othah day an' by de time he got tuh de end o' de row wid de mule, de corn done growed up an' popped all ovah de

groun'—de mule thinkin' hit wuz snow laid down in hit an' froze
tuh death."

Antonymous to these rich-soil tales are the poor land anecdotes
springing from the barren soil district of Alabama. These yarns
are said to have been woven by the sons of farmers also, but for the
purpose of ridiculing the land owned, or rented by some comrade's
father, rather than boasting about the rich quality of the land hold-
ings of their own fathers. For example, one boy would say "The lan'
on yo' papa's farm is so po' 'til grass won' even down grow on it."
Then the boy whose father was referred to in the first instance
would retort "Yeah, the lan' on yo' papa's farm is so po' 'til even if
you built a church on it, you couldn't raise a hymn lessen you put
fertilizer under the church house first." Without a doubt, the favorite folk-tale of the Arkansas Negro is the "court story" in which a
Negro is accused of some felony and habitually comes clear. Almost
invariably, when Arkansas Negro narrators of tales are asked for a
story, they will give you a "court story."

One of the best is about Sandy Johnson—a Negro farmhand
who is arrested the same day that two white farm workers in the
same county are apprehended by the police. Sandy and the two
white men are charged with the same offense—theft. Sandy is to be
tried on the same day, at the same hour, and in the same court, as
the white men. Knowing that the two white men will be tried first
Sandy decides to listen carefully to their replies and fashion his
answers after theirs.

The day for the trial comes, the three prisoners are brought in
and the Judge calls the court to order. The first prisoner called to
the stand is one of the white men. He is accused of stealing a cow.
"Guilty, or not guilty," asks the Judge.

"Not guilty," replies the defendant. "I've owned that cow ever
since she was a calf." The case was dismissed.

Then the second white man was arraigned for trial. He was
accused of stealing a horse. "Guilty, or not guilty," asks the Judge.

"Not guilty," replies the accused. "I've owned that horse ever
since he was a colt." The case was dismissed.

Then the Negro, Sandy Johnson, was called to the stand. He
was accused of stealing a wagon. "Guilty, or not guilty," asks the
Judge.

"Not guilty," replies Sandy, "I'se owned dat wagon evuh since
hit wuz a wheelbarrow." The case was dismissed.

In Texas there is the Mexican-Negro anecdote of the Negro
interpreter of Spanish who accompanies his boss-man on horse

trading and land purchasing expeditions near the Mexican border.

A popular tale told in the Rio Grande valley section of Texas is the one about Uncle Aaron, the ranch-hand, who has been bragging to his boss-man about his ability to speak Spanish, and who is carried along on a land purchasing trip to interpret for his boss.

On the way to the Mexican border they met a Mexican in the road and Uncle Aaron's boss-man asks him to inquire who owns the land in the vicinity. So they get down off their horses and Uncle Aaron walks up to the Mexican and says—pointing to the east, "Who hombre who ownee de lanee?"

The Mexican, who does not understand Uncle Aaron's brand of Spanish, replies, "Quien sabe?" which means, "Who knows?," or "I don't know," when translated into English.

Uncle Aaron, who does not understand what the Mexican said, turns to his boss-man and says, "Boss, Mr. Quien Sabe own dis lan' to de Eas'."

Then, pointing to the west, Uncle Aaron asks the Mexican the same question and gets the same reply, "Quien sabe?"

Uncle Aaron then turns to his boss-man again and says, "Boss, Mr. Quien Sabe own dis lan' to de wes' too."

Then turning toward the Mexican for the third time he directs the same question to the Mexican about the South and gets the same response as before, "Quien sabe?"

"Boss," said Uncle Aaron for his third report, "dis Mescan say Mr. Quien Sabe own dis lan' to de Souf, too, but I b'lieves he's lyin'."

With these remarks, Uncle Aaron picks up the branch off a tree limb beside the road and starts to beating the Mexican, asking the same time, "Now who own dis lan' to de Norf?"

"Cuidad" (Be careful), yelled the Mexican, as Uncle Aaron whaled him with the stick of wood.

Then turning to his boss-man, this time with a broad smile of satisfaction, Uncle Aaron says: "Boss, Mr. Cuidad own dis lan' to de Norf'—ah knowed dat Mescan was lyin' all de time."

John, the clever Negro, has promise of becoming a folk-hero. Wherever he goes he is forever outwitting some one. One summer John's boss-man suspected John of stealing his water-melons from his favorite water-melon patch, but he had not been able to catch him.

Finally one day, however, as the owner of the plantation was returning from a neighboring plantation he saw John coming from the direction of the water-melon patch with a large melon on his shoulder. "John," said the boss-man, "I've been missing a lot of melons out of my patch lately and the tracks lead towards your house."

"Things ain't allus what dey seems, Boss," replies John.

"And another thing," the plantation owner continues, "that looks like one of my melons you have on your back now, and you're coming from the direction of my patch."

"What direction got tuh do wid a hones' man?" replies John.

The prize stories of the Georgia Negro are the tales of race-prejudice, savoring always of the maltreatment of Negroes in what they call "Marse Charlie's country."

Among those that are told most repeatedly by the dispensers of tales is the one about the South Carolina Negro who went to New York, to live, and who decided to visit his home state after being away for a number of years. The Negro's name was Joe and his native town was near the Georgia state line. During the trip home he fell asleep and did not know when the train arrived at the little town where his mother and father lived. So he slept through it until the train reached a small town in Northern Georgia, where the conductor, realizing that Joe had gone past his destination, put him off the train.

As soon as the train pulled out from the station some white men who had seen Joe get off the train walked up and caught him by the collar and shook him saying: "Don't you know we don't 'low no nigguhs here, we gonna whip you good."

"Naw suh, Boss, naw suh, please don't whip me," pleaded Joe, "Ah didn't know whar ah wuz."

"Well," replied one of the white men, "if we let you off, will you catch the first train out of here?"

"Yas suh, yas suh," replied Joe, trembling with fear. "Ah'll go yuh one better'n dat. If you gimme two minits, ah'l ketch dat un what done jus' went."

[ARNA BONTEMPS
Introduction to The Book of
Negro Folklore]

THE LORE of the Negro turned out to be a deeper vein than was at
first suspected. Once represented principally by Uncle Remus and
the Brer Rabbit tales, it has since found its way into such entertain-
ments as the minstrel shows of the late nineteenth and early twentieth centuries and the monologues of Bert Williams (on phonograph
records as well as in vaudeville and the *Ziegfield Follies*), not to
mention recent characterizations like those projected by *Stepin
Fetchet, Rochester,* and the *Amos n' Andy* ensemble. A carry-over
from Negro folktales into the American writing by and about Negroes, from Mark Twain to William Faulkner and Ralph Ellison, is
also conspicuous.

But the tales, as varied and intriguing as they are, give only a
partial indication of the range and capacity of the folk who created
them. For many Americans these are still apt to evoke memories of
favored house servants, trusting and trusted Aunties, Uncles, and
Grannies. But a less cozy, less contented side of folk life is recaptured by ballads like "John Henry," by work and prison songs, by
the blues, and even by the spirituals. Still another mood of the folk
may be detected in sermons, prayers, and testimonials. These expressions of life's hardship, its stress and strain, did not lend themselves so quickly to exploitation, but ways were eventually found.
The blues provided a tap-root of tremendous vitality for season
after season, vogue after vogue of popular music, and became an
American idiom in a broad sense. A time came when even "Dry
Bones," "When the Saints go Marching In," and "He's Got the
Whole World in His Hand" seemed to express a national mood. Nor
was the art of the old-time Negro preacher overlooked in the scram-
ble.

Interestingly, too, folk expression of this kind continues. The
"Black and Unknown Bards," eulogized by James Weldon Johnson
as creators of the spirituals, have now come out as the composers of
gospel songs such as those sung by Mahalia Jackson, but their
intimate links with the folk, personal as well as musical, remain

intact. Louis Armstrong is himself a bridge between the sporting houses in which Jelly Roll Morton introduced his special piano style and "invented" jazz for seduction and the era of television, goodwill tours, and jazz as a secret weapon of diplomacy. Uncle Remus finds a very hep Harlem counterpart in Langston Hughes' "Simple Minded Friend."

Close reading, so called, can become a bad habit, possibly a vice, where simple appreciation is concerned, but never does it start more quarrels than when the folk are involved. So let it be said quickly that Negro folklore, like almost any other kind, can be traced in its origins to a dim past when it drew on a common cultural heritage, which most of the folk of the world appear to have shared. In any case, the telling of tales is a time honored custom in Africa. By what steps the fables of Æsop (Ethiop) became the animal stories of West Africa, of the West Indies, and of the slave states of the U.S.A. is a lively question but not to the point here. What does concern us is that the slaves brought with them to the New World their ancient habit of story telling as pastime, together with a rich bestiary.

While the masters of slaves went to some length to get rid of tribal languages and some tribal customs, like certain practices of sorcery, they accepted the animal stories as a harmless way to ease the time or entertain the master's children. That the folk tales of these Negro slaves were actually projections of personal experiences and hopes and defeats in terms of symbols appears to have gone unnoticed.

In the African prototypes of the American Negro tales the heroes were generally the jackal, the hare, the tortoise, and the spider. The African jackal survived as the American fox, the African hare as the American rabbit, and the African tortoise as the American dry-land turtle or terrapin. The spider came only as near as the West Indies, where it reappeared in the Anansi tales of Jamaica. As a villain the African hyena was replaced by the American wolf, but that role is sometimes assigned to the fox or the bear in the American tale. The rest of the cast of characters, the lions, leopards, tigers, and monkeys was safely transported.

Much has sometimes been made of the fact that a study of some three hundred versions of "The Tar Baby" story tends to leave the impression that its origin was in India, or that the well-liked "Playing Godfather," for example, is in the Reynard cycle and reappears in Grimm's fairy tales. This, however, is not true of the great majority of the tales brought over from Africa, and even where it is, the American Negro fables, as has been pointed out by anthropologists, "have been so modified with new beasts and local color added, different themes, and different experiences, that an almost new, certainly a quite different thing results." Written literature, of course, does the same thing.

The American Negro slave, adopting Brer Rabbit as hero, represented him as the most frightened and helpless of creatures. No hero-animals in Africa or elsewhere were so completely lacking in strength. But the slaves took pains to give Brer Rabbit other significant qualities. He became in their stories by turn a practical joker, a braggart, a wit, a glutton, a lady's man, and a trickster. But his essential characteristic was his ability to get the better of bigger and stronger animals. To the slave in his condition the theme of weakness overcoming strength through cunning proved endlessly fascinating.

Also satisfying, for related reasons, were accounts of the defeat, if not destruction, of the powerful Brer Wolf, the stupid Brer Bear, and the sly Brer Fox. Variations on these themes permitted the story tellers to invest Brer Squirrel, Sis Goose, Brer Rooster, Brer Alligator, and the rest with traits equally recognizable, equally amusing, and equally instructive.

The Brer Rabbit lore owes its wide vogue among Americans in general to the Uncle Remus stories of Joel Chandler Harris, but his were not the first or the last collections of these tales. Much of the special appeal of his versions may be attributed to the setting in which the old Uncle entertains the Young Master. To this extent they do not conform as fully to the definition of a folktale as one *by the folk for the folk* as do versions like "Brer Rabbit Fools Buzzard," collected by Arthur Huff Fauset, or "Brer Fox and the Goobers," collected by Carl Carmer. Such a story as "Ole Sis Goose," collected by A. W. Eddins, appears to belong to a time more recent than the Joel Chandler Harris tales and to suggest, by its reference to the problem of justice in the courts, that the possibilities of this genre have not even yet been exhausted by the Negro folk.

Another body of Negro folktales, equally dear to the slaves themselves, stemmed from the familiar trickster theme. In slavery the trickster, most frequently called John or Jack, had a made-to-order setting. Surprised in his folly or his wrong-doing by Ole Master, Old Miss, the "patterollers," or even the devil, he would attempt to clear himself by his wit. He did not always succeed, but the happy ending was when he avoided a whipping or, better still, obtained his freedom. In the course of the tales the story tellers

poked as much fun at themselves as they did at their masters, but
pretentiousness was unfailingly exposed.

Stories of enormous exaggeration, sometimes called "lies" by
the folk themselves, a large body of "why" stories, accounting humorously for the beginnings of almost everything, from the creation
of man and beast to explanations of the peculiar ways of women,
together with humanized accounts of heaven, continue to amuse the
folk after nearly a century of Emancipation. Equally durable is the
preacher story, likewise of slavery time origin.

The Negro "preacher tale" is in the tradition of the religious
tales of antiquity and the "exempla" of medieval Europe, as well as
of the anecdotes used so effectively by Lorenzo Dow and other
Methodist and Baptist preachers in proclaiming the protestant religion to the plantation folk in the latter part of the 18th century.
While frequently failing to moralize and generally taking off into
directions not suggested by their respected predecessors, the Negro
religious tales retained at least one important characterisic of the
genre: they aimed to entertain.

To the folk the Negro "preacher tale" included both the stories
told by their preachers in the pulpit and the stories told *about* their
preachers when not in the pulpit. In either case, whether borrowed
or adapted originally, they took root in one section of the South or
another and became a part of the cultural heritage of the local folk.
Sometimes a popular preacher tale was *no lie,* as in the case of the
story told about the Reverend L. K. Williams, later pastor of the
huge Olivet Baptist Church in Chicago and vice-president of the
Baptist World Alliance.

In the Brazos Bottoms of Texas, where he was born and
raised, L. K. was known as a gambler in his youth. His father, a
deacon in the church, did all he could to make a Christian of the
boy, but to no avail. Young L. K. went right on shooting dice on the
banks of the Brazos River while the good folk of the Bottom were in
church singing hymns on Sunday morning. But a time came, as the
old folks used to say, and as J. Mason Brewer has recorded, when
the spirit overcame him, and young L. K. Williams gave up his
"worldly ways" and "put on de armuh of de Lawd." Here is how it
was remembered by one of his contemporaries:

"We was all listenin' to de preachuh an' jes' beginnin' to feel
de sperrit movin' in our haa'ts, when all of a sudden we heahs a
hoss gallopin' up to'a'ds de chu'chhouse es fas' ez he kin trot.
Evuhbody wonder what de trouble be an' staa't lookin' outen de
windows. Putty soon dey seed a roan hoss stop out at de fence roun'

de chu'chhouse an a boy git offen 'im. De boy staa'ted runnin' up to de chu'chhouse an' when he gits close 'nuff we seed dat hit was L. K. Williams. He had on his duckins an' dey was dirty ez dey could be an' his hair ain't been combed, but he runned in de do' straight up to whar de preachuh was preachin' say, 'Elduh, ah wants to jine de chu'ch an' be a Christun.' His pappy was settin' on de front row an' soon as L. K. said dis his pappy grab 'im an' staa't cryin' an' say, 'Bless de Lawd! Bless de Lawd. Mah prayers done been answered.' From dat day on L. K. comed to chu'ch all day evuh Sunday, an' putty soon he come to be a exhorter (dat's a preachuh tryin' to git on foot preachin', you know). So putty soon dey calls 'im to pastuh a li'l ole chu'ch, and he comed to be one of de bes' preachuhs in de Bottoms. Dey say dat de why he comed an' jined de chu'ch dat Sunday was 'caze he losed all his money in a dice game down to Falls on de Brazos, and de Lawd meck hit come to 'im to git shed of his sinful ways an' live a good life."

While life has changed a great deal down on the Brazos since L. K. Williams was a crap-shooting boy, and many of the folk have gone away, as he himself did long ago, his kind and theirs survive, and many of them are never more delighted than when they have a chance to tell you about what happened to their preacher or the story he told in a recent sermon. This should not surprise. Writing about the Negro church in the United States in 1903, W. E. B. Du-Bois observed that "there is a church organization for every sixty Negro families. This institution, therefore, naturally assumed many functions which the harshly suppressed social organ had to surrender; the church became the center of amusements, of what little spontaneous economic activity remained, of education and of all social intercourse." The picture is still recognizable.

The tempo of the singing, as represented by the Negro spirituals, has been stepped up and a jazz note added to make the gospel songs, and the "moaning" of the preacher has given way (well, more or less) to a more ordered discourse, but the "gravy" is still there, as the folk themselves would testify.

James Weldon Johnson recognized in the sermons of the old-time Negro preacher an important form of folk expression. He reproduced a number of these as poetry. Other folklorists have gone to the same sources and made literal transcriptions or prose adaptations. All have confirmed one point. There was a wonderful creativity behind this preaching, which fully warrants the esteem in which it was held by its rapt, hand-clapping, foot-patting, and vocally responsive hearers.

Many of the more successful sermons of the old-time Negro preacher were repeated time and again and gradually took on the set pattern of a work of folk art. John Jasper of Richmond became famous for his "De Sun Do Move," and thousands of people, white and black, flocked to his church to hear it. Other old-time preachers imitated it, adapted it, and added it to their own repertories. The same happened with such numbers as "Dry Bones in the Valley," "The Heavenly March," and the "Train Sermon," sometimes called "The Black Diamond Express, running between here and hell, making thirteen stops and arriving in hell ahead of time."

The old-time Negro preacher himself belonged to a unique breed. Entertaining, comic when comedy was needed, he was in every sense the shepherd of the flock. It was he who gave the slave hope and inspiration. It was he who eased the hard journey with the comforting sentiment, "You may have all dis world, but give me Jesus." It was he who created the setting in which the spirituals were born.

Before the Revolutionary War the Negroes George Liele and Andrew Bryan were preaching to whites and blacks alike in Augusta and Savannah, Georgia, respectively. John Ledman in his *History of the Rise of Methodism in America* tells about Black Harry who preached from the same platform with the other founders of that church in the United States and concludes, "The truth was that Harry was a more popular speaker than Mr. Asbury (Bishop Francis Asbury) or almost anyone else in his day." The old-time preacher was among the first slaves to learn to read and write. He became a teacher. When the time came for courageous action, he took a hand in the Underground Railroad, while his counterpart in the North became an effective Abolitionist speaker. So the tradition to which Martin Luther King of Montgomery, Alabama, belongs is a long one. The Negro preacher has had a vital role, not the least important aspect of which has been the awakening and encouragement of folk expression. He is forever memorialized in the spirituals, the preacher stories, and to a lesser extent, since the whole setting cannot be recaptured (the moaning and the hand-clapping and the responses of the audience, for example), in the sermons themselves.

As an indication of the kind of backing the old-time preacher could count on, we have the testimonials and remembrances of his members. The church folk answered him back, and the answer was strong and affirmative. What he gave, and what they picked up was hope, confidence, a will to survive. The lore that stemmed from the religious experiences of the Negro in slavery, like that which found expression in the animal tales and the pastime rhymes, was always fundamentally optimistic. But this is not the whole story.

Just as sure as God had his heaven, the devil had his hell. And the box (guitar), as all the older folk know, has always been a special device of the devil's. I can remember what happened to one of these careless minstrels who made the mistake of wandering onto the church grounds during an intermission between services back in my childhood. The sisters of the church lit into him like a flock of mother hens attacking a garter snake. He protested. He was just fixing to play a couple of hymns, he explained. But this did not save him. He was obliged to leave in a hurry. The deaconesses knew from bitter experience, no doubt, that the church yard was no place for a box. They also knew that the songs with which the guitar was associated were not for the ears of children.

The blues, like the work and prison songs and most of the folk ballads, seemed at first shockingly incompatable with the new condition and aspirations of freedmen. But this was not actually the case. Behind these earthy lyrics was the beginning of a new racial consciousness and self conception. It recognized difference but without the usual connotations of disparity. It made no apology, asked no pity, offered no defense. It insisted only on being itself, as the young poets of the Harlem Renaissance loved to say.

Because of this a distinguished sociologist could observe some thirty years ago that "Who would know something of the core and limitations of this life (Negro folk) should go to the *Blues*. In them is the curious story of disillusionment without a saving philosophy and yet without defeat. They mark these narrow limits of life's satisfactions, its vast treacheries and ironies. Stark, full human passions crowd themselves into an uncomplex expression, so simple in their power that they startle. If they did not reveal a fundamental and universal emotion of the human heart, they would not be noticed now as the boisterous and persistent intruders in the polite society of lyrics that they are. . . . Herein lies one of the richest gifts of the Negro to American life. . . . These are the *Blues,* not of the Negro intellectuals any more than of the white ones, but, of those who live beneath the range of polite respect."

Ellison has called the blues "an autobiographical chronicle of personal catastrophe expressed lyrically" and added, "Their attraction lies in this, that they at once express both the agony of life and the possibility of conquering it through sheer toughness of spirit. They fall short of tragedy only in that they provide no solution, offer no scapegoat but the self."

It is not surprising, under the circumstances, that Negro writers, and the many others who have used the Negro as a subject, should continue to dip into the richness of Negro folk life. The novelist and the sociologist just quoted were born into a folk culture. The same was true of Paul Laurence Dunbar, James Weldon Johnson, Jean Toomer, Sterling Brown, Zora Neale Hurston, Richard Wright, Margaret Walker, Gwendolyn Brooks, and James Baldwin, to name but a few. It shows, indeed it is conspicuous, in their writing. But does this fact, this tendency to lean more heavily on Negro folk tradition than on "standard" or "white" models, set the Negro writer of the United States outside the main stream of Western literature?

It should not. Stanley Edgar Hyman has noted that in this matter contemporary Negro writers, employing what we have called the folk manner, are in line with Aristophanes, Shakespeare, and St. Paul, all of whom drew similarly from *their* folk sources in myth and ritual. So, Mr. Hyman concludes, correctly, I believe, "High Western culture and the Negro folk tradition thus do not appear to pull the writer in opposite directions, but to say the same thing in their different vocabularies, to come together and reinforce insight with insight."

W. E. B. DUBOIS
Of the Sorrow Songs

I walk through the churchyard
    To lay this body down;
I know moon-rise, I know star-rise;
I walk in the moonlight, I walk in the starlight;
I'll lie in the grave and stretch out my arms,
I'll go to judgment in the evening of the day,
And my soul and thy soul shall meet that day,
    When I lay this body down.

NEGRO SONG.

THEY THAT walked in darkness sang songs in the olden days—
Sorrow Songs—for they were weary at heart. And so before each
thought that I have written in this book I have set a phrase, a
haunting echo of these weird old songs in which the soul of the
black slave spoke to men. Ever since I was a child these songs have
stirred me strangely. They came out of the South unknown to me,
one by one, and yet at once I knew them as of me and of mine. Then
in after years when I came to Nashville I saw the great temple
builded of these songs towering over the pale city. To me Jubilee
Hall seemed ever made of the songs themselves, and its bricks were
red with the blood and dust of toil. Out of them rose for me morning, noon, and night, bursts of wonderful melody, full of the voices
of my brothers and sisters, full of the voices of the past.

Little of beauty has America given the world save the rude

grandeur God himself stamped on her bosom; the human spirit in this new world has expressed itself in vigor and ingenuity rather than in beauty. And so by fateful chance the Negro folk-song—the rhythmic cry of the slave—stands to-day not simply as the sole American music, but as the most beautiful expression of human experience born this side the seas. It has been neglected, it has been, and is, half despised, and above all it has been persistently mistaken and misunderstood; but notwithstanding, it still remains as the singular spiritual heritage of the nation and the greatest gift of the Negro people.

Away back in the thirties the melody of these slave songs stirred the nation, but the songs were soon half forgotten. Some, like "Near the lake where drooped the willow," passed into current airs and their source was forgotten; others were caricatured on the "minstrel" stage and their memory died away. Then in war-time came the singular Port Royal experiment after the capture of Hilton Head, and perhaps for the first time the North met the Southern slave face to face and heart to heart with no third witness. The Sea Islands of the Carolinas, where they met, were filled with a black folk of primitive type, touched and moulded less by the world about them than any others outside the Black Belt. Their appearance was uncouth, their language funny, but their hearts were human and their singing stirred men with a mighty power. Thomas Wentworth Higginson hastened to tell of these songs, and Miss McKim and others urged upon the world their rare beauty. But the world listened only half credulously until the Fisk Jubilee Singers sang the slave songs so deeply into the world's heart that it can never wholly forget them again.

There was once a blacksmith's son born at Cadiz, New York, who in the changes of time taught school in Ohio and helped defend Cincinnati from Kirby Smith. Then he fought at Chancellorsville and Gettysburg and finally served in the Freedman's Bureau at Nashville. Here he formed a Sunday-school class of black children in 1866, and sang with them and taught them to sing. And then they taught him to sing, and when once the glory of the Jubilee songs passed into the soul of George L. White, he knew his life-work was to let those Negroes sing to the world as they had sung to him. So in 1871 the pilgrimage of the Fisk Jubilee Singers began. North to Cincinnati they rode,—four half-clothed black boys and five girl-women,—led by a man with a cause and a purpose. They stopped at Wilberforce, the oldest of Negro schools, where a black bishop blessed them. Then they went, fighting cold and starvation, shut out of hotels, and cheerfully sneered at, ever northward; and ever the magic of their song kept thrilling hearts, until a burst of applause in the Congregational Council at Oberlin revealed them to the world. They came to New York and Henry Ward Beecher dared to welcome them, even though the metropolitan dailies sneered at his "Nigger Minstrels." So their songs conquered till they sang across the land and across the sea, before Queen and Kaiser, in Scotland and Ireland, Holland and Switzerland. Seven years they sang, and brought back a hundred and fifty thousand dollars to found Fisk University.

Since their day they have been imitated—sometimes well, by the singers of Hampton and Atlanta, sometimes ill, by straggling quartettes. Caricature has sought again to spoil the quaint beauty of the music, and has filled the air with many debased melodies which vulgar ears scarce know from the real. But the true Negro folk-song still lives in the hearts of those who have heard them truly sung and in the hearts of the Negro people.

What are these songs, and what do they mean? I know little of music and can say nothing in technical phrase, but I know something of men, and knowing them, I know that these songs are the articulate message of the slave to the world. They tell us in these eager days that life was joyous to the black slave, careless and happy. I can easily believe this of some, of many. But not all the past South, though it rose from the dead, can gainsay the heart-touching witness of these songs. They are the music of an unhappy people, of the children of disappointment; they tell of death and suffering and unvoiced longing toward a truer world, of misty wanderings and hidden ways.

The songs are indeed the siftings of centuries; the music is far more ancient than the words, and in it we can trace here and there signs of development. My grandfather's grandmother was seized by an evil Dutch trader two centuries ago; and coming to the valleys of the Hudson and Housatonic, black, little, and lithe, she shivered and shrank in the harsh north winds, looked longingly at the hills, and often crooned a heathen melody to the child between her knees, thus:

Do ba - na co - ba, ge - ne   me,   ge - ne me!

Do   ba - na co - ba, ge - ne   me,   ge - ne me!

Ben d'   nu - li, nu - li, nu - li, nu - li, ben d'   le.

The child sang it to his children and they to their children's children, and so two hundred years it has traveled down to us and we sing it to our children, knowing as little as our fathers what its words may mean, but knowing well the meaning of its music.

This was primitive African music; it may be seen in larger form in the strange chant which heralds "The Coming of John":

> *You may bury me in the East,*
> *You may bury me in the West,*
> *But I'll hear the trumpet sound in that morning,*

—the voice of exile.

Ten master songs, more or less, one may pluck from this forest of melody—songs of undoubted Negro origin and wide popular currency, and songs peculiarly characteristic of the slave. One of these I have just mentioned. Another whose strains begin this book is "Nobody knows the trouble I've seen." When, struck with a sudden poverty, the United States refused to fulfill its promises of land to the freedmen, a brigadier-general went down to the Sea Islands to carry the news. An old woman on the outskirts of the throng began singing this song; all the mass joined with her, swaying. And the soldier wept.

The third song is the cradle-song of death which all men know, —"Swing low, sweet chariot,"—whose bars begin the life story of "Alexander Crummell." Then there is the song of many waters, "Roll, Jordan, roll," a mighty chorus with minor cadences. There were many songs of the fugitive like that which opens "The Wings of Atalanta," and the more familiar "Been a-listening." The seventh is the song of the End and the Beginning—"My Lord, what a mourning! when the stars begin to fall"; a strain of this is placed before "The Dawn of Freedom." The song of groping—"My way's cloudy"—begins "The Meaning of Progress"; the ninth is the song of this chapter—"Wrestlin' Jacob, the day is a-breaking,"—a pæan of hopeful strife. The last master song is the song of songs—"Steal away,"—sprung from "The Faith of the Fathers."

There are many others of the Negro folk-songs as striking and characteristic as these, as, for instance, the three strains in the third, eighth, and ninth chapters; and others I am sure could easily make a selection on more scientific principles. There are, too, songs that seem to be a step removed from the more primitive types: there is the maze-like medley, "Bright sparkles," one phrase of which heads "The Black Belt"; the Easter carol, "Dust, dust and ashes"; the dirge, "My mother's took her flight and gone home"; and that burst of melody hovering over "The Passing of the First-Born"—"I hope my mother will be there in that beautiful world on high."

These represent a third step in the development of the slave song, of which "You may bury me in the East" is the first, and songs like "March on" (chapter six) and "Steal away" are the second. The first is African music, the second Afro-American, while the third is a blending of Negro music with the music heard in the foster land. The result is still distinctively Negro and the method of blending original, but the elements are both Negro and Caucasian. One might go further and find a fourth step in this development, where the songs of white America have been distinctively influenced by the slave songs or have incorporated whole phrases of Negro melody, as "Swanee River" and "Old Black Joe." Side by side, too, with the growth has gone the debasements and imitations—the Negro "minstrel" songs, many of the "gospel" hymns, and some of the contemporary "coon" songs,—a mass of music in which the novice may easily lose himself and never find the real Negro melodies.

In these songs, I have said, the slave spoke to the world. Such a message is naturally veiled and half articulate. Words and music have lost each other and new and cant phrases of a dimly under-stood theology have displaced the older sentiment. Once in a while we catch a strange word of an unknown tongue, as the "Mighty Myo," which figures as a river of death; more often slight words or mere doggerel are joined to music of singular sweetness. Purely secular songs are few in number, partly because many of them were turned into hymns by a change of words, partly because the frolics

were seldom heard by the stranger, and the music less often caught.
Of nearly all the songs, however, the music is distinctly sorrowful.
The ten master songs I have mentioned tell in word and music of
trouble and exile, of strife and hiding; they grope toward some
unseen power and sigh for rest in the End.

The words that are left to us are not without interest, and,
cleared of evident dross, they conceal much of real poetry and
meaning beneath conventional theology and unmeaning rhapsody.
Like all primitive folk, the slave stood near to Nature's heart. Life
was a "rough and rolling sea" like the brown Atlantic of the Sea
Islands; the "Wilderness" was the home of God, and the "lonesome
valley" led to the way of life. "Winter'll soon be over," was the
picture of life and death to a tropical imagination. The sudden wild
thunder-storms of the South awed and impressed the Negroes—at
times the rumbling seemed to them "mournful," at times imperious:

> *My Lord calls me,*
> *He calls me by the thunder,*
> *The trumpet sounds it in my soul.*

The monotonous toil and exposure is painted in many words.
One sees the ploughmen in the hot, moist furrow, singing:

> *Dere's no rain to wet you,*
> *Dere's no sun to burn you,*
> *Oh, push along, believer,*
> *I want to go home.*

The bowed and bent old man cries, with thrice-repeated wail:

> *O Lord, keep me from sinking down,*

and he rebukes the devil of doubt who can whisper:

> *Jesus is dead and God's gone away.*

Yet the soul-hunger is there, the restlessness of the savage, the wail
of the wanderer, and the plaint is put in one little phrase:

My   soul   wants some - thing that's   new,   that's new

Over the inner thoughts of the slaves and their relations one
with another the shadow of fear ever hung, so that we get but

glimpses here and there, and also with them, eloquent omissions and silences. Mother and child are sung, but seldom father; fugitive and weary wanderer call for pity and affection, but there is little of wooing and wedding; the rocks and the mountains are well known, but home is unknown. Strange blending of love and helplessness signs through the refrain:

> *Yonder's my ole mudder,*
> *Been waggin' at de hill so long;*
> *'Bout time she cross over,*
> *Git home bime-by.*

Elsewhere comes the cry of the "motherless" and the "Farewell, farewell, my only child."

Love-songs are scarce and fall into two categories—the frivolous and light, and the sad. Of deep successful love there is ominous silence, and in one of the oldest of these songs there is a depth of history and meaning:

Poor Ro - sy, poor__ gal; Poor Ro - sy,
poor__ gal; Ro - sy break my poor heart,
Heav'n shall - a - be my home.

A black woman said of the song, "It can't be sung without a full heart and a troubled sperrit." The same voice sings here that sings in the German folk-song:

> *Jetz Geh i' an's brunele, trink' aber net.*

Of death the Negro showed little fear, but talked of it familiarly and even fondly as simply a crossing of the waters, perhaps— who knows?—back to his ancient forests again. Later days transfigured his fatalism, and amid the dust and dirt the toiler sang:

Dust, dust and ashes, fly over my grave,
But the Lord shall bear my spirit home.

The things evidently borrowed from the surrounding world undergo characteristic change when they enter the mouth of the slave. Especially is this true of Bible phrases. "Weep, O captive daughter of Zion," is quaintly turned into "Zion, weep-a-low," and the wheels of Ezekiel are turned every way in the mystic dreaming of the slave, till he says:

There's a little wheel a-turnin' in-a-my heart.

As in olden time, the words of these hymns were improvised by some leading minstrel of the religious band. The circumstances of the gathering, however, the rhythm of the songs, and the limitations of allowable thought, confined the poetry for the most part to single or double lines, and they seldom were expanded to quatrains or longer tales, although there are some few examples of sustained efforts, chiefly paraphrases of the Bible. Three short series of verses have always attracted me,—the one that heads this chapter, of one line of which Thomas Wentworth Higginson has fittingly said, "Never, it seems to me, since man first lived and suffered was his infinite longing for peace uttered more plaintively." The second and third are descriptions of the Last Judgment,—the one a late improvisation, with some traces of outside influence:

Oh, the stars in the elements are falling,
And the moon drips away into blood,
And the ransomed of the Lord are returning unto God,
Blessed be the name of the Lord.

And the other earlier and homelier picture from the low coast lands:

Michael, haul the boat ashore,
Then you'll hear the horn they blow,
Then you'll hear the trumpet sound,
Trumpet sound the world around,
Trumpet sound for rich and poor,
Trumpet sound the Jubilee,
Trumpet sound for you and me.

Through all the sorrow of the Sorrow Songs there breathes a hope—a faith in the ultimate justice of things. The minor cadences of despair change often to triumph and calm confidence. Sometimes it is faith in life, sometimes a faith in death, sometimes assurance of boundless justice in some fair world beyond. But whichever it is, the meaning is always clear: that sometime, somewhere, men will judge men by their souls and not by their skins. Is such a hope justified? Do the Sorrow Songs sing true?

The silently growing assumption of this age is that the probation of races is past, and that the backward races of to-day are of proven inefficiency and not worth the saving. Such an assumption is the arrogance of peoples irreverent toward Time and ignorant of the deeds of men. A thousand years ago such an assumption, easily possible, would have made it difficult for the Teuton to prove his right to life. Two thousand years ago such dogmatism, readily welcome, would have scouted the idea of blond races ever leading civilization. So wofully unorganized is sociological knowledge that the meaning of progress, the meaning of "swift" and "slow" in human doing, and the limits of human perfectibility, are veiled, unanswered sphinxes on the shores of science. Why should Æschylus have sung two thousand years before Shakespeare was born? Why has civilization flourished in Europe, and flickered, flamed, and died in Africa? So long as the world stands meekly dumb before such questions, shall this nation proclaim its ignorance and unhallowed prejudices by denying freedom of opportunity to those who brought the Sorrow Songs to the Seats of the Mighty?

Your country? How came it yours? Before the Pilgrims landed we were here. Here we have brought our three gifts and mingled them with yours: a gift of story and song—soft, stirring melody in an ill-harmonized and unmelodious land; the gift of sweat and brawn to beat back the wilderness, conquer the soil, and lay the foundations of this vast economic empire two hundred years earlier than your weak hands could have done it; the third, a gift of the Spirit. Around us the history of the land has centred for thrice a hundred years; out of the nation's heart we have called all that was best to throttle and subdue all that was worst; fire and blood, prayer and sacrifice, have billowed over this people, and they have found peace only in the altars of the God of Right. Nor has our gift of the Spirit been merely passive. Actively we have woven ourselves with the very warp and woof of this nation,—we fought their battles, shared their sorrow, mingled our blood with theirs, and generation after generation have pleaded with a headstrong, careless people to despise not Justice, Mercy, and Truth, lest the nation be smitten with a curse. Our song, our toil, our cheer, and warning have been given to this nation in blood-brotherhood. Are not these gifts worth

the giving? Is not this work and striving? Would America have
been America without her Negro people?

Even so is the hope that sang in the songs of my fathers well
sung. If somewhere in this whirl and chaos of things there dwells
Eternal Good, pitiful yet masterful, then anon in His good time
America shall rend the Veil and the prisoned shall go free. Free,
free as the sunshine trickling down the morning into these high
windows of mine, free as yonder fresh young voices welling up to
me from the caverns of brick and mortar below—swelling with
song, instinct with life, tremulous treble and darkening bass. My
children, my little children, are singing to the sunshine, and thus
they sing:

long   the   heav - en - ly   way.

And the traveller girds himself, and sets his face toward the
Morning, and goes his way.

> ALAIN LOCKE
> *The Negro Spirituals*

THE SPIRITUALS are really the most characteristic product of the
race genius as yet in America. But the very elements which make
them uniquely expressive of the Negro make them at the same time
deeply representative of the soil that produced them. Thus, as
unique spiritual products of American life, they become nationally
as well as racially characteristic. It may not be readily conceded
now that the song of the Negro is America's folk-song; but if the
Spirituals are what we think them to be, a classic folk expression,
then this is their ultimate destiny. Already they give evidence of this
classic quality. Through their immediate and compelling universality of appeal, through their untarnishable beauty, they seem assured
of the immortality of those great folk expressions that survive not
so much through being typical of a group or representative of a
period as by virtue of being fundamentally and everlastingly human. This universality of the Spirituals looms more and more as
they stand the test of time. They have outlived the particular generation and the peculiar conditions which produced them; they have
survived in turn the contempt of the slave owners, the conventional-
izations of formal religion, the repressions of Puritanism, the cor-
ruptions of sentimental balladry, and the neglect and disdain of
second-generation respectability. They have escaped the lapsing

conditions and the fragile vehicle of folk art, and come firmly into the context of formal music. Only classics survive such things.

In its disingenuous simplicity, folk art is always despised and rejected at first; but generations after, it flowers again and transcends the level of its origin. The slave songs are no exception; only recently have they come to be recognized as artistically precious things. It still requires vision and courage to proclaim their ultimate value and possibilities. But while the first stage of artistic development is yet uncompleted, it appears that behind the deceptive simplicity of Negro song lie the richest undeveloped musical resources anywhere available. Thematically rich, in idiom of rhythm and harmony richer still, in potentialities of new musical forms and new technical traditions so deep as to be accessible only to genius, they have the respect of the connoisseur even while still under the sentimental and condescending patronage of the amateur. Proper understanding and full appreciation of the Spirituals, in spite of their present vogue, is still rare. And the Negro himself has shared many of the common and widespread limitations of view with regard to them. The emotional intuition which has made him cling to this folk music has lacked for the most part that convinced enlightenment that eventually will treasure the spirituals for their true musical and technical values. And although popular opinion and the general conception have changed very materially, a true estimate of this body of music cannot be reached until many prevailing preconceptions are completely abandoned. For what general opinion regards as simple and transparent about them is in technical ways, though instinctive, very intricate and complex, and what is taken as whimsical and child-like is in truth, though naïve, very profound.

It was the great service of Dr. Du Bois in his unforgettable chapter on the Sorrow Songs in *The Souls of the Black Folk* to give them a serious and proper social interpretation, just as later Mr. Krehbiel in his *Afro-American Folk Songs* gave them their most serious and adequate musical analysis and interpretation. The humble origin of these sorrow songs is too indelibly stamped upon them to be ignored or overlooked. But underneath broken words, childish imagery, peasant simplicity, lies, as Dr. Du Bois pointed out, an epic intensity and a tragic profundity of emotional experience, for which the only historical analogy is the spiritual experience of the Jews and the only analogue, the Psalms. Indeed they transcend emotionally even the very experience of sorrow out of which they were born; their mood is that of religious exaltation, a degree of ecstasy indeed that makes them in spite of the crude vehicle a classical expression of the religious emotion. They lack the grand style, but never the sublime effect. Their words are colloquial, but their mood is epic. They are primitive, but their emotional artistry is perfect. Indeed, spiritually evaluated, they are among the most genuine and outstanding expressions of Christian mood and feeling, fit musically and emotionally, if not verbally, of standing with the few Latin hymns, the handful of Gregorian tunes, and the rarest of German chorals as a not negligible element in the modicum of strictly religious music that the Christian centuries have produced.

Perhaps there is no such thing as intrinsically religious music; certainly the traceable interplay of the secular and the religious in music would scarcely warrant an arbitrary opinion in the matter. And just as certainly as secular elements can be found in all religious music are there discoverable sensuous and almost pagan elements blended into the Spirituals. But something so intensely religious and so essentially Christian dominates the blend that they are indelibly and notably of this quality. The Spirituals are spiritual. Conscious artistry and popular conception alike should never rob them of this heritage, it is untrue to their tradition and to the folk genius to give them another tone. That they are susceptible of both crude and refined secularization is no excuse. Even though their own makers worked them up from the "shout" and the rhythmic elements of the sensuous dance, in their finished form and basic emotional effect all of these elements were completely sublimated in the sincere intensities of religious seriousness. To call them Spirituals and treat them otherwise is a travesty.

It was the Negro himself who first took them out of their original religious setting, but he only anticipated the inevitable by a generation—for the folk religion that produced them is rapidly vanishing. Noble as the purpose of this transplanting was, damage was done to the tradition. But we should not be ungrateful, for surely it was by this that they were saved to posterity at all. Nevertheless it was to an alien atmosphere that the missionary campaigning of the Negro schools and colleges took these songs. And the concert stage has but taken them an inevitable step further from their original setting. We should always remember that they are essentially congregational, not theatrical, just as they are essentially a choral not a solo form. In time, however, on another level, they will get back to this tradition,—for their next development will undoubtedly be, like that of the modern Russian folk music, their use in the larger choral forms of the symphonic choir, through which they will reachieve their folk atmosphere and epic spirituality.

It is a romantic story told in the *Story of the Jubilee Singers*, and retold in Professor Work's *Folk Song of the American Negro;* the tale of that group of singers who started out from Fisk University in 1871, under the resolute leadership of George L. White, to make this music the appeal of the struggling college for philanthropic support. With all the cash in the Fisk treasury, except a dollar held back by Principal Adam K. Spence, the troupe set out to Oberlin, where, after an unsuccessful concert of current music, they instantly made an impression by a program of Negro Spirituals. Henry Ward Beecher's invitation to Brooklyn led to fame for the singers, fortune for the college, but more important than these things, recognition for the Spirituals. Other schools, Hampton, Atlanta, Calhoun, Tuskegee joined the movement, and spread the knowledge of these songs far and wide in their concert campaigns. Later they recorded and published important collections of them. They thus were saved over that critical period of disfavor in which any folk product is likely to be snuffed out by the false pride of the second generation. Professor Work rightly estimates it as a service worth more racially and nationally than the considerable sums of money brought to these struggling schools. Indeed, as he says, it saved a folk art and preserved as no other medium could the folk temperament, and by maintaining them introduced the Negro to himself. Still the predominant values of this period in estimating the Spirituals were the sentimental, degenerating often into patronizing curiosity on the one side, and hectic exhibitionism on the other. Both races condescended to meet the mind of the Negro slave, and even while his moods were taking their hearts by storm, discounted the artistry of genius therein.

It was only as the musical appreciation of the Spirituals grew that this interest changed and deepened. Musically I think the Spirituals are as far in advance of their moods as their moods are in advance of their language. It is as poetry that they are least effective. Even as folk poetry, they cannot be highly rated. But they do have their quaint symbolisms, and flashes, sometimes sustained passages of fine imagery, as in the much quoted

> *I know moonlight, I know starlight*
> *I lay dis body down*
> *I walk in de graveyard, I walk troo de graveyard*

> *To lay dis body down.*

> *I lay in de grave an' stretch out my arms,*
>   *I lay dis body down.*
> *I go to de judgment in de evenin' of de day*
>   *When I lay dis body down,*
> *An' my soul an' yo' soul will meet de day*
>   *I lay dis body down.*

or

> *Bright sparkles in de churchyard*
>   *Give light unto de tomb;*
> *Bright summer, spring's over—*
>   *Sweet flowers in their bloom.*

> *My mother once, my mother twice, my mother,*
>   *she'll rejoice,*
> *In the Heaven once, in the Heaven twice,*
>   *she'll rejoice.*
>   *May the Lord, He will be glad of me*
>   *In the Heaven, He'll rejoice.*

or again

> *My Lord is so high, you can't get over Him,*
> *My Lord is so low, you can't get under Him,*
>   *You must come in and through de Lamb.*

In the latter passages, there is a naïveté, and also a faith and
fervor, that are mediæval. Indeed one has to go to the Middle Ages
to find anything quite like this combination of childlike simplicity
of thought with strangely consummate artistry of mood. A quaintly
literal, lisping, fervent Christianity, we feel it to be the evangelical
and Protestant counterpart of the naïve Catholicism of the tenth to
the thirteenth centuries. And just as there we had quaint versions of
Bernard of Clairvaux and Saint Francis in the Virgin songs and
Saints Legends, so here we have Bunyan and John Wesley perco-
lated through a peasant mind and imagination, and concentrated
into something intellectually less, but emotionally more vital and
satisfying. If the analogy seems forced, remember that we see the
homely colloquialism of the one through the glamorous distance of
romance, and of the other, through the disillusioning nearness of
social stigma and disdain. How regrettable though, that the very
qualities that add charm to the one should arouse mirthful ridicule
for the other.

Over-keen sensitiveness to this reaction, which will completely pass within a half generation or so, has unfortunately caused many singers and musicians to blur the dialect and pungent colloquialisms of the Spirituals so as not to impede with irrelevant reactions their proper artistic and emotional effect. Some have gone so far as to advocate the abandonment of the dialect versions to insure their dignity and reverence. But for all their inadequacies, the words are the vital clues to the moods of these songs. If anything is to be changed, it should be the popular attitude. One thing further may be said, without verging upon apologetics, about their verbal form. In this broken dialect and grammar there is almost invariably an unerring sense of euphony. Mr. Work goes so far as to suggest—rightly, I think—that in many instances the dropped, elided, and added syllables, especially the latter, are a matter of instinctive euphonic sense following the requirements of the musical rhythm, as, for example, "The Blood came a twinklin' down" from "The Crucifixion" or "Lying there fo' to be heal" from "Blind Man at the Pool." Mr. Work calls attention to the extra beat syllable, as in "De trumpet soun's it in-a' my soul," which is obviously a singing device, a subtle phrase-molding element from a musical point of view, even if on verbal surface value, it suggests illiteracy.

Emotionally, these folk songs are far from simple. They are not only spread over the whole gamut of human moods, with the traditional religious overtone adroitly insinuated in each instance, but there is further a sudden change of mood in the single song, baffling to formal classification. Interesting and intriguing as was Dr. Du Bois's analysis of their emotional themes, modern interpretation must break with that mode of analysis, and relate these songs to the folk activities that they motivated, classifying them by their respective song-types. From this point of view we have essentially four classes, the almost ritualistic prayer songs or pure Spirituals, the freer and more unrestrained evangelical "shouts" or camp-meeting songs, the folk ballads so overlaid with the tradition of the Spirituals proper that their distinctive type quality has almost been unnoticed until lately, and the work and labor songs of strictly secular character. In choral and musical idiom closely related, these song types are gradually coming to be regarded as more and more separate, with the term Spiritual reserved almost exclusively for the songs of intensest religious significance and function. Indeed, in the pure Spirituals one can trace the broken fragments of an evangelical folk liturgy, with confession, exhortation, "mourning," conversion and "love-feast" rejoicing as the general stages of a Protestant folk-mass. The instinctive feeling for these differences is almost wholly lost, and it will require the most careful study of the communal life as it still lingers in isolated spots to set the groupings even approximately straight. Perhaps after all the final appeal will have to be made to the sensitive race interpreter, but at present many a half secularized ballad is mistaken for a "spiritual," and many a camp-meeting shout for a folk hymn. It is not a question of religious content or allusion,—for the great majority of the Negro songs have this—but a more delicate question of caliber of feeling and type of folk use. From this important point of view, Negro folk song has yet to be studied.

The distinctiveness of the Spirituals after all, and their finest meaning resides in their musical elements. It is pathetic to notice how late scientific recording has come to the task of preserving this unique folk art. Of course the earlier four-part hymn harmony versions were travesties of the real folk renditions. All competent students agree in the utter distinctiveness of the melodic, harmonic and rhythmic elements in this music. However, there is a regrettable tendency, though a very natural one in view of an inevitable bias of technical interest, to over-stress as basically characteristic one or other of these elements in their notation and analysis. Weldon Johnson thinks the characteristic beauty of the folk song is harmonic, in distinction to the more purely rhythmic stress in the secular music of the Negro, which is the basis of "ragtime" and "jazz"; while Krehbiel more academically balances these elements, regarding the one as the African component in them, and the other as the modifying influence of the religious hymn. "In the United States," he says, "the rhythmic element, though still dominant, has yielded measurably to the melodic, the dance having given way to religious worship, sensual bodily movement to emotional utterance." But as a matter of fact, if we separate or even over-stress either element in the Spirituals, the distinctive and finer effects are lost. Strain out and emphasize the melodic element *a la* Foster, and you get only the sentimental ballad; emphasize the harmonic idiom, and you get a cloying sentimental glee; over-emphasize the rhythmic idiom and instantly you secularize the product into syncopated dance elements. It is the fusion, and that only, that is finely characteristic; and so far as possible, both in musical settings and in the singing of the Negro Spirituals, this subtle balance of musical elements should be sought after and maintained. The actual mechanics of the native singing, with its syllabic quavers, the off-tones and tone glides, the improvised interpolations and, above all, the subtle rhythmic phrase balance, has much to do with the preservation of the vital qualities of these songs.

Let us take an example. There is no more careful and appreciative student of the Spirituals than David Guion; as far as is possible from a technical and outside approach, he has bent his skill to catch the idiom of these songs. But contrast his version of "God's Goin' to Set Dis Worl' on Fire" with that of Roland Hayes. The subtler rhythmic pattern, the closer phrase linkage, the dramatic recitative movement, and the rhapsodic voice glides and quavers of the great Negro tenor's version are instantly apparent. It is more than a question of musicianship, it is a question of feeling instinctively qualities put there by instinct. In the process of the art development of this material the Negro musician has not only a peculiar advantage but a particular function and duty. Maintaining spiritual kinship with the best traditions of this great folk art, he must make himself the recognized vehicle of both its transmission and its further development.

At present the Spirituals are at a very difficult point in their musical career; for the moment they are caught in the transitional stage between a folk-form and an art-form. Their increasing concert use and popularity, as Carl Van Vechten has clearly pointed out in a recent article, has brought about a dangerous tendency toward sophisticated over-elaboration. At the same time that he calls attention to the yeoman service of Mr. Henry T. Burleigh in the introduction of the Spirituals to the attention and acceptance of the concert stage, Mr. Van Vechten thinks many of his settings tincture the folk spirit with added concert furbelows and alien florid adornments. This is true. Even Negro composers have been perhaps too much influenced by formal European idioms and mannerisms in setting these songs. But in calling for the folk atmosphere, and insisting upon the folk quality, we must be careful not to confine this wonderfully potential music to the narrow confines of "simple versions" and musically primitive molds. While it is proper to set up as a standard the purity of the tradition and the maintenance of idiom, it is not proper to insist upon an arbitrary style or form. When for similar reasons, Mr. Van Vechten insists in the name of the folk spirit upon his preference for the "evangelical renderings" of Paul Robeson's robust and dramatic style as over against the subdued, ecstatic and spiritually refined versions of Roland Hayes, he overlooks the fact that the folk itself has these same two styles of singing, and in most cases discriminates according to the mood, occasion and song type, between them. So long as the peculiar quality of Negro song is

maintained, and the musical idiom kept unadulterated, there is and
can be no set limitation. Negro folk song is not midway its artistic
career as yet, and while the preservation of the original folk forms
is for the moment the most pressing necessity, an inevitable art
development awaits them, as in the past it has awaited all other
great folk music.

The complaint to be made is not against the art development of
the Spirituals, but against the somewhat hybrid treatment characteristic of the older school of musicians. One of the worst features of
this period has been the predominance of solo treatment and the
loss of the vital sustained background of accompanying voices. In
spite of the effectiveness of the solo versions, especially when com-
petently sung by Negro singers, it must be realized more and more
that the proper idiom of Negro folk song calls for choral treatment.
The young Negro musicians, Nathaniel Dett, Carl Diton, Ballanta
Taylor, Edward Boatner, Hall Johnson, Lawrence Brown and others, while they are doing effective solo settings, are turning back
gradually to the choral form. Musically speaking, only the superficial resources in this direction have been touched as yet; just as
soon as the traditional conventions of four-part harmony and the
oratorio style and form are broken through, we may expect a choral
development of Negro folk song that may equal or even outstrip the
phenomenal choral music of Russia. With its harmonic versatility
and interchangeable voice parts, Negro music is only conventionally
in the four-part style, and with its skipped measures and interpolations it is at the very least potentially polyphonic. It can therefore
undergo without breaking its own boundaries, intricate and original
development in directions already the line of advance in modernistic
music.

Indeed one wonders why something vitally new has not already
been contributed by Negro folk song to modern choral and orchestral musical development. And if it be objected that it is too far a
cry from the simple folk spiritual to the larger forms and idioms of
modern music, let us recall the folk song origins of the very tradition which is now classic in European music. Up to the present, the
resources of Negro music have been tentatively exploited in only
one direction at a time,—melodically here, rhythmically there, har-
monically in a third direction. A genius that would organize its
distinctive elements in a formal way would be the musical giant of
his age. Such a development has been hampered by a threefold
tradition, each aspect of which stands in the way of the original use
of the best in the Negro material. The dominance of the melodic

tradition has played havoc with its more original harmonic features, and the oratorio tradition has falsely stereotyped and overlaid its more orchestral choral style, with its intricate threading in and out of the voices. Just as definitely in another direction has the traditional choiring of the orchestra stood against the opening up and development of the Negro and the African idioms in the orchestral forms. Gradually these barriers are being broken through. Edgar Varese's *Integrales*, a "study for percussion instruments," presented last season by the International Composers' Guild, suggests a new orchestral technique patterned after the characteristic idiom of the African "drum orchestra." The modernistic, *From the Land of Dreams*, by Grant Still, a young Negro composer who is his student and protégé, and Louis Grünberg's setting for baritone and chamber orchestra of Weldon Johnson's *The Creation: a Negro Sermon*, are experimental tappings in still other directions into the rich veins of this new musical ore.

[ON POETRY]

Jupiter Hammon, Phillis Wheatley, George Moses Horton

1

THE LITERATURE of the Negro in America, motivated as it is by his very practical desire to adjust himself to the American environment, is "literature of necessity." Until recent years the Negro writer has not known what it is to write without this motivation, and even now, of the dozens of writers who have published in the last twenty years the work of but two seems wholly independent of this influence. At the very heart of this literature, then, lies the spore of a cankerous growth. This might be said to be the necessity of ends. But there is also a necessity of means. Negro writers have been obliged to have two faces. If they wished to succeed they have been obliged to satisfy two different (and opposed when not entirely opposite) audiences, the black and the white. This necessity of means, perhaps, has been even stronger than the necessity of ends, and as writers have increased, the necessity has grown almost to the point of desperation.

From Jupiter Hammon, the first Negro writer in America, to Countee Cullen and Langston Hughes, these two necessities can be traced with varying degrees of clarity—now one and now the other predominant—like threads through the whole cloth. With the very earliest writers the needs did not encompass more than personal self, but as consciousness of others awakened in later writers and as the simplicity of the Negro's primary position in America changed successively to the complexity of the times of abolition agitation, freedom, enfranchisement, and social self-determination, the artless personality of his literature dropped away and he became the sometimes frenzied propagandist of racial consciousness and advancement.

2

Jupiter Hammon was the first American Negro to see his name in print as a maker of verse. The date of his birth is uncertain, but the earliest reference to him is found in a letter dated May 19, 1730, when he was probably a little more than ten years old. At this time he was the slave of Henry Lloyd of Queens Village, Long Island. The date of his death is likewise uncertain, but was very probably not earlier than 1806.

Hammon's first published work was "An Evening Thought: Salvation by Christ, with Penetential Cries" in 1760. His next work, "A Poetical Address to Phillis Wheatley," was published eighteen years later, but it is improbable that the intervening years were devoid of literary activity, especially considering that Hammon was something of a preacher among his people, a fact which plainly had a bearing upon his work. "An Essay on the Ten Virgins," of which no copy is extant, was printed in 1779. In 1782 he published "A Winter Piece" with "A Poem for Children with Thoughts on Death" and "An Evening's Improvement" to which was appended a rhymed dialogue entitled "The Kind Master and Dutiful Servant." The last of his printed work, "An Address to Negroes in the State of New York," was issued in 1787 and reached three editions.

Hammon was an intelligent and privileged slave, respected by the master class for his skill with tools and by the slaves for his power as a preacher. His verse is rhymed prose, doggerel, in which the homely thoughts of a very religious and superstitious man are expressed in limping phrases. Now and then his lines have a lyric swing that seems to mark them as having been chanted spontaneously in the sermons he preached. Undoubtedly some lines from "An Evening Thought" have this lyric significance. The alternately rhyming lines lend themselves very easily and nicely to religious chanting.

> *Salvation comes by Christ alone,*
> *The only son of God;*
> *Redemption now to every one,*
> *That love his holy word.*

Dear Jesus unto Thee we cry,
Give us the preparation;
Turn not away thy tender eye;
We seek thy true salvation.

Of the work of this kind, the piece addressed to Phillis Wheatley is the best. Hammon must have struck responsive chords in the breast of the young Massachusetts slave who already at this time had been acclaimed in England as an unusual poet. Both were extremely religious, and both preferred slavery in America to freedom in Africa. Each of the twenty-one quatrains of "The Address to Phillis Wheatley" has a marginal note of reference to the Bible.

I

O come you pious youth! Adore
  The wisdom of thy God,
In bringing thee from distant shore
  To learn his holy word.

II

Thou mightst been left behind,
  Amidst a dark abode;
God's tender mercy still combin'd,
  Thou hast the holy word.

IV

God's tender mercy brought thee here;
  Tost o'er the raging main;
In Christian faith thou hast a share,
  Worth all the gold of Spain.

IX

Come you, Phillis, now aspire,
  And seek the living God,
So step by step thou mayest go higher,
  Till perfect in the word.

Almost did Miss Wheatley express Hammon's exact thought in her lines "To The University of Cambridge."

'T was not long since I left my native shore,
The land of errors and Egyptian gloom:
Father of mercy! 't was thy gracious hand
Brought me in safety from those dark abodes.

On the whole, Hammon's untutored art offered but narrow scope for the fullest expression. His most substantial contribution to

Negro literature prior to the Civil War is in prose, and whatever of literary merit he possessed must be looked for in his single prose piece, "An Address to the Negroes in the State of New York." This work reveals more of Hammon's workaday character than all his poetry together. The thoughts expressed in "An Address to Negroes" are not typical of the thoughts of slaves, especially those who were unfortunate enough to have had some education. With the notable exception of Phillis Wheatley, the slave writers were bitterly reproachful of bondage. Many slaves who could neither read nor write but who were nonetheless truly poetic burned themselves out in revolt. To the splendid folly of their deeds Hammon's equivocal statement is an outrage. A summation of his philosophy and a clearcut statement of his resignation to a life of servitude is found in his words:

"Respecting obedience to masters. Now whether it is right and lawful in the sight of God, for them to make slaves of us or not, I am certain that while we are slaves, it is our duty to obey our masters in all their lawful commands, and mind them. . . . As we depend upon our masters for what we eat and drink and wear, we cannot be happy unless we obey them."

Hammon's life was motivated by the compulsion of obedience to his earthly and his heavenly master. Perhaps the inevitability of his position tended to wilt his moral fiber. Perhaps the beneficence of his masters lightened the burden of his bondage. Though he was the first Negro slave to publish an adverse opinion on the institution of slavery, his opinion was robbed of its force by the words "though for my own part I do not wish to be free." Perhaps it was the very weakness of the statement that recommended it for publication. At the same time, however, his hedging was not without its wisdom. He says:

"Now I acknowledge that liberty is a great thing, and worth seeking for, if we can get it honestly; and by our good conduct prevail upon our masters to set us free: though for my own part I do not wish to be free, yet I should be glad if others, especially the young negroes, were to be free; for many of us who are grown up slaves, and have always had masters to take care of us, should hardly know how to take care of themselves. . . . That liberty is a great thing we may know from our own feelings, and we may likewise judge so from the conduct of the white people in the late war. How much money has been spent and how many lives have been lost to defend their liberty! I must say that I have hoped that

God would open their eyes, when they were so much engaged for
liberty, to think of the state of the poor blacks, and to pity us."

As to literary values, there is not much to choose between
Hammon's poetry and prose. Though he was not without the romantic gift of spontaneity, he lacked any knowledge of metrics and
sought only to make rhymes. In prose the artlessness of his construction, the rambling sentences, the repetitions reveal, sometimes
at the expense of thought, his not unattractive personality. When he
is most lucid there is force in the quaintness of his thought evocative of the highly personal flavor of early American letters.

3

Little more is known of the birth of Phillis Wheatley than of Jupiter
Hammon. At the time of her purchase by John Wheatley in 1761
she was judged to be in her seventh or eighth year from "the
circumstance of shedding her front teeth." She was a scrawny child,
alert with the precocity so often associated with physical frailty.
Mrs. Wheatley was quick to realize Phillis's unusual intelligence,
but she could not possibly tell that this little slave girl, scarcely
more than a useless luxury at first, was to become in England the
best-known of contemporary American poets.

Phillis's life with the Wheatleys was in every way exceptional.
Taught to read and write, nurtured and tutored with the greatest
care, within a year and a half of her arrival from Africa she had
acquired a sufficient command of the English language "to read
any, the most difficult parts of the sacred writings." Two years later
she had written her first poems.

There is no question but that Miss Wheatley considered herself
a Negro poet: the question is to what degree she felt the full significance of such a designation. Certainly she was not a *slave* poet in
any sense in which the term can be applied to many who followed
her. She stood far outside the institution that was responsible for
her. As for the question of degree, though she refers to herself time
and again as an "Ethiop," she seems to make such reference with a
distinct sense of abnegation and self-pity.

> *Father of mercy! 'T was thy gracious hand*
> *Brought me in safety from those dark abodes.*

This attitude on the part of Miss Wheatley was the result of the
training and conduct of her life. Treated as one of the Wheatley
family on terms of almost perfect equality, petted and made much

of, she was sagacious enough to see that this was due in part at least to her exotic character and sensitive enough to feel that her color was really a bar to a more desirable, if less flattering, attention. At best this life was not too dear to Phillis. She recounts the joys of the life to come in the strains of one who looks upon this life as though it were a strange and bitter preparation for an eternity of bliss. The Wheatleys had adopted her, but she had adopted their terrific New England conscience. Her conception of the afterlife was different from that of most of the slaves as we find it expressed in songs and spirituals. No contemplation of physical luxuries of feastings, jeweled crowns, and snowy robes enticed her. Her heaven must be a place of the purest sublimation of spirit. Less than this would serve but to remind her of this dark bourne of flesh and blood.

But if the degree to which she felt herself a Negro poet was slight, the extent to which she was attached spiritually and emotionally to the slaves is even slighter. By 1761 slavery was an important, almost daily topic. The Boston home of the Wheatleys, intelligent and alive as it was, could not have been deaf to the discussions of restricting the slave trade, especially since by 1770 Massachusetts, Pennsylvania, and Virginia had each taken steps in that direction. Nothing so hard and definite as the abolition movement had been put forward, but when Miss Wheatley landed in England in 1773 freedom was a vital topic in pulpit and Parliament. Not once, however, did she express in either word or action a thought on the enslavement of her race; not once did she utter a straightforward word for the freedom of the Negro. When she did speak of freedom in a letter to the Earl of Dartmouth, it was:

> *No more, America, in mournful strain,*
> *Of wrongs and grievances unredressed complain;*
> *No longer shall thou dread the iron chain*
> *Which wanton Tyranny with lawless hand,*
> *Had made, and with it meant t' enslave the land.*

Toward the end of this poetic epistle she says the only thing that may be taken as an indictment of human slavery. Yet even in these lines the effect is vitiated.

> *Should you, my lord, while you peruse my song,*
> *Wonder from whence my love of freedom sprung,*
> *Whence flow these wishes for the common good,*
> *By feeling hearts alone best understood,*
> *I, young in life, by seeming cruel fate*
> *Was snatched from Afric's fancied happy seat.*

"Seeming cruel" and "fancied happy" give her away as not
believing either in the cruelty of the fate that had dragged thousands of her race into bondage in America nor in the happiness of
their former freedom in Africa. How different the spirit of her
work, and how unracial (not to say unnatural) are the stimuli that
release her wan creative energies. How different are these from the
work of George Horton who twenty-five years later could cry out
with bitterness, without cavil or fear:

> *Alas! and am I born for this,*
> *To wear this slavish chain?*

It is this negative, bloodless, unracial quality in Phillis Wheatley that makes her seem superficial, especially to members of her
own race. Hers is a spirit-denying-the-flesh attitude that somehow
cannot seem altogether real as the essential quality and core of one
whose life should have made her sensitive to the very things she
denies. In this sense none of her poetry is real. Compared to the
Negro writers who followed her, Miss Wheatley's passions are tame,
her skill the sedulous copy of established techniques, and her
thoughts the hand-me-downs of her age. She is chilly. Part of her
chill is due to the unmistakable influence of Pope's neoclassicism
upon her. She followed the fashion in poetry. Overemphasis of
religion was a common fault of the time. She indulged it in poetic
epistles, eulogistic verse, verses written in praise of accomplishments. Her ready submission to established forms was a weakness
of the period. First and last, she was the fragile product of three
related forces—the age, the Wheatley household, and New England
America. Her work lacks spontaneity because of the first, enthusiasm because of the second, and because of the third it lacks an
unselfish purpose that drives to some ultimate goal of expression.

And yet she had poetic talent, was in fact a poet. No one who
reads the following lines from "Thoughts on the Works of Providence" can deny it.

> *Infinite love, where'r we turn our eyes,*
> *Appears: this ev'ry creatures want supplies;*
> *This most is heard in nature's constant voice;*
> *This makes the morn, and this the eve, rejoice;*
> *This bids the fostering rains and dews descend*
> *To nourish all, to serve one gen'ral end,*
> *The good of man: yet man ungrateful pays*
> *But little homage, and but little praise.*

> *To Him whose works arrayed in mercy shine,*
> *What songs should rise, how constant, how divine!*

Judged in the light of the day in which she wrote, judged by that day's standards and accomplishments, she was an important poet. As a Negro poet she stands out remarkably, for her work lacks the characteristics of thought one would expect to find. She was the first Negro woman in America to write and publish poetry.

The story of her life following her return from England is soon told by the anonymous writer of the *Memoirs of Phillis Wheatley.* Her health, never sound, grew precarious. In 1778 she married a Negro doctor, lawyer, and groceryman named John Peters, by whom she had two children. Peters proved worthless, deserting her in her utmost need, when the older Wheatleys were dead and the younger ones scattered.

"In a filthy apartment, in an obscure part of the metropolis, lay the dying mother and child. The woman who had stood honored and respected by the wise and good in that country which was hers by adoption, or rather compulsion, who had graced the ancient halls of old England, and had rolled about in the splendid equipages of the proud nobles of Britain, was now numbering the last hours of her life in a state of the most abject misery, surrounded by all the emblems of squalid poverty. . . .

"The friends of Phillis who had visited her in her sickness, knew not of her death. . . . A grand-niece of Phillis's benefactress, passing up Court Street, met the funeral of an adult and a child: a by-stander informed her that they were bearing Phillis to that silent mansion."

4

What Hammon lacked in audacity and color and what Miss Wheatley failed to show in enthusiasm and racial kinship is more than supplied by George Moses Horton. If the former were motivated only by an aimless urge to write, finding as they went along, willy-nilly, ideas, emotions, and thoughts to give expression to, Horton started from an emotional basis. He first wanted to say something. Hammon and Miss Wheatley were negative; Horton was positive. He felt, albeit selfishly, the motivation derived from the Negro's position in America. He felt, too, something of the wonder and mystery, the tragic beauty, and the pathetic ugliness of life. Above all, he had the gift of laughter. He was the first "natural-born" poet of the Negro race in America.

Horton was born a slave in North Carolina about the year

1797. The exact date is uncertain. At a reception given him in Philadelphia in 1866, he was said to have remarked that his former master reckoned his age by looking into his mouth, judged the state of his health by whipping him, and determined the condition of his immortal soul by damning him to hell. Horton was an incorrigible actor and laugh-baiter, never missing an opportunity (at the cost of no matter what falsehood) to dramatize himself. When his first volume, *Hope of Liberty*, was published in 1829, Weston R. Gales, editor of the *Raleigh Register* and one of the men interested in helping Horton gain his freedom, judged him to be about thirty-two years old.

Though Horton very soon gave evidence of hating slavery, it does not seem that he was more than nominally restrained by his slave status. What Horton's occupations and wanderings were we do not know, but he gained somehow considerably more knowledge of the world than fell to the lot of most slaves. By the 1820's he had become known in Raleigh and was proabably at that time working around the State University at Chapel Hill and writing for students the poems that made him something of a campus celebrity.

The poems of this period are not available, but they must have been light and more or less humorously concerned with love, the sort of jingles that would delight young college students. Certainly it is inconceivable that the provincial sons of the South, many of them slaveholders, would have paid the poet for poems in which he railed against slavery. Indeed it may be that at this time Horton's feelings about slavery had not crystallized into hatred. It seems fair to judge these earlier poems, then, by later work of the same kind.

Later Horton learned to hate. Perhaps his disappointment over his failure to purchase his freedom had something to do with it. As early as 1822 he had had elaborate dreams of migrating to the free colony of Liberia. Perhaps from the North there had drifted down to him some word of the sympathetic interest his scattered poems had created. At any rate, he was fully aware of the desirability of a life of freedom. Though only three poems on slavery appeared in *Hope of Liberty*, one is inclined to the belief that "some of the poems deleted in the interest of the author" were of this nature. Since the volume was manifestly published to obtain funds with which to purchase Horton's freedom, this seems all the more likely.

Though throughout the book he shows a consistently good and original nature, dwelling much on religion, nature, and love, now and then he expresses the dark bitterness with which his lot afflicted him. From the hopeful hymn that opens the volume,

Creation fires my tongue!
  Nature, thy anthems raise;
And spread the universal song
  Of thy Creator's praise!

he could come to the following lament, the meter of which was
certainly inspired by the Methodist hymns with which he was familiar:

Alas! and am I born for this,
  To wear this slavish chain?
Deprived of all created bliss,
  Through hardship, toil, and pain?

How long have I in bondage lain,
  And languished to be free!
Alas! and must I still complain,
  Deprived of liberty?

The financial purpose of the book failed, and from 1829 on
there is increasing evidence that Horton "played" his misfortunes,
real or imaginary, "to the grandstand." It is not known who inspired the editor's hint in the preface to the Philadelphia edition of
Hope of Liberty (1837) that Weston Gales had retained the money
realized from the Raleigh printing, but an impartial judgment of
Horton's later character makes one believe it was likely Horton
himself. Naïvely selfish and stuffed with the vanity of a child, his
conduct after his escape to Philadelphia and freedom toward the
close of the civil struggle was said to have been unbearable. The free
Negroes, of which at the time there were considerable numbers in
Philadelphia, could not tolerate his demeanor, the childish strutting
that had made him a character in the South. After a few weeks, they
dropped him so completely that John Hawkins, who was a boy of
thirteen in 1880, and whose parents knew Horton well, could not
recall when or where the poet died.

Though Horton fully realized the bitterness of bondage, he
tasted its gall only for himself. He seems to have thought that
slavery was created for himself alone. In this he differs from Miss
Wheatley in that she seemed never fully to appreciate her slave
status. If she was not aroused by it for others, neither was she
aroused by it for herself. Horton, wholly aware, satisfied himself
with but one expressed thought for others:

> *Love which can ransom every slave,*
>   *And set the pris'ner free;*
> *Gild the dark horrors of the grave,*
>   *And still the raging sea.*

Even later when the *New York Tribune,* probably America's greatest paper at that time, began to publish antislavery sentiment and
the editor, Horace Greeley, became interested in Horton, it was the
same. The best that Horton could attain was a conceited plea for his
own deliverance:

> *Let me no longer be a slave,*
>   *But drop the fetters and be free.*
>
> .   .   .   .   .
>
> *Oh, listen all who never felt*
>   *For fettered genius heretofore,*
> *Let hearts of petrification melt,*
>   *And bid the gifted negro soar.*

After 1837 various of Horton's poems appeared in northern
periodicals of abolitionist leanings or declaration, like the *North
Star,* Frederick Douglass's Rochester paper, the *Liberator,* and the
Lancaster (Pa.) *Gazette.* In 1838, George Light published in Boston
an edition of Horton's *Hope of Liberty* and bound it with the
memoir and poems of Phillis Wheatley. The full title of this edition
was, *Memoir and Poems of Phillis Wheatley, a Native African and
Slave: Also, Poems by a Slave.* In 1865 there was printed at Raleigh the second and final volume of Horton's poems, *Naked Genius,*
which seems to contain a great many earlier poems not published
before.

Between 1829 and 1865 Horton seems not to have grown at all,
though the later pieces in *Naked Genius* reveal a return of that good
humor that helped the sale of his earlier poems to the university
students. He never lost his naïve conceit. His poems are concerned
with love and nature, heavenly grace and divine miracles. Remarkable among his characteristics is his imagery, generally as confused
and wasteful and rich as a tropic sunset, but sometimes astonish-
ingly fine and telling.

> *'T was like fair Helen's sweet return to Troy.*

> *At his command the water blushed*
>   *And all was turned to wine.*

Remarkable, too, are the turns of humor which deny the simplicity of his mind and character. It is unfortunate that so much of his Chapel Hill verse was lost, for in those days of his youth the humor must have been much more audacious and sparkling, though perhaps less sophistical. It may be that those early verses are an important loss to American humor. The finger-snapping flippancy of "Jeff Davis in a Tight Place" and "Creditor to His Proud Debtor" are not unworthy of a Holmes.

My duck bill boots would look as bright,
Had you in justice served me right;
Like you, I then could step as light,
   Before a flaunting maid.
As nicely could I clear my throat,
And to my tights my eyes devote;
But I'd leave you bare, without the coat
   For which you have not paid.

Then boast and bear the crack,
With the sheriff at your back,
Huzzah for dandy Jack,
My jolly fop, my Jo!

Beside the gray-mantled figures of Hammon and Phillis Wheatley, Horton appears dressed in motley. His humor, his audacious and homely wit, his lack of dignity give him important historical place as the forerunner of the minstrel poets, and this consideration outweighs whatever of intrinsic poetical value his poems possess.

WALLACE THURMAN
Negro Poets and Their Poetry

JUPITER HAMMON, the first Negro in this country to write and publish poetry, was a slave owned by a Mr. Joseph Lloyd of Queens Village, Long Island. Hammon had been converted to the religion of Jesus Christ and all of his poems are religious exhortations, incoherent in thought and crudely excepted. His first poem was published in 1761, his second, entitled "An Address to Miss Phillis

Wheatley, Ethiopian Poetess in Boston, who came from Africa at eight years of age and soon became acquainted with the Gospel of Jesus Christ", in 1768.

This Miss Phillis Wheatley, who had been bought from a slave-ship by a family named Wheatley in Boston Harbor and educated by them, wrote better doggerel than her older contemporary Hammon. She knew Alexander Pope and she knew Ovid—Hammon only knew the Bible—and she knew Pope so well that she could write like a third-rate imitator of him. Phillis in her day was a museum figure who would have caused more of a sensation if some contemporary Barnum had exploited her. As it was, she attracted so much attention that many soft hearted (and, in some cases, soft headed) whites and blacks have been led to believe that her poetry deserves to be considered as something more than a mere historical relic. This is an excerpt from her best poem:

> *Imagination! who can sing thy force?*
> *Or who describe the swiftness of thy course?*
> *Soaring through the air to find the bright abode,*
> *The empyreal palace of the thundering God,*
> *We on thy pinions can surpass the wind,*
> *And leave the rolling universe behind,*
> *From star to star the mental optics rove,*
> *Measure the skies, and range the realms above,*
> *There is one view we grasp the mighty whole,*
> *Or with new worlds amaze the unbounded soul.*

She never again equalled the above, far less surpassed it. And most of the time she wrote as in the following excerpt from "On Major General Lee". (This poem would warm the heart of "Big Bill" Thompson of Chicago; he really should know about it.) A captured colonial soldier is addressing a British general:

> *O Arrogance of tongue!*
> *And wild ambition, ever prone to wrong!*
> *Believ'st thou, chief, that armies such as thine*
> *Can stretch in dust that heaven defended line?*
> *In vain allies may swarm from distant lands,*
> *And demons aid in formidable bands,*
> *Great as thou art, thou shun'st the field of fame,*
> *Disgrace to Britain and the British name.*

She continues in this vein, damning the British and enshrining the Americans until she reaches a climax in the following priceless lines:

Find in your train of boasted heroes, one
To match the praise of Godlike Washington.
Thrice happy chief in whom the virtues join,
And heaven taught prudence speaks the man divine.

Thomas Jefferson is quoted as saying that "Religion has produced a Phillis Wheatley, but it could not produce a poet. Her poems
are beneath contempt". Nevertheless, Phillis had an interesting and
exciting career. The Wheatleys carried her to London, where her
first volume was published in 1773. She was exhibited at the Court
of George III, and in the homes of the nobility much as the Negro
poets of today are exhibited in New York drawing rooms. She wrote
little about slavery, which is not surprising considering that save for
her epic trip across the Atlantic in a slave-ship, she had never
known slavery in any form. She often mentioned her homeland and
once spoke of herself as "Afric's muse", but she was more interested
in the religion of Jesus Christ and in the spreading of piety than in
any more worldly items, save perhaps in her patriotic interest for
the cause of the American colonists.

Heretofore every commentator, whether white or black, when
speaking of Phillis Wheatley, has sought to make excuses for her
bad poetry. They have all pointed out that Phillis lived and wrote
during the eighteenth century, when, to quote from the introduction
to White and Jackson's "Poetry of American Negro Poets", "the
great body of contemporary poetry was turgid in the style of debased Pope". It would be too much, they continue, to expect "a poet
of Phillis Wheatley's rather conventional personality to rise above
this influence". In his preface to "The Book of American Negro
Poetry", James Weldon Johnson contends that "had she come under
the influence of Wordsworth, Byron, Keats or Shelley, she would
have done greater work". Does it smack too much of lese majesty to
suggest that perhaps Phillis wrote the best poetry she could have
written under any influence, and that a mediocre imitation of Shelly
would have been none the less mediocre than a mediocre imitation
of Pope? Phillis was also influenced by the Bible, but her paraphrases of the scripture are just as poor as her paraphrases of
"debased Pope".

Phillis died in 1784 and until Paul Lawrence Dunbar published
his "Oak and Ivy", in 1892, American Negro poetry stayed at the
level at which she had left it, although there must have been over
one hundred Negroes who wrote and published poetry during this
period. Most of them came into prominence during and after the

Civil War, and were encouraged by abolitionists to write of their race and their race's trials. Frances Ellen Harper is probably the best of this period. One volume, "On Miscellaneous Subjects", was published with an introduction by William Lloyd Garrison. Over ten thousand copies were circulated. Mrs. Harper also wrote and published "Moses, a Story of the Nile", in verse covering fifty-two closely printed pages. Many of her contemporaries were equally ambitious. Length was a major poetic virtue to them.

It seems highly probable that these people wrote in verse because neither their minds nor their literary tools and backgrounds were adequate for the task of writing readable and intelligent prose. They could be verbose and emotional in verse, and yet attain a degree of coherence not attainable when they wrote in prose. George M. Horton is a good illustration. He was born a slave in Chatham County, North Carolina, in 1797. It is said that he "was not a good farm worker on account of devoting too much time to fishing, hunting and attending religious meetings". He taught himself to read with the aid of a Methodist hymn-book and a red-backed speller. In 1830 he secured work as a janitor at Chapel Hill, the seat of the University of South Carolina. Here he made extra money writing love poems for amorous students. Desiring to obtain his freedom and migrate to Liberia, Horton, aided by some of his white friends, published a volume of verse entitled "The Hope of Liberty", but the returns from the sale of this volume were not sufficient for his purpose. But he remained more or less a free agent, and was allowed to hire himself out instead of having to remain on his master's plantation. In 1865, a troop of Federal soldiers, who had been quartered in Chapel Hill, were ordered north. Horton left with them and went to Philadelphia where he eventually died.

Here is a sample of his prose: "By close application to my book and at night my visage became considerably emaciated by extreme perspiration, having no lucubratory apparatus, no candle, no lamp, not even lightweed, being chiefly raised in oaky woods". And here is a sample of his verse:

> *Come liberty. Thou cheerful sound*
> *Roll through my ravished ears;*
> *Come, let my griefs in joy be drowned*
> *And drive away my fears.*

Further comment would be superfluous.

After the Civil War, the Negro found himself in a dilemma. He was supposed to be free, yet his condition was little changed. He was worse off in some respects than he had been before. It can be understood, then, that the more articulate Negroes of the day spent most of their time speculating upon this thing called freedom, both as it had been imagined and as it was in actuality.

However, none of the poetry written at this time is worthy of serious critical consideration. It was not even a poetry of protest. Although Negro poets objected to the mistreatment of their people, they did not formulate these objections in strong, biting language, but rather sought sympathy and pled for pity. They wept copiously but seldom manifested a fighting spirit. The truth is, only one American Negro poet has been a fighting poet, only one has really written revolutionary protest poetry, and that is Claude McKay, who will be considered later.

Paul Lawrence Dunbar was the first American Negro poet whose work really merited critical attention. Dunbar was the son of two ex-slaves, but supposedly full-blooded Negroes, a fact flagrantly paraded by race purists, to controvert the prevalent Nordic theory that only Negroes with Caucasian blood in their veins ever accomplish anything. He was born in Dayton, Ohio, June 27th, 1872. His father had escaped from his master and fled to Canada, but later returned to the States and enlisted for military service during the Civil War in a Massachusetts regiment. Dunbar may have inherited his love for letters and writing from his mother, whose master had often read aloud in her presence.

Dunbar attended the public school in his home town, and was graduated from the local high-school, where he had edited the school paper. Then he found employment as an elevator operator. In 1892 he delivered an address in verse to the Western Association of Writers, and shortly afterwards he published his first volume, "Oak and Ivy". In 1896, through the subscription method, he was able to publish another volume entitled, "Majors and Minors". William Dean Howells wrote a most favorable review of this volume and later paved the way for Dodd, Mead and Company to publish "Lyrics of Lowly Life", for which he wrote an introduction. Meanwhile Dunbar had visited England, and had become a great friend with Coleridge Taylor, the Negro composer, with whom he collaborated on many songs. On his return to the United States, another friend, Robert G. Ingersoll, helped him to get a position in the Library of Congress. He was only able to keep this job two years, for meanwhile he had developed pulmonary tuberculosis, and despite pilgrimages to such lung-soothing climates as the Adirondacks, the Rockies, and Florida, he finally succumbed to the disease and died in Dayton, Ohio, on February 9, 1908.

From 1892 until the time of his death, Dunbar published five volumes of verse, four volumes of collected short stories, and four novels. Not only was he the first Negro to write poetry which had real merit and could be considered as having more than merely sentimental or historical value, but he was also the first Negro poet to be emancipated from Methodism, the first American Negro poet who did not depend on a Wesleyan hymn-book for inspiration and vocabulary. Most of the poets preceding him were paragons of piety. They had all been seized upon by assiduous missionaries and put through the paces of Christianity, and their verses were full of puerile apostrophizing of the Almighty, and leaden allusions to Scriptural passages.

Yet Dunbar was far from being a great poet. First of all, he was a rank sentimentalist, and was content to let surface values hold his interest. He attempted to interpret the soul of his people, but as William Stanley Braithwaite has said, he succeeded "only in interpreting a folk temperament". And although he was, as William Dean Howells affirmed, the first "man of pure African blood of American civilization to feel Negro life aesthetically and express it lyrically", neither his aesthetic feeling nor his expression ever attained enough depth to be of permanent value.

Dunbar is famous chiefly for his dialect poetry. Yet he often regretted that the world turned to praise "a jingle in a broken tongue". He was ambitious to experiment in more classical forms, and to deal with something less concrete than the "smile through your tears" plantation larky of reconstruction times. Here perhaps was his greatest limitation. Being anxious to explore the skies, he merely skimmed over the surface of the earth.

After Dunbar, there was a whole horde of Negro poets who, like him, wrote in dialect. The sum total of their achievement is zero, but happily, in addition to these parasitic tyros there were also two new poets who had more originality and more talent than their contemporaries. And though neither of these men produced anything out of the ordinary, they did go beyond the minstrel humor and peasant pathos of Dunbar, and beyond the religious cant and doggerel jeremiads of Dunbar's predecessors. One of these men, William Stanley Braithwaite, is best known as a student and friend of poets and poetry rather than as a poet. He has yearly, since 1913, issued an anthology of American magazine verse, and has also published some academic studies of English literature.

The second, James Weldon Johnson, achieved little as a poet until recently, when he published "God's Trombones", a volume of Negro sermons done in verse. His first volume, "Fifty Years And

Other Poems", contains little of merit. The title poem, which recounts in verse the progress of the race from 1863 to 1913, has,
because of its propagandist content, been acclaimed as a great
poem. No comment or criticism is necessary of this opinion when
part of the poem itself can be quoted:

> *Far, far, the way that we have trod*
> *From heathen trails and jungle dens*
> *To freedmen, freedmen, sons of God,*
> *Americans and citizens.*

Mr. Johnson, it seems, has also been fairly intimate with Methodist
hymnbooks.

His sermon poems, while at times awkward and faulty in technique, have an ecstatic eloquence and an individual rhythm which
immediately place them among the best things any Negro has ever
done in poetry. Although this may not be saying much, and although, as a poet Mr. Johnson may not be adequate to the task of
fully realizing the promise of these sermon poems, he has at least
laid a foundation upon which a new generation of Negro poets can
build. He will have to be remembered as something more than just a
historical or sentimental figure. He, like Dunbar, is an important, if
a minor bard; and if the Negro poet of the future is to make any
individual contribution to American literature he must derive almost as much from the former's "God's Trombones" as from the
latter's "Lyrics of Lowly Life".

To consider all the Negro poets who since 1913 have lifted up
their voices in song would necessitate using an entire issue of any
journal. It is not only an impossible task but one not worth the time
and space it would require. For our present study we will touch only
the high spots, passing over such people as Fenton Johnson, whose
early promise has never been fulfilled; Joseph Cotter, Jr., who, it is
alleged by most critics in this field, would have been a great poet
had he lived but whose extant work belies this judgment; Georgia
Douglas Johnson, whose highly sentimental and feminine lyrics
have found favor; Arna Bontemps, who specializes in monotonous
and wordy mystic evocations which lack fire and conviction, and
Helene Johnson, who alone of all the younger group seems to have
the "makings" of a poet.

But taking up the contemporary triumvirate—McKay, Cullen,
and Hughes—all of whom have had volumes published by reputable
houses and are fairly well known to the poetry-reading public, we
have poets of another type. Each one of them represents a different
trend in Negro literature and life.

Claude McKay was born in Jamaica, British West Indies, where he received his elementary education, served a while in the constabulary, and wrote his first poems. A friend financed his journey to America to finish his scholastic work, but McKay found himself at odds with the second-rate schools he attended here and finally fled to New York City where he became a member of the old *Masses, Seven Arts, Liberator* group of radicals and artists. During this period he received a legacy which, he tells us, was spent in riotous living. Broke, he attempted to make a living by washing dishes, operating elevators, doing porter work—the usual occupations engaged in by Negro artists and intellectuals.

McKay's first volume was published while he was still in Jamaica, a compilation of folk verse done in the native dialect. The Institute of Arts and Sciences of Jamaica gave him a medal in recognition of this first book. It is in many ways remarkable, and in it the poet gives us a more substantial portrait and delves far deeper into the soul of the Jamaican than Dunbar was ever able to in the soul of the southern Negro in America.

McKay's latter poetry is often marred by bombast. He is such an intense person that one can often hear the furnace-like fire within him roaring in his poems. He seems to have more emotional depth and spiritual fire than any of his forerunners or contemporaries. It might be added that he also seems to have considerably more mental depth too. His love poems are not as musical or as haunting as Mr. Cullen's, but neither are they as stereotyped. His sonnet to a Harlem dancer may not be as deft or as free from sentiment as "Midnight Man" by Langston Hughes, but it is far more mature and moving. All of which leads us to say that a study of Claude McKay's and of the other better Negro poetry convinces us that he, more than the rest, has really had something to say. It is his tragedy that his message was too alive and too big for the form he chose. His poems are for the most part either stilted, choked, or over-zealous. He could never shape the flames from the fire that blazed within him. But he is the only Negro poet who ever wrote revolutionary or protest poetry. Hence:

> *If we must die, let it be not like hogs*
> *Hunted and penned in an inglorious spot,*
>
> .   .   .
>
> *Oh, Kinsman! We must meet the common foe;*
> *Though far outnumbered let us still be brave,*
> *And for their thousand blows, deal one death blow!*
> *What though before us lies the open grave?*

Like men we'll face the murderous pack,
Pressed to the wall, dying—but fighting back.

There is no impotent whining here, no mercy-seeking prayer to the white man's God, no mournful jeremiad, no "ain't it hard to be a nigger", no lamenting of or apologizing for the fact that he is a member of a dark-skinned minority group. Rather he boasts:

Be not deceived, for every deed you do,
I could match—out match; Am I not Africa's son,
Black of that black land where black deeds are done?

This is propaganda poetry of the highest order although it is crude and inexpert. Contrast it with these lines from Countee Cullen's sonnet "From The Dark Tower":

We shall not always plant while others reap
The golden increment of bursting fruit,
Nor always countenance abject and mute
That lesser men should hold their brothers cheap.

Countee Cullen is the symbol of a fast disappearing generation of Negro writers. In him it reaches its literary apogee. On the other hand Langston Hughes announces the entrance of a new generation, while Claude McKay, glorious revolutionary that he is, remains uncatalogued. For two generations Negro poets have been trying to do what Mr. Cullen has succeeded in doing. First, trying to translate into lyric form the highly poetic urge to escape from the blatant realities of life in America into a vivid past, and, second, fleeing from the stigma of being called a *Negro* poet, by, as Dunbar so desired to do, ignoring folk-material and writing of such abstractions as love and death.

There is hardly anyone writing poetry in America today who can make the banal sound as beautiful as does Mr. Cullen. He has an extraordinary ear for music, a most extensive and dexterous knowledge of words and their values, and an enviable understanding of conventional poetic forms. Technically, he is almost precocious, and never, it may be added, far from the academic; but he is also too steeped in tradition, too influenced mentally by certain conventions and taboos. When he does forget these things as in his greatest poem, "Heritage":

What is Africa to me:
Copper sun or scarlet sea,
Jungle star or jungle track,

> *Strong bronzed men, or regal black*
> *Women from whose loins I sprang*
> *When the birds of Eden sang?*
> *One three centuries removed*
> *From the scenes his fathers loved,*
> *Spicy grove, cinnamon tree,*
> *What is Africa to me?*

and the unforgettable:

> *All day long and all night through,*
> *One thing only must I do:*
> *Quench my pride and cool my blood,*
> *Lest I perish in the flood,*
> *Lest a hidden ember set*
> *Timber that I thought was wet*
> *Burning like the dryest flax,*
> *Melting like the merest wax,*
> *Lest the grave restore its dead,*
> *Not yet has my heart and head*
> *In the least way realized*
> *They and I are civilized*

or his (to illustrate another tendency) :

> *I climb, but time's*
> *Abreast with me;*
> *I sing, but he climbs*
> *With my highest C.*

and in other far too few instances, he reaches heights no other Negro poet has ever reached, placing himself high among his contemporaries, both black or white. But he has not gone far enough. His second volume is not as lush with promise or as spontaneously moving as his first. There has been a marking time or side-stepping rather than a marching forward. If it seems we expect too much from this poet, we can only defend ourselves by saying that we expect no more than the poet's earlier work promises.

Mr. Cullen's love poems are too much made to order. His race poems, when he attempts to paint a moral, are inclined to be sentimental and stereotyped. It is when he gives vent to the pagan spirit and lets it inspire and dominate a poem's form and context that he does his most impressive work. His cleverly turned rebellious poems are also above the ordinary. But there are not enough of these in comparison to those poems which are banal, though beautiful.

Langston Hughes has often been compared to Dunbar. At first this comparison seems far-fetched and foolish, but on closer examination one finds that the two have much in common, only that where Dunbar failed, Langston Hughes succeeds. Both set out to interpret "the soul of his race"; one failed, the other, just at the beginning of his career, has in some measure already succeeded.

The younger man has not been content to assemble a supply of stock types who give expression to stock emotions which may be either slightly amusing or slightly tragic, but which are never either movingly tragic or convincingly comic. When Langston Hughes writes of specific Negro types he manages to make them more than just ordinary Negro types. They are actually dark-skinned symbols of universal characters. One never feels this way about the people in Dunbar's poetry. For he never heightens them above their own particular sphere. There is never anything of the universal element in his poems that motivates Mr. Hughes.

Moreover, Langston Hughes has gone much farther in another direction than any other Negro poet, much farther even than James Weldon Johnson went along the same road in "God's Trombones". He has appropriated certain dialects and rhythms characteristically Negroid as his poetic properties. He has borrowed the lingo and locutions of migratory workers, chamber-maids, porters, boot-blacks, and others, and woven them into rhythmic schemes borrowed from the blues songs, spirituals and jazz and with them created a poetic diction and a poetic form all his own. There is danger in this, of course, for the poet may and often does consider these things as an end in themselves rather than as a means to an end. A blues poem such as:

I'm a bad, bad man
'Cause everybody tells me so.
I'm a bad, bad man,
Everybody tells me so.
I takes ma meanness and ma licker
Everywhere I go.

or:

Ma sweet good man has
Packed his trunk and left.
Ma sweet good man has
Packed his trunk and left.
Nobody to love me:
I'm gonna kill ma self.

may be poignant and colorful but the form is too strait-laced to allow much variety of emotion or context. The poems produced are apt to prove modish and ephemeral. But when this blues form is expanded, as in:

> *Drowning a drowsy syncopated tune,*
> *Racking back and forth to a mellow croon,*
> *I heard a Negro play.*
> *Down on Lenox Avenue the other night*
> *By the pale dull pallor of an old gas light*
> *He did a lazy sway*
> *He did a lazy sway*
> *To the tune o' those Weary Blues.*
> *With his ebony hands on each ivory key*
> *He made that poor piano mean with melody.*
> *O Blues!*
> *Swaying to and fro on his rickety stool*
> *He played that sad raggy tune like a musical fool.*
> *Sweet Blues!*
> *Coming from a black man's soul.*

the poet justifies his experiment, and ends at the same time the most felicitous and fruitful outlet for his talent.

Mr. Hughes, where his race is concerned, is perfectly objective. He is one of them so completely that he, more than any other Negro poet, realizes that after all they are human beings; usually the articulate Negro either regards them as sociological problems or as debased monstrosities. To Mr. Hughes, certain types of Negroes and their experiences are of permanent value. He is not afraid of, nor does he ignore, them. He can calmly say:

> *Put on yo' red silk stockings*
> *Black gal.*
> *Go an' let de white boys*
> *Look at yo' legs.*
>
> .   .   .
>
> *An' tomorrow's chile'll*
> *Be a high yaller.*

or:

> *My old man's a white old man*
> *And my old mother's black*
>
> .   .   .

My old man died in fine big house.
My ma died in a shack.
I wonder where I'm gonna die,
Being neither white nor black?

and reach the heights of his achievement in "Mulatto", one of the finest and most vivid poems written in the past few years. But Mr. Hughes has also written some of the most banal poetry of the age, which has not, as in the case of Mr. Cullen, even sounded beautiful.

The future of Negro poetry is an unknown quantity, principally because those on whom its future depends are also unknown quantities. There is nothing in the past to crow about, and we are too close to the present to judge it more than tentatively. McKay is called in France, an alien and a communist, barred from returning to this country. Once in a while a poem of his appears, but the period of his best work in this field seems to be at an end. Langston Hughes and Countee Cullen are both quite young, as poets and as individuals. Neither can be placed yet, nor can their contributions be any more than just intelligently commented upon. Whether they are going or will continue to go in the right direction is no more than a matter of individual opinion. All of us do know that as yet the American Negro has not produced a great poet. Whether he will or not is really not at all important. What does matter is that those who are now trying to be great should get intelligent guidance and appreciation. They seem to have everything else except perhaps the necessary genius.

ARNA BONTEMPS
Negro Poets, Then and Now

THE POETRY of the Negro is hard to pin down. Like his music, from spirituals and gospel songs to blues, jazz and be-bop, it is likely to be marked by a certain special riff, an extra glide, a kick where none is expected and a beat for which there is no notation. It follows the literary traditions of the language it uses, but it does not hold them sacred. As a result, there has been a tendency for critics to put it in a category by itself, outside the main body of American poetry.

But Negroes take to poetry as they do to music. In the Harlem Renaissance poetry led the way for the other arts. It touched off the awakening that brought novelists, painters, sculptors, dancers, dramatists and scholars of many kinds to the notice of a nation that had nearly forgotten about the gifts of its Negro people. And almost the first utterance of the revival struck a note that disturbed poetic traditions:

> *I've known rivers ancient as the world and older than the flow of human blood in human veins.*

Soon thereafter the same generation responded to a poem that had been written even earlier and which Claude McKay included in his *Harlem Shadows* under the title of "Flame-Heart" in 1922. "So much have I forgotten in ten years," the first stanza began. It closed with

> *I have forgotten much, but still remember*
> *The poinsettia's red, blood-red in warm December.*

And before these notes subsided, Countee Cullen raised his voice:

> *O lovers never barter love*
> *For gold or fertile lands,*
> *For love is meat and love is drink,*
> *And love heeds love's commands.*
> *And love is shelter from the rain,*
> *And scowling stormy skies;*
> *Who casts off love must break his heart,*
> *And rue it till he dies.*

The Renaissance was on, and it was richly quotable, with Helene Johnson saying:

> *Ah little road, brown as my race is brown,*
> *Dust of the dust, they must not bruise you down.*

And Jean Toomer:

> *Pour O pour that parting soul in song,*
> *O pour it in the sawdust glow of night. . . .*
> *And let the valley carry it along.*

And Frank Horne:

> *I buried you deeper last night*
> *You with your tears and your tangled hair.*

And Georgia Douglas Johnson:

> *I'm folding up my little dreams*
> *Within my heart tonight.*

And Donald Jeffrey Hayes:

> *No rock along the road but knows*
> *The inquisition of his toes;*
> *No journey's end but what can say:*
> *He paused and rested here a day!*

And Waring Cuney:

> *She does not know*
> *Her beauty,*
> *She thinks her brown body*
> *Has no glory.*

But in those days a good many of the group went to The Dark Tower to weep because they felt an injustice in the critics' insistence upon calling them Negro poets instead of just poets. That attitude was particularly displeasing to Countee Cullen. But some who are writing today are not so sure. Considering the general state of poetry, the isolation of so many major poets from the everyday problems of mankind, their private language, their rarified metaphysical subject matter, one or two Negroes have even dared to suggest that being a Negro poet may not be so bad after all. Certainly there is nothing noticeably tragic about the lusty singers who carry the tunes today.

Gwendolyn Brooks, twice a Guggenheim fellow, once recipient of a grant from the American Academy of Arts and Letters, and more recently a Pulitzer Prize winner, has gathered a basket of laurels while keeping house for her husband and her young son in Chicago. Of all the post-Renaissance group of Negro poets in the U. S. she has received the most substantial critical approval. Her early poems won prizes in the Midwestern Writers' Conference and at Northwestern University, and after the publication of her collection *A Street in Bronzeville* in 1945 she was selected by *Mademoiselle* as one of the ten American women of the year. *Annie Allen,* her second book of poems, became the first by a Negro American poet to win the Pulitzer honor.

Comparable distinctions are probably in store for several of Miss Brooks' contemporaries. Robert E. Hayden, a member of the English faculty at Fisk University, received the Hopwood Award at the University of Michigan in 1938 and again in 1942. The Special Services Committee of Ann Arbor gave him a fellowship in 1946 and the Julius Rosenwald Fund selected him for one in 1947. His poems have appeared in *The Atlantic Monthly, Poetry, Cross Section* and other periodicals and anthologies. A first collection of them was called *Heart-Shape in the Dust* and was published in 1940 in Detroit. Seriously dedicated to his work, Hayden is a conscious artist rather than a spontaneous one, a deliberate worker, a careful polisher. While he does not scorn Negro themes and has used them in his most successful poems to date, he would like his work to stand or fall by objective poetic standards. As was the case with Countee Cullen, one gets the impression that Hayden is bothered by this Negro thing. He would like to be considered simply as a poet.

The opposite is true of Frank Marshall Davis and Melvin Beaunearus Tolson. The very titles of Davis' books tell his story: *Black Man's Verse, I Am the American Negro* and *47th Street*. The poetry is about as the titles would indicate. Its main quality is ruggedness. Perhaps this is not surprising in a poet who worked with street construction gangs in his youth and who has since lived the rough-and-tumble life of a newspaper man. He helped to start the Atlanta *Daily World* before beginning a long connection with the *Associated Negro Press* in 1935. Jazz music and the Negro's struggle for civil rights are his great concerns aside from journalism and poetry.

Tolson too is on the rugged side, and racial awareness emerges from nearly every line he has written. He never worked with street gangs, but during his twenty-two years on the faculty of Wiley College he barnstormed with many a winning debating team as its coach. He tried to promote little theatre groups among the sharecroppers in the surrounding country. And he is now doing some of the same things at Langston University. As a poet he first attracted attention when his "Dark Symphony" won a prize at the Negro American Exposition in Chicago and later appeared in the *Atlantic Monthly*. A volume of his poems followed, under the title *Rendezvous With America*, and it is so clearly and unmistakably Negro in every way that the government of Liberia recently reached across the sea to place a laurel wreath on the poet's brow. It has named Tolson its poet laureate.

Somewhere between Hayden and Tolson, in subject matter as in prosody, are Margaret Walker and Owen Dodson, both awkward fits for any rigid category. Margaret Walker is the vivacious daughter of a southern minister and attended Gilbert Academy in New Or-

leans before going to Northwestern University. The State University
of Iowa gave her a Master's degree in creative writing, accepting a
collection of her poems in place of a thesis. This same sheaf of
poems, when entered in the Yale University Younger Poets competition, won the prize in 1942 and was published as *For My People*. A
Rosenwald Fellowship, a lecture tour, and other exciting honors and
adventures followed. Miss Walker is now teaching at Jackson College in Mississippi.

Dodson's father was a Brooklyn minister. Educated there, at
Bates College and at Yale University, where he earned a Master of
Fine Arts degree, Dodson saw two of his plays produced at Yale before he went out to teach and direct drama at various Negro colleges, including Howard University, where he is now located. *Powerful Long Ladder*, his first book, was a collection of poems. His
poems have appeared in a number of magazines, and he too has
benefited by a Rosenwald Fellowship.

A still younger group is already taking shape. To it belong
such writers as Moses Carl Holman and Bruce McWright. Of these
Myron O'Higgins seems nearest to recognition at this date, and
Bette Latimer is the youngest. Both of these have had magazine and
anthology publication, and O'Higgins is co-author with Robert
Hayden of the attractive brochure *The Lion and the Archer*. He has
been a Rosenwald Fellow. Bette Latimer graduated from Fisk in
1948, the year of her twenty-first birthday. Another newcomer is
Mason Jordan Mason whose work is not widely known but whose
admirers are most outspoken. Of none of the new group have more
exciting things been predicted. A book of his poems is promised by
the Twayne Publishers, Inc., whose poetry editor is John Ciardi.

As a whole, however, neither members of the post-Renaissance
group nor the youngest group were as precocious as Langston
Hughes and Countee Cullen, Claude McKay and Paul Laurence
Dunbar. Hughes wrote "The Negro Speaks of Rivers" the summer
after his graduation from Central High School in Cleveland. It has
been translated into a dozen or two languages. Countee Cullen wrote
"I Have a Rendezvous with Life" as a high school student at De
Witt Clinton in New York, the poems of his first book while an un-
dergraduate at New York University. The *Songs of Jamaica* by
Claude McKay were written by the time he was nineteen, and all the
poems in Dunbar's first book were apparently written before he
reached twenty-one. Cullen and Hughes achieved important books at
twenty-two and twenty-four respectively, books which received seri-

ous attention and widespread approval among top critics every-where.

By far the most productive of the survivors of the Harlem Re-naissance poets is Langston Hughes, of course. But Sterling Brown, who belongs to the same age group, though his poetry came to no-tice a little later, is still active, a distinguished teacher at Howard University as well as a respected critic and a poet with a deep feel-ing for folk materials. He is unsurpassed as a teller of tales and a reader of his own narrative verse and character pieces, and the Uni-versity of Minnesota and Vassar College have both borrowed him for semesters on their campuses. Donald Jeffrey Hayes, the quality of whose lyrics remains dulcet, lives quietly in Atlantic City, but continues to contribute short lyrics to magazines like *Harper's Ba-zaar, Good Housekeeping* and *This Week.* Neither racial nor high-brow, Hayes' position among Negro poets, is in some respects like that of Frank Yerby among fiction writers. His hobby is setting his own lyrics to music. Helene Johnson, youngest of the Harlem group, stopped publishing poetry long ago, despite the promise of her early verse. She lives in Brooklyn with her husband and children. Clarissa Scott Delany, beautiful daughter of Emmett Scott and first wife of Hubert Delany, died young. And Frank Horne still turns a few poignant phrases in verse between his duties as a Housing expert in the government at Washington.

There is also among us a sedate and unobtrusive company of mature singers whose careers go back, in at least one case, to the turn of this century and whose quiet achievements have encouraged both subsequent groups of Negro American poets. William Stanley Braithwaite stands out among these. A selected edition of Braith-waite's poems has just been published by Coward-McCann, calling to mind again such early collections as his *Lyrics of Life and Love* (1904) and *The House of Falling Leaves* (1908) as well as his fa-mous series of annual *Anthologies of Magazine Verse,* 1913 to 1929, in which the works of American poets like Edgar Lee Masters, Vachel Lindsay, Carl Sandburg and many others were introduced to book readers. During all those years Braithwaite's service to poetry in the United States was of the greatest importance. He was seldom thought of as a Negro, but eventually recognition came from this direction as well. Now in his aerie at 409 Edgecomb Avenue in Har-lem this veteran singer devotes his time to biographical and critical studies.

Angelina W. Grimké, Anne Spencer, Georgia Douglas Johnson

and Jessie Redmond Fauset, all younger than Braithwaite, also belong to a span of singing years that began before the Renaissance in
Harlem and reaches to the present. All are women of unusual charm
—and reticence. Since her retirement as teacher of English in the
Dunbar High School in Washington, D. C., Miss Grimké has lived in
New York City. Anne Spencer, a librarian in Lynchburg, Virginia,
was once described by another poet as "a lady in her garden." She
has more than justified this by recently announcing a crowning
achievement: a pink candy-striped Chinese peony, eight years from
seed. Georgia Douglas Johnson worked with an organization of
women in behalf of the Republican candidates in the last elections.
Many other poets, past and present, have found politics quite com-
patible with creative composition. One gathers that Georgia Douglas Johnson's has not flagged as a result. Jessie Redmond Fauset, an
influence in the Harlem Renaissance by reason of her literary editorship of the *Crisis* as well as her four well-known novels, now appears to have returned to poetry, an even earlier love.

In the nation as a whole the suffering poet is still a prevailing
type. There is no premium on sensitiveness. And the lot of the Negro poet has much in common with the plight of the whole species.
This explains, no doubt, the tendency of some writers of poetry to
apologize for the habit, others to keep it a secret. All have to face
the hard problem of making a living. Since the income from poetry
is extremely small, one may wonder how poets manage to keep body
and soul together.

Well, Pauli Murray, one member of the young group, is a distinguished lawyer. Frank Horne, as has been indicated, continues in
government service. Some, like Moses Carl Holman, Robert Hayden, Melvin B. Tolson and Sterling Brown, are college professors.
Others, Helene Johnson and Gwendolyn Brooks, are housewives.
Richard Wright, a sometime poet, is an important American novelist and probably the most distinguished American now living on the
Left Bank in Paris. Myron O'Higgins and Bette Darcie Latimer are
at the age of youthful pilgrimages and journeys.

Langston Hughes is the only Negro poet since Dunbar who has
succeeded in making a living from poetry. But a poem must be used
many ways to yield enough sustenance to keep a hearty individual
like Mr. Hughes in the kind of food he likes. Therefore it is not surprising to find his poems being danced by Pearl Primus on the stage
while they are sung by Juanita Hall in night clubs and on radio and
television, and by Muriel Rahn in Town Hall concerts, and while
Paul Robeson is reciting "Freedom Train" in the United States, the

West Indies and Central America. But it is a living, and as a result Mr. Hughes has had only one job—one semester as guest professor at Atlanta University—since the publication of *The Weary Blues,* his first book, in 1926. Poetry has turned a pretty penny for the Negro who spoke of rivers the summer after graduating from high school in 1920. And there is an eager and talented band of newer singers who hope that it will do as much for them.

[
MARGARET WALKER
New Poets
]

DURING THE past twenty years of literary history in America, Negroes have enjoyed unusual prominence as poets. At least ten books of poetry by new poets have received serious critical comment in leading literary magazines and columns. If we can believe the additional comments in anthologies of American poetry and books of literary criticism, Negroes writing poetry have gone a long way toward achieving full literary status as American writers; and they have thus attained a measure of integration into contemporary schools of literary thought.

A backward look into American life during these two decades should provide a reason for this literary development and resurgence. It must also accountably tell the background of such poetry, and at the same time provide a basis for predicting the future of poetry written by Negroes in America. Let us, therefore, consider, first, the socio-economic and political factors which have influenced the poetry of the past twenty years.

During the Twenties we spoke of the New Negro and the Negro Renaissance. At that time such figures as James Weldon Johnson, Langston Hughes, Countee Cullen, Claude McKay, and Jean Toomer emerged as the spokesmen of the New Negro. Rich white patrons or "angels" who could and did underwrite the poetry of Negroes by helping to support Negroes who were interested in writing poetry did so as a fad to amuse themselves and their guests at some of the fabulous parties of the Twenties. They considered the intelligent, sensitive, and creative Negro as the talented tenth, exotic, bizarre, and unusual member of his race; and they indulgently regarded the poetry of the Negro as the prattle of a gifted child. Negro people as a mass showed little appreciation for poetry and offered very little audience for the Negro writing poetry. Whatever Negro people thought about the poetry written about Negro life did not seem to matter. In the final analysis the audience and the significant critics were white. Negroes as a whole knew too little about their own life to analyze correctly and judge astutely their own literary progress as poets. Isolated from the literary life of whites and confused by the segregated pattern of economic and political life, it was only natural that the point of view of these writers was limited. They lacked social perspective and suffered from a kind of literary myopia. They seemed constantly to beg the question of the Negro's humanity, perhaps as an answer to the white patron's attitude that Negroes are only children anyway. *God's Trombones* by James Weldon Johnson, *The Weary Blues* by Langston Hughes, *Color* and *Copper Sun* by Countee Cullen, and *Harlem Shadows* by Claude McKay were published during the Twenties. Each was received as justification that the Negro race could produce geniuses and that it was nothing short of remarkable that "God should make a poet black and bid him sing." Titles of books as well as eloquent short lyrics such as "O Black and Unknown Bards," and "I, too, sing America . . . I am the darker brother" all reflected an intense desire to justify the Negro as a human being. These books sold well among whites but none of them ranked in a "best-seller" class. People did not buy poetry, certainly not poetry by Negroes. It was a day of individual literary patronage when a rich "angel" adopted a struggling poor artist and made an exotic plaything out of any "really brilliant Negro."

The halcyon days of individual patronage of the arts were ended with the stockmarket crash at the end of the Twenties. The gay hayride of the flaming and gilded Twenties had come to a jolting stop and the depression of the Thirties began to make its first inroads into American life. Hoover persisted so long in predicting that prosperity was just around the corner that it became a standing joke. Men appeared on street corners selling apples, and there was talk of an American dole such as England had already experienced. Early in 1932 before the repeal of prohibition and the ending of the speakeasies that had been an institution of the Twenties, it was a common sight to see streets of large cities littered with sprawling drunkards. The parks were full of unemployed men, shabby and helpless, wearing beaten and hopeless faces. Grant Park in Chicago was a notable example. Evictions were common and Communism was on the march. What chance did the luxury of art have at such a time?

Roosevelt's New Deal not only averted a bloody social revolution in 1932 and 1933 by bracing the tottering economic structure of the country, but it also ushered into existence the boon to art and letters in the form of the Works Progress Administration. The WPA meant two things of far-reaching significance to Negroes who were writers. It meant, first (as it meant to whites), money on which to exist and provision for the meager security necessary in order to create art. It meant, second, that Negroes who were creative writers, and poets especially, were no longer entirely isolated from other writers. In cities above the Mason-Dixon line where the Writers Projects drew no color line, a new school of black and white writers mushroomed over-night into being.

The cry of these writers was the cry of social protest: protest against the social ills of the day which were unemployment, slums, crime and juvenile delinquency, prejudice, poverty, and disease. The New Deal struggled to alleviate these social ills while the writers led the vanguard of literary protest and agitation for a better world. The decade of the nineteen-thirties therefore became known as the socially conscious Thirties. Negroes joined the ranks of these socially conscious writers and Negroes who were writing poetry in particular were poets of social protest. At least three new poets appeared during the Thirties with books of poetry of obvious social significance.

Southern Road by Sterling Brown appeared in 1932. It was chiefly concerned with the plight of Negroes in the South. Ballads in this volume such as the "Slim Greer Series" are some of the finest in the annals of American poetry regardless of the color of the author. One of Mr. Brown's later poems, "Old Lem," which first appeared in magazines and anthologies in the Thirties, is an outstanding example of social protest and clearly reflects the mood of the period.

> *I talked to old Lem*
> *And old Lem said:*
> *"They weigh the cotton*
> *They store the corn*
> *We only good enough*
> *To work the rows;*
> *They run the commissary*
> *They keep the books*

We gotta be grateful
For being cheated;
Whippersnapper clerks
Call us out of our name
We got to say mister
To spindling boys
They make our figgers
Turn somersets
We buck in the middle
Say, 'Thankyuh, sah.'
    They don't come by ones
    They don't come by twos
    But they come by tens."

Black Man's Verse and *I Am the American Negro* by Frank Marshall Davis appeared in 1935 and 1937 respectively. These two volumes of poetry, although technically rough and uneven, were scathing books of social protest. An example of such social protest may be seen in the following excerpt from one of Mr. Davis' poems, "Portrait of the Cotton South":

Well, you remakers of America
You apostles of Social Change
Here is pregnant soil
Here are grass roots of a nation.
But the crop they grow is Hate and Poverty.
By themselves they will make no change
Black men lack the guts
Po' whites have not the brains
And the big land owners want Things as They Are.

Black Labor Chant by David Wadsworth Cannon, who died before his volume of verse was published in 1939, celebrated the Negro's joining ranks with the upsurging Labor movement, particularly the CIO, and continued in general in the vein of social protest.

Although the outbreak of the Second World War changed the note of social significance, bringing as it did prosperity at home in the United States, and ushering into the world the Atomic Age, the strong note of anxiety it bred was not felt at first in the literature of the period. For at least a decade longer the poetry of American Negroes continued to reflect the mood of the Thirties. A half dozen books of poetry published during the Forties reflect either a note of social protest or a growing concern with the terrible reality of war.

Heart-Shape in the Dust by Robert Hayden appeared in 1940

followed by *For My People* by Margaret Walker in 1942. *Rendez-vous With America* by Melvin Tolson was published in 1944; *A Street in Bronzeville* by Gwendolyn Brooks in 1945; and *Powerful Long Ladder* by Owen Dodson appeared in 1946. The first three poets each reflected in varying degrees the note of social protest in their respective volumes of poetry. The last two poets showed a growing concern with the grim reality of war.

Contrast the tone of the poems of the Twenties with examples of the poetry of the early Forties reflecting as they did the social consciousness of the Thirties. From Robert Hayden's early work, *Heart-Shape in the Dust,* an excerpt from the poem, "Speech," follows:

> *Hear me, white brothers,*
> *Black brothers, hear me:*
> *I have seen the hand*
> *Holding the blowtorch*
> *To the dark, anguish-twisted body;*
> *I have seen the hand*
> *Giving the high-sign*
> *To fire on the white pickets;*
> *And it was the same hand,*
> *Brothers, listen to me,*
> *It was the same hand.*

From Margaret Walker's poem, "For My People":

> *For my people standing staring trying to fashion a better way from confusion, from hypocrisy and misunderstanding, trying to fashion a world that will hold all the people, all the faces, all the Adams and Eves and their countless generations;*
>
> *Let a new earth rise. Let another world be born. Let a bloody peace be written in the sky. Let a second generation full of courage issue forth; let a people loving freedom come to growth. Let a beauty full of healing and a strength of final clenching be the pulsing in our spirits and our blood. Let the martial songs be written, let the dirges disappear. Let a race of men now rise and take control.*

From Melvin Tolson's poem, "Dark Symphony":

> *Out of abysses of Illiteracy*
> *Through labyrinths of Lies,*
> *Across wastelands of Disease . . .*
> *We advance!*

> *Out of dead-ends of Poverty,*
> *Through wildernesses of Superstition,*
> *Across barricades of Jim Crowism*
> *We advance!*
> *With the Peoples of the World . . .*
> *We advance!*

In each of these three illustrations of poetry published during the early Forties may be detected the note of social protest, a growing perspective beyond the point of view of race, and a militant attitude not evidenced in the poets of the Twenties.

Gwendolyn Brooks and Owen Dodson published in 1945 and 1946 and their works show a growing concern with the problem of war. They show more than any of the aforementioned poets a growing global perspective which has become a keynote of current poetry. In her volume, *A Street in Bronzeville*, Miss Brooks writes about "Gay Chaps at the Bar":

> *We knew how to order . . .*
> *But nothing ever taught us to be islands*
> *. . . No stout*
> *Lesson showed how to chat with death. We brought*
> *No brass fortissimo, among our talents,*
> *To holler down the lions in this air.*

In Owen Dodson's poems, "Black Mother Praying" and "Conversation on V," the question of race is presented within the framework of war. The following excerpt is taken from "Conversation on V":

> *V stands for Victory.*
> *Now what is this here Victory?*
> *It what we get when we fight for it.*
> *Ought to be Freedom, God do know that.*

Common Peoples Manifesto by Marcus Christian was published in 1948. It has probably not received as widespread critical notice as it deserves, but in several reviews mention has been made of its "considerable merit." It, too, reflects the social note of protest that was typical of the poetry of the Thirties.

The period of greatest intensification of the social note in poetry written by Negroes extends roughly from 1935 to 1945. Sum-

ming up the period, generally speaking, we can see that the New
Negro came of age during the Thirties. He grew away from the
status of the exotic, the accidentally unusual Negro, the talented
tenth of what the white audience chose to consider an otherwise
mentally infantile minority group whose masses were illiterate, disfranchised, exploited, and oppressed. Negroes became members of a
new school of writers who were no longer isolated because of color,
who were integrated around the beliefs that created the New Deal.
They were the poets of social protest who began to catch a glimmer
of a global perspective, who as spokesmen for their race did not beg
the question of their humanity, and who cried out to other peoples
over the earth to recognize race prejudice as a weapon that is as
dangerous as the atomic bomb in the threat to annihilation of culture and peace in the western world.

Any literary development of the Negro in the Thirties was directly due to his social development. During the Thirties the Negro
people made great social strides. The New Deal opened many avenues of opportunity and development to the masses of Negro people.
The economic standards of the Negro race rose higher than ever in
the history of his life in this country. As a result of free art for all
the people a cultural renaissance in all the arts swept the United
States. This created a new intelligentsia with a genuine appreciation
for the creative arts and a recognition for all cultural values. Labor
was stimulated by the unionization together of black and white
labor and this in turn strengthened the political voice of the people.
Consequently the literary audience widened and the Negro people
themselves grew in intellectual awareness.

Three books published during the Forties, however, show a
marked departure from the note of social protest. These books are
From the Shaken Tower by Bruce McWright, published in Great
Britain in 1944; *The Lion and the Archer* by Robert Hayden and
Myron O'Higgins, published as a brochure in 1948; and Gwendolyn
Brooks' Pulitzer Prizewinning volume, *Annie Allen*, which was published in 1949. Each one of these books is less preoccupied with the
theme of race as such. Race is rather used as a point of departure
toward a global point of view than as the central theme of one obsessed by race. This global perspective is an important new note in
poetry. The tendency is toward internationalism rather than toward
nationalism and racism. Because modern inventions have shortened
the time involved in transportation and communications to such an
amazing degree our world has shrunk to a small community of na-

tions and mankind is forced to recognize the kinship of all peoples. Thus we have a basis for new conceptions that of necessity lead us in new directions.

These new poets of the late Forties also remind us that there are other factors in the writing of poetry that are equally as important as perspective. They focus our attention on craftsmanship with their return to an emphasis on form. The new poetry has universal appeal coupled with another definite mark of neo-classicism, the return to form. They show an emphasis placed on technique rather than subject matter, and a moving toward intellectual themes of psychological and philosophical implications which border on obscurantism. These poems are never primitive, simple, and commonplace.

What technical advances have these poets of our new classical age shown over the poets of the Twenties and the Thirties?

Looking back to the Twenties one quickly recognizes that the poets of the Negro Renaissance varied technically from the strictly classical and conventional poetry to the utterly unconventional. Countee Cullen was an outstanding example of the true classicist who had been schooled thoroughly in versification and all the types and forms of poetry. His classical education was clearly reflected in his poetry. On the other hand, Langston Hughes introduced the pattern of the "blues" into poetry. He made no pretense of being the poets' poet, of writing intellectual poetry, or conforming to any particular school of aesthetics. The pattern of the "blues" was, nevertheless, the first new Negro idiom introduced into American poetry since the time of Paul Laurence Dunbar and his Negro dialect that was typical of the ante-bellum plantation life. The poetry of Negroes that was published during the Thirties was primarily free verse. Technically there were no innovations.

Currently, the new poets, however, are so concerned with form that they are often interested in form to the exclusion of everything else and thus are in danger of sacrificing sense for sound, or meaning for music. As a result of this tendency much of recent poetry by white writers in America has been labelled obscurantist. Can this charge be safely levelled at recent poetry by Negroes?

Such a charge has already been levelled at *Annie Allen* when the book was mentioned in a recent issue of *Phylon*. It was then stated that the poem, "the birth in a narrow room," has too many elliptical or truncated lines. This seems a minor technical matter of not too great importance since it does not actually destroy the meaning of the poem. The lines under question follow:

> *Weeps out of western country something new.*
> *Blurred and stupendous. Wanted and unplanned.*
> *Winks. Twines, and weakly winks*
> *Upon the milk-glass fruit bowl, iron pot,*
> *The bashful china child tipping forever*
> *Yellow apron and spilling pretty cherries.*

Does this make sense? Obviously when one reads the entire poem in terms of the title, the poem does make sense, and that should be all that really matters.

The fact that Miss Brooks displays an excellent knowledge of form, whether in the versatile handling of types of forms of poetry included in *Annie Allen* or in the metrical variations in the volume, can be readily seen as proof of this new emphasis upon conventional form. She skillfully handles a number of stanzaic forms including couplets, quatrains, the Italian Terza Rima, and even in the Anniad, the difficult rime-royal or the seven line stanza named for Chaucer. Here is a perfect example:

> *Think of thaumaturgic lass*
> *Looking in her looking-glass*
> *At the unembroidered brown;*
> *Printing bastard roses there;*
> *Then emotionally aware*
> *Of the black and boisterous hair*
> *Taming all that anger down.*

In addition to these conventional forms she includes several poems written in free verse as well as occasional lines of blank verse. In regard to types she includes short lyrics, ballads, and sonnets written with veteran aplomb. As a whole, *Annie Allen* is a fine delineation of the character of a young Negro woman from childhood through adolescence to complete maturity, but with slight racial exceptions it could apply to any female of a certain class and society. The entire volume is tinged with an highly sophisticated humor and is not only technically sure but also vindicates the promise of *A Street in Bronzeville*. Coming after the long hue and cry of white writers that Negroes as poets lack form and intellectual acumen, Miss Brooks' careful craftsmanship and sensitive understanding reflected in *Annie Allen* are not only personal triumphs but a racial vindication.

There may be more reason to level the charge of obscurantism at the poetry of Myron O'Higgins in *The Lion and the Archer*, written in collaboration with Robert Hayden. Although the vocabulary is no more intellectual than that of Miss Brooks, and there are several magnificent poems in this brochure—new in note, and vital—there seems more obscurity and ambiguity in the use of poetic symbols and imagery, as for example:

> But that day in between
> comes back with two lean cats
> who run in checkered terror
> through a poolroom door
> and bolting from a scream
> a keen knife marks with sudden red
> the gaming green
> . . . a purple billiard ball
> explodes the color scheme.

Robert Hayden shows a decided growth and advance in this volume over his first, *Heart-Shape in the Dust,* which was uneven and lacked the grasp of a true Negro idiom which he seemed to be seeking at that time. His sense of choric movement and his understanding and perspective of peoples have increased to a telling degree and he writes now with due maturity and power:

> Now as skin-and-bones Europe hurts all over from the swastika's
>   hexentanz: oh think of Anton, Anton brittle, Anton crystalline;
> think what the winter moon, the leper beauty of a Gothic tale,
>   must see:
> the ice-azure likeness of a young man reading, carved most
>   craftily.

In Bruce McWright there is authentic reporting of World War II but even the title of his book, *From the Shaken Tower,* reflects the questions of our present-day age. War has further denounced the ivory towers because war is the grim reality that ends the romantic dreams and airy castle building. The poets of the Thirties said that ivory towers were not fit habitations for poets anyway; they should be social prophets, preachers, teachers, and leaders. Now, with the threat of annihilation hanging over the civilized world of western culture, whether by atomic or hydrogen bomb, with the tremendous wave of social revolution sweeping through the world, men have felt themselves spiritually bankrupt. There is therefore a wave of religious revival, especially in America, whether through fear and hysteria, or from a genuine desire for inner self analysis, reflection and introspective knowledge that may lead, thereby, to a spiritual panacea which we seek for the ills of the world. Whether to Catholicism, Existentialism, or Communism, modern man is turning to some definite belief around which to integrate his life and give it true wholeness and meaning. Consequently there has already been noted among white writers a decided religious revival. Whereas Marxism was the intellectual fad of the Thirties, religion has become the intellectual fad at present in America where the political and economic structures have definitely reverted to an extremely conservative position. The religious pathway of T. S. Eliot, prophet of the spiritual wasteland, technical pioneer, and most influential name among poets during the Thirties, has been followed by W. H. Auden. Robert Lowell, a Pulitzer Prize poet of a few years ago, is a Catholic convert. Thus far no Negro recently writing poetry has reflected this religious revival, but we may well expect this tendency.

Negroes not only have grown up as poets technically with volumes of poetry showing a growing concern with craftsmanship, social perspective, and intellectual maturity, but they have also begun to reap the rewards in the form of laurels due them for their labors. They have received a greater measure of consideration from literary critics and judges of literary competitions than ever before in the history of writing by Negroes in America. Not only have Negroes succeeded in winning many philanthropic grants such as Rosenwalds and Guggenheims which have provided the wherewithal to pursue creative projects and develop burgeoning talents, but also many other honors and awards have been granted to poets of the Negro race. These have included grants from the Academy of Arts and Letters and the Yale Award for a promising younger poet. Now in 1950 has come the signal achievement with the awarding of the Pulitzer Prize for Poetry to Gwendolyn Brooks for her volume, *Annie Allen*. This is the first time in the history of this Prize that a Negro has won this national honor. With this announcement comes not only the recognition of the fact that poetry by Negroes has come of age but also that the Negro has finally achieved full status in the literary world as an American poet.

What, then, is the future of the Negro writing poetry in America? It would seem from these remarks that the outlook is bright and hopeful. It is a fact that some of the most significant poetry written in America during the past two decades has been written by Negroes. Now, what is the promise? Is there hope that it will be fulfilled? Is the Negro as a poet doomed to annihilation because he is part of a doomed Western world, or is that Western culture really doomed? Is our society already a fascist society? If it is, what hope has our literature? If these are only bogey-men, then whither are we turning? Is our path toward religious revival, neo-classicism, internationalism as a result of global perspectives and world government, or what?

From such young poets as M. Carl Holman must come the answer. Deeply concerned with the psychological, yet aware of our physical world, he shares a growing understanding of our spiritual problems with some of the most mature craftsmen practicing the art of poetry. He bears watching as a poet who is technically aware and intellectually worthy of his salt.

If we are truly in a transitional stage of social evolution, a state of flux, of cataclysmic socio-economic and political upheaval that will ultimately and inevitably shape our literary life, this will soon be clear. Now, the shape of our emerging society is dimly shadowed by many imponderables. The future of the Negro writing poetry in America is bright only if the future of the world is bright, and if he with the rest of his world can survive the deadly conflicts that threaten him and his total freedom, the awful anticipation of which now hangs over his head like the sword of Damocles.

JAMES A. EMANUEL
The Future of Negro Poetry:
A Challenge for Critics

THE FUTURE reputation of poetry written by Negro Americans is guaranteed by its past distinction (scarcely known to us) and by its present flourishing. Enough able Negro craftsmen are at work to infuse a continual stream of worthy poetry into our national literature. Enough Negro critics are on hand to illuminate that stream with sensitive explications, needed surely by readers of their own race and also by the university community at large, whose blindness to the artistry and power in the works of black poets writing since the 1740's has prolonged the exclusion of Negro poetry from standard school textbooks.

The open-eyed exploration of Negro poetry may be one of the last cultural frontiers to challenge the American mind as we know it. The best poets of any country and of any race, working in their most creative moments to record the inexpressible, to give verbal

order to tensions and fragmented perceptions often of national significance, comprise a group whose publications offer profound evidence of the condition of the human spirit in their time and place.
The black man in America has long been the tuning fork of the national soul. His shudders under the lash of slavery, his anxieties under the fragrant promises of democracy, and his now glimmering
realization of himself as the embodiment of America's destiny—all
have been evolutionary and prophetic. The black poet—as James
Weldon Johnson recognized in his "O Black and Unknown Bards"
—has been fated to personify and to transcribe the miracle of human survival against demoniac odds. In our present years of shock
and menace, literary men, like others devoted to the humanities, feel
moved to pursue some special inquiry responsive to their need for
the truth about shadowed recesses in the American past. Negro poetry at its best, brilliant and deft and passionate in all modes, contains such corrective instruction; and when closely studied, it often
approximates the effect of revelation.

It will be the privilege of Negro scholars in particular to bring
their professional and racial sensitivities to bear in the examination
of techniques used by Negro poets to express their unique fusion of
the human, the American, and the individual. Awaiting Negro critics is the rare opportunity to satisfy a poignant racial need deepened by centuries of unconscionable bondage and generations of sophisticated collusion inflicted by countrymen who today lie shackled
in the very "mind-forged manacles" (as William Blake would describe them) that they so oppressively devised for black men. But
racial need—the need, in this case, for a sympathetic but thorough
and high-principled estimate of the best contributions of Negro
poets—has motivated relatively few Negro critics to study systematically works by men and women of their own race. (This stagnation
can be termed either black failure or white success, or both, depending upon one's view of the possibilities of Negro individualism and
vision within family and institutional structures affected by the assumption of inferiority in the deeds and persons of Negroes.) The
pages of *CLA Journal,* to select but one representative Negro-
managed scholarly publication, are regularly filled with excellent
Negro commentary on the works of white authors. If more of such
professionally trained Negro critics were to turn their energies to
the explication of literature by authors of their race, the enrichment
in the feeling and knowledge of both black and white readers would
be imponderable.

The problems of the white critic attentive to this enterprise have taken on a few of the complexities characteristic of the end of the 1960's. "Black pride," one of the rallying cries authentically attributed to "Black Power" as conceived and described by Negroes before its redefinition and distortion by the national press, has complicated the role of traditional scholarship. The sense of estrangement and isolation that has eroded interracial cooperation in general has moved some Negro literary men to advocate a hands-off policy for white critics disposed to evaluate writings by Negroes, while others have stood on middle ground by arguing the inability of white critics to understand subtle—and even overt—racial allusions and substance employed by Negro craftsmen. Other Negroes see such advocacy as nonsense and deem insignificant the degree to which white critics would fall short of a full understanding of undercurrents in the content and style of racial art.

Although the controversy is largely academic, its ultimate meaning—like the meaning and outcome of other more demanding issues in America—will steadily materialize in the minds of the Negroes concerned, and its ultimate effect will serve the nation through that interracial activity without which the America that we know will not survive. The question of the white critic's participation in a new, complete examination of Negro poetry is academic simply because financial profit dominates our society. The competent—and not so competent—white critic's easy access to publishers guarantees his continued involvement with Negro literature as long as either black or white readers will buy his books or the magazines in which his essays appear. David Littlejohn will give the public more of his opinions of Negro authors, if Publishers Row is willing, despite what Hoyt W. Fuller, editor of *Negro Digest,* declared about that white critic's *Black on White:* "It is glib, opinionated nonsense. . . . Avoid this book like the plague." Robert A. Bone, a sincere, scholarly white critic, author of *The Negro Novel in America,* will surely continue to publish his thoughtful judgments, despite the controversial nature of some of his conclusions.

It is in the mind of the Negro—the storehouse of so much that is vital and even mysterious in the American character—that the resolution of the question of the criticism of Negro poetry will implant its most meaningful effect. It is there that America's most valuable democratic concept, that the individual must retain proportionate and practical control of his own destiny, is now being tested. The black man's wrestling with this concept in politics and in education is being reported by our news media. The speculative structure of the new "black university" spans both political and educational principles, and the conjectural new "black aesthetic" bridges both educational and literary traditions. All this ferment is increasing the watchfulness of the well-informed Negro, whatever his personal station; and although the primary object of that watchfulness is Negro leadership, new attention is being given to the attitudes of authors and critics. The crucial question in the mind of the Negro, whether his interest is mainly political, educational, or broadly cultural, seems to be this: Is Negro leadership finally ready to assume full practicable responsibility for the guidance and welfare of its black constituency?

To Negro literary scholars who have a special affinity for poetry, "black constituency" means all the black people who have, or who could be induced to have, an abiding interest in poetry: undifferentiated readers, students of various levels, and other scholars. The bond between the Negro scholar and his special actual or potential reader is the bond of color, and both realize this truth today with an apocalyptic certainty made changeless in this century by its accommodation to cynicism and fear as well as to optimism and love. Even to acknowledge this bond in unequivocal terms, let alone to act in conformity with its dictates, has been allowed to seem narrow-minded and, in the terrible close of the 1960's, almost subversive. But the bond thickens and both leadership and its street-corner anchor in the flesh of the workingman grow more precious amid the brutal facts of racist murders and concentration camps (as revealed in *Look*, May 28, 1968) in "the land of the free and the home of the brave."

In the mind, then, of Black Man Thinking (to develop an Emersonian phrase), a literary question has become a question of courage. When Negro scholars in substantial numbers begin to turn their lives into a pathway that circles through the ghetto freighted with evidence of defensible respect for the many contributions of black people to America, the man on the street will believe two probabilities without which he can no longer believe anything: that America is maturing fast enough to save itself, and that black men of vision are culminating their race's gifts to the nation in actions loyal to their beleaguered color. Such actions by Negro critics could indeed be called courageous now. When a black man trained by the educational Establishment turns to the study of poetry about which he himself has been taught little or nothing, he shows the courage of a man willing to suffer the labors of a new start in a difficult and avoidable endeavor. When a Negro scholar turns his back on the preoccupations of university colleagues (black and white) who

know or care little about Negro poetry and other forms of literature
written by black people, he exhibits the courage of a dissenter
whose new cause identifies him with objects of near disdain and
alienates him from the professional sympathies that ease the many
irritations of a researcher. Although the normal, incredible ordeals of
black academicians are detailed in John Hope Franklin's essay,
"The Dilemma of the American Negro Scholar," in *Soon, One
Morning,* most readers would derive from their own experiences in
racist surroundings adequate knowledge of the probable causes and
consequences of an "accepted" Negro critic's turnabout from the
norms of the literary power structure. And the sidewalk sense of the
ordinary black man is sufficient to tell him that when middle-class–
oriented Negro scholars begin to modify their careers because of his
own special needs, a prophetic humanity with a uniquely racial
courage is alive and working.

The seemingly narrow question, then, of whether Negro critics
will reveal the beauties and the substance of Negro poetry or allow
that privilege to white critics with more connections in the market
place is really inseparable from fatefully related questions now
pressing Negro leadership in many disciplines and sectors. It can be
isolated, however, in terms of its specific challenges for critics of
different aesthetic persuasions and of different races. The matter can
be briefly simplified by reference to the variety of Negro poetry, so
inexhaustible that black and white critics of all dispositions can accommodate their tastes. In both content and style, in both the nineteenth and twentieth centuries—though much more often, of course,
in the latter—it can nourish and exercise temperaments as diverse
as those of the black nationalist, the genteel aesthete, and the formal
classroom analyst. Within its abundance, Negro poetry contains rebellious fury, flower-petal delicacy, and shrewdly complex literary
and historical allusions.

The kind of analysis merited by the best Negro poetry can be
demonstrated by the following admittedly incomplete observations
on two sonnets written by Negroes (their lines numbered for con-
venience of discussion). The highly disciplined, traditional sonnet
form is chosen here because of its appeal to conventional scholarly
tastes—and because its rigidity would seem to make it resistant to
the needs of a modern black poet bent on expressing his racial self
or his unique kind of social fury. The attempt to resolve the question of which particular insights into the meaning and style of each
sonnet might occur more naturally to Negro critics than to white
can be made by each reader in his own way.

The first sonnet, by Gwendolyn Brooks, which appeared in 1949 in *Annie Allen* (number 4 in the section "the children of the poor"), reads as follows:

First fight. Then fiddle. Ply the slipping string	1
With feathery sorcery; muzzle the note	2
With hurting love; the music that they wrote	3
Bewitch, bewilder. Qualify to sing	4
Threadwise. Devise no salt, no hempen thing	5
For the dear instrument to bear. Devote	6
The bow to silks and honey. Be remote	7
A while from malice and from murdering.	8
But first to arms, to armor. Carry hate	9
In front of you and harmony behind.	10
Be deaf to music and to beauty blind.	11
Win war. Rise bloody, maybe not too late	12
For having first to civilize a space	13
Wherein to play your violin with grace.	14

One ought first to conclude what the poem is about—and remain, to borrow a phrase from Keats, "capable of being in uncertainties." A violinist, a professional soldier, a militant civil rights leader, and a mother protective of her disadvantaged children might each perceptively defend a different total interpretation. The largest theme of the sonnet, however, is the relationship between art and life, meaningfully comparable to themes in such diverse works as Langston Hughes' "The Blues I'm Playing," a short story; Robinson Jeffers' "The Bloody Sire," a poem; and E. M. Forster's "What I Believe," an essay. It suffices for our purpose to allow the final three lines to state the societal meaning, modified to individual dimensions most discernibly in the reference to "hurting love" in line 3.

The poet's mastery appears not so much in the meaning as in the style. The allusive imagery mounts richly around the basic image of a stringed instrument, ostensibly the violin of the final line, the "dear instrument" of line 6, plied with the "bow" of line 7. The "fiddle" of line 1, however, is but a disarming contrast to the violent image that swiftly magnifies the word "fight" in a historical context meaningful to racially oppressed people. The subsequent "slipping string," "sorcery," and "muzzle," even though they can refer to the actions of a virtuoso in the parlor or concert hall, also can refer to thuggee, the disciplined kind of murder offered to the

goddess Kali by the courteous assassins of India finally suppressed
by the British in the nineteenth century. The running noose of the
Thugs, their unusual religious rites, and their silent three-on-one
killing are thus brought subtly to the fore. The "hempen thing" of
line 5, then, is the killer's strangling rope, unfavorably compared by
the poet with the violin's "wise thread" (my inversion is as deliberate as hers), just as the "salt" of the same line is indirectly compared with rosin—and further contrasted with the "honey" of line
7, itself reminiscent of the raw sugar eaten by Thugs in rituals after
slayings. And the Thugs were indeed "remote/ A while . . . from
murdering" (as in lines 7 and 8), often acting for long periods as
delightful servants of their intended victims, awaiting thuggee.

One could discuss at length the poet's verbal skill: her crucial,
compact, almost humorous imperatives; her deft consonance and
soft assonance (as in lines 1 and 2, respectively); her other double
images and oppositions ("feathery" versus "hurting" and "silks"
versus hemp); her ironic near-comparisons ("sorcery" and bewil-
derment, "dear" and "honey"); her internal partial rhymes (as in
lines 2, 5, 6, and 14); her pert, feminine sententiousness (as in
"Qualify to sing/ Threadwise"). A similar command of form at-
taches to her transition in the sestet, for line 9 enhances both whole
meaning and particular style; it enlarges the initial advice of line 1
through the figurative use of "armor" to define "hate" as a shield to
protect a harmonizing purpose. Thus hate in this poem is to be bat-
tered; music and beauty, because they are to be temporarily ignored, are to be saved, are to be revitalized in that civilized "space"
of time which always follows the cessation of hateful violence.

A rigorous examination of this poem from Gwendolyn
Brooks's Pulitzer prize-winning volume yields more to contemplate
than has been suggested here; for example, the civil rights leader
imagined as an explicator would not stop at this point. The fact to
be remembered is that critics heretofore have almost always stopped
far too soon in their discussions of the works of Negroes. Such is
the case with the other sonnet, "The White House," selected by
Claude McKay as one of his best and preserved in his *Selected
Poems* (1953). The poem by McKay (whose famous sonnet "If We
Must Die" was quoted by Winston Churchill in his address to the
Congress of the United States before our entry into World War II
reads as follows:

> *Your door is shut against my tightened face,*   1
> *And I am sharp as steel with discontent;*   2

> But I possess the courage and the grace   3
> To bear my anger proudly and unbent.   4
> The pavement slabs burn loose beneath my feet,   5
> A chafing savage, down the decent street;   6
> And passion rends my vitals as I pass,   7
> Where boldly shines your shuttered door of glass.   8
> Oh, I must search for wisdom every hour,   9
> Deep in my wrathful bosom sore and raw,   10
> And find in it the superhuman power   11
> To hold me to the letter of your law!   12
> Oh, I must keep my heart inviolate   13
> Against the potent poison of your hate.   14

The subject of this perfect sonnet, Shakespearean in form except for the rhyme *ccdd* instead of *cdcd* in the second quatrain, is more quickly ascertainable than that of Gwendolyn Brooks's poem. McKay uses discrimination in housing, made national in its sanction by his choice of title, and generalized to encompass all forms of legally enforced racism, to concretize the situation to which the protagonist is responding. That response is the poem. The heart and mind of the Negro—to use the most profound and most quickly forgotten phrase of the famous Supreme Court decision of May 17, 1954—is McKay's foremost concern. The technique with which the poet conveys his feeling is so distinctive that it deserves recognition through some new critical terminology (such as "homicidal art") occasionally or significantly applicable to the style of other Negro poets, among them Melvin B. Tolson and LeRoi Jones, and even Georgia Douglas Johnson and Gloria C. Oden.

The title of the poem, then, denotes the setting, the stimulus to the protagonist's anguished response: the prejudiced intellectual and perceptual abode of racist whites. The words "shut" and "tightened" in line 1 pair off as the psychological tension, the rejection begetting rejection, caused by instances of discrimination. What I have named "homicidal art" begins in line 2, where language itself becomes a weapon, a proud thrust at bigotry. Lines 3 and 4 are sociologically important, are part of the philosophical creed that awaits synthesis for group usage by Black Man Thinking: the Negro, denied the attributes of "courage" and "grace" by America, must through his own leaders assign them to himself as qualities befitting the repute of people who proudly restrain their expressions of anger against a society whose "door is shut." The word "unbent" shows clearly, however, that McKay is not advocating passivity.

Line 5, returning to homicidal art, expresses perfectly the kind of "crime in the streets" that every Negro with any self-respect whatsoever commits in his "vitals" (line 7) every time he is victimized by racism. In this line, the heat of the protagonist's resentment literally, although only in wish-fulfillment, tears up the "decent" street. And as he feels this emotion, he realizes, in line 6, that the white bigots before whom he is controlling himself are thinking of him as a "savage" trespassing their "decent" neighborhood.

Line 7 conveys a scarcely recognized personal tragedy that often repeats itself in the life of a Negro: psychically brutalized by society, he brutalizes himself in harboring such fierce, self-destructive resentment so often under the pressure of so few opportunities for release without incurring more oppression; and, knowing that racist society is responsible for these episodes of self-dehumanization, he "rends [his] vitals" in knowing further that the cycle is beyond his control. The octave ends with the right transition, the circumstance that gives extra moral urgency to the sestet, for "boldly shines" in line 8 pictures racial discrimination as both an affront and a temptation. The self-contradiction in that temptation (the temptation to strike back justifiably at a vulnerable offender) is contained in the words "shuttered door of glass." Playing on "shut" in line 1, McKay in line 8 suggests that bigotry hides behind a glass door, that it has a fragility, a final untenability, that invites violent retaliation from its victims.

The emotional access in the "Oh" that begins the sestet in line 9 is itself a response, a restraint, in the face of the temptation that the protagonist continues to struggle with by searching for "wisdom," a satirical contrast to the word "savage" in line 6. The struggle occurs in his heart and mind, McKay's steady concern, an arena of anger, "sore and raw" (in line 10) from the abrasions of repeated contests of the will. It should be noted in passing that the poet skillfully and relevantly uses different levels of diction when suggesting the protagonist's varieties of anger indicated by "wrathful," "sore," and "raw." A classroom question, about the antecedent of "it" in line 11, yields the conclusion that the reference is not to "wrathful bosom"—the restraint mentioned in lines 11 and 12 not being a logical product of anger—but is to "wisdom," in which the reputed "savage" must find "the superhuman power" of self-control, for the highly civilized purpose of honoring the idea of law and order, even when law confirms the practice of racism. This action proves "the courage and the grace" claimed for the Negro in line 3. The little word "Oh" beginning line 13 hints at the emotional

cost of this courage. Whereas the same word in line 9 reflected temptation, this second usage indicates the Negro's determination, a determination to protect the sanctity of his spirit, to keep his "heart
inviolate." The words "potent poison of your hate" in the final line
define the menace that bigoted whites present to the heart and mind
of the Negro. McKay ends with desperate optimism, for he balances
precariously the evil potency of racism with the Negro's continuous
resolve to save himself.

The case for Negro poetry can hopefully be allowed to rest
upon the evidence of these two representative poems. As is demonstrated by their obvious merit, not yet explicated by the critical Establishment, the best work of Negro poets, like the best work of
their brothers of color in other endeavors, must be justly assessed
and made easily available to general readers, students, and scholars.
Negro critics who are able to do so must divert some of their professional activity to this necessity, to the end that black Americans
of the next generation might know that black men before them,
trained in formal institutions to recognize and explain literary excellence, were also trained by personal experience to honor the needs
of men bonded to them by the deepest of claims.

> DUDLEY RANDALL
> *Black Poetry*

WHEN TWO of the Broadside poets were asked for poems for a new
little magazine, they refused, saying they preferred not to appear in
a white publication. This is a great change from Phillis Wheatley,
the second published black poet in this country. Whatever references she made to her African heritage were derogatory, reflecting
her status as a favored house slave and a curiosity, a black woman
slave who could write poetry, and write it better than most of her
contemporaries.

Her black contemporary, Jupiter Hammon, wrote in the same
vein. His "An Evening Thought" advised slaves to obey their
masters.

The black poets who followed them were different, however.
George Moses Horton attacked slavery in his poetry, and this theme

was foremost in the work of the few black poets in pre-Emancipation days. Because of the situation of the Negro in this country, it was only natural that much of his poetry would be concerned with social struggle. Even the folk poetry reflected this desire for freedom, from spirituals like "Go Down, Moses" to folk seculars like "Promises of Freedom."

> *My ole Mistiss promise me,*
> *W'en she died, she'd set me free,*
> *She lived so long dat 'er head got bal',*
> *An' she give out'n de notion a-dyin' at all.*

Even after Emancipation, when promises of freedom did not materialize, this theme of freedom was dominant. Paul Laurence Dunbar's dialect verses painted plantation and rural life in humorous or sentimental colors, but in his standard English pieces he repeated the theme, in "Sympathy" and "We Wear the Mask."

His contemporary, James Weldon Johnson, turned to folk sermons for his best-known work, *God's Trombones.*

The Harlem Renaissance of the 1920's nurtured a brilliant group of poets, Claude McKay, Jean Toomer, Langston Hughes, Countee Cullen, Arna Bontemps, Sterling Brown, and Melvin B. Tolson, although Tolson's books were not published until much later. Their work was anthologized by Alain Locke in *The New Negro* (1925), by Countee Cullen in *Caroling Dusk* (1927), and by James Weldon Johnson in *The Book of American Negro Poetry* (1922 and 1931). Kerlin's *Negro Poets and Their Poems* and Sterling Brown's, Arthur Davis', and Ulysses Lee's *The Negro Caravan* (1941) include, in addition to these poets, some of the poets of the Depression, Robert Hayden and others. Hayden, in his "Speech," voiced the Depression's ideology of black and white solidarity in organizing labor unions.

The next generation of poets included, besides Hayden, Gwendolyn Brooks, Margaret Walker, Owen Dodson, Frank Marshall Davis, Moses Carl Holman, and Margaret Danner. Most of these were included in Langston Hughes' and Arna Bontemps' anthology *The Poetry of the Negro 1746–1949* (1949).

Outside of Beatrice Murphy's *Ebony Rhythm* (1948) and Herman Dreer's *American Literature by Negro Authors* (1950), there were no other comprehensive anthologies of black poetry until 1958. Curiously, these were published abroad. Rosey E. Pool, a Dutch woman living in London, in 1958 edited *Black and Unknown Bards* with Eric Walrond and a bilingual English-Dutch collection of Negro verse called *Ik Zag Hoe Zwart Ik Was* (*I Saw How Black I Was*) with Paul Breman. Breman, a Dutchman also living in London, issued *Sixes and Sevens* in 1962, which included the work of thirteen younger Negro poets, James Thompson, Conrad Kent Rivers, James Emanuel, Russell Atkins, Ray Durem, Calvin C. Hernton, Audre Lorde, Raymond Patterson, and others.

A work wider in scope was Rosey Pool's *Beyond the Blues* (1962), which included fifty-six poets. It not only contained old and new poems by the established poets, but included the work of new poets such as LeRoi Jones, Bobb Hamilton, Julia Fields, and Mari Evans. Rosey Pool's introduction is perhaps the best short history of Afro-American poetry yet written. An anecdote underlining American neglect of black writers is that when Rosey Pool was dining with a Negro critic, she mentioned Ray Durem. "Who in the hell is Ray Durem?" the critic asked.

Beyond the Blues seemed to release the flood. There followed in 1963 Arna Bontemps' *American Negro Poetry*; in 1964 Langston Hughes' *New Negro Poets: USA*; in 1965 Rosey Pool's *Ik Ben die Nieuwe Neger*; in 1966 Hughes' *La Poésie Négro Américaine*; in 1967 Robert Hayden's *Kaleidoscope* and Dudley Randall's and Margaret Burrough's *For Malcolm: Poems on the Life and the Death of Malcolm X*, which included many of the younger black poets; in 1968 Arnold Adoff's *I Am the Darker Brother*, with still others scheduled for publication.

The work of the younger poets is similar in theme but different in emphasis from that of the older poets. In an essay in the *Journal of Black Poetry*, poet Ronald Stone compares a poem of Langston Hughes with a poem of LeRoi Jones. The one by Jones is not mild in tone like that of Hughes, but is angry and defiant. The younger poets no longer plead, or ask for rights from the white man. Instead of searching themselves for faults which engender the contempt of the white man, they examine the white man, and, after regarding his wars, his hypocritical religion, his exploitation, his dehumanization, they dub him—"the Beast." They no longer pity themselves, like James A. Corrothers—"To be a Negro in a day like this." Instead, they say, "I am black and beautiful." They reject whiteness and white standards. They call themselves blacks, rejecting the word Negro, which they say was given to them by white men. Some poets have taken African names. Le Graham is now Ahmed Alhamisi, Rolland Snellings is Askia Muhammad Touré.

This intensified pride in blackness has made the new poets indifferent to a white audience. *Negro Digest, Journal of Black Po-*

*etry, Free Lance, Umbra, Broadside Series, Soulbook, Dasein, Black
Dialogue, Freedomways, Uhuru, Black Expression* are periodicals
where they can publish for a black audience without white censor-
ship. In addition, there are the older publications, *Phylon, The
Crisis, Journal of Negro History.* There are publishers like Joe Goncalves of Journal of Black Poetry Press, Dudley Randall of Broadside Press, Ahmed Alhamisi of Black Arts Publications, LeRoi
Jones of Jihad Press, Robert Hayden of Counterpoise Series, and
Paul Breman (a Dutchman) of Heritage Series, who publish pamphlets of poetry and free black poets from the dependence upon
commercial publishers. There has been a proliferation of black
bookstores which afford outlets for their books. In New York, Detroit, Chicago, Los Angeles, San Francisco, Boston, Wilmington,
and other cities, stores specializing in Afro-American history and
literature are doing a flourishing business.

Writing for a black audience out of black experience, the
poets seek to make their work relevant and to direct their audience
to black consciousness, black unity, and black power. This may be
called didacticism or propaganda, but they are indifferent to labels
put upon it. They consider such labels as part of white standards,
and they reject white standards. They are indifferent as to whether
their work survives, just so it is effective today.

The bellwether of the revolutionary black poets is LeRoi Jones.
Talented and precocious, he has studied at Howard and Columbia.
He has rejected his background of middle-class parents—a postal
worker and a social worker; marriage to a white woman; editorship
of an avant-garde periodical *Jugen* where few black poets appeared;
and association with white poets of the Black Mountain and Greenwich Village schools. With his arrest for possession of a pistol during the Newark uprising and his conviction for writing poems the
judge did not like, he has become a symbol of black rebellion to the
younger poets, who imitate him and learn from him.

The younger poets have a teacher of great talent, and while
they think they are rejecting white standards, they are learning
from Jones, a man versed in German philosophy, conscious of literary traditions (see his preface to *The Moderns*), who uses the
structure of Dante's *Divine Comedy* in his *The System of Dante's
Hell,* and the punctuation, spelling, and line divisions of sophisticated contemporary poets.

No other of the younger poets has such outstanding talent as
Jones. Perhaps it would be better to mention them by location. Of
the New York and Eastern poets, Raymond Patterson writes con-

trolled, logical poetry. Bobb Hamilton writes scathing satire, but can be lyrically lovely. Larry Neal's long, random lines are packed with emotion and images. Ed Spriggs has a delicate lyric gift. James Thompson has a penchant for sound effects and unusual phrases. Julia Fields has nobility and dignity in her *Poems*, with Biblical overtones. Samuel Allen's *Ivory Tusks* has force and humor. Welton Smith has a gift for moving, magical phrases. Gloria Catherine Oden is a sophisticated, careful craftsman. James A. Emanuel's lyrics in *The Treehouse* are distinguished for their economy and concentration. Audre Lorde uses words and images well in *The Lost Cities*. A. B. Spellman is one of the better younger poets. Nikki Giovanni is both enigmatic and revolutionary in *Black Feeling Black Talk*.

In the Midwest, Ahmed Le Graham Alhamisi, author of *The Black Narrator* and *Black Spiritual Gods*, writes fierce, angry verses, in which his rage and his hate are reinforced with varied technical devices. Russell Atkins writes rollicking satiric verse. In *Star by Star* Naomi Long Madgett enriches the texture of her poetry with more complexity. Dudley Randall has published *Poem Counterpoem* (with Margaret Danner) and *Cities Burning*. Don L. Lee, whose *Think Black* and *Black Pride* have sold widely, writes with clarity and corrosive wit. Mari Evans' poems are sensitive and probing. Etheridge Knight, in *Poems from Prison*, ranges from stark portraits of prisoners to delicate haiku. The late Conrad Kent Rivers in *The Still Voice of Harlem* was developing in depth. Oliver LaGrone is sometimes entangled in his exuberant imagery and complex syntax. Alicia Johnson, Jewel Latimore, and Carolyn Rodgers are promising Chicago poets.

In the West, Sonia Sanchez in *Homecoming* writes with a fierce directness. Sarah Webster Fabio is versatile and sophisticated. Askia Muhammad Touré's long lines have an orator's sweep and sometimes an orator's clichés. Bob Kaufman, in *Solitudes Full of Loneliness*, writes experimental, sometimes surrealistic poetry. From Holland and Africa, Ted Joans writes seemingly spontaneous but carefully structured poems. William Kereopatse Kgositsile, exile from South Africa, writes revolutionary poetry that sometimes explodes syntax. Marvin X, in exile in Canada, in *Black Man, Listen* voices the philosophy of the Nation of Islam in clear, direct lines.

Along with all the activity of the younger poets, the poets of the previous generations have not been inactive. Robert Hayden's *A Ballad of Remembrance* in 1966 won first prize for poetry in English at the World Conference of Negro Arts in Dakar, Senegal.

This was followed by his *Selected Poems* containing his best work over the years. Besides the long, famous showpieces like "Runagate" and "Middle Passage," several shorter pieces show his humanity and are memorable—"The Whipping," with its insight into the frustrations of a mother whipping her son; "Those Winter Mornings," with its belated sympathy for his father making the fires and shining his son's shoes on cold winter mornings; and "The Wheel," with its emanations of evil.

The late Melvin B. Tolson published *Harlem Gallery* in 1965, which was a storehouse of erudition and dazzling poetic technique. Despite his occasional obscurity, Tolson often wrote with clarity and power, as in the section "The Sea Turtle and the Shark," with its horrifying imagery.

Langston Hughes' posthumous *The Panther and the Lash* showed the poet still of the folk and still holding his finger to the pulse of the times. It included his timely "Backlash Blues."

Margaret Danner has the distinction of producing a whole book of poems about Africa, *Impressions of African Art Forms*. She has also published *To Flower, Poem Counterpoem* (with Dudley Randall), and *The Iron Lace*. Her flexible verse has a sensuous delight in color, texture, and form.

Gwendolyn Brooks' latest book, *In the Mecca*, shows the influence of her association in her workshop with militant young Chicago South Side writers. There are still the precise, glittering, startling phrases, but there are fewer "feminine" epithets, and certain passages have a raw power that overwhelms. As well as her piercing insight into people's minds, there are violence, horror, and tragedy in this book.

In spite of my emphasis on the black consciousness of the poets, I do not wish to leave the impression of a monolithic sameness. There are all shades of opinion and militancy among the poets. Some are proudly black, and others would prefer to be colorless. In fact, just as the two Broadside poets refused their poems to a white magazine, recently two Negro poets declined to submit their poems to a black periodical.

> SARAH WEBSTER FABIO
> *Who Speaks Negro?*

KARL SHAPIRO plays oneupsmanship with Robert Penn Warren in the question he begs both in his *Negro Digest* article, "Decolonization of American Literature," and in his "*Introduction to Harlem Gallery*"; while Warren searches, vainly but profitably, by editing a book by the same name, to learn "Who speaks for the Negro?", Shapiro asks a more loaded one, "Who speaks Negro?" His answer is the late Melvin Tolson; his identification of Tolson's language as being authentically "Negro" is a gross inaccuracy which would mislead us into a familiar trap of liking someone for the wrong reason.

Tolson was aware of the solons and sages asking, "What is a Negro?" Searching for his own identity from what he refers to as the ruins of his Afroirishjewish Grandpa and other racially mixed ancestors, he asks, "Who is a Negro?" His answer that "The Negro is a dish in the white man's kitchen—a *potpourri* . . .", given in *Harlem Gallery,* is too simple a truth; any notion of Negritude which extols the virtue of being a rotten pot with flowers and petals for scent is lacking a full understanding of this concept.

Melvin Tolson's language is most certainly not "Negro" to any significant degree. The weight of that vast, bizarre, pseudo-literary diction is to be placed back into the American mainstream where it rightfully and wrongmindedly belongs. Allen Tate recognized the distorted mirror image of the pseudo neo-classical Anglo-American diction and, I think, rightfully interpreted this language as a device of parody.

Much of the dialogue in *Harlem Gallery* suggests a satirization of the one-dimensional and contradictory stereotypes of Negroes whipped up in the kitchens of the white man's fantasy world. Although I must admit to some difficulty in trying to establish a pattern of tone which would serve as a signpost to the degree of sincerity the poet had for his subject, in certain instances, Tolson's use of the grotesque, overstatement, excesses of diction at each end of the spectrum suggest that his language was very much a part of the parody. Language, for Tolson, was a device which enabled him to make his statement about life as he observed it, a statement which all but defies paraphrase.

The language of the Negro is classical in the sense that it never gets too far from concrete realities, from the "thingy" quality of objects, persons, places, matter perceived in all its immediacy by the senses and not through oblique references and artificially created allusory illuminations.

"Negro", if anything, is a language—largely unassimilated and unlettered—which cuts through, penetrates things as they are reflected in spirituals, blues or jazz lyrics to a core of meaning eliciting a soulful response, to a moment of realization of what it means to be a human being in a world with a stranglehold on this awareness.

Such a language is truly poetic in its lyrical impulse and cannot be faked. Paul Laurence Dunbar, Phillis Wheatley, Bessie Smith, Mahalia Jackson, Ray Charles, Willie Mae Thornton, Langston Hughes and LeRoi Jones can come to a lyric with a widely diverse body of diction and still, I think, speak "Negro." Karl Shapiro is not expected to understand this. It is very difficult, although not impossible, for a non-Negro to be able to assess this quality. LeRoi Jones mulls over this difficulty in *The Dutchman* when Clay says, "You don't know anything except what's there for you to see. An Act. Lies. Device. Not the pure heart, the pumping black heart. You don't ever know that."

Karl Shapiro, in his "Decolonization of American Literature," decries the fact that American literature is a "country-cousin literature of England." He describes it as a three century old child yet clinging to the mother's apron strings, an orphan in a far away place, filled with sentimental longing for "home." New culture in every country except ours, Mr. Shapiro reminds us, "is based on Home country, settler, and native." In order for an American to become so attached to English literature it is necessary for him to lead an imaginary life. Shapiro feels and laments the fact that he suffers from this common addiction which amounts to cultural amnesia for a Jew. He expresses his concern in the statement that, "Living an imaginary English life meant living a phony life of the mind, for I was not English in any sense of the word."

He speaks of the three phases of decolonization in our culture and refers to them as "nostalgia, assimilation and Negritude." Of these he comments, "Nostalgia is homesickness not for the good old days but for the bad old days. *Assimilation* means a cultural *entente* at the expense of any *mystique*. *Negritude* means assertion of the realities, historical and mystical as well." The Negro, he feels is luckier than the Jew because, "There he is, unassimilable and un-nostalgic, the biggest fact of life in the modern world." Of language he says, "A language in itself is nothing. *A literature in itself is nothing. A literature is the expression of a nation's soul, and a great literature leaves nothing out—that is its greatness.*"

Shapiro assisted Untermeyer in editing *The Modern American and Modern British Poetry* in 1955, and by his own above defini-tion of greatness the exclusion of Claude McKay, Paul Laurence Dunbar, James Weldon Johnson, Langston Hughes, Melvin Tolson and Pulitzer prize winner Gwendolyn Brooks, and all black poets writing in English, fosters the "status quo mediocrity" which he de-plores. To say that the American artist who reaches back to the Tradition is by his standards unauthentic is to place almost the total body of mainstream creativity into a bag. The authenticity which he lauds would by its very nature be idiosyncratic and difficult and its significance stands very little chance of being recognized.

Shapiro answers the question, "Is Negro Literature possible?" , by reminding us that, given the context of his life in America, only a pseudo-literature, an Uncle Tom poem could be created by him, and that it would be necessary for him, as was the case of Paul Lau-rence Dunbar, to use a phony Negro dialect as a medium because Oxford English gave him no choice. He then asks himself, "If there were to be an authentic Negro medium, where would it come from?", and timidly suggests the spiritual or blues as a likely source.

The difficulty inherent in Shapiro launching a crusade to loosen the hold of the academic mind over poetry which refers back to prior commitments is apparent; he must first free himself who would others free. Cultural amnesia is a historical reality of Ameri-can Negro existence; a violent severance of past language, customs and human relationships became a necessary prerequisite to the op-pressed state that was to become his lot. Negro contraband culture traveled the long underground railroad of race poetry, race music, race folklore, which is only recently surfacing, switching to the main track.

A concept of Negritude forged from historical realities and physical necessity and a race's stubborn determination *to be* is the rich heritage of modern Negro poets. There are volumes of race po-etry, records of blues and spirituals to be rediscovered; there is a growing body of world Negro poetry to explore, there is yet the too real daily confrontation of what it means to be Negro. There is still time to create myths from these realities in all their authenticity, and it is a disservice to young Negro poets to make them feel a necessity for an artificially created literary frame of reference. It is sound advice that he gives when he says ". . . it would be better to ignore the existence of the literature of reference and to create whatever we think valid than to go on tilting at windmills. This is what the beat writers did; they were successful because they refused to *take part in the academic dialogue.*"

Melvin Tolson was not a beat poet; he was a part of the neo-classical scene who—although as able as any to attempt the Quixotic feat of reviving a dead horse, albeit a Trojan horse—was denied a rightful place in this theatre of the absurd. Like many Negroes of this period, he was told to go back and perfect the art, and, then, in the great democratic tradition, he would be accepted into the society of the neo-classicists.

He accepted and perfected the art of classical reference as a pillar for an American tradition in literature but became victimized by the cultural lag that is common between the white and Negro worlds. About this time Allen Tate, the Nashville Agrarian poets, and other champions of this movement, gave up this vain pursuit of doing battle with tilting windmills. Therefore, while Tolson busied himself out-pounding Pound, his fellow poets forgot to send him the message that Pound was out.

Negro poets who did not go out on that kind of a limb could watch the public literary spectacle of mainstream American men-of-letters and, at the same time, nurture their own contraband art. The fact that Negro literary history cannot be traced through mainstream anthologies makes a pointed statement about mainstream American literature and life and the racist nature of this life. At the same time it says nothing about the tradition of a developing body of poetry by American and West Indian Negroes from the Revolutionary Period to the present. Negro anthologizers, fortunately, such as Langston Hughes and Arna Bontemps, have aptly anthologized this development.

Only a writer who overestimates the innocence of the Negro reading public would attempt to sell them on an unseasonable image of the modern Negro poet. Negroes are very hip consumers whether the commodity is clothing or poetry. Poets, like clothes, must appeal to the moment and reflect the spirit, tempo, tastes of the time. There is a bold slim line in the Mod look; an unadorned sophistication. Outmoded are not only the colonial frock coats of the "great

white fathers" but also the zoot suits, the double breasteds, even the
traditional pinstripe Oxford grey with the wide grotesque lapels.
Negroes are tailoring their own fashions this season; the new gar-
ments promise to be better fits than any of the traditional second-
hand outfits which were pawned off as models which suited their
fancy.

Who speaks Negro? Any black man who is on top of What's
happening.

ON
DRAMA

The Drama of Negro Life

DESPITE THE fact that Negro life is somehow felt to be particularly
rich in dramatic values, both as folk experience and as a folk temperament, its actual yield, so far as worth-while drama goes, has
been very inconsiderable. There are many reasons behind this paradox; foremost of course the fact that drama is the child of social
prosperity and of a degree at least of cultural maturity. Negro life
has only recently come to the verge of cultural self-expression, and
has scarcely reached such a ripening point. Further than this, the
quite melodramatic intensity of the Negro's group experience has
defeated its contemporaneous dramatization; when life itself moves
dramatically, the vitality of drama is often sapped. But there have
been special reasons. Historical controversy and lowering social
issues have clouded out the dramatic colors of Negro life into the
dull mass contrasts of the Negro problem. Until lately not even good
problem drama has been possible, for sentiment has been too partisan for fair dramatic balancing of forces and too serious for either
aesthetic interest or artistic detachment. So although intrinsically
rich in dramatic episode and substance, Negro life has produced for
our stage only a few morally hectic melodramas along with innumerable instances of broad farce and low comedy. Propaganda, pro-
Negro as well as anti-Negro, has scotched the dramatic potentialities
of the subject. Especially with the few Negro playwrights has the
propaganda motive worked havoc. In addition to the handicap of
being out of actual touch with the theatre, they have had the dramatic motive deflected at its source. Race drama has appeared to
them a matter of race vindication, and pathetically they have

123

pushed forward their moralistic allegories or melodramatic protests as dramatic correctives and antidotes for race prejudice.

A few illuminating plays, beginning with Edward Sheldon's *Nigger* and culminating for the present in O'Neill's *All God's Chillun Got Wings*, have already thrown into relief the higher possibilities of the Negro problem-play. Similarly, beginning with Ridgeley Torrence's *Three Plays for a Negro Theatre* and culminating in *Emperor Jones* and *The No 'Count Boy*, a realistic study of Negro folk-life and character has been begun, and with it the inauguration of the artistic Negro folk play. The outlook for a vital and characteristic expression of Negro life in drama thus becomes immediate enough for a survey and forecast of its prospects and possibilities. Of course, in the broad sense, this development is merely the opening up of a further vein in the contemporary American drama, another step in the path of the dramatic exploration and working out of the native elements of American life. At the same time, especially in the plan and effort of the Negro dramatist, it becomes a program for the development of the Negro drama as such and of a Negro Theatre. Fortunately this special motive in no way conflicts with the sectional trend and local color emphasis of American drama today with its Wisconsin, Hoosier, Carolina and Oklahoma projects. It is this coincidence of two quite separate interests that has focussed the attention of both white and Negro artists upon the same field, and although we should naturally expect the most intimate revelations to come from the race dramatist, the present situation sustains a most desirable collaboration in the development of this new and fertile province. Indeed the pioneer efforts have not always been those of the Negro playwright and in the list of the more noteworthy recent exponents of Negro drama, Sheldon, Torrence, O'Neill, Howard Culbertson, Paul Green, Burghardt DuBois, Angelina Grimke, and Willis Richardson, only the last three are Negroes.

The development of Negro drama at present owes more to the lure of the general exotic appeal of its material than to the special program of a racial drama. But the motives of race drama are already matured, and just as inevitably as the Irish, Russian and Yiddish drama evolved from the cultural programs of their respective movements, so must the Negro drama emerge from the racial stir and movement of contemporary Negro life. Projects like the Hapgood Players (1917–18), The Horizon Guild (1920), The Howard Players (1921–24), The Ethiopian Art Theatre (1923), The National Ethiopian Art Theatre founded in Harlem last year and The Shadows, a Negro "Little Theatre" just started in Chicago, though

short-lived and handicapped for an adequate and competent reper-
tory, are nevertheless unmistakable signs of an emerging Negro
drama and the founding of a Negro Theatre.

But the path of this newly awakened impulse is by no means as
clear as its goal. Two quite contrary directions compete for the artist's choice. On the one hand is the more obvious drama of social
situation, focussing on the clash of the race life with its opposing
background; on the other the apparently less dramatic material of
the folk life and behind it the faint panorama of an alluring race
history and race tradition. The creative impulse is for the moment
caught in this dilemma of choice between the drama of discussion
and social analysis and the drama of expression and artistic interpretation. But despite the present lure of the problem play, it ought
to be apparent that the real future of Negro drama lies with the
development of the folk play. Negro drama must grow in its
own soil and cultivate its own intrinsic elements; only in this way
can it become truly organic, and cease being a rootless derivative.

Of course the possibilities of Negro problem drama are great
and immediately appealing. The scheme of color is undoubtedly one
of the dominant patterns of society and the entanglement of its
skeins in American life one of its most dramatic features. For a long
while strong social conventions prevented frank and penetrating
analysis, but now that the genius of O'Neill has broken through
what has been aptly called "the last taboo," the field stands open.
But for the Negro it is futile to expect fine problem drama as an
initial stage before the natural development in due course of the capacity for self-criticism. The Negro dramatist's advantage of psychological intimacy is for the present more than offset by the disad-
vantage of the temptation to counter partisan and propagandist attitudes. The white dramatist can achieve objectivity with relatively
greater ease, though as yet he seldom does, and has temporarily an
advantage in the handling of this material as drama of social situation. Proper development of these social problem themes will require the objectivity of great art. Even when the crassest conventions are waived at present, character stereotypes and deceptive
formulae still linger; only genius of the first order can hope to penetrate to the materials of high tragedy—and, for that matter, high
comedy also—that undoubtedly are there. For with the difference
that modern society decrees its own fatalisms, the situations of race
hold tragedies and ironies as deep and keen as those of the ancient
classics. Eventually the Negro dramatist must achieve mastery of a
detached, artistic point of view, and reveal the inner stresses and

dilemmas of these situations as from the psychological point of view
he alone can. The race drama of the future will utilize satire for the
necessary psychological distance and perspective, and rely upon
irony as a natural corrective for the sentimentalisms of propaganda.
The objective attack and style of younger contemporary writers like
Jean Toomer, who in *Kabnis* has written a cryptic but powerful
monologue, promise this not too distantly.

The folk play, on the other hand, whether of the realistic or the
imaginative type, has no such conditioned values. It is the drama of
free self-expression and imaginative release, and has no objective
but to express beautifully and colorfully the folk life of the race. At
present, too, influenced perhaps by the social drama, it finds tentative expression in the realistic genre plays of Paul Green, Willis
Richardson and others. Later no doubt, after it learns to beautify
the native idioms of our folk life and recovers the ancestral folk tradition, it will express itself in a poetic and symbolic style of drama
that will remind us of Synge and the Irish Folk Theatre or Ansky
and the Yiddish Theatre. There are many analogies, both of temperament, social condition and cultural reactions, which suggest this.
The life which this peasant drama imperfectly reflects is shot
through with emotion and potential poetry; and the soggy, somewhat sordid realism of the plays that now portray it does not develop its full possibilities. The drabness of plays like Culbertson's
Jackey and *Goat Alley* and of *Granny Boling* and *White Dresses* is
in great part due to the laborious effort of first acquaintance. They
are too studied, too expository. Even in such a whimsical and poetically conceived folk comedy as Paul Green's *No 'Count Boy,* with
which the Dallas Little Theatre group won a recent amateur dramatic contest in New York, there is this same defect of an overstud-
ied situation lacking spontaneity and exuberant vitality. It seems
logical to think that the requisite touch must come in large measure
from the Negro dramatists. It is not a question of race, though, but
of intimacy of understanding. Paul Green, for example, is a close
student of, almost a specialist in, Negro folk life, with unimpeach-
able artistic motives, and a dozen or more Negro plays to his credit.
But the plays of Willis Richardson, the colored playwright, whose
Chip Woman's Fortune was the first offering of the Chicago Ethiopian Art Theatre under Raymond O'Neill, are very much in the
same vein. Though the dialogue is a bit closer to Negro idiom of
thought and speech, compensating somewhat for his greater ama-
teurishness of technique and structure, there still comes the impression that the drama of Negro life has not yet become as racy, as

gaily unconscious, as saturated with folk ways and the folk spirit as it could be, as it eventually will be. Decidedly it needs more of that poetic strain whose counterpart makes the Irish folk drama so captivating and irresistible, more of the joy of life even when life flows tragically, and even should one phase of it remain realistic peasant drama, more of the emotional depth of pity and terror. This clarification will surely come as the Negro drama shifts more and more to the purely aesthetic attitudes. With life becoming less a problem and more a vital process for the younger Negro, we shall leave more and more to the dramatist not born to it the dramatization of the race problem and concern ourselves more vitally with expression and interpretation. Others may anatomize and dissect; we must paint and create. And while one of the main reactions of Negro drama must and will be the breaking down of those false stereotypes in terms of which the world still sees us, it is more vital that drama should stimulate the group life culturally and give it the spiritual quickening of a native art.

The finest function, then, of race drama would be to supply an imaginative channel of escape and spiritual release, and by some process of emotional reenforcement to cover life with the illusion of happiness and spiritual freedom. Because of the lack of any tradition or art to which to attach itself, this reaction has never functioned in the life of the American Negro except at the level of the explosive and abortive release of buffoonery and low comedy. Held down by social tyranny to the jester's footstool, the dramatic instincts of the race have had to fawn, crouch and be amusingly vulgar. The fine African tradition of primitive ritual broken, with the inhibitions of Puritanism snuffing out even the spirit of a strong dramatic and mimetic heritage, there has been little prospect for the development of strong native dramatic traits. But the traces linger to flare up spectacularly when the touch of a serious dramatic motive once again touches them. No set purpose can create this, only the spontaneous play of the race spirit over its own heritage and traditions. But the deliberate turning back for dramatic material to the ancestral sources of African life and tradition is a very significant symptom. At present just in the experimental stage, with historical curiosity the dominating motive, it heralds very shortly a definite attempt to poetize the race origins and supply a fine imaginative background for a fresh cultural expression. No one with a sense for dramatic values will underestimate the rich resources of African material in these respects. Not through a literal transposing, but in some adaptations of its folk lore, art-idioms and symbols, African

material seems as likely to influence the art of drama as much as or
more than it has already influenced some of its sister arts. Certainly
the logic of the development of a thoroughly racial drama points in-
dependently to its use just as soon as the Negro drama rises to the
courage of distinctiveness and achieves creative independence.

[
    MONTGOMERY GREGORY
    The Drama of Negro Life
]

PRESIDENT-EMERITUS Charles William Eliot of Harvard University
recently expressed the inspiring thought that America should not be
a "melting-pot" for the diverse races gathered on her soil but that
each race should maintain its essential integrity and contribute its
own special and peculiar gift to our composite civilization: not a
"melting-pot" but a symphony where each instrument contributes
its particular quality of music to an ensemble of harmonious
sounds. Whatever else the Negro may offer as his part there is already the general recognition that his folk-music, born of the pangs
and sorrows of slavery, has made America and the world his eternal
debtor. The same racial characteristics that are responsible for this
music are destined to express themselves with similar excellence in
the kindred art of drama. The recent notable successes of Negro
actors and of plays of Negro life on Broadway point to vast potentialities in this field. Eugene O'Neill, who more than any other person
has dignified and popularized Negro drama, gives testimony to the
possibilities of the future development of Negro drama as follows:
"I believe as strongly as you do that the gifts the Negro can—and
will—bring to our native drama are invaluable ones. The possibilities are limitless and to a dramatist open up new and intriguing opportunities." Max Reinhardt, the leading continental producer,
while on his recent visit to New York commented enthusiastically
upon the virgin riches of Negro drama and expressed a wish to utilize elements of it in one of his projected dramas.

Before considering contemporary interest in Negro drama it
will be well to discover its historical background. William Shakespeare was the first dramatist to appreciate the "intriguing opportunities" in the life of the darker races and in his master-tragedy

Othello, he has given us the stellar rôle of the Moor in a study of the effect of jealousy upon a nature of simple and overpowering emotion. So great an embarrassment has this "Black-a-moor" been to the Anglo-Saxon stage that the "supreme tragedy of English drama" has suffered a distinct unpopularity, and its chief interpreters have been compelled to give a bleached and an adulterated presentation of the black commander of the Venetian army. Thus O'Neill had an excellent precedent for his *Emperor Jones.*

The example of Shakespeare was not followed by his immediate successors. In fact, a character of sable hue does not appear in the pages of English literature until a century later when Aphra Behn wrote that sentimental romance, *Oronooko,* portraying the unhappy lot of a noble Negro prince in captivity. This tearful tragedy had numerous imitators in both fiction and drama, an example of the latter being the *Black Doctor,* written by Thomas Archer and published in London in 1847. It was not long after this publication that London and the continent were treated to an extraordinary phenomenon,—the appearance of a Maryland Negro in *Othello* and other Shakespearean rôles in the royal theaters. Ira Aldridge is thus the first Negro to surmount the bars of race prejudice and to receive recognition on the legitimate English-speaking stage.

Up until the Civil War, then, there was but meager interest in the drama of the African or Negro in England, and practically none in the United States. That great sectional conflict aroused a tremendous sentimental interest in the black population of the South and gave us Harriet Beecher Stowe's *Uncle Tom's Cabin,* which also enjoyed a wide popularity as a drama. *The Octoroon,* written on the same pattern, soon followed on the American stage. These works mark the first instance where an attempt is made to present to the American public in a realistic manner the authentic life of the Negro. They accustomed the theater-goer to the appearance of a number of Negro characters (played by blacked-face white actors) on the stage, and this fact was in itself a distinct gain for Negro drama.

Although *Uncle Tom's Cabin* passed into obscurity, "Topsy" survived. She was blissfully ignorant of any ancestors, but she has given us a fearful progeny. With her, popular dramatic interest in the Negro changed from serious moralistic drama to the comic phase. We cannot say that as yet the public taste has generally recovered from this descent from sentimentalism to grotesque comedy, and from that in turn to farce, mimicry and sheer burlesque. The earliest expression of Topsy's baneful influence is to be found in the minstrels made famous by the Callenders, Lew Dockstader, and Primrose and West. These comedians, made up into grotesque caricatures of the Negro race, fixed in the public taste a dramatic stereotype of the race that has been almost fatal to a sincere and authentic Negro drama. The earliest Negro shows were either imitations of these minstrels or slight variations from them. In fact, the average play of Negro life to-day, whether employing white or black actors, reeks with this pernicious influence.

It was not until 1895 that the Negro attempted to break with the minstrel tradition, when John W. Isham formed *The Octoroons*, a musical show. Minor variety and vaudeville efforts followed, but the first all-Negro comedy to receive Broadway notice was Williams and Walker's *In Dahomey*, which played at the Forty-sixth Street Theatre for several weeks. Williams and Walker, Cole and Johnson, S. H. Dudley, and Ernest Hogan now presented a succession of shows in which the Negro still appeared in caricature but which offered some compensation by the introduction of a slight plot and much excellent music and dancing. Such shows as *Abyssinia, Rufus Rastus, Bandana Land*, and *Mr. Lode of Coal*, are still familiar names to the theater-goers between 1900 and 1910. During the latter year "Bert" Williams' inimitable genius was fully recognized, and from then until his death he was an idol of the American public. It may not be amiss to state that it was Williams' ambition to appear in a higher type of drama, and David Belasco states in the introduction to *The Son of Laughter*, a biography of "Bert" Williams by Margaret Rowland, that his death probably prevented him from appearing under his direction as a star. Negro drama will always be indebted to the genius of this great comedian and appreciative of the fact that by breaking into *The Follies* "Bert" Williams unlocked the doors of the American theater to later Negro artists.

The reader will probably be familiar with the extraordinary successes of the latest Negro musical comedies, *Shuffle Along, Runnin' Wild*, and *From Dixie to Broadway*, and with the names of their stars—Sissle and Blake, Miller and Lyles, and Florence Mills. In many respects these shows represent notable advances over the musical shows that preceded them, yet fundamentally they carry-on the old minstrel tradition. Ludwig Lewisohn, the eminent New York critic, thus evaluates their work: "Much of this activity, granting talent and energy, is of slight interest; much of it always strikes me as an actual imitation of the white 'blacked-face' comedian—an imitation from the Negro's point of view of a caricature of himself. All of these things have little or no value as art, as an expression of either the Negro individual or the Negro race." Yet in all justice it should be said that these shows have given a large number of talented Negroes their only opportunity for dramatic expression and have resulted in the development of much stage ability. "Bert" Williams and Florence Mills are examples of dramatic geniuses who have elevated their work in these productions to the highest art. Certainly historically these musical shows are a significant element in the groping of the Negro for dramatic expression, and who knows but that they may be the genesis for an important development of our drama in the future?

Serious Negro drama is a matter of recent growth and still is in its infancy. It is in this field of legitimate drama that the Negro must achieve success if he is to win real recognition in the onward sweep of American drama. The year 1910 may be said to mark the first significant step in this direction, for it witnessed the production with a distinguished cast, including Guy Bates Post and Annie Russell, at the New Theatre in New York City, of Edward Sheldon's *The Nigger* (later called *The Governor*), a somewhat melodramatic treatment of the tragedy of racial admixture in the South. It marks the first sincere attempt to sound the depths of our racial experience for modern drama. A more sympathetic and poetic utilization of this dramatic material appears a few years later in the composition of three one-act plays (*Granny Maumee, The Rider of Dreams,* and *Simon the Cyrenian*), by Ridgely Torrence. Of equal importance was the artistic staging of these plays with a cast of talented Negro actors by Sheldon, Mrs. Norman Hapgood, and others. The venture was a pleasing artistic success, and but for the intervention of the World War might have resulted in the establishment of a permanent Negro Little Theatre in New York City. Not only had the public been impressed with the artistic value of such plays, but it also had been given its first demonstration of the ability of the Negro actor in other than burlesque parts. Opal Cooper especially won the plaudits of the critics, and, like John the Baptist, he proved to be only the forerunner of one who was to touch the peaks of histrionic accomplishment.

Then by a *tour-de-force* of genius—for the histrionic ability of Charles Gilpin has been as effective as the dramatic genius of Eugene O'Neill—the serious play of Negro life broke through to public favor and critical recognition. Overnight this weird psychological study of race experience was hailed as a dramatic masterpiece and an unknown Negro was selected by the Drama League as one of the ten foremost actors on the American stage. In any further development of Negro drama, *The Emperor Jones,* written by O'Neill, interpreted by Gilpin, and produced by the Provincetown Players, will tower as a beacon-light of inspiration. It marks the breakwater plunge of Negro drama into the main stream of American drama.

In 1923 Raymond O'Neill assembled a noteworthy group of Negro actors in Chicago and formed the "Ethiopian Art Theatre." Following successful presentation there he launched his interesting theater on Broadway. Whereas Torrence started out with several original race plays, O'Neill attempted the adaptation of Oscar Wilde's *Salome* and Shakespeare's *Comedy of Errors*. His chief success was the production of *The Chip Woman's Fortune*, a one-act race play by the young Negro dramatist, Willis Richardson. The acting of Evelyn Preer, the Kirkpatricks, Olden and Solomon Bruce was equal to the best traditions of the American theater—but even great acting could not atone for an unwise selection of plays. This untimely collapse of a most promising enterprise should hold a valuable lesson for other promoters of Negro drama.

Since these passing successes of the Negro on the regular stage, there have been several hopeful experiments in the Little Theatre and educational fields, with larger likelihood of permanent results. At Howard University, in Washington, D.C., the writer, with the enthusiastic co-operation of Marie-Moore-Forrest, Cleon Throckmorton, Alain Leroy Locke and the University officials, undertook to establish on an enduring basis the foundations of Negro drama through the institution of a dramatic laboratory where Negro youth might receive sound training in the arts of the theater. The composition of original race plays formed the pivotal element in the project. The Howard Players have given ample evidence of having the same significance for Negro drama that the erstwhile "47 Workshop" at Harvard University and the North Carolina University Players have had for American drama in general. Atlanta University, Hampton Institute, and Tuskegee Institute have been making commendable efforts in the same direction. In Harlem, the Negro quarter of New York City, Anne Wolter has associated with her an excellent corps of dramatic workers in the conduct of "The Ethiopian Art Theatre School."

Finally, mention must be made of two young Negro actors who have been maintaining the same high standard of artistic performance as established by Gilpin. Paul Robeson has succeeded to the rôle of *The Emperor Jones*, and has appeared in the leading part in O'Neill's latest Negro drama, *All God's Chillun Got Wings*. Eugene Corbie has likewise given a creditable performance as the "Witch Doctor" in *Cape Smoke*. Thus a sufficient demonstration has been made that Gilpin's achievement was not merely a comet-flare across the dramatic horizon but a trustworthy sign of the histrionic gift of his race.

The past and present of Negro drama lies revealed before us. It is seen that the popular musical comedies with their unfortunate minstrel inheritance have been responsible for a fateful misrepresentation of Negro life. However, the efforts toward the development of a sincere and artistic drama have not been altogether in vain. O'Neill and Torrence have shown that the ambitious dramatist has a rich and virgin El Dorado in the racial experiences of black folk. As the spirituals have risen from the folk-life of the race, so too will there develop out of the same treasure-trove a worthy contribution to a native American drama. The annual prizes now being offered through the vision of Charles S. Johnson of *The Opportunity* magazine and of W. E. B. DuBois and Jessie Fauset of *The Crisis* magazine for original racial expression in the various literary forms are acting as a splendid stimulus to Negro writers to begin the adequate expression of their race life.

Our ideal is a national Negro Theater where the Negro playwright, musician, actor, dancer, and artist in concert shall fashion a drama that will merit the respect and admiration of America. Such an institution must come from the Negro himself, as he alone can truly express the soul of his people. The race must surrender that childish self-consciousness that refuses to face the facts of its own life in the arts but prefers the blandishments of flatterers, who render all efforts at true artistic expression a laughing-stock by adorning their characters with the gaudy gowns of cheap romance. However disagreeable the fact may be in some quarters, the only avenue of geniune achievement in American drama for the Negro lies in the development of the rich veins of folk-tradition of the past and in the portrayal of the authentic life of the Negro masses of to-day. The older leadership still clings to the false gods of servile reflection of the more or less unfamiliar life of an alien race. The "New Negro," still few in number, places his faith in the potentialities of his own people—he believes that the black man has no reason to be ashamed of himself, but that in the divine plan he too has a worthy and honorable destiny.

The hope of Negro drama is the establishment of numerous small groups of Negro players throughout the country who shall simply and devotedly interpret the life that is familiar to them for the sheer joy of artistic expression.

THERE STILL seem to be a great many bothersome questions—for those who care to be bothered—in the use of the term Negro drama. An all-inclusive term to cover the long history of our singing strength? including the recent search for the authentic black voice? Should a survey course include African writers, West Indian, the minstrel past? Should an anthology make a distinction between white and black playwrights? And what of all-Negro casts in white shows? Negro scenes in white plays? And so forth. But there are, it would seem, very few questions with the term Black Theater. It is simply—the theater of Black People. Our theater of the sixties.

It began sometime between the Baldwin opening and the Black Arts School closing. It began sometime between the death gasps of the Civil Rights Movement and the birth of the Black Liberation Movement. It is a birthday tribute to Malcolm X, a memorial to Langston Hughes. A program of poetry by LeRoi Jones with music by Graves and Pullens, a dance by Tally Beatty. It is Alvin Ailey and Eleo Pomare. It is the musical performances of Sun Ra, Archie Shepp. It is a New Breed Fashion show. It is children reciting poetry on an improvised stage on Speakers' Corner. It is a fund raising for Huey Newton. It is improvisational exercises by students' workshops. It is a survey course by Voices Inc., the Afro-American Folkloric troupe, and Pauline Meyers. It is even argued that Blacks playing Shakespeare, Bach, Ibsen, Folkine, Shaw, CBS is black theater, for "They put their own thing on it so tough these days—like what Ray Charles did for that sad ass song 'Margie'—indelible style, ya dig. That's what it's all about in the sixties—Black Theater." Just as the labor movement established the agit-prop theater, and the New Negro Movement established protest theater, the Black Liberation Movement established Black Theater.

Every time a southern sheriff unleashed the dogs, we moved further away from the dark town folly-blackbird revue mentality. Every political push within the colonized zones all over the world made the super neuter nigger hero on film seem all the more absurd. Every electric prod helped cauterize those dead tissues that layered over the vehement blackness just beneath the skin. Every assassin bullet propelled us toward historical awareness, a new sense of ourselves. And in the grips of grief and pride, the masks crumbled, the intricate network of etiquette between black and white began to crumble too. And finally, some have gotten free from the superficiality and the mimicry to speak plainly and to tap that dramatic storehouse of black-white, black-black, black-self encounters. And Black Theater takes shape.

What seems to provide the essential conflict for the playwright, a tension which is invariably invested in the work, is that never yet resolved vacillation between assimilation and separateness, between the social responsibility of the black artist and the autonomy of art, the rogue's gallery of personae from polemicist, machine-gunner, troubadour, liquidator, colloborationist, witness, recorder, Kamikaze. The movement, though, seems to be an impulse away from. As Jones raises in *Blues People* and others have discussed at length, this impulse stems from the old assumption that Afro-Americans are as earnest and devoted in the defense of the American system as are American whites. The sixties' playwright as well as other thinkers have stepped back to smile at that assumption as they decide what parts of that system, which values are worth saving, adopting; which of those so-called mainstream preoccupations are worth transforming by injecting which of the so-called minority values; which of those forked-tongued values that have formed the American reality of fine sentiment and broken treaties, broken spirits, broken bodies are real for black people.

When James Baldwin returned from his terrifying journey South in the fifties, he had the germ of a play in the Emmett Till case. The young black boy had been mauled and murdered in Mississippi in 1955, and the white man who had gone to trial and been acquitted sold his story of the crime, confessional details and all, to William Bradford Huie for a magazine article. When the boy appeared on stage several years later as Richard Henry in *Blues for Mister Charlie*, the predominantly black audience of that preview evening cheered the bitter, bold ass bad braggart nigger who had come home to scream on everybody, pass his photos of white-women-I-have-had around, and wear away the already eroding dialogue between Cap'n and Rastus. They stood up for Juanita, the spirited young woman who loves Richard and has been holding onto her rage at all the games all the jiveass-mothers have been running on her and her people for so long. They fell in love with

Mother Henry the wry old grandmother whose uhhunhs helped her survive and survive with dignity. They embraced Meridian Henry, the mixed-up minister who should've known better. They checked out the white editor, Parnell, as he narrated, interpreted, and got involved in the tensions—they found him impotent and laughable. They booed Lyle Britten the ofaypeckerwoodredneckcrackerbastard murderer. They dug where his wife Jo was at, they'd met her often enough. Complete strangers slapped palms, gave five, stomped feet, punched shoulders at every four-letter invective that boomed across the dark and stormy stage. And when the white actor yelled "You dirty nigger," "You black bastard," his counterparts in the auditorium tensed up and shouted out. No one at that moment seemed to mind the turpid rhetoric, the sprawling staging, the very nearly clumsy flash-back flash-forth whodunit machinery, the embarrassingly inept acting of the playwright's brother, the flat white cardboard grotesques, the oversharped cliché of black virility—white impotency, the pitiful-po'-me underneath the black characters' tirades. It was a rally. It was fire. It was energetic, vital, relevant, cathartic, upsetting. It was beautiful. It was the beginning—the beginning of polarization on stage and in the house. It was a distinct voice—distinct from the fairly muted voice of Negro drama of the fifties.

Black theater, however, did not grow on Broadway. It took hold in the community—in the community theaters, the library and school auditoriums, the writers' workshop studios, acting school lofts, the Y's, the mobile units of Harlem primarily, and in the off-Broadway areas where blacks were growing in numbers, and in the various counties of the Black Belt, the various ghettoes where troupes began to form and to tour. Black theater became a workshop for playwrights like Douglas Turner Ward, LeRoi Jones, Ron Milner, Ed Bullins; a showcase for performers like Lou Gossett, James Earl Jones, Cynthia Belgrave, Helen Ellis, Eleo Pomare, Milford Grave, Don Pullens, Moses Gunn; a forum for the spectators, musicians, designers, poets, dancers of Harlem, Bedford-Stuyvesant, the Lower East Side, the Village, the South, the campuses, the communities. Black theater became a possibility.

At the time of the *Blues* opening, the St. Mark's production of Jean Genet's *The Blacks* was about to go on tour. This production and the Sheridan Square production of Duberman's *In White America* were a beginning too. In the past, the black actor playing roles written by whites and directed by whites was severely hampered and tended to reveal, in spite of talent and craftmanship, the handicap—the inability to tap himself, to make use of whatever truth he was aware of, of what it means to be black, to somehow not get caught up and frozen in that other "truth," the stage truth, the stuff of his life as seen by someone else. The Duberman script, a survey of historic ordeals, a series of testimony and narrative, was at least flexible enough in its historical "truth" to allow the performers to finally, as the actor James Earl Jones has often stated, say something about what's behind the black face, to force the Other to see me through my color. And no one, sitting down with one or two actors from the Genet cast, can fail to notice how racialized many of those actors became in their attempt to translate the Africans into Afro-Americans, to translate the Outsider view to a Black view. Some agonizing moments occurred, it would seem, in those actors' attempts to decipher the text, to animate the roles, to fashion the charades into meaningful drama. The play called for obviously African-looking actors. Afro hair was important for the masque. Knowledge of that double life, the envy and mimicry of the oppressor, the rage and self-hate, the need for revenge—all were necessary to prevent the essentially anti-people script from breaking into a series of gratuitously aggressive episodes. And while the play was sinisterly biased in its assumption that revenge is what it is all about, not liberation but simply substitution of evil, there was nothing about the text that cut deeply into the essential truth of black anger or compromised the black actor too dreadfully. That play— staged with definite hostility—was a beginning too.

The LeRoi Jones plays from 1962 to 1964 were more than a beginning of Black Theater. It was. *Dutchman,* the game between the man on the margin and the seductive assassin, said all there is to say about the whole continuous pattern of the lure and the murder of black people. Jennifer West portrayed the white, sexy, bizarre Lula who entraps. And Robert Hooks portrayed the Negro-Black victim Clay who has imprisoned his self in Ivy League acceptance and is smoked out of his corner by the paranoia and promise of the girl and stabbed to death. *The Toilet,* an anecdotal short piece set in a boys' high school bathroom, was about a gang who beat up the lonely white boy who's made homosexual overtures to one of the group. When the others leave the bloody mess behind, Ray, another marginal type even on the outskirts of his own group, remains behind to minister the boy's wounds—sympathetic, in touch, caught up in the need to touch and be touched. *The Slave,* by far the most ambitious piece of dramaturgy, is about Walker, a black intellectual jammed between his Western-valued education and his people's call to arms. In the midst of revolution in the streets, he invades the home of his former wife, a white woman who just couldn't find personal immunity in his anti-whitey campaign. He speaks of their marriage, their children, identifies with the new husband, white, who shares his taste in music, philosophy, literature—one minute identifying, the next hell bent on extricating himself from everything white including those parts of himself that have been tainted. A tormented character, another Jones victim—portraying again the crisis drama within the "native" too much immersed in the colonial culture.

During the '64 season, several off-off Broadway and off-Broadway houses featured playlets and improvisations that attempted to dramatize the anguish of the black-white relationship. One of the more notable pieces was the Crickett production of Fugard's *The Blood Knot* with James Earl Jones, later Lou Gossett, and J. D. Cannon. It was a domestic-racial drama of two half brothers, white and black, who are living in a shanty in Port Elizabeth, South Africa. They play out the tensions of brothers who have various degrees of mobility and opportunity, they play out the horrors of that country's racial policies.

What signalled the new trend in the black-white relationship was not only the tension but the acknowledgment that the whole conquistador mentality was as murderous to the white psyche as to the black. And the tension did not arise out of some melodramatic moment when a white slipped and told a darky joke. New too was the curtain scene—no clasp of hands, no reaching toward brotherhood as the black forgives all past atrocities and promises not to marry his new ally's sister. The curtain tended to fall on an announcement that the end was near—the end of the traditional dialogue, the end of control, the end of the world as we knew it.

Since World War II, numerous writers have sounded the doomsday note: The West was in its decline. The big powers were on their way out. American life was falling apart. At the heart of white culture was a void. No one could any longer be convinced that the future lay in the adoption of a Western style of life. That way was suicide. LeRoi Jones' Walker says this, as he attempts to exorcise those parts of himself that harbor the seeds of decay. Jones had often argued the point in many of the essays of *Home* and in numerous sections of *Blues People*. He states in "The Revolutionary Theatre" that theater must teach white people their death. In many ways, the theater of the sixties—Black theater, Radical theater, and even mainstream theater—has done just that. Before Jones numerous people had made the case. Norman Mailer argued in "The White Negro" that the only hope for survival, the only way the white could move away from the wall, was in the adoption of the Blacks' hip life style. Sartre in "Black Orpheus" parallels the Mailer theme, indicating that the only alive literature, the only vital impulse left in letters, is negritude—the Cesaire–Senghor–Diop movement that might be shorthanded in the vernacular as soul plus revolt. George Orwell tolled the bell years ago. And Susan Sontag, Bob Dylan, the young Gutheries, and others have recently chimed in. Allen Ginsburg has told us what happened to the best minds of his time. And even a quick glance at the films, literature, and social science disciplines of the majority culture seems to reveal the yes— our men are Madison Ave automatons, our women hungry and shorted out, love perverted and distorted by money and power, social realities built on lies, our heroes are murderers, bandits, degenerates, we're all caught up in mechanical habits, in love with broken-down institutions, our leaders the very dregs of the bestial swamps, and all the greedy grabbing for the top hasn't evolved a race of taller men. So some white people scamper away from white culture. Others study Chinese while the Third World rises. Others organize to tear it down. And others are just waiting for the end.

Several plays give voice to this theme. In many ways, Archie Shepp's not enough seen "jazz allegory" *Junebug Graduates Tonight* investigates the dying off of America and the alternative routes of survival—at least as some see them. An uneven production, hampered more by cowardly direction (at least a reluctance or inability to push actors to the center of their characters to find the seat of tensions and to provide the various pulls in the play) than by the loudmouth symbolism, it is a serious though patchwork discussion of the Muslim route, the Marxist view, the integrationist's stand, the fascist order. The protagonist Junebug is to make the valedictorian address on graduation night and more than wanting to make good or to look right, he wants to be right. The play depicts the forces in his life that will determine the spirit and content of his address.

The prologue opens with a song in a bombed-out church with one of the oddest curtain raiser lines I've ever heard—"A nigger is like a tree—dispensable." It makes more sense after we have met Uncle Sam, the huckster-con artist who insists he is a dirty ole man but is actually impotent except where money and power and gain are concerned, and America, a fat-leg predator all too eager to take the confused Junebug under her wing and skirt. The first scene, a five-part fugue in a kitchen, presents the family. There is the hard, bitter, nastymouth dike Jessie (played by Minnie Gentry who can burn any stage down with a little help from a gutsy director) who if unleashed could put a little muscle in the radical movement; Sonja, a young trick who is too easy bait for the white man and his dusky-negress fantasies despite her street hipness; a silly bloated aunt with babies who probably meets every crisis, personal and racial, with a trip to Rose Meta; Billy the pimp, a sorry commentary on what happens to black manhood caught between the white supremacist and the black matriarch—"You could've been a big time pimp," Julia sings to him, which prompts him to erectionless soapsuds of lyrical love which provoke raucous laughter from Jessie. "I'm a virgin," he laments. In the next scenes we meet the Muslim father, a cottonwood cracker, some Nazis and minutemen, Y.A.F.ers, hecklers and uncommitted bystanders. Junebug, recently immersed in Marx, delivers his speech. America is betrayed, Uncle Sam is outraged. An interesting piece, "Junebug"—pity it wasn't a Negro Ensemble or New Lafayette property.

The Douglas Turner Ward plays, *Days of Absence* and *Happy Ending*, present the notion that blacks and whites are more tied up with each other than either cares to admit. In *Happy Ending* a young militant nephew is scandalized because his aunts, two domestics, are weeping over the fact that their employers are getting a divorce. Good, he argues, their world is crashing around them, crumbling apart, and so forth. The aunts interrupt their tears long enough to point out that all these years they've been living comfortably by taking food, "losing" clothes, padding the bills, etc. The nephew quiets down. The other play, extremely well done in white face and natural, is about the whites of a Southern town who gradually notice to their confusion and finally realize to their horror that all the blacks in the town and from neighboring counties have mysteriously disappeared. Pandemonium breaks loose. An interesting comment on the old colonial myth that if the settlers should withdraw, the natives would fall back into their brutish ways and be lost forever.

The recent productions of the Negro Ensemble Company, particularly *Kongi's Harvest*, New Lafayette, American Place, particularly Bullins' plays, and two evenings of theater—the Malcolm X birthday tribute of the Onyx Society at the Mary McLeod Bethune school and the Black Theater for Black Panthers at the Fillmore East —seem to point the direction to total theater—dance, poetry, music, drama, films, song; and to the creation of a nationalist myth—

international Blackness as the cultural matrix, homage to revolutionary heroes, institutionalization of Negritude, foregone conclusion of white decadence, the turning of the back.

Opening first at the American Place and later at the Martinique were three pieces by Ed Bullins, Minister of Culture of the Black Panther Party and resident playwright of the New Lafayette. *A Son Come Home*, an ephemeral playlet staged with a somewhat flabby montage effect, the mood sustained by the music of Gordon Watkins, portrays a mother-son relationship. He, recently out of jail for some nationalist(?) activities and now earnest in his desire to be a musician, returns home after nearly ten years to find that she, having done with sacrificing and travail, having decided that the best way to end the struggle is to abandon it, has sought refuge in a very exacting and bloodless religious sect. As they go over the past, upstage actors depict those experiences they cannot put words to, those background ordeals that have let the family fall to pieces. And the son, bewildered to find that his mother can no longer help him or even love him, is dismayed, too, realizing he can no longer fit into any of those old relationships anyway.

The second play, the very lively *Electronic Nigger*, is a scary bit of hilarity. Carpentier, an electronic eavesdropper agent from the Department of Correction, enters a creative writing class and usurps the position of the teacher—first night nerves, first novel failure, anxious, earnest, cultivated, well-read, square, co-opted. Carpentier is at first obnoxious, absurd in his jargon, and his program is wiretapping and socio-eco-politico-case-history-computerized drama. The teacher feels that he is a disgrace to the race. A white student even calls him "Uncle Tom." But his madness, his program, his power prove very seductive and he pied-pipers the students to his corner while the teacher disintegrates like some breakaway bannister . . . or better yet like a machine gone wild: "Plato, Faulkner, Shaw, Ellison, Emily Dick—."

The last play, *Clara's Ole Man*, starts out like any other local color documentary with some of the folks coming and going through the slice of life. Then it moves into nightmare territory. Clara has invited young Jack in for the day while her ole man is supposed to be at work. Jack, a gentle, mildly ambitious ex-marine currently going to college prep school, enters the kitchen, which rapidly becomes more and more claustrophobic, and meets the somewhat bizarre family—Big Girl, a none too pleasant butch who displaces the air around her with fat, power, and profanity; Baby Girl, the spastic in the corner who seems to be the embodiment of disease and corruption once Big Girl goes into her spiel; some strange neighbors on strange missions; some street corner hardheads fresh in from a mugging. Jack's out-of-itness amuses Big Girl and the thugs; eventually his innocence irritates them. Finally, it aggravates them to the point of violence as Jack, finally realizing that Big Girl is Clara's ole man, attempts to leave only to have his exit cut off by the wandering-in wino.

The Bullins play at the Black Panther program, *How Do You Do,* is a duet between a black poet on stage creating and two conjured-up sassy types who move in and out of the various postures black folks are known to adopt—ladeda, down home, blackerthan-thou, middle-class, whiter-than-bright, I've-got-a-brand-newthis and dig-my-shoes, Sapphire is a grim sister, Rastus shouts black but sleeps white. A delight. What characterizes Bullins work is a complete nonchalance about mainstream acceptance. Many of the reviewers were forced to mention that they found the spirit of the plays somewhat "alien to the white liberal conscience."

The Jones plays on the Panther program portrayed a black revolutionary (or maybe he was only an armed second-story man) who invades the home of a white family, played in white masks with gibberish language and haphazard gestures, only to be thoroughly confused by their foreignness, their toylike, not even childlike, behavior. He's come with some sinister (or is it revolutionary?) purpose but stays on amused as he directs the poor fools. A friend joins him, they damn near die laughing, pulling the strings with alarming expertise.

The work at the Malcolm program was a musical drama based on various Jones' poems, taking some of his more catchy lines for virtuoso playing. What informs most of Jones' work, unlike Bullins', is a messianic zeal to teach whites how stupid, how hateful, how doomed they are. I wonder if Albert Murray, in his essay "Something Different, Something More," isn't absolutely right when he maintains that the fuck-you-charlie school of drama is just a safe game in which whites read underneath that they are being envied and wooed. I think perhaps the ignore-'em school makes better drama and perhaps better propaganda too.

What characterizes Black Theater, then, is a newness in content, direction, attitude, and purpose. Miscegenation is no longer the great dramatic moment on stage. The black character is no longer just a good guy like the boy next door with smoked cork on his face. The playwright need not any longer accommodate his vision to what the white conscience believes is the truth about this country,

its past, its people, and their relationships. There is an undercurrent
of pedogogy, sometimes called radicalism, that feels obliged to
bomb blacks out of their corners, smoke whites out of hiding, and
flush the shit out of the system. There is a concern for the details
that make up the black world, its kitchens, its flamboyantly angry
men, its torn women, its ambivalences, its fluctuating moods, its
spirit distilled in the walk, the music, the language. Revolution was
talked to death on the stages of the thirties. The residue hung in the
air till the sixties. But at least revolutionary upheaval is taking place
in a realer sense in our time which will either sustain dramatic writing or bump it off completely, made irrelevant. And even if the angry hero becomes too fixed and the white-man-listen spring dries
up, the theatrical adventures of the sixties will at least have provided the lessons for the more genuine, more separate, more black,
more liberated revolutionary theater of the seventies.

> ED BULLINS
> *The So-called Western*
> *Avant-garde Drama*

IT WOULD seem that in America there is no way to break away from
the historical (in the Western sense) definitions of drama, though
never-ending revolutions occur in theater which are usually inap-
propriately named "avant-garde." These "avant-garde" movements
are not attempts, in most cases, to break or separate from Western
theater's history, conventions and traditions, but are efforts to extend Western dramatic art, to perpetuate and adapt the white man's
theater, to extend Western reality, and finally to *rescue* his culture
and have it benefit *his* needs.

Avant-garde theater is difficult to recognize, for it may not be
truly indicative of the future and may have little other effect upon
the current drama other than to be pretentious. Its characteristics
may only be bizarre, e.g., penis worship, masturbation, incestuous
narcissism and ego projection. And often avant-garde mannerisms
are a collection of rediscovered conventions of a forgotten era,
newly foisted upon the new generation to become cliches in themselves.

Most conventions fall into a series or set of mannerisms. After a time men (usually of the coming generation) rebel against these arbitrary rules; they break "tradition," rail against dogma and smash the molds established by custom and time, as well as complacence. These are the avant-garde. But, nevertheless, they work within a tradition which is particular to the West.

So are they avant-garde? Are they not actually only so-called avant-garde? Is what they are doing really new? Is there anything under the sun that is new, especially in the theater, in the Western tradition of that institution?

Currently, the so-called avant-garde theater, as opposed to contemporary commercial, academic and "experimental" theater, is identified chiefly with France and the absurdist school of writing (defined not by the playwrights but by critics) or with Piscator and Brecht and the Epic theater, or with actor/director movements, e.g., The Polish Lab, The Living Theater, Peter Brooke's *Experiments* at the Royal Shakespearian Theater Club or The Berlin Ensemble. (I shall not even enter into a parallel argument concerning Black Drama and Western Theater, for the separation is so innovative and startling that they cannot be spoken of in the same vocabulary, much less classifications. This statement should be approached as a jumping-off place to various discussions which will lead to that unique entity known as Black Drama.)

But is any of the above really new? For instance, the paragon of *their* movement and history, *Waiting for Godot* by Samuel Beckett, has a linear story action, a timelessness, universal characters and a plot with continual expansion of meaning. (This is the white man's language, which I use in connection with his culture; in speaking of Black culture, we Black artists are continually developing a vocabulary and dialogue.) Many of the other plays in this tradition have similar effects and are equally as identifiable. These effects are all found in previous dramatic literature, conventional or archaic, in our period, but equally vanguard in theirs. But to cut through the academic and critical verbiage, it is the white man's vision of reality that is most identifiable in his drama, and Black dramatists are not heir to that type of madness.

The trick or innovation that the present-day absurdists seem to have come upon, out of their conscious or unconscious wills and motivations, is the ability to express *disbelief*. They disbelieve in themselves, in their sources, in their creation, in their present moment in time. The conventional drama aims at telling a story. The absurdists feel little or no story is necessary. The tradition of theater has been to deal in character. *Krapp's Last Tape* by Beckett has a tape recorder as one of the principal characters, not giving it anthropomorphic characteristics like Mr. Ed, the talking horse, but leaving it in the realm of being an object. Objects remain the phenomenological items they are and humans become dehumanized in this drama. Quite a step away from traditional humanistic thought, but not too far removed from Medusa (of Greek legend) turning men to stone or of Lot's wife who couldn't allow her damned city to burn without a backward glance (the portrayal of the great white Bitch figure in Western literature and philosophy has some interesting associative material for contemporary Black writers).

The new technological culture (ology) seems to be the one factor or aggregation of factors which might change Western theater drastically [Western theater: a theater which shies away from social, political, psychological or *any* disturbing (revolutionary) reforms, just as the reactionary society which it reflects does] and may throw this backward institution into the twentieth century. (If the media is the message, we Black arists have been far ahead of anything the white man has conceived.)

For the white man there are no new stories, or plots, or characters; and somehow, by the time they filter down to present-day theater, there are *no* really new ideas in his culture. His sense of reality cannot extend far enough to encompass what is not merely himself, or to perceive what is really happening, i.e., *Black*.

So, the electric light hasn't really changed *Hamlet*. The arena stage was known when the threshing floor existed and the hero-warriors danced the lion and spear dance. All are there and remain, and not just as some footnoted reference in anthropological data. The use of mechanical sound and film devices were used before Piscator and Brecht.

There may be nothing which can really be properly regarded as avant-garde in Western theater. (Surely, Black Drama doesn't wish to exploit this pretentious, effete, white bourgeois term.) And this pale label (avant-garde) must not be confused with "experimental." "Experimental" is generally the refuge of the inept. Experiments, and especially in theater, must be designed to go somewhere, to have a positive direction and goal, even if that place is predetermined to be "nowhere," e.g. (and only in rare cases) a *happening*.

An experiment can only be a handmaiden to the so-called avant-garde and quite in keeping with the times; for as stated above, there may be no such thing as avant-garde in white America.

To paraphrase Brother LeRoi Jones: It is a post-American

form of Black theater we Black Artists should be seeking. It is Black
Art that is like a dagger pointed at the vitals of America, and
through the rips "we" (US) can enter the New Epoch.

[
K. WILLIAM KGOSITSILE
Towards Our Theater:
A Definitive Act
]

"These are the words of lovers. Of dancers, of dynamite sing-
ers. These are the songs if you have the music"—LeRoi Jones,
"Three Movements and a Coda"

TESTIFYING. And what shapes people your mind? Our theatre will
be a definitive act, a decisive song. There will be portions of actual
life unveiled. All the things we could have been. All the things we
are. All the things we will be. There will be instruction. There will
be construction. There will also be destruction. Really grinding. All
the faggoty frankensteins crapping their balls and eating them piece-
meal before our very eyes, forming our negative references, detest-
able and detested. Check out LeRoi Jones' *Black Mass*, his most
accomplished play to date, in my opinion.

Jacoub, a Black magician, in the pursuit of creation for creation's sake (a perversion, like art for art's sake), creates this
monster. The monster runs around like crazy, vomiting and eating
the vomit. No one can communicate with it. Long before its only
understandable sound, "Me . . . White . . .", reaches us, we have
identified this beast. It has no regard for human life. Everything it
touches undergoes a horrible distortion. It touches Tila, a beautiful
Black woman who suddenly turns into a half-white monster, hop-
ping and slobbering around like this inhuman monster. May you die
a most horrible death if you claim you do not recognize this monster and its victims!

Theater as poetry, be it comic or tragic, be it instruction or
entertainment, remains an act which, through language as complementary vehicle—image, rhythm, symbol—carves from life, reveals
and celebrates future direction. It weaves past and present together
to clarify future points of reference which exist now as desire or the
artist's imagination. The language is necessarily complementary to

the action, to clarify some aspects of the experience, psychic or physical. So there will be very little dialogue because speech or words will come in only when other sounds or the action cannot clearly supply the necessary image.

The images and symbols will be national, put up for clarification and illustration by the sharp-edged sensibility of the artist whose impulse throbs with the nation's desire and pulse. The desired and desirable will be seen through elegant image and symbol abstracted from life. The undesirable, the corrupting, the destructive, will be portrayed in a grotesque manner, its sinister qualities driving us to the mercy killing of the villain.

Don't get me wrong. This will not be life in its entirety. It will be portions of life because art is not life. Art is contained in life. Life is the bigger body from which art cuts out bleeding portions for illustration, revelation, celebration and whatever moves the capable sensibility leaping from the corner where a spade is a spade. Yes, we will finally be coming to grips with *where we are really at*, historically. We will be destroying the symbols which have facilitated our captivity. We will be creating and establishing symbols to facilitate our necessary constant beginning.

Old decadent would-be Black woman, this theatre will straighten out your mind instead of your hair. If you are too twisted and/or petrified to be straightened out, it will pulp you to death, your hideous little imitation life pungent like the stench of stale menstrual flow. It will be a cleaning up for a theatre (life portions) of sheer beauty; paths towards a life of construction after the necessary destruction. How do you relate to that stupid powdery mask you wear every morning? Or all that junk in your toilet? I understand now they even wear blonde wigs in South Africa!! Are you some imitation Caucasian bitch? Have mercy on the male counterpart ". . . selling black for a quick screw," as Welton Smith so clearly points out.

The villains in the theatre, as in real life, will be alienated and destroyed; fear-ridden, no-ball cowards drowned in their own filth, forced to yield place to a better order of things. We want to love and laugh unrestrained. For this now-lost simple natural right, our new heroes will giant-walk and destroy any and everything that attempts to militate against that desire, as indeed we have to do in real life.

All the anti-life crap that must vacate our minds will go up in flames. Jehovah, J.C., Capitalism, Hollywood, "art for art's sake"— the whole jive. All points of reference will emerge from within the nation. So will our heroes, literary and national—Dedan Kimathi, Malcolm, Du Bois, Nkrumah, Nyerere, Babu, Touré, Fanon, and many more living and being born every day, pulsating with visions of a world worth killing and dying for. The European game will be over in the arts as in our real life. For a long time this theatre will not be liked because it will make many people uncomfortable; because it will be a portrayal of truth; because we have been trained in Western freak institutions to be afraid of truth. Is it then surprising that confrontation with truth, unveiled, is not always particularly pleasant? Again like Jones sings:

> *. . . these are natural*
> *things. No one is*
> *threatening anybody*
> *that's just the way life*
> *is . . .*

> LOFTEN MITCHELL
> *The Negro Theatre and the*
> *Harlem Community*

The majority of the history contained herein was originally the subject of two articles prepared for European publications —the Encyclopedia Della Spetta Colo in Rome and the Oxford Companion to the Theatre.

A SCENE in the play, *Star of the Morning*, describes the disbanding of the Williams and Walker Company in 1909. Bert Williams asks Jesse Shipp, the company director: "Jesse, where'll you go?" Jesse answers: "Uptown. 100,000 Negroes in New York now. Lots of them moving to Harlem. I'll go there. Maybe they'll be needing a theatre."

Fifty-three years after Jesse Shipp's statement, Ed Cambridge, the director of *Star of the Morning*, read these lines at an audition. The shoulders of a number of theatre people sagged as the lines left Cambridge's lips. A sharp pain stabbed me. I wished the lines had not been written.

Later that night Gertrude Jeanette, Esther Rolle, Lynn Hamilton, Louis Gossett, Rick Ferrell and Irving Burgie sat in the home

of Michael Allen, rector of St. Marks-in-the-Bouwerie, discussing
the fact that there was a theatre in Harlem when there were only
100,000 Negroes in the city and not one at present when the population totalled approximately one and a half million black people. Our
trembling fingers spilled coffee into overflowing saucers and onto
Priscilla Allen's tablecloth. Ed Cambridge shuddered, banged his
cup into the saucer, and growled: "It's a good thing Jesse Shipp
didn't go up there this year looking to work in theatre. He'd have
been hungry as hell!"

The Harlem to which Jesse Shipp went—like the Harlem of
today—was peculiarly a part of this society—this society created by
an impoverished, decaying Europe reaching out, searching for a
new route to India and finding instead a new Eldorado in the west.
The European underprivileged raced to these shores, staked claims,
then warred with the red man and with rival European groups.
Other Europeans found the rich African continent, enslaved its
people, then attempted to justify these atrocities. "The image of
Africa," says John Henrik Clarke in his essay, "Reclaiming the Lost
African Heritage," "was deliberately distorted by Europeans who
needed a moral justification for the rape, pillage and destruction of
African cultural patterns and ways of life."

The image of the African was also distorted in America where
a ruling aristocracy sought to break its ties to the old world.
Grandiloquent phrases declared equality of all—with the exception
of those who were black or those who were white and owned no
property. Patrick Henry demanded liberty or death, but he ignored
the twenty-three slaves in his possession.

America was, for the African, a strange, hostile land. Everywhere people spoke of freedom, yet he was not free. Everywhere he
heard others speak of their glorious ancestry, yet he was told his
Africa was a huge jungle, inhabited by cannibals. Sometimes the
Negro believed these distortions and saw himself as others saw
him—as something sub-human, deserving a cruel fate. Yet, somehow he dared to dream that someday he would be free.

His dreams were not idle ones. He fought the nation's wars.
His hands built the economy. His cultural gifts were either stolen or
ignored by white historians who interpreted the nation's history in
biased terms. In his essay, "Negritude and Its Relevance to the
American Negro Writer," Samuel Allen describes the Negro's subjection to the cultural imprint of a powerful, dominant majority in an
unfriendly land. Mr. Allen tells us that the American Negro group
became—if not the only—one of the few black minorities in world

history. Despite colonialism, those in Africa had the sheer weight of numbers for allies, plus the realization that the land was rightfully theirs. The West Indian Negro also had the advantage of numerical strength, plus an infrequency of contacts with the ruling group.

The American Negro, however, underwent a physical and spiritual alienation without parallel in modern history. He was overwhelmed militarily and economically, transplanted from his native soil, then subjected not only to a dominant elite, but to what the poet Claude McKay called a cultural hell—a hell created by a powerful, materialistic, brutal frontier society that was uncertain of its own identity, yet seeking to assure itself of status by denying status to its victims.

After the Civil War

The slave system crumbled. The Reconstruction Era followed, but this was sabotaged by those who sold the Negro back to his former owners. Jimcrow legislation further oppressed him. The southern slaveholding oligarchy remain unchallenged and now, more than one hundred years later, as the Negro struggles to complete the first American Revolution, it seems remarkable indeed that he ever owned a house, let alone a theatre.

Despite hostility, the Negro was part of the drama long before the United States became a nation. John Leacock's *The Fall of British Tyranny* (1776) described recalcitrant slaves who promised to kill their masters upon attaining freedom. *Yorker's Stratagem* (1795) dealt with a New Yorker's marriage to a West Indian mulatto. Murdock's *The Triumph of Love* (1795) featured the cackling, comic servant; despite the fact that black Crispus Attucks was not comic when he shed the first blood in the American Revolution and black Phoebe Fraunces did not cackle when she saved the life of George Washington.

In the early part of the nineteenth ceutury a group of free New York Negroes, spearheaded by James Hewlett, organized the African Company at Bleecker and Grove Streets. In 1821 this group performed Shakespearean plays before mixed audiences. Disorderly whites forced the management to segregate them and also to lament that whites did not know how to behave at entertainment designed for ladies and gentlemen of color. This theatre, eventually destroyed by white hoodlums, is reported to have influenced the great Ira Aldridge who went abroad where he was acclaimed by European royalty.

Origin of minstrel tradition

In the middle of the nineteenth century a number of plays attempted to deal with the Negro as subject matter. J. T. Trowbridge's *Neighbor Jackwood* (1857) and Stowe's *Uncle Tom's Cabin* were notable efforts. Dion Bouccault's *The Octoroons* reflected many of the traditional attitudes towards the Negro—that he was either a happy-go-lucky creature or a person with "unclean blood." The nineteenth century was, however, chiefly the era of the minstrel tradition—*the tradition originally created by slaves to satirize their masters*. White performers copied this pattern, popularized it, and spread the concept of the shuffling, chicken-stealing Negro to a society willing to embrace any representation of the Negro that denied his humanity. Following the Civil War, Negroes themselves joined the minstrel tradition, blackened their faces and imitated whites imitating them.

The wave of minstrelsy overflowed into the latter part of the nineteenth century. A group of showmen objected to it. Sam T. Jack's *The Creole Show* (1890) broke with the minstrel pattern. Later came *The Octoroons*, then Bob Cole's *A Trip to Coontown* (1898), the first show to be written, directed and produced by Negroes. In 1898 Will Marion Cook and Paul Laurence Dunbar offered *Clorindy—the Origin of the Cakewalk*. Bert Williams, George Walker, Ernest Hogan, Alex Rogers, Jesse Shipp, S. H. Dudley and J. Rosamond Johnson saw to it that the break with minstrelsy was complete. They produced a series of musicals with plot, characterization and meaning.

But, Thomas Dixon's *The Clansman*, later filmed as *The Birth of a Nation*, echoed existing attitudes towards the Negro. Race riots flared. The robber barons built their empires and the Theatrical Trust Syndicate brought the big business concept to the American theatre. This syndicate controlled the theatre and, because Mrs. Fiske and Sarah Bernhardt incurred their disfavor, the former was compelled to play in second rate theaters and the latter in a tent. The Negro artist found himself unable to get inside the Broadway theatre as performer or patron. Only Bert Williams worked on the Broadway stage. In 1910 the Negro performer had to go to Harlem.

He went because the fabric of theatre life excluded him. Some Negro actors welcomed the exile to Harlem. There they could perform roles previously denied them. They could play love scenes— something that was "taboo" while performing before whites. There, too, they could escape the raging hostility rampant in downtown areas. Many remembered too well the 1900 race riot when the mob yelled: "Get Williams and Walker!" Many knew, too, that comedian Ernest Hogan had to lock himself in a theatre overnight to escape from a lynch mob.

Harlem, therefore, offered the new Negro resident a haven from an unfriendly world despite the fact that he often had to fight neighboring whites in hand-to-hand battles. Many classes of Negroes poured into Harlem. Although a large number came from the South, this group had either heard about the theatre or seen Negro touring companies. In America at the turn of the century there existed approximately five thousand theatres as well as tent shows and civic auditoriums. To these came the Williams and Walker Company, Black Patti's Troubadors, and others. The movie industry had not yet challenged the economics of theatre. Despite the rise of the Syndicate, theatre was then a primary form of entertainment. It had not yet become a totally middle class luxury.

The Negro who moved to Harlem, therefore, was receptive to the theatre movement that grew around him. For one thing, he could not go into any other theatre. Had he been able to go, he would have witnessed vapid Cinderella stories unrelated to his daily life. Therefore, he flocked readily to the Crescent Theatre, opened by Eddie Hunter on 135th Street. Lester Walton leased the Lafayette Theatre and later stock companies appeared at the Lincoln and Alhambra Theatres. These groups presented Negro versions of Broadway plays, originals, dance-dramas, classics and musicals. The carriage trade often journeyed uptown to openings. Florenz Ziegfeld bought the finale of *Darktown Follies* for his own production. Another show, *Darkydom,* saw many of its sketches sold to Broadway producers.

On April 5, 1917 the Negro drama again moved towards downtown circles. Ridgely Torrence's *Three Plays for a Negro Theatre,* directed by Robert Edmond Jones, opened at the Old Garden Theatre. Charles Gilpin appeared in John Drinkwater's *Abraham Lincoln* and in Eugene O'Neill's *The Emperor Jones* (1920) at the Provincetown Theatre. Later, O'Neill's *All God's Chillun Got Wings* fanned flaming headlines because the play dealt with miscegenation. The Negro theatre artist had returned to the downtown area, doing what he felt whites would pay to see, or performing plays that reflected a white point of view.

The Negro Renaissance flowered. *Shuffle Along, Goat Alley* (1921), *Strut Miss Lizzie* (1922), *The Plantation Revue* (1922), *How Come?* (1923), *The Chipwoman's Fortune* (1923), *Chocolate Dandies* (1924), *Dixie to Broadway* (1924), *Topsy and Eva,* and

Paul Robeson in a revival of *The Emperor Jones* (1925) were major downtown offerings during the 1920's. 1925 ushered in the first Negro-written Broadway drama, Garland Anderson's *Appearances*. Also seen were such offerings as *Lucky Sambo, My Magnolias, Deep River, In Abraham's Bosom, Show Boat,* and Wallace Thurman's *Harlem.* Later, too, came *Porgy,* then *The Green Pastures.*

Effect of movies on theatre

Theatrical activity continued in Harlem. Night clubs flourished. This was the period when the Negro was in vogue. Commercialism flooded the community. Stage presentations gave way to vaudeville sketches as the commercial-minded sought to sell to whites what they wanted to see and hear about Negroes. And then the movie industry reared its head. Where there had been approximately five thousand American theatres in 1900, the arrival of talking pictures reduced this amount drastically. By 1940 there were only 200 in the nation. The moving picture replaced the stage and, in addition to the novel form, the prices were considerably cheaper. And many Negroes frankly sought this type of entertainment because at least it was honest. It did not attempt to represent them in any light.

One of the ventures that suffered as the movies rose to power was the Theatrical Owners and Bookers Association. This group, known as "Toby" was organized, owned and managed by Negroes who controlled a nation-wide circuit. Negro performers were assured of continued work.

The depression, the movies and the extended influences of white managers destroyed Toby. Veterans Sidney Easton and Elsworth Wright have declared that Negro actors did not know unemployment until Toby went out of business.

The depression of 1929 temporarily halted the Harlem theatre movement. Negroes appeared in a number of professional shows: *Hot Rhythm, Brown Buddies, Lew Leslie's Blackbirds, Sweet Chariot, Fast and Furious, Swinging the Blues, The House of Connelly, Sugar Hill, Savage Rhythm, Never No More, Bloodstream, Black Souls* and *Blackberries* of 1932. Negroes were in a sober mood during the depression years. Hall Johnson's *Run, Little Children,* Langston Hughes' *Mulatto,* John Wexley's *They Shall Not Die* and the Paul Peters'—George Sklar's *Stevedore,* were serious works. This era ushered in, too, such vehicles as *Four Saints in Three Acts, Mamba's Daughters, Roll Sweet Chariot, Porgy and Bess, The Swing Mikado* and *The Hot Mikado.*

The nineteen-thirties brought professional attempts to the
Harlem area. Rose McClendon and Dick Campbell organized the
Negro People's Theatre. The Harlem Players, a stock company, presented Negro versions of *Sailor, Beware* and *The Front Page* at the
Lafayette Theatre. This group tried to speak to a community that
concerned itself with eating regularly, with being dispossessed, and
with relatives being lynched in the southland. The troubles of a
sailor and the problems of a newspaperman hardly interested Harlem. The Harlem Players soon went out of business. Another group,
the Harlem Experimental Players, produced Regina Andrews' plays,
directed by Harold Jackman. The Harlem Suitcase Theatre presented
Langston Hughes' *Don't You Want To Be Free?* and Dick Campbell
and Muriel Rahn organized the Rose McClendon Players. Housed at
the 124th Street Library Auditorium, this group produced George
Norford's *Joy Exceeding Glory* and Abraham Hill's *On Strivers
Row.*

Best known of the uptown groups, however, was the Negro
Unit of the Federal Theatre. It presented at the Lafayette such plays
as George McEntee's *The Case of Philip Lawrence*, J. Augustus
Smith's *Turpentine* (written with Peter Morrell), Frank Wilson's
Walk Together, Chillun, Rudolph Fisher's *Conjure Man Dies*,
Shaw's *Androcles and the Lion*, William Du Bois' *Haiti* and George
Kelly's *The Show Off*. Its most highly acclaimed production was the
Orson Welles–John Houseman offering, *Macbeth* on April 14,
1936. Canada Lee was a member of the cast. This Federal Unit was
a solvent, skillful group that attracted theatregoers of all incomes.
When an act of Congress ended the Works Progress Administration,
it left Harlem without a low-priced professional theatre.

The Negro Playwrights Company, organized towards the end
of the nineteen-thirties, attempted to supply the community with
professional theatre. Theodore Ward's *The Big White Fog*, directed
by Powell Lindsay, opened at the Lincoln Theatre and introduced
Frank Silvera to New York audiences. Financial difficulties brought
this organization to an untimely end.

During the 1940's the Negro was involved on Broadway as well
as in Harlem. The Richard Wright–Paul Green play, *Native Son*,
starring Canada Lee, and Paul Robeson's *Othello* were significant
achievements. *Cabin in the Sky* enjoyed a successful run. In Harlem, Abram Hill, Frederick O'Neill, Austin Briggs-Hall, and a number of talented theatre people formed the American Negro Theatre,
and housed it in the auditorium of the 135th Street Library. In
addition to Hill's two plays, *On Striver's Row* and *Walk Hard*, such

worthwhile ventures as Theodore Brown's *Natural Man* and Owen
Dodson's *Garden of Time* were shown. But, it was the Abram Hill–
Harry Wagstaff Gribble adaptation of *Anna Lucasta* that created a
sensation and later moved to Broadway. That sensation also
brought the American Negro Theatre into commercial focus—a
move not welcomed by the group's founders. Despite its continued
efforts to build a community theatre, the group found that, because
of its success with *Anna Lucasta*, it was judged in terms of Broadway fare.

With the end of World War II a number of dramatists turned
to the post-war adjustment of the Negro. *Deep Are the Roots, Jeb,
Strange Fruit* and *On Whitman Avenue* appeared. *St. Louis
Woman, Carib Song, Lysistrata, Mr. Pebbles and Mr. Hooker, Bal
Negre, Beggar's Holiday, Finian's Rainbow, Street Scene, Our Lan',*
and *Set My People Free* all involved Negro artists.

American attitudes towards the Negro underwent a change in
the post-war world, a change reflected in many avenues of the
nation's life. Nationalism roared from colonial lands. American
Negroes echoed this roar. Some whites found it easier to accept this
roar as the voice of the "New Negro." To some extent this concept
alleviated numerous guilt complexes and permitted the ruling group
to believe it had only subjugated the "old, non-protesting Negro."
What was not faced was the truth that Negroes had been protesting,
agitating and fighting for human rights since 1619. But, now, after
World War II, sharper lines of communication brought the revolts
in Asia and Africa into the lives of Americans. The revolt of suppressed peoples became a reality that had to be met.

A number of barriers relaxed. Negroes now found they could
purchase seats to Broadway houses—seats that were not on the
aisle. Prior to 1945 only three Broadway houses sold seats to Negroes that were not on the aisle. This practice was based on the
belief that whites did not want Negroes climbing over them. The
Playwrights Company's declaration of principles in 1945 had much
to do with this shift in policy. In addition, the company also declared its members would deal specifically with Negroes in dramatic
terms. Interesting examples of the integration of the Negro in
"white shows" followed. *Detective Story* (1948) and *The Shrike*
(1951–52) featured Negro actors in roles that were not specifically
Negroid. Actors Equity Association launched repeated drives, urg-
ing the continuation of this pattern. The Greenwich Mews Theatre,
a professional Off-Broadway company, followed this pattern in productions of *Widower's Houses, Major Barbara, Time of Storm* and

Monday's Heroes. Broadway, however, continued to use the Negro actor in specified roles, and in roles the Negro himself did not always find to his liking. *The Member of the Wedding, Lost in the Stars, The Wisteria Trees, The Autumn Garden, The Climate of Eden* and *The Crucible* are plays involving Negroes.

In November, 1950 a group of Negro playwrights met in Harlem with representatives of four community theatre groups: the Harlem Showcase, the Committee for the Negro in the Arts, Ed Cambridge and the "Y" drama group, and the Elks Community Theatre. The American Negro Theatre had disbanded and many of its charter members wandered into the aforementioned groups. At the meeting a Council on the Harlem Theatre was formed. A resolution noted that the use of Negro actors in non-Negro roles offered limited employment to a large group of actors. In addition, it neither encouraged nor assisted in disseminating the cultural values of the Negro people. The Council noted, too, that the commercial failure of Theodore Ward's *Our Lan'* (1947)—after its initial Off-Broadway success—suggested that the commercial theatre wanted to tolerate the Negro, but it did not want to deal with him in strong, truthful, dramatic terms. The Council members declared that the serious play of Negro life met repeated commercial failure because it was often written from a "white point of view." Generally, plays involving Negroes had a "good" white character helping the black people out of trouble. The obvious implication, the Council noted, was that white theatregoers faced psychological barriers and could not identify with central, sympathetic Negro characters.

The Council urged the representative groups to produce plays by Negro writers and to mutually assist one another in casting, producing and promoting. The target was the Off-Broadway area. A number of Negro-written plays appeared in library basements, in community auditoriums and lodge halls, financed quite often because the group collected money from its members and launched a production. Some of the plays shown were: Harold Holifield's *Cow in the Apartment* and *J. Toth,* this writer's *The Bancroft Dynasty* and *The Cellar,* Gertrude Jeanette's *This Way Forward* and *Bolt From the Blue,* Julian Mayfield's *The Other Foot,* Ossie Davis' *Alice in Wonder* and Alice Childress' *Just A Little Simple.* These plays, written, directed and produced by Negroes, appeared primarily during the 1950–51 period.

In the midst of what Harlemites considered a renaissance, the Apollo Theatre sponsored two shabby productions of "white" plays with Negro actors: *Detective Story* and *Rain.* Both productions were artistically and commercially unsuccessful. The Apollo's management stated publicly that Harlemites did not care for serious drama. The Council on the Harlem Theatre issued a statement declaring: "The owner of the Apollo has insulted the Negro people by bringing to this community two inferior pieces with little meaning to our lives. Ridiculous prices were charged and, when we exercised the buyer's right [of withholding patronage] we were accused of lacking taste."

The Apollo management's charge, however, served as a catalytic agent for productions by Negro authors. On October 15, 1951 William Branch's *A Medal for Willie* was presented by the Committee for the Negro in the Arts at the Club Baron on Lenox Avenue. The critics hailed the play which posed in strong dramatic terms the question: should the Negro soldier fight and die abroad or should he take arms against the prejudiced southland. In September, 1952, Ossie Davis' *Alice in Wonder* opened at the Elks Community Theatre and it, too, roared the truth about the Negro's plight in America.

The early nineteen fifties witnessed another significant event. Large numbers of Negroes moved from Harlem to Long Island, Brooklyn, the Bronx and Westchester. Many theatre workers and playgoers moved, too. Apartment houses became rooming houses, occupied by those who fled the South in terror. There was a shift, too, in methods of producing plays. Community theatres all over the city broke down. The Yiddish Theatre saw an era approaching when it would no longer profit on Second Avenue. Producers were no longer anxious to own theatres, but rather to rent them, produce a play there and let someone else worry about maintaining the property. Those Negroes who had sought so valiantly to build a theatre in the Harlem area now turned towards Broadway and Greenwich Village.

Most of the professional theatre work since that time has been performed in those areas. On September 24, 1953 Louis Peterson's *Take A Giant Step* opened on Broadway. The Charles Sebree–Greer Johnston play, *Mrs. Patterson*, also appeared on Broadway. On October 24, 1954 William Branch's *In Splendid Error* excited audiences at the Greenwich Mews Theatre. In 1955 Alice Childress' satire, *Trouble in Mind*, delighted audiences at the same theatre. Luther James produced an all-Negro version of *Of Mice and Men* in the Greenwich Village area and, on March 29, 1956 Earl Hyman appeared as *Mr. Johnson* on Broadway. Despite Mr. Hyman's remarkable performance, the play failed.

The 1956–57 season brought three Negro-written plays to Off-Broadway stages: Louis Peterson's *Take A Giant Step*, revived at the Jan Hus House, this writer's *A Land Beyond the River* at the Greenwich Mews, and the Langston Hughes–David Martin folk musical, *Simply Heavenly* at the 84th Street Theatre. These plays should have ended the bromide that Negro audiences do not support theatre. Negro theatregoers were directly responsible for the financial success of these plays.

On March 11, 1959 Lorraine Hansberry's *A Raisin in the Sun* opened on Broadway to acclaim and later won the Critics Circle Award. It enjoyed a long and successful run, then later toured. During the 1961–62 season Errol John's *The Moon on A Rainbow Shawl* was shown on the Lower East Side and in May, 1961 Jean Genet's *The Blacks* settled down at the St. Mark's Playhouse for a long run. *Fly Blackbirds*, a revue, won critical acclaim Off-Broadway while the Ossie Davis satire, *Purlie Victorious* was hailed by Broadway theatregoers during the 1961–62 season.

In reviewing this brief—and, of necessity, superficial—survey, it seems amazing that Negro theatre workers have managed such a considerable output. It should be remembered that many of the venturers discussed here were written, directed and produced under harrowing circumstances. The artists generally worked full time at other jobs. They had no well-to-do relatives who could maintain them. They performed at night while working or struggling during the day to pay their rents. And, too, these plays were supported by people whose incomes were, at most, uncertain.

Whether it is possible to build a Harlem community theatre in an era when community theatres are almost nonexistent remains a tantalizing question. However, people like Maxwell Glanville, Jay Brooks and other tireless workers continue their efforts in Harlem. They fight eternally rising costs, the omnipotence of Broadway, cheap movie and television fare and a changing community.

For the theatre worker outside Harlem, we can only foresee an occasional successful production. One cannot resist noting, however, that the produced plays will be written by whites dealing with the strings attached to an interracial love affair or some other area of Negro life receptive to white audiences. We may even have the Birmingham story brought to the stage, but it will probably be written by a white author who will deal with the problem of a "good" white caught in the throes of an uprising. Theatre in America remains a middle class luxury wherein the playwright speaks, cajoles, seduces, and lies to an expense-account audience. Until it becomes once again an art form willing to attract all people, we see no change in the type of play being produced.

Yet, a courageous producer has before him a rich opportunity. Negro playwrights are numerous and they wait eagerly for a producer who has not been "brainwashed." One of the most needed theatre workers at present is the Negro producer. He could utilize the rich dramatic history of these times, the wonderful artists and the splendid audiences that can be attracted if the theatre speaks to them in terms of the truth of their daily lives.

JESSIE FAUSET
The Gift of Laughter

THE BLACK man bringing gifts, and particularly the gift of laughter, to the American stage is easily the most anomalous, the most inscrutable figure of the century. All about him and within himself stalks the conviction that like the Irish, the Russian and the Magyar, he has some peculiar offering which shall contain the very essence of the drama. Yet the medium through which this unique and intensely dramatic gift might be offered has been so befogged and misted by popular preconception that the great gift, though divined, is as yet not clearly seen.

Popular preconception in this instance refers to the pressure of white opinion by which the American Negro is surrounded and by which his true character is almost submerged. For years the Caucasian in America has persisted in dragging to the limelight merely one aspect of Negro characteristics, by which the whole race has been glimpsed, through which it has been judged. The colored man who finally succeeds in impressing any considerable number of whites with the truth that he does not conform to these measurements is regarded as the striking exception proving an unshakable rule. The medium then through which the black actor has been presented to the world has been that of the "funny man" of America. Ever since those far-off times directly after the Civil War when white men and colored men too, blacking their faces, presented the antics of plantation hands under the caption of "Georgia Minstrels" and the like, the edict has gone forth that the black man on the stage must be an end-man.

In passing one pauses to wonder if this picture of the black American as a living comic supplement has not been painted in order to camouflage the real feeling and knowledge of his white compatriot. Certainly the plight of the slaves under even the mildest of masters could never have been one to awaken laughter. And no genuinely thinking person, no really astute observer, looking at the Negro in modern American life, could find his condition even now a first aid to laughter. That condition may be variously deemed hopeless, remarkable, admirable, inspiring, depressing; it can never be dubbed merely amusing.

It was the colored actor who gave the first impetus away from this buffoonery. The task was not an easy one. For years the Negro was no great frequenter of the theater. And no matter how keenly he felt the insincerity in the presentation of his kind, no matter how ridiculous and palpable a caricature such a presentation might be, the Negro auditor with the helplessness of the minority was powerless to demand something better and truer. Artist and audience alike were in the grip of the minstrel formula. It was at this point in the eighteen-nineties that Ernest Hogan, pioneer comedian of the better type, changed the tradition of the merely funny, rather silly "end-man" into a character with a definite plot in a rather loosely constructed but none the less well outlined story. The method was still humorous, but less broadly, less exclusively. A little of the hard luck of the Negro began to creep in. If he was a buffoon, he was a buffoon wearing his rue. A slight, very slight quality of the Harlequin began to attach to him. He was the clown making light of his troubles but he was a wounded, a sore-beset clown.

This figure became the prototype of the plays later presented by those two great characters, Williams and Walker. The ingredients of the comedies in which these two starred usually consisted of one dishonest, overbearing, flashily dressed character (Walker) and one kindly, rather simple, hard-luck personage (Williams). The interest of the piece hinged on the juxtaposition of these two men. Of course these plays, too, were served with a sauce of humor because the public, true to its carefully taught and rigidly held tradition, could not dream of a situation in which colored people were anything but merely funny. But the hardships and woes suffered by Williams, ridiculous as they were, introduced with the element of folk comedy some element of reality.

Side by side with Williams and Walker, who might be called the apostles of the "legitimate" on the stage for Negroes, came the merriment and laughter and high spirits of that incomparable pair, Cole and Johnson. But they were essentially the geniuses of musical comedy. At that time their singers and dancers outsang and out-danced the neophytes of contemporary white musical comedies even as their followers to this day outsing and outdance in their occasional appearances on Broadway their modern neighbors. Just what might have been the ultimate trend of the ambition of this partnership, the untimely death of Mr. Cole rendered uncertain; but speaking offhand I should say that the relation of their musical comedy idea to the fixed plot and defined dramatic concept of the Williams and Walker plays molded the form of the Negro musical show which still persists and thrives on the contemporary stage. It was they who capitalized the infectious charm of so much rich dark beauty, the verve and abandon of Negro dancers, the glorious fullness of Negro voices. And they produced those effects in the *Red Shawl* in a manner still unexcelled, except in the matter of setting, by any latter-day companies.

But Williams and Walker, no matter how dimly, were seeking a method whereby the colored man might enter the "legitimate." They were to do nothing but pave the way. Even this task was difficult but they performed it well.

Those who knew Bert Williams say that his earliest leanings were toward the stage; but that he recognized at an equally early age that his color would probably keep him from ever making the "legitimate." Consequently, deliberately, as one who desiring to become a great painter but lacking the means for travel and study might take up commercial art, he turned his attention to minstrelsy. Natively he possessed the art of mimicry; intuitively he realized that his first path to the stage must lie along the old recognized lines of "funny man." He was, as few of us recall, a Jamaican by birth; the ways of the American Negro were utterly alien to him and did not come spontaneously; he set himself therefore to obtaining a knowledge of them. For choice he selected, perhaps by way of contrast, the melancholy out-of-luck Negro, shiftless, doleful, "easy" ; the kind that tempts the world to lay its hand none too lightly upon him. The pursuit took him years, but at length he was able to portray for us not only that "typical Negro" which the white world thinks is universal but also the special types of given districts and localities with their own peculiar foibles of walk and speech and jargon. He went to London and studied under Pietro, greatest pantomimist of his day, until finally he, too, became a recognized master in the field of comic art.

But does anyone who realizes that the foibles of the American Negro were painstakingly acquired by this artist, doubt that Williams might just as well have portrayed the Irishman, the Jew, the Englishman abroad, the Scotchman or any other of the vividly etched types which for one reason or another lend themselves so readily to caricature? Can anyone presume to say that a man who travelled *north, east, south* and *west* and even abroad in order to acquire accent and jargon, aspect and characteristic of a people to which he was bound by ties of blood but from whom he was natively separated by training and tradition, would not have been able to portray with equal effectiveness what, for lack of a better term, we must call universal rôles?

There is an unwritten law in America that though white may imitate black, black, even when superlatively capable, must never imitate white. In other words, grease-paint may be used to darken but never to lighten.

Williams' color imposed its limitations upon him even in his chosen field. His expansion was always upward but never outward. He might portray black people along the gamut from roustabout to unctuous bishop. But he must never stray beyond those limits. How keenly he felt this few of us knew until after his death. But it was well known to his intimates and professional associates. W. C. Fields, himself an expert in the art of amusing, called him "the funniest man I ever saw and the saddest man I ever knew."

He was sad with the sadness of hopeless frustration. The gift of laughter in his case had its source in a wounded heart and in bleeding sensibilities.

That laughter for which we are so justly famed has had in late years its over-tones of pain. Now for some time past it has been used by colored men who have gained a precarious footing on the stage to conceal the very real dolor raging in their breasts. To be by force of circumstances the most dramatic figure in a country; to be possessed of the wells of feeling, of the most spontaneous instinct for effective action and to be shunted no less always into the rôle of the ridiculous and funny,—that is enough to create the quality of bitterness for which we are ever so often rebuked. Yet that same laughter influenced by these same untoward obstacles has within the last four years known a deflection into another channel, still productive of mirth, but even more than that of a sort of cosmic gladness, the joy which arises spontaneously in the spectator as a result of the sight of its no less spontaneous bubbling in others. What hurt most in the spectacle of the Bert Williams' funny man and his forerunners was the fact that the laughter which he created must be objective. But the new "funny man" among black comedians is essentially funny himself. He is joy and mischief and rich, homely native humor personified. He radiates good feeling and happiness; it is with him now a state of being purely subjective. The spectator is infected with his high spirits and his excessive good will; a stream of well-being is projected across the footlights into the consciousness of the beholder.

This phenomenon has been especially visible in the rendition of the colored musical "shows," *Shuffle Along, Runnin' Wild, Liza*, which livened up Broadway recently for a too brief season. Those of us who were lucky enough to compare with the usual banality of musical comedy, the verve and pep, the liveliness and gayety of those productions will not soon forget them. The medley of shades, the rich colorings, the abundance of fun and spirits on the part of the players all combined to produce an atmosphere which was actually palpable, so full was it of the ecstasy and joy of living. The singing was inimitable; the work of the chorus apparently spontaneous and unstudied. Emotionally they garnished their threadbare plots and comedy tricks with the genius of a new comic art.

The performers in all three of these productions gave out an impression of sheer happiness in living such as I have never before seen on any stage except in a riotous farce which I once saw in Vienna and where the same effect of superabundant vitality was induced. It is this quality of vivid and untheatrical portrayal of sheer emotion which seems likely to be the Negro's chief contribution to the stage. A comedy made up of such ingredients as the music of Sissle and Blake, the quaint, irresistible humor of Miller and Lyles, the quintessence of jazzdom in the Charleston, the superlativeness of Miss Mills' happy abandon could know no equal. It would be the line by which all other comedy would have to be measured. Behind the banalities and clap-trap and crudities of these shows, this supervitality and joyousness glow from time to time in a given step or gesture or in the teasing assurance of such a line as: "If you've never been vamped by a brown-skin, you've never been vamped at all."

And as Carl Van Vechten recently in his brilliant article, *Prescription for the Negro Theater*, so pointedly advises and prophesies, once the spirit breaks through the silly "childish adjuncts of the minstrel tradition" and drops the unworthy formula of unoriginal imitation of the stock revues, there will be released on the American stage a spirit of comedy such as has been rarely known.

The remarkable thing about this gift of ours is that it has its rise, I am convinced, in the very woes which beset us. Just as a person driven by great sorrow may finally go into an orgy of laughter, just so an oppressed and too hard driven people breaks over into compensating laughter and merriment. It is our emotional salvation. There would be no point in mentioning this rather obvious fact were it not that it argues also the possession on our part of a histrionic endowment for the portrayal of tragedy. Not without reason has tradition made comedy and tragedy sisters and twins, the capacity for one argues the capacity for the other. It is not surprising then that the period that sees the Negro actor on the verge of great comedy has seen him breaking through to the portrayal of serious and legitimate drama. No one who has seen Gilpin and Robeson in the portrayal of *The Emperor Jones* and of *All God's Chillun* can fail to realize that tragedy, too, is a vastly fitting rôle for the Negro actor. And so with the culminating of his dramatic genius, the Negro actor must come finally through the very versatility of his art to the universal rôle and the main tradition of drama, as an artist first and only secondarily as a Negro.

Nor when within the next few years, this question comes up,— as I suspect it must come up with increasing insistence, will the more obvious barriers seem as obvious as they now appear. For in this American group of the descendants of Mother Africa, the question of color raises no insuperable barrier, seeing that with chameleon adaptability we are able to offer white colored men and women for *Hamlet*, *The Doll's House* and the *Second Mrs. Tanqueray;* brown men for *Othello;* yellow girls for *Madam Butterfly;* black men for *The Emperor Jones.* And underneath and permeating all this bewildering array of shades and tints is the unshakable precision of an instinctive and spontaneous emotional art.

All this beyond any doubt will be the reward of the "gift of laughter" which many black actors on the American stage have proffered. Through laughter we have conquered even the lot of the jester and the clown. The parable of the one talent still holds good and because we have used the little which in those early painful days was our only approach we find ourselves slowly but surely moving toward that most glittering of all goals, the freedom of the American stage. I hope that Hogan realizes this and Cole and Walker, too, and that lastly Bert Williams, the inimitable, will clap us on with those tragic black-gloved hands of his now that the gift of his laughter is no longer tainted with the salt of chagrin and tears.

$$\begin{bmatrix} \text{ON} \\ \text{FICTION} \end{bmatrix}$$

WILLIAM STANLEY BRAITHWAITE
*The Negro in
American Literature*

TRUE TO his origin on this continent, the Negro was projected into literature by an over-mastering and exploiting hand. In the generations that he has been so voluminously written and talked about he has been accorded as little artistic justice as social justice. Antebellum literature imposed the distortions of moralistic controversy and made the Negro a wax-figure of the market place: post-bellum literature retaliated with the condescending reactions of sentiment and caricature, and made the Negro a *genre* stereotype. Sustained, serious or deep study of Negro life and character has thus been entirely below the horizons of our national art. Only gradually through the dull purgatory of the Age of Discussion, has Negro life eventually issued forth to an Age of Expression.

Perhaps I ought to qualify this last statement that the Negro was *in* American literature generations before he was part of it as a creator. From his very beginning in this country the Negro has been, without the formal recognition of literature and art, creative. During more than two centuries of an enslaved peasantry, the race has been giving evidence, in song and story lore, of an artistic temperament and psychology precious for itself as well as for its potential use and promise in the sophisticated forms of cultural expression. Expressing itself with poignancy and a symbolic imagery unsurpassed, indeed, often unmatched, by any folk-group, the race in servitude was at the same time the finest national expression of emotion and imagination and the most precious mass of raw material for literature America was producing. Quoting these stanzas of James Weldon Johnson's *O Black and Unknown Bards*, I want you

169

to catch the real point of its assertion of the Negro's way into the domain of art:

> *O black and unknown bards of long ago,*
>   *How came your lips to touch the sacred fire?*
> *How, in your darkness, did you come to know*
>   *The power and beauty of the minstrel's lyre?*
> *Who first from midst his bonds lifted his eyes?*
>   *Who first from out the still watch, lone and long,*
> *Feeling the ancient faith of prophets rise*
>   *Within his dark-kept soul, burst into song?*
>
> *There is a wide, wide wonder in it all,*
>   *That from degraded rest and servile toil*
> *The fiery spirit of the seer should call*
>   *These simple children of the sun and soil.*
> *O black slave singers, gone, forgot, unfamed,*
>   *You—you, alone, of all the long, long line*
> *Of those who've sung untaught, unknown, unnamed,*
>   *Have stretched out upward, seeking the divine.*

How misdirected was the American imagination, how blinded by the dust of controversy and the pall of social hatred and oppression, not to have found it irresistibly urgent to make literary use of the imagination and emotion it possessed in such abundance.

Controversy and moral appeal gave us *Uncle Tom's Cabin,*— the first conspicuous example of the Negro as a subject for literary treatment. Published in 1852, it dominated in mood and attitude the American literature of a whole generation; until the body of Reconstruction literature with its quite different attitude came into vogue. Here was sentimentalized sympathy for a down-trodden race, but one in which was projected a character, in Uncle Tom himself, which has been unequalled in its hold upon the popular imagination to this day. But the moral gain and historical effect of Uncle Tom have been an artistic loss and setback. The treatment of Negro life and character, overlaid with these forceful stereotypes, could not develop into artistically satisfactory portraiture.

Just as in the anti-slavery period, it had been impaled upon the dilemmas of controversy, Negro life with the Reconstruction, became involved in the paradoxes of social prejudice. Between the Civil War and the end of the century the subject of the Negro in literature is one that will some day inspire the literary historian with a magnificent theme. It will be magnificent not because there is any sharp emergence of character or incidents, but because of the immense paradox of racial life which came up thunderingly against the principles and doctrines of democracy, and put them to the severest test that they had known. It was a period when, in literature, Negro life was a shuttlecock between the two extremes of humor and pathos. The Negro was free, and was not free. The writers who dealt with him for the most part refused to see more than skin-deep,—the grin, the grimaces and the picturesque externalities. Occasionally there was some penetration into the heart and flesh of Negro characters, but to see more than the humble happy peasant would have been to flout the fixed ideas and conventions of an entire generation. For more than artistic reasons, indeed against them, these writers refused to see the tragedy of the Negro and capitalized his comedy. The social conscience had as much need for this comic mask as the Negro. However, if any of the writers of the period had possessed gifts of genius of the first caliber, they would have penetrated this deceptive exterior of Negro life, sounded the depths of tragedy in it, and produced a masterpiece.

American literature still feels the hold of this tradition and its indulgent sentimentalities. Irwin Russell was the first to discover the happy, care-free, humorous Negro. He became a fad. It must be sharply called to attention that the tradition of the ante-bellum Negro is a post-bellum product, stranger in truth than in fiction. Contemporary realism in American fiction has not only recorded his passing, but has thrown serious doubts upon his ever having been a very genuine and representative view of Negro life and character. At best this school of Reconstruction fiction represents the romanticized high-lights of a régime that as a whole was a dark, tragic canvas. At most, it presents a Negro true to type for less than two generations. Thomas Nelson Page, kindly perhaps, but with a distant view and a purely local imagination, did little more than paint the conditions and attitudes of the period contemporary with his own manhood, the restitution of the over-lordship of the defeated slave owners in the Eighties. George W. Cable did little more than idealize the aristocratic tradition of the Old South with the Negro as a literary foil. The effects, though not the motives of their work, have been sinister. The "Uncle" and the "Mammy" traditions, unobjectionable as they are in the setting of their day and generation, and in the atmosphere of sentimental humor, can never stand as the great fiction of their theme and subject: the great period novel of the South has yet to be written. Moreover, these type pictures have degenerated into reactionary social fetishes, and from that descended into libelous artistic caricature of the Negro, which has hampered art quite as much as it has embarrassed the Negro.

Of all of the American writers of this period, Joel Chandler Harris has made the most permanent contribution in dealing with the Negro. There is in his work both a deepening of interest and technique. Here at least we have something approaching true portraiture. But much as we admire this lovable personality, we are forced to say that in the Uncle Remus stories the race was its own artist, lacking only in its illiteracy the power to record its speech. In the perspective of time and fair judgment the credit will be divided, and Joel Chandler Harris regarded as a sort of providentially provided amanuensis for preserving the folk tales and legends of a race. The three writers I have mentioned do not by any means exhaust the list of writers who put the Negro into literature during the last half of the nineteenth century. Mr. Howells added a shadowy note to his social record of American life with *An Imperative Duty* and prophesied the Fiction of the Color Line. But his moral scruples—the persistent artistic vice in all his novels—prevented him from consummating a just union between his heroine with a touch of Negro blood and his hero. It is useless to consider any others, because there were none who succeeded in creating either a great story or a great character out of Negro life. Two writers of importance I am reserving for discussion in the group of Negro writers I shall consider presently. One ought perhaps to say in justice to the writers I have mentioned that their nonsuccess was more largely due to the limitations of their social view than of their technical resources. As white Americans of their day, it was incompatible with their conception of the inequalities between the races to glorify the Negro into the serious and leading position of hero or heroine in fiction. Only one man, that I recall, had the moral and artistic courage to do this, and he was Stephen Crane in a short story called *The Monster.* But Stephen Crane was a genius, and therefore could not besmirch the integrity of an artist.

With Thomas Dixon, of *The Leopard's Spots*, we reach a distinct stage in the treatment of the Negro in fiction. The portraiture here descends from caricature to libel. A little later with the vogue of the "darkey-story," and its devotees from Kemble and McAllister to Octavus Roy Cohen, sentimental comedy in the portrayal of the Negro similarly degenerated to blatant but diverting farce. Before the rise of a new attitude, these represented the bottom reaction,

both in artistic and social attitude. Reconstruction fiction was passing out in a flood of propagandist melodrama and ridicule. One
hesitates to lift this material up to the plane of literature even for
the purposes of comparison. But the gradual climb of the new literature of the Negro must be traced and measured from these two
nadir points. Following *The Leopard's Spots,* it was only occasionally during the next twenty years that the Negro was sincerely
treated in fiction by white authors. There were two or three tentative efforts to dramatize him. Sheldon's *The Nigger* was the one
notable early effort. And in fiction Paul Kester's *His Own Country*
is, from a purely literary point of view, an outstanding performance. This type of novel failed, however, to awaken any general
interest. This failure was due to the illogical treatment of the human
situations presented. However indifferent and negative it may seem,
there is the latent desire in most readers to have honesty of purpose
and a full vision in the artist: and especially in fiction, a situation
handled with gloves can never be effectively handled.

The first hint that the American artist was looking at this subject with full vision was in Torrence's *Granny Maumee.* It was
drama, conceived and executed for performance on the stage, and
therefore had a restricted appeal. But even here the artist was concerned with the primitive instincts of the Race, and, though faithful
and honest in his portrayal, the note was still low in the scale of
racial life. It was only a short time, however, before a distinctly new
development took place in the treatment of Negro life by white
authors. This new class of work honestly strove to endow the Negro
life with purely aesthetic vision and values, but with one or two exceptions, still stuck to the peasant level of race experience, and gave,
unwittingly, greater currency to the popular notion of the Negro as
an inferior, superstitious, half-ignorant and servile class of folk.
Where they did in a few isolated instances recognize an ambitious
impulse, it was generally defeated in the course of the story.

Perhaps this is inevitable with an alien approach, however well-
intentioned. The folk lore attitude discovers only the lowly and the
naïve: the sociological attitude finds the problem first and the
human beings after, if at all. But American art in a reawakened
seriousness, and using the technique of the new realism, is gradually
penetrating Negro life to the core. George Madden Martin, with her
pretentious foreword to a group of short stories, *The Children in
the Mist,*—and this is an extraordinary volume in many ways—
quite seriously tried, as a Southern woman, to elevate the Negro to
a higher plane of fictional treatment and interest. In succession, fol-

lowed Mary White Ovington's *The Shadow*, in which Miss Ovington
daringly created the kinship of brother and sister between a black
boy and white girl, had it brought to disaster by prejudice, out of
which the white girl rose to a sacrifice no white girl in a novel had
hitherto accepted and endured; then Shands' *White and Black*, as
honest a piece of fiction with the Negro as a subject as was ever
produced by a Southern pen—and in this story, also, the hero,
Robinson, making an equally glorious sacrifice for truth and justice, as Miss Ovington's heroine; Clement Wood's *Nigger*, with de-
fects of treatment, but admirable in purpose, wasted though, I
think, in the effort to prove its thesis on wholly illogical material;
and lastly, T. S. Stribling's *Birthright*, more significant than any of
these other books, in fact, the most significant novel on the Negro
written by a white American, and this in spite of its totally false
conception of the character of Peter Siner.

Mr. Stribling's book broke ground for a white author in giving
us a Negro hero and heroine. There is an obvious attempt to see
objectively. But the formula of the Nineties—atavistic race-
heredity—still survives and protrudes through the flesh and blood of
the characters. Using Peter as a symbol of the man tragically linked
by blood to one world and by training and thought to another,
Stribling portrays a tragic struggle against the pull of lowly origins
and sordid environment. We do not deny this element of tragedy in
Negro life—and Mr. Stribling, it must also be remembered,
presents, too, a severe indictment in his painting of the Southern
conditions which brought about the disintegration of his hero's
dreams and ideals. But the preoccupation, almost obsession of
otherwise strong and artistic work like O'Neill's *Emperor Jones, All
God's Chillun Got Wings*, and Culbertson's *Goat Alley* with this
same theme and doubtful formula of hereditary cultural reversion
suggests that, in spite of all good intentions, the true presental of the
real tragedy of Negro life is a task still left for Negro writers to perform. This is especially true for those phases of culturally representative race life that as yet have scarcely at all found treatment by
white American authors. In corroborating this, let me quote a passage from a recent number of the *Independent*, on the Negro novelist which reads:

> During the past few years stories about Negroes have been
> extremely popular. A magazine without a Negro story is hardly
> living up to its opportunities. But almost every one of these
> stories is written in a tone of condescension. The artists have
> caught the contagion from the writers, and the illustrations are

ninety-nine times out of a hundred purely slapstick stuff. Stories and pictures make a Roman holiday for the millions who are convinced that the most important fact about the Negro is that his skin is black. Many of these writers live in the South or are from the South. Presumably they are well acquainted with the Negro, but it is a remarkable fact that they almost never tell us anything vital about him, about the real human being in the black man's skin. Their most frequent method is to laugh at the colored man and woman, to catalogue their idiosyncrasies, their departure from the norm, that is, from the ways of the whites. There seems to be no suspicion in the minds of the writers that there may be a fascinating thought life in the minds of the Negroes, whether of the cultivated or of the most ignorant type. Always the Negro is interpreted in the terms of the white man. White-man psychology is applied and it is no wonder that the result often shows the Negro in a ludicrous light.

I shall have to run back over the years to where I began to survey the achievement of Negro authorship. The Negro as a creator in American literature is of comparatively recent importance. All that was accomplished between Phillis Wheatley and Paul Laurence Dunbar, considered by critical standards, is negligible, and of historical interest only. Historically it is a great tribute to the race to have produced in Phillis Wheatley not only the slave poetess in eighteenth century Colonial America, but to know she was as good, if not a better, poetess than Ann Bradstreet whom literary historians give the honor of being the first person of her sex to win fame as a poet in America.

Negro authorship may, for clearer statement, be classified into three main activities: Poetry, Fiction, and the Essay, with an occasional excursion into other branches. In the drama, until very recently, practically nothing worth while has been achieved, with the exception of Angelina Grimke's *Rachel,* notable for its sombre craftsmanship. Biography has given us a notable life story, told by himself, of Booker T. Washington. Frederick Douglass's story of his life is eloquent as a human document, but not in the graces of narration and psychologic portraiture, which has definitely put this form of literature in the domain of the fine arts. Indeed, we may well believe that the efforts of controversy, of the huge amount of discursive and polemical articles dealing chiefly with the race problem, that have been necessary in breaking and clearing the impeded pathway of racial progress, have absorbed and in a way dissipated the literary energy of many able Negro writers.

Let us survey briefly the advance of the Negro in poetry. Behind Dunbar, there is nothing that can stand the critical test. We shall always have a sentimental and historical interest in those forlorn and pathetic figures who cried in the wilderness of their ignorance and oppression. With Dunbar we have our first authentic lyric utterance, an utterance more authentic, I should say, for its faithful rendition of Negro life and character than for any rare or subtle artistry of expression. When Mr. Howells, in his famous introduction to the *Lyrics of Lowly Life*, remarked that Dunbar was the first black man to express the life of his people lyrically, he summed up Dunbar's achievement and transported him to a place beside the peasant poet of Scotland, not for his art, but precisely because he made a people articulate in verse.

The two chief qualities in Dunbar's work are, however, pathos and humor, and in these he expresses that dilemma of soul that characterized the race between the Civil War and the end of the nineteenth century. The poetry of Dunbar is true to the life of the Negro and expresses characteristically what he felt and knew to be the temper and condition of his people. But its moods reflect chiefly those of the era of Reconstruction and just a little beyond,—the limited experience of a transitional period, the rather helpless and subservient era of testing freedom and reaching out through the difficulties of life to the emotional compensations of laughter and tears. It is the poetry of the happy peasant and the plaintive minstrel. Occasionally, as in the sonnet to *Robert Gould Shaw* and the *Ode to Ethiopia* there broke through Dunbar, as through the crevices of his spirit, a burning and brooding aspiration, an awakening and virile consciousness of race. But for the most part, his dreams were anchored to the minor whimsies; his deepest poetic inspiration was sentiment. He expressed a folk temperament, but not a race soul. Dunbar was the end of a régime, and not the beginning of a tradition, as so many careless critics, both white and colored, seem to think.

After Dunbar many versifiers appeared,—all largely dominated by his successful dialect work. I cannot parade them here for tag or comment, except to say that few have equalled Dunbar in this vein of expression, and none have deepened it as an expression of Negro life. Dunbar himself had clear notions of its limitations;—to a friend in a letter from London, March 15, 1897, he says: "I see now very clearly that Mr. Howells has done me irrevocable harm in the dictum he laid down regarding my dialect verse." Not until James W. Johnson published his *Fiftieth Anniversary Ode* on the emancipation in 1913, did a poet of the race disengage himself from the background of mediocrity into which the imitation of Dunbar snared Negro poetry. Mr. Johnson's work is based upon a broader contemplation of life, life that is not wholly confined within any racial experience, but through the racial he made articulate that universality of the emotions felt by all mankind. His verse possesses a vigor which definitely breaks away from the brooding minor undercurrents of feeling which have previously characterized the verse of Negro poets. Mr. Johnson brought, indeed, the first intellectual substance to the content of our poetry, and a craftsmanship which, less spontaneous than that of Dunbar's, was more balanced and precise.

Here a new literary generation begins: poetry that is racial in substance, but with the universal note, and consciously the background of the full heritage of English poetry. With each new figure somehow the gamut broadens and the technical control improves. The brilliant succession and maturing powers of Fenton Johnson, Leslie Pinckney Hill, Everett Hawkins, Lucien Watkins, Charles Bertram Johnson, Joseph Cotter, Georgia Douglas Johnson, Roscoe Jameson and Anne Spencer bring us at last to Claude McKay and the poets of the younger generation and a poetry of the masterful accent and high distinction. Too significantly for mere coincidence, it was the stirring year of 1917 that heard the first real masterful accent in Negro poetry. In the September *Crisis* of that year, Roscoe Jameson's *Negro Soldiers* appeared:

> *These truly are the Brave,*
> *These men who cast aside*
> *Old memories to walk the blood-stained pave*
> *Of Sacrifice, joining the solemn tide*
> *That moves away, to suffer and to die*
> *For Freedom—when their own is yet denied!*
> *O Pride! A Prejudice! When they pass by*
> *Hail them, the Brave, for you now crucified.*

The very next month, under the pen name of Eli Edwards, Claude McKay printed in *The Seven Arts,*

THE HARLEM DANCER

> *Applauding youths laughed with young prostitutes*
> *And watched her perfect, half-clothed body sway;*
> *Her voice was like the sound of blended flutes*
> *Blown by black players upon a picnic day.*
> *She sang and danced on gracefully and calm,*

> *The light gauze hanging loose about her form;*
> *To me she seemed a proudly-swaying palm*
> *Grown lovelier for passing through a storm.*
>
> *Upon her swarthy neck black, shiny curls*
> *Profusely fell; and, tossing coins in praise*
> *The wine-flushed, bold-eyed boys, and even the girls*
> *Devoured her with their eager, passionate gaze;*
> *But, looking at her falsely-smiling face*
> *I knew her self was not in that strange place.*

With Georgia Johnson, Anne Spencer and Angelina Grimke, the Negro woman poet significantly appears. Mrs. Johnson especially has voiced in true poetic spirit the lyric cry of Negro womanhood. In spite of lapses into the sentimental and the platitudinous, she has an authentic gift. Anne Spencer, more sophisticated, more cryptic but also more universal, reveals quite another aspect of poetic genius. Indeed, it is interesting to notice how to-day Negro poets waver between the racial and the universal notes.

Claude McKay, the poet who leads his generation, is a genius meshed in this dilemma. His work is caught between the currents of the poetry of protest and the poetry of expression; he is in turn the violent and strident propagandist, using his poetic gifts to clothe arrogant and defiant thoughts, and then the pure lyric dreamer, contemplating life and nature with a wistful sympathetic passion. When the mood of *Spring in New Hampshire* or the sonnet *The Harlem Dancer* possesses him, he is full of that spirit and power of beauty that flowers above any and all men's harming. How different in spite of the admirable spirit of courage and defiance, are his poems of which the sonnet *If We Must Die* is a typical example. Negro poetic expression hovers for the moment, pardonably perhaps, over the race problem, but its highest allegiance is to Poetry—it must soar.

Let me refer briefly to a type of literature in which there have been many pens, but a single mind. Dr. Du Bois is the most variously gifted writer which the race has produced. Poet, novelist, sociologist, historian and essayist, he has produced books in all these fields with the exception, I believe, of a formal book of poems, and has given to each the distinction of his clear and exact thinking, and of his sensitive imagination and passionate vision. *The Souls of Black Folk* was the book of an era; it was a painful book, a book of tortured dreams woven into the fabric of the sociologist's document. This book has more profoundly influenced the spiritual temper of the race than any other written in its generation. It is only through the intense, passionate idealism of such substance as makes *The Souls of Black Folk* such a quivering rhapsody of wrongs endured and hopes to be fulfilled that the poets of the race with compelling artistry can lift the Negro into the only full and complete nationalism he knows—that of the American democracy. No other book has more clearly revealed to the nation at large the true idealism and high aspiration of the American Negro.

In this book, as well as in many of Dr. Du Bois's essays, it is often my personal feeling that I am witnessing the birth of a poet, phoenix-like, out of a scholar. Between *The Souls of Black Folk* and *Darkwater*, published four years ago, Dr. Du Bois has written a number of books, none more notable, in my opinion, than his novel *The Quest of the Silver Fleece*, in which he made Cotton the great protagonist of fate in the lives of the Southern people, both white and black. I only know of one other such attempt and accomplishment in American fiction—that of Frank Norris—and I am somehow of the opinion that when the great epic novel of the South is written this book will prove to have been its forerunner. Indeed, the Negro novel is one of the great potentialities of American literature. Must it be written by a Negro? To recur to the article from which I have already quoted:

> The white writer seems to stand baffled before the enigma and so he expends all his energies on dialect and in general on the Negro's minstrel characteristics. . . . We shall have to look to the Negro himself to go all the way. It is quite likely that no white man can do it. It is reasonable to suppose that his white psychology will always be in his way. I am not thinking at all about a Negro novelist who shall arouse the world to the horror of the deliberate killings by white mobs, to the wrongs that condemn a free people to political serfdom. I am not thinking at all of the propaganda novel, although there is enough horror and enough drama in the bald statistics of each one of the annual Moton letters to keep the whole army of writers busy. But the Negro novelist, if he ever comes, must reveal to us much more than what a Negro thinks about when he is being tied to a stake and the torch is being applied to his living flesh; much more than what he feels when he is being crowded off the sidewalk by a drunken rowdy who may be his intellectual inferior by a thousand leagues. Such a writer, to succeed in a big sense, would have to forget that there are

white readers; he would have to lose self-consciousness and
forget that his work would be placed before a white jury. He
would have to be careless as to what the white critic might
think of it; he would need the self-assurance to be his own
critic. He would have to forget for the time being, at least,
that any white man ever attempted to dissect the soul of a
Negro.

What I here quote is both an inquiry and a challenge! Well informed as the writer is, he does not seem to detect the forces which
are surely gathering to produce what he longs for.

The development of fiction among Negro authors has been, I
might almost say, one of the repressed activities of our literary life.
A fair start was made the last decade of the nineteenth century when
Chesnutt and Dunbar were turning out both short stories and
novels. In Dunbar's case, had he lived, I think his literary growth
would have been in the evolution of the Race novel as indicated in
The Uncalled and the *Sport of the Gods*. The former was, I think,
the most ambitious literary effort of Dunbar; the latter was his most
significant; significant because, thrown against the background of
New York City, it displayed the life of the race as a unit, swayed by
currents of existence, of which it was and was not a part. The story
was touched with that shadow of destiny which gave to it a purpose
more important than the mere racial machinery of its plot. But
Dunbar in his fiction dealt only successfully with the same world
that gave him the inspiration for his dialect poems, though his ambition was to "write a novel that will deal with the educated class of
my own people." Later he writes of *The Fanatics:* "You do not
know how my hopes were planted in that book, but it has utterly
disappointed me." His contemporary, Charles W. Chesnutt, was
concerned more primarily with the fiction of the Color Line and the
contacts and conflicts of its two worlds. He was in a way more successful. In the five volumes to his credit, he has revealed himself as
a fiction writer of a very high order. But after all Mr. Chesnutt is a
story-teller of genius transformed by racial earnestness into the
novelist of talent. His natural gift would have found freer vent in a
flow of short stories like Bret Harte's, to judge from the facility and
power of his two volumes of short stories, *The Wife of His Youth
and Other Stories* and *The Conjure Woman*. But Mr. Chesnutt's
serious effort was in the field of the novel, where he made a brave
and partially successful effort to correct the distortions of Reconstruction fiction and offset the school of Page and Cable. Two of
these novels, *The Marrow of Tradition* and *The House Behind the*

Cedars, must be reckoned among the representative period novels of their time. But the situation was not ripe for the great Negro novelist. The American public preferred spurious values to the genuine; the coinage of the Confederacy was at literary par. Where Dunbar, the sentimentalist, was welcome, Chesnutt, the realist, was barred. In 1905 Mr. Chesnutt wrote *The Colonel's Dream,* and thereafter silence fell upon him.

From this date until the past year, with the exception of *The Quest of the Silver Fleece,* which was published in 1911, there has been no fiction of importance by Negro authors. But then suddenly there comes a series of books, which seems to promise at least a new phase of race fiction, and possibly the era of the major novelists. Mr. Walter White's novel *The Fire in the Flint* is a swift moving straightforward story of the contemporary conflicts of black manhood in the South. Coming from the experienced observation of the author, himself an investigator of many lynchings and riots, it is a social document story of first-hand significance and importance, too vital to be labelled and dismissed as propaganda, yet for the same reason too unvarnished and realistic a story to be great art. Nearer to the requirements of art comes Miss Jessie Fauset's novel *There Is Confusion.* Its distinction is to have created an entirely new milieu in the treatment of the race in fiction. She has taken a class within the race of established social standing, tradition and culture, and given in the rather complex family story of *The Marshalls* a social document of unique and refreshing value. In such a story, race fiction, detaching itself from the limitations of propaganda on the one hand and genre fiction on the other, emerges from the color line and is incorporated into the body of general and universal art.

Finally in Jean Toomer, the author of *Cane,* we come upon the very first artist of the race, who with all an artist's passion and sympathy for life, its hurts, its sympathies, its desires, its joy, its defeats and strange yearnings, can write about the Negro without the surrender or compromise of the artist's vision. So objective is it, that we feel that it is a mere accident that birth or association has thrown him into contact with the life he has written about. He would write just as well, just as poignantly, just as transmutingly, about the peasants of Russia, or the peasants of Ireland, had experience brought him in touch with their existence. *Cane* is a book of gold and bronze, of dusk and flame, of ecstasy and pain, and Jean Toomer is a bright morning star of a new day of the race in literature.

BENJAMIN GRIFFIN BRAWLEY
*The Negro in
American Fiction*

EVER SINCE Sydney Smith sneered at American books a hundred years ago, honest critics have asked themselves if the literature of the United States was not really open to the charge of provincialism. Within the last year or two the argument has been very much revived; and an English critic, Mr. Edward Garnett, writing in *The Atlantic Monthly*, has pointed out that with our predigested ideas and made-to-order fiction we not only discourage individual genius, but make it possible for the multitude to think only such thoughts as have passed through a sieve. Our most popular novelists, and sometimes our most respectable writers, see only the sensation that is uppermost for the moment in the mind of the crowd—divorce, graft, tainted meat or money—and they proceed to cut the cloth of their fiction accordingly. Mr. Owen Wister, a "regular practitioner" of the novelist's art, in substance admitting the weight of these charges, lays the blame on our crass democracy which utterly refuses to do its own thinking and which is satisfied only with the tinsel and gewgaws and hobbyhorses of literature. And no theme has suffered so much from the coarseness of the mob-spirit in literature as that of the Negro.

As a matter of fact, the Negro in his problems and strivings offers to American writers the greatest opportunity that could possibly be given to them to-day. It is commonly agreed that only one other large question, that of the relations of capital and labor, is of as much interest to the American public; and even this great issue fails to possess quite the appeal offered by the Negro from the social standpoint. One can only imagine what a Victor Hugo, detached and philosophical, would have done with such a theme in a novel. When we see what actually has been done—how often in the guise of fiction a writer has preached a sermon or shouted a political creed, or vented his spleen—we are not exactly proud of the art of novel-writing as it has been developed in the United States of America. Here was opportunity for tragedy, for comedy, for the subtle portrayal of all the relations of man with his fellow man, for faith and hope and love and sorrow. And yet, with the Civil War fifty years in the distance, not one novel or one short story of the first rank has found its inspiration in this great theme. Instead of such work we have consistently had traditional tales, political tracts, and lurid melodramas.

Let us see who have approached the theme, and just what they have done with it, for the present leaving out of account all efforts put forth by Negro writers themselves.

The names of four exponents of Southern life come at once to mind—George W. Cable, Joel Chandler Harris, Thomas Nelson Page, and Thomas Dixon; and at once, in their outlook and method of work, the first two become separate from the last two. Cable and Harris have looked toward the past, and have embalmed vanished or vanishing types. Mr. Page and Mr. Dixon, with their thought on the present (though for the most part they portray the recent past), have used the novel as a vehicle for political propaganda.

It was in 1879 that "Old Creole Days" evidenced the advent of a new force in American literature; and on the basis of this work, and of "The Grandissimes" which followed, Mr. Cable at once took his place as the foremost portrayer of life in old New Orleans. By birth, by temperament, and by training he was thoroughly fitted for the task to which he set himself. His mother was from New England, his father of the stock of colonial Virginia; and the stern Puritanism of the North was mellowed by the gentler influences of the South. Moreover, from his long apprenticeship in newspaper work in New Orleans he had received abundantly the knowledge and training necessary for his work. Setting himself to a study of the Negro of the old régime, he made a specialty of the famous—and infamous—quadroon society of Louisiana of the third and fourth decades of the last century. And excellent as was his work, turning his face to the past in manner as well as in matter, from the very first he raised the question propounded by this paper. In his earliest volume there was a story entitled " 'Tite Poulette," the heroine of which was a girl amazingly fair, the supposed daughter of one Madame John. A young Dutchman fell in love with 'Tite Poulette, championed her cause at all times, suffered a beating and stabbing for her, and was by her nursed back to life and love. In the midst of his perplexity about joining himself to a member of another race, came the word from Madame John that the girl was not her daughter, but the child of yellow fever patients whom she had nursed until they died, leaving their infant in her care. Immediately upon the publication of this story, the author received a letter from a young woman who had actually lived in very much the same situation as that portrayed in " 'Tite Poulette," telling him that his story was not true to life and that he knew it was not, for Madame John really *was* the mother of the heroine. Accepting the criticism, Mr. Cable set about the composition of "Madame Delphine," in which the situation is somewhat similar, but in which at the end the mother tamely makes a confession to a priest. What is the trouble? The artist is so bound by circumstances and hemmed in by tradition that he simply has not the courage to launch out into the deep and work out his human problems for himself. Take a representative portrait from "The Grandissimes":

> Clemence had come through ages of African savagery, through fires that do not refine, but that blunt and blast and blacken and char; starvation, gluttony, drunkenness, thirst, drowning, nakedness, dirt, fetichism, debauchery, slaughter, pestilence, and the rest—she was their heiress; they left her the cinders of human feelings. . . . She had had children of assorted colors—had one with her now, the black boy that brought the basil to Joseph; the others were here and there, some in the Grandissime households or field-gangs, some elsewhere within occasional sight, some dead, some not accounted for. Husbands—like the Samaritan woman's. We know she was a constant singer and laugher.

Very brilliant of course; and yet Clemence is a relic, not a prophecy.

Still more of a relic is Uncle Remus. For decades now, this charming old Negro has been held up to the children of the South as the perfect expression of the beauty of life in the glorious times "befo' de wah," when every Southern gentleman was suckled at the bosom of a "black mammy." Why should we not occasionally attempt to paint the Negro of the new day—intelligent, ambitious, thrifty, manly? Perhaps he is not so poetic; but certainly the human element is greater.

To the school of Cable and Harris belong also of course Miss Grace King and Mrs. Ruth McEnery Stuart, a thoroughly representative piece of work being Mrs. Stuart's "Uncle 'Riah's Christmas Eve." Other more popular writers of the day, Miss Mary Johnston and Miss Ellen Glasgow for instance, attempt no special analysis of the Negro. They simply take him for granted as an institution that always has existed and always will exist, as a hewer of wood and drawer of water, from the first flush of creation to the sounding of the trump of doom.

But more serious is the tone when we come to Thomas Nelson Page and Thomas Dixon. We might tarry for a few minutes with Mr. Page to listen to more such tales as those of Uncle Remus; but we must turn to living issues. Times have changed. The grandson of Uncle Remus does not feel that he must stand with his hat in his hand when he is in our presence, and he even presumes to help us in the running of our government. This will never do; so in "Red Rock" and "The Leopard's Spots" it must be shown that he should never have been allowed to vote anyway, and those honorable gentlemen in the Congress of the United States in the year 1865 did not know at all what they were about. Though we are given the characters and setting of a novel, the real business is to show that the Negro has been the "sentimental pet" of the nation all too long. By all means let us have an innocent white girl, a burly Negro, and a burning at the stake, or the story would be incomplete.

We have the same thing in "The Clansman," a "drama of fierce revenge." But here we are concerned very largely with the blackening of a man's character. Stoneman (Thaddeus Stevens very thinly disguised) is himself the whole Congress of the United States. He is a gambler, and "spends a part of almost every night at Hall & Pemberton's Faro Place on Pennsylvania Avenue." He is hysterical, "drunk with the joy of a triumphant vengeance." "The South is conquered soil," he says to the President (a mere figure-head, by the way), "I mean to blot it from the map." Further: "It is but the justice and wisdom of heaven that the Negro shall rule the land of his bondage. It is the only solution of the race problem. Wait until I put a ballot in the hand of every Negro, and a bayonet at the breast of every white man from the James to the Rio Grande." Stoneman, moreover, has a mistress, a mulatto woman, a "yello vampire" who dominates him completely. "Senators, representatives, politicians of low and high degree, artists, correspondents, foreign ministers, and cabinet officers hurried to acknowledge their fealty to the uncrowned king, and hail the strange brown woman who held the keys of his house as the first lady of the land." This, let us remember, was for some months the best-selling book in the United States. A slightly altered version of it has very recently commanded such prices as were never before paid for seats at a moving-picture entertainment; and with "The Traitor" and "The Southerner" it represents our most popular treatment of the gravest social question in American life! "The Clansman" is to American literature exactly what a Louisiana mob is to American democracy. Only too frequently, of course, the mob represents us all too well.

Turning from the longer works of fiction to the short story, I have been interested to see how the matter has been dealt with here. For purposes of comparison I have selected from ten representative periodicals as many distinct stories, no one of which was published more than ten years ago; and as these are in almost every case those stories that first strike the eye in a periodical index, we may assume that they are thoroughly typical. The ten are: "Shadow," by Harry Stillwell Edwards, in the *Century* (December, 1906); "Callum's Co'tin': A Plantation Idyl," by Frank H. Sweet, in the *Craftsman* (March, 1907); "His Excellency the Governor," by L. M. Cooke, in *Putnam's* (February, 1908); "The Black Drop," by Margaret Deland in *Collier's Weekly* (May 2 and 9, 1908); "Jungle Blood," by Elmore Elliott Peake, in *McClure's* (September, 1908); "The Race-Rioter," by Harris Merton Lyon, in the *American* (February, 1910); "Shadow," by Grace MacGowan Cooke and Alice Mac-Gowan, in *Everybody's* (March, 1910); "Abram's Freedom," by Edna Turpin, in the *Atlantic* (September, 1912); "A Hypothetical Case," by Norman Duncan, in *Harper's* (June, 1915); and "The Chalk Game," by L. B. Yates, in the *Saturday Evening Post* (June 5, 1915). For high standards of fiction I think we may safely say that, all in all, the periodicals here mentioned are representative of the best that America has to offer. In some cases the story cited is the only one on the Negro question that a magazine has published within the decade.

"Shadow" (in the *Century*) is the story of a Negro convict who for a robbery committed at the age of fourteen was sentenced to twenty years of hard labor in the mines of Alabama. An accident disabled him, however, and prevented his doing the regular work for the full period of his imprisonment. At twenty he was a hostler, looking forward in despair to the fourteen years of confinement still waiting for him. But the three little girls of the prison commissioner visit the prison. Shadow performs many little acts of kindness for them, and their hearts go out to him. They storm the governor and the judge for his pardon, and present the Negro with his freedom as a Christmas gift. The story is not long, but it strikes a note of genuine pathos.

"Callum's Co'tin' " is concerned with a hard-working Negro, a blacksmith, nearly forty, who goes courting the girl who called at his shop to get a trinket mended for her mistress. At first he makes himself ridiculous by his finery; later he makes the mistake of coming to a crowd of merrymakers in his working clothes. More and more, however, he storms the heart of the girl, who eventually capitulates. From the standpoint simply of craftsmanship, the story is an excellent piece of work.

"His Excellency the Governor" deals with the custom on Southern plantations of having, in imitation of the white people, a Negro "governor" whose duty it was to settle minor disputes. At the death of old Uncle Caleb, who for years had held this position of responsibility, his son Jubal should have been the next in order. He was likely to be superseded, however, by loud-mouthed Sambo, though urged to assert himself by Maria, his wife, an old house-servant who had no desire whatever to be defeated for the place of honor among the women by Sue, a former field-hand. At the meeting where all was to be decided, however, Jubal with the aid of his fiddle completely confounded his rival and won. There are some excellent touches in the story; but, on the whole, the composition is hardly more than fair in literary quality.

"The Black Drop," throughout which we see the hand of an experienced writer, analyzes the heart of a white boy who is in love with a girl who is almost white, and who when the test confronts him suffers the tradition that binds him to get the better of his heart. "But you will still believe that I love you?" he asks, ill at ease as they separate. "No, of course I can not believe that," replies the girl.

"Jungle Blood" is the story of a simple-minded, simple-hearted Negro of gigantic size who in a moment of fury kills his pretty wife and the white man who has seduced her. The tone of the whole may be gleaned from the description of Moss Harper's father: "An old darky sat drowsing on the stoop. There was something ape-like about his long arms, his flat, wide-nostriled nose, and the mat of gray wool which crept down his forehead to within two inches of his eyebrows."

"The Race-Rioter" sets forth the stand of a brave young sheriff to protect his prisoner, a Negro boy, accused of the assault and murder of a little white girl. Hank Egge tries by every possible subterfuge to defeat the plans of a lynching party, and finally dies riddled with bullets as he is defending his prisoner. The story is especially remarkable for the strong and sympathetic characterization of such contrasting figures as young Egge and old Dikeson, the father of the dead girl.

"Shadow" (in *Everybody's*) is a story that depends for its force very largely upon incident. It studies the friendship of a white boy, Ranny, and a black boy, Shadow, a relationship that is opposed by both the Northern white mother and the ambitious and

independent Negro mother. In a fight, Shad breaks a collar-bone for
Ranny; later he saves him from drowning. In the face of Ranny's
white friends, all the harsher side of the problem is seen; and yet
the human element is strong beneath it all. The story, not without
considerable merit as it is, would have been infinitely stronger if the
friendship of the two boys had been pitched on a higher plane. As it
is, Shad is very much like a dog following his master.

"Abram's Freedom" is at the same time one of the most clever
and one of the most provoking stories with which we have to deal.
It is a perfect example of how one may walk directly up to the light
and then deliberately turn his back upon it. The story is set just before the Civil War. It deals with the love of the slave Abram for a
free young woman, Emmeline. "All his life he had heard and used
the phrase 'free nigger' as a term of contempt. What, then, was this
vague feeling, not definite enough yet to be a wish or even a longing?" So far, so good. Emmeline inspires within her lover the highest ideals of manhood, and he becomes a hostler in a livery-stable,
paying to his master so much a year for his freedom. Then comes
the astounding and forced conclusion. At the very moment when,
after years of effort, Emmeline has helped her husband to gain his
freedom (and when all the slaves are free as a matter of fact by
virtue of the Emancipation Proclamation), Emmeline, whose husband has special reason to be grateful to his former master, says to
the lady of the house: "Me an' Abram ain't got nothin' to do in dis
worl' but to wait on you an' master."

In "A Hypothetical Case" we again see the hand of a master-
craftsman. Is a white boy justified in shooting a Negro who has
offended him? The white father is not quite at ease, quibbles a good
deal, but finally says Yes. The story, however, makes it clear that
the Negro did not strike the boy. He was a hermit living on the
Florida coast and perfectly abased when he met Mercer and his two
companions. When the three boys pursued him and finally overtook
him, the Negro simply held the hands of Mercer until the boy had
recovered his temper. Mercer in his rage really struck himself.

"The Chalk Game" is the story of a little Negro jockey who
wins a race in Louisville only to be drugged and robbed by some
"flashlight" Negroes who send him to Chicago. There he recovers
his fortunes by giving to a group of gamblers the correct "tip" on
another race, and he makes his way back to Louisville much richer
by his visit. Throughout the story emphasis is placed upon the
superstitious element in the Negro race, an element readily considered by men who believe in luck.

Of these ten stories, only five strike out with even the slightest degree of independence. "Shadow" (in the *Century*) is not a powerful piece of work, but it is written in tender and beautiful spirit. "The Black Drop" is a bold handling of a strong situation. "The Race-Rioter" also rings true, and in spite of the tragedy there is optimism in this story of a man who is not afraid to do his duty. "Shadow" (in *Everybody's*) awakens all sorts of discussion, but at least attempts to deal honestly with a situation that might arise in any neighborhood at any time. "A Hypothetical Case" is the most tense and independent story in the list.

On the other hand, "Callum's Co'tin'" and "His Excellency the Governor," bright comedy though they are, belong, after all, to the school of Uncle Remus. "Jungle Blood" and "The Chalk Game" belong to the class that always regards the Negro as an animal, a minor, a plaything—but never as a man. "Abram's Freedom," exceedingly well written for two-thirds of the way, falls down hopelessly at the end. Many old Negroes after the Civil War preferred to remain with their former masters; but certainly no young woman of the type of Emmeline would sell her birthright for a mess of pottage.

Just there is the point. That the Negro is ever to be taken seriously is incomprehensible to some people. It is the story of "The Man That Laughs" over again. The more Gwynplaine protests, the more outlandish he becomes to the House of Lords.

We are simply asking that those writers of fiction who deal with the Negro shall be thoroughly honest with themselves, and not remain forever content to embalm old types and work over outworn ideas. Rather should they sift the present and forecast the future. But of course the editors must be considered. The editors must give their readers what the readers want; and when we consider the populace, of course we have to reckon with the mob. And the mob does not find anything very attractive about a Negro who is intelligent, cultured, manly, and who does not smile. It will be observed that in no one of the ten stories above mentioned, not even in one of the five remarked most favorably, is there a Negro of this type. Yet he is obliged to come. America has yet to reckon with him. The day of Uncle Remus as well as of Uncle Tom is over.

Even now, however, there are signs of better things. Such an artist as Mr. Howells, for instance, has once or twice dealt with the problem in excellent spirit. Then there is the work of the Negro writers themselves. The numerous attempts in fiction made by them have most frequently been open to the charge of crassness already

considered; but Paul Laurence Dunbar, Charles W. Chesnutt, and
W. E. Burghardt DuBois have risen above the crowd. Mr. Dunbar,
of course, was better in poetry than in prose. Such a short story as
"Jimsella," however, exhibited considerable technique. "The Uncalled" used a living topic treated with only partial success. But for
the most part, Mr. Dunbar's work looked toward the past. Somewhat stronger in prose is Mr. Chesnutt. "The Marrow of Tradition" is not much more than a political tract, and "The Colonel's
Dream" contains a good deal of preaching; but "The House Behind
the Cedars" is a real novel. Among his short stories, "The Bouquet"
may be remarked for technical excellence, and "The Wife of His
Youth" for a situation of unusual power. Dr. DuBois's "The Quest
of the Silver Fleece" contains at least one strong dramatic situation,
that in which Bles probes the heart of Zora; but the author is a
sociologist and essayist rather than a novelist. The grand epic of the
race is yet to be produced.

Some day we shall work out the problems of our great country.
Some day we shall not have a state government set at defiance, and
the massacre of Ludlow. Some day our little children will not slave
in mines and mills, but will have some chance at the glory of God's
creation; and some day the Negro will cease to be a problem and
become a human being. Then, in truth, we shall have the Promised
Land. But until that day comes let those who mold our ideals and
set the standards of our art in fiction at least be honest with themselves and independent. Ignorance we may for a time forgive; but a
man has only himself to blame if he insists on not seeing the sunrise
in the new day.

> LEROI JONES
> *The Myth of a*
> *"Negro Literature"* *

THE MEDIOCRITY of what has been called "Negro Literature" is one
of the most loosely held secrets of American culture. From Phillis
Wheatley to Charles Chesnutt, to the present generation of American Negro writers, the only recognizable accretion of tradition read-

* An address given at the American Society for African Culture, March 14,
1962.

ily attributable to the black producer of a formal literature in this country, with a few notable exceptions, has been of an almost agonizing mediocrity. In most other fields of "high art" in America, with the same few notable exceptions, the Negro contribution has been, when one existed at all, one of impressive mediocrity. Only in music, and most notably in blues, jazz, and spirituals, *i.e.*, "Negro Music," has there been a significantly profound contribution by American Negroes.

There are a great many reasons for the spectacular vapidity of the American Negro's accomplishment in other formal, serious art forms—social, economic, political, etc.—but one of the most persistent and aggravating reasons for the absence of achievement among serious Negro artists, except in Negro music, is that in most cases the Negroes who found themselves in a position to pursue some art, especially the art of literature, have been members of the Negro middle class, a group that has always gone out of its way to cultivate *any* mediocrity, as long as that mediocrity was guaranteed to prove to America, and recently to the world at large, that they were not really who they were, *i.e.*, Negroes. Negro music alone, because it drew its strengths and beauties out of the depth of the black man's soul, and because to a large extent its traditions could be carried on by the lowest classes of Negroes, has been able to survive the constant and willful dilutions of the black middle class. Blues and jazz have been the only consistent exhibitors of "Negritude" in formal American culture simply because the bearers of its tradition maintained their essential identities as Negroes; in no other art (and I will persist in calling Negro music, Art) has this been possible. Phillis Wheatley and her pleasant imitations of 18th century English poetry are far and, finally, ludicrous departures from the huge black voices that splintered southern nights with their *hollers, chants, arwhoolies,* and *ballits*. The embarrassing and inverted paternalism of Charles Chesnutt and his "refined Afro-American" heroes are far cries from the richness and profundity of the blues. And it is impossible to mention the achievements of the Negro in any area of artistic endeavor with as much significance as in spirituals, blues and jazz. There has never been an equivalent to Duke Ellington or Louis Armstrong in Negro writing, and even the best of contemporary literature written by Negroes cannot yet be compared to the fantastic beauty of the music of Charlie Parker.

American Negro music from its inception moved logically and powerfully out of a fusion between African musical tradition and the American experience. It was, and continues to be, a natural, yet highly stylized and personal version of the Negro's life in America. It is, indeed, a chronicler of the Negro's movement, from African slave to American slave, from Freedman to Citizen. And the literature of the blues is a much more profound contribution to Western culture than any other literary contribution made by American Negroes. Moreover, it is only recently that formal literature written by American Negroes has begun to approach the literary standards of its model, *i.e.*, the literature of the white middle class. And only Jean Toomer, Richard Wright, Ralph Ellison, and James Baldwin have managed to bring off examples of writing, in this genre, that could succeed in passing themselves off as "serious" writing, in the sense that, say, the work of Somerset Maugham is "serious" writing. That is, serious, if one has never read Herman Melville or James Joyce. And it is part of the tragic naïveté of the middle class (brow) writer, that he has not.

Literature, for the Negro writer, was always an example of "culture." Not in the sense of the more impressive philosophical characteristics of a particular social group, but in the narrow sense of "cultivation" or "sophistication" by an individual within that group. The Negro artist, because of his middle-class background, carried the artificial social burden as the "best and most intelligent" of Negroes, and usually entered into the "serious" arts to exhibit his familiarity with the social graces, *i.e.*, as a method or means of displaying his participation in the "serious" aspects of American culture. To be a writer was to be "cultivated," in the stunted bourgeois sense of the word. It was also to be a "quality" black man. It had nothing to do with the investigation of the human soul. It was, and is, a social preoccupation rather than an aesthetic one. A rather daring way of status seeking. The cultivated Negro leaving those ineffectual philanthropies, Negro colleges, looked at literature merely as another way of gaining prestige in the white world for the Negro middle class. And the literary and artistic models were always those that could be socially acceptable to the white middle class, which automatically limited them to the most spiritually debilitated imitations of literature available. Negro music, to the middle class, black and white, was never socially acceptable. It was shunned by blacks ambitious of "waking up white," as low and degrading. It was shunned by their white models simply because it was produced by blacks. As one of my professors at Howard University protested one day, "It's amazing how much bad taste the blues display." Suffice it to say, it is in part exactly this "bad taste" that has continued to keep Negro music as vital as it is. The abandonment of one's local (*i.e.*, place or group) emotional attachments in favor of the abstract emotional response of what is called "the general public" (which is notoriously white and middle class) has always been the great diluter of any Negro culture. "You're acting like a nigger," was the standard disparagement. I remember being chastised severely for daring to eat a piece of watermelon on the Howard campus. "Do you realize you're sitting near the highway?" is what the man said, "This is the capstone of Negro education." And it is too, in the sense that it teaches the Negro how to make out in the white society, using the agonizing overcompensation of pretending he's also white. James Baldwin's play, *The Amen Corner*, when it appeared at the Howard Players theatre, "set the speech department back ten years," an English professor groaned to me. The play depicted the lives of poor Negroes running a store-front church. Any reference to the Negro-ness of the American Negro has always been frowned upon by the black middle class in their frenzied dash toward the precipice of the American mainstream.

High art, first of all, must reflect the experiences of the human being, the emotional predicament of the man, as he exists, in the defined world of his being. It must be produced from the legitimate emotional resources of the soul in the world. It can *never* be produced by evading these resources or pretending that they do not exist. It can never be produced by appropriating the withered emotional responses of some strictly social idea of humanity. High art, and by this I mean any art that would attempt to describe or characterize some portion of the profound meaningfulness of human life with any finality or truth, cannot be based on the superficialities of human existence. It must issue from *real* categories of human activity, *truthful* accounts of human life, and not fancied accounts of the attainment of cultural privilege by some willingly preposterous apologists for one social "order" or another. Most of the formal literature produced by Negroes in America has never fulfilled these conditions. And aside from Negro music, it is only in the "popular traditions" of the so-called lower class Negro that these conditions are fulfilled as a basis for human life. And it is because of this "separation" between Negro life (as an emotional experience) and Negro art, that, say, Jack Johnson or Ray Robinson is a larger cultural hero than any Negro writer. It is because of this separation, even evasion, of the emotional experience of Negro life, that Jack Johnson is a more modern political symbol than most Negro writers. Johnson's life, as proposed, certainly, by his career, reflects much more accurately the symbolic yearnings for singular values

among the great masses of Negroes than any black novelist has yet
managed to convey. Where is the Negro-ness of a literature written
in imitation of the meanest of social intelligences to be found in
American culture, *i.e.*, the white middle class? How can it even
begin to express the emotional predicament of black Western man?
Such a literature, even if its "characters" *are* black, takes on the
emotional barrenness of its model, and the blackness of the characters is like the blackness of Al Jolson, an unconvincing device. It is
like using black checkers instead of white. They are still checkers.

The development of the Negro's music was, as I said, direct
and instinctive. It was the one vector out of African culture impossible to eradicate completely. The appearance of blues as a native
American music signified in many ways the appearance of American Negroes where once there were African Negroes. The emotional
fabric of the music was colored by the emergence of an American
Negro culture. It signified that culture's strength and vitality. In the
evolution of form in Negro music it is possible to see not only the
evolution of the Negro as a cultural and social element of American
culture, but also the evolution of that culture itself. The "Coon
Shout" proposed one version of the American Negro—and of
America; Ornette Coleman proposes another. But the point is that
both these versions are accurate and informed with a legitimacy of
emotional concern nowhere available in what is called "Negro Literature," and certainly not in the middlebrow literature of the
white American.

The artifacts of African art and sculpture were consciously
eradicated by slavery. Any African art that based its validity on the
production of an artifact, *i.e.*, some *material* manifestation such as
a wooden statue or a woven cloth, had little chance of survival. It
was only the more "abstract" aspects of African culture that could
continue to exist in slave America. Africanisms still persist in the
music, religion, and popular cultural traditions of American Negroes. However, it is not an African art American Negroes are
responsible for, but an American one. The traditions of Africa must
be utilized within the culture of the American Negro where they *actually* exist, and not because of a defensive rationalization about the
worth of one's ancestors or an attempt to capitalize on the recent
eminence of the "new" African nations. Africanisms do exist in
Negro culture, but they have been so translated and transmuted by
the American experience that they have become integral parts of
that experience.

The American Negro has a definable and legitimate historical tradition, no matter how painful, in America, but it is the only place such a tradition exists, simply because America is the only place the American Negro exists. He is, as William Carlos Williams said, "A pure product of America." The paradox of the Negro experience in America is that it is a separate experience, but inseparable from the complete fabric of American life. The history of Western culture begins for the Negro with the importation of the slaves. It is almost as if all Western history before that must be strictly a learned concept. It is only the American experience that can be a persistent cultural catalyst for the Negro. In a sense, history for the Negro, before America, must remain an emotional abstraction. The cultural memory of Africa informs the Negro's life in America, but it is impossible to separate it from its American transformation. Thus, the Negro writer if he wanted to tap his legitimate cultural tradition should have done it by utilizing the entire spectrum of the American experience from the point of view of the emotional history of the black man in this country: as its victim and its chronicler. The soul of such a man, as it exists outside the boundaries of commercial diversion or artificial social pretense. But without a deep commitment to cultural relevance and intellectual purity this was impossible. The Negro as a writer, was always a social object, whether glorifying the concept of white superiority, as a great many early Negro writers did, or in crying out against it, as exemplified by the stock "protest" literature of the thirties. He never moved into the position where he could propose his own symbols, erect his own personal myths, as any great literature must. Negro writing was always "after the fact," *i.e.*, based on known social concepts within the structure of bourgeois idealistic projections of "their America," and an emotional climate that never really existed.

The most successful fiction of most Negro writing is in its emotional content. The Negro protest novelist postures, and invents a protest quite amenable with the tradition of bourgeois American life. He never reaches the central core of the America which *can* cause such protest. The intellectual traditions of the white middle class prevent such exposure of reality, and the black imitators reflect this. The Negro writer on Negro life in America postures, and invents a Negro life, and an America to contain it. And even most of those who tried to rebel against that *invented* America were trapped because they had lost all touch with the reality of their experience within the *real* America, either because of the hidden emotional allegiance to the white middle class, or because they did not realize where the reality of their experience lay. When the serious Negro writer disdained the "middlebrow" model, as is the case with a few contemporary black American writers, he usually rushed headlong into the groves of the Academy, perhaps the most insidious and clever dispenser of middlebrow standards of excellence under the guise of "recognizable tradition." That such recognizable tradition is necessary goes without saying, but even from the great philosophies of Europe a contemporary usage must be established. No poetry has come out of England of major importance for forty years, yet there are would-be Negro poets who reject the gaudy excellence of 20th century American poetry in favor of disembowelled academic models of second-rate English poetry, with the notion that somehow it is the only way poetry should be written. It would be better if such a poet listened to Bessie Smith sing *Gimme a Pigfoot*, or listened to the tragic verse of a Billie Holiday, than be content to imperfectly imitate the bad poetry of the ruined minds of Europe. And again, it is this striving for *respectability* that has it so. For an American, black or white, to say that some hideous imitation of Alexander Pope means more to him, emotionally, than the blues of Ray Charles or Lightnin' Hopkins, it would be required for him to have completely disappeared into the American Academy's vision of a Europeanized and colonial American culture, or to be lying. In the end, the same emotional sterility results. It is somehow much more tragic for the black man.

A Negro literature, to be a legitimate product of the Negro experience in America, must get at that experience in exactly the terms America has proposed for it, in its most ruthless identity. Negro reaction to America is as deep a part of America as the root causes of that reaction, and it is impossible to accurately describe that reaction in terms of the American middle class; because for them, the Negro has never really existed, never been glimpsed in anything even approaching the complete reality of his humanity. The Negro writer has to go from where he actually is, completely outside of that conscious white myopia. That the Negro does exist is the point, and as an element of American culture he is completely misunderstood by Americans. The middlebrow, commercial Negro writer assures the white American that, in fact, he doesn't exist, and that if he does, he does so within the perfectly predictable fingerpainting of white bourgeois sentiment and understanding. Nothing could be further from the truth. The Creoles of New Orleans resisted "Negro" music for a time as raw and raucous, because they thought they had found a place within the white society which would preclude their being Negroes. But they were unsuccessful in their at-

tempts to "disappear" because the whites themselves reminded them
that they were still, for all their assimilation, "just coons." And this
seems to me an extremely important idea, since it is precisely this
bitter insistence that has kept what can be called "Negro Culture" a
brilliant amalgam of diverse influences. There was always a border
beyond which the Negro could not go, whether musically or socially. There was always a possible limitation to any dilution or excess of cultural or spiritual reference. The Negro could not ever
become white and that was his strength; at some point, always, he
could not participate in the dominant tenor of the white man's culture, yet he came to understand that culture as well as the white
man. It was at this juncture that he had to make use of other resources, whether African, sub-cultural, or hermetic. And it was this
boundary, this no-man's-land, that provided the logic and beauty of
his music. And this is the only way for the Negro artist to provide
his version of America—from that no-man's-land outside the mainstream. A no-man's-land, a black country, completely invisible to
white America, but so essentially part of it as to stain its whole
being an ominous gray. Were there really a Negro literature, now it
could flower. At this point when the whole of Western society might
go up in flames, the Negro remains an integral part of that society,
but continually outside it, a figure like Melville's Bartleby. He is an
American, capable of identifying emotionally with the fantastic cultural ingredients of this society, but he is also, forever, outside that
culture, an invisible strength within it, an observer. If there is ever a
Negro literature, it must disengage itself from the weak, heinous
elements of the culture that spawned it, and use its very existence as
evidence of a more profound America. But as long as the Negro
writer contents himself with the imitation of the useless ugly inele-
gance of the stunted middle-class mind, academic or popular, and
refuses to look around him and "tell it like it is"—preferring the
false prestige of the black bourgeois or the deceitful "acceptance" of
buy and sell America, something never included in the legitimate
cultural tradition of "his people"—he will be a failure, and what is
worse, not even a significant failure. Just another dead American.

[
RICHARD WRIGHT
*The Literature of the Negro in
the United States*
]

To MOST people the literature of the American Negro is fairly well-known. So for me to give you merely a bare, bald recital of what Negroes have written would, in my opinion, be shirking a duty and a responsibility. Indeed, it would be the easy and the lazy way out, and I don't like the easy and lazy ways out of things.

As we all know, anthologists are legion today; to make an anthology requires simply this: Get a big pile of books on a given subject together, a big pot of glue, and a pair of sharp scissors and start clipping and pasting.

I do most seriously want to tell you about Negro writing, but I also want to try to tell you what some of that writing means, how it came to be written, what relationship it had to its time, and what it means to us today. In short, I'd like to try to interpret some of it for you; but one cannot interpret without thinking, without comparing. And, for the most part, I'm going to use Negro poets and their poems as my examples; for poets and poems have a way of telling a lot in a compressed manner.

But, first, I'm going to try to deposit certain concepts in your mind about the world in which we live; then, using these concepts as a magnifying glass, we will look at some of the literary utterances of the American Negro. The concepts I shall deal with are familiar, though I doubt if they've been applied to American Negro expression before. Let me start by making a general comparison.

A few years ago I spent some months living in the heart of French Quebec, on an island in the St. Lawrence River, about fifteen miles from the city of Quebec. As you no doubt know, the Province of Quebec represents one of the few real surviving remnants of feudal culture on the American continent. It has a Catholic culture, a close, organic, intimate, mainly rural, way of life. For more than three hundred years, many of the customs and habits of life of French Canadians have not changed.

Never before had I the experience of living intimately in a culture so different from the Protestant, Puritan culture of my own native land. And, like most travelers, I saw French Canadian culture with two pairs of eyes: I saw the Catholic culture of French Quebec, and, at the same time, I saw how different that culture was from the culture of industrial, Protestant America.

Now you may feel that I'm going rather far astray in talking about Negro literature by describing a culture in which there are practically no Negroes, but I have my reasons for this.

In French Quebec the Catholic church dominates all personal and institutional and political phases of life from the cradle to the grave. There is no split between the personal and the political; they are one. In telling you these facts, please understand I'm making no judgment upon the culture of French Quebec. I'm merely trying to present a few facts for the purpose of establishing a basis of comparison. The people of French Quebec are at one with their culture; they express themselves in and through it. The personalities of the people I met were serene, even-tempered; no one strove too hard for a personal or an individualistic vision of life. No one sought a separate or unique destiny; they were not a romantic people. The secular and the sacred are united in French Quebec; the social and the personal are integrated; the individual and his group are one.

How different this is from our culture! In America we are split up in almost every imaginable way. We have no central unity; our church and state are separate. With but a tiny area of agreement, each individual lives in his own world.

This break with the past was accomplished when we broke with the feudal world, and we call this Freedom, and it is the crowning development of the industrial West; it has given us the most powerful civilization the world has ever known. But, also, it has given us millions of wrecked lives, millions of oppressed. It has given us anti-Semitism, anti-Negroism. It has given us spectacular crime, corruption, violence, and a singular disregard for the individual. Yet I feel that we were right in breaking with the feudal world. We do not have and we do not need an official creed to which all must bow. Yet we have an industrial civilization that breeds restlessness, eagerness, an almost neurotic anxiety that there is a hidden meaning that each must wring from life before he dies lest he feel that he has failed.

How does this relate to the Negro in America? In this way: The Negro, like everybody else in America, came originally from a simple, organic way of life, such as I saw in French Quebec. And you must remember that your forefathers also came from the feudal cultures of Europe. It was from the total, oppressive cultures like those of French Quebec that men fled three centuries ago to settle in the New World. You are now adjusted to industrial life and perhaps you have forgotten that your forefathers once endured the agony of leaving their homes and native lands to settle in America. So, in historical outline, the lives of American Negroes closely resemble your own.

There are, of course, some few important differences; most whites left Europe voluntarily; the American Negro was snatched by force from the organic, warm, tribal culture of Africa, transported across the Atlantic in crowded, stinking ships, and sold into slavery. Held in bondage, stripped of his culture, denied family life for centuries, made to labor for others, the Negro tried to learn to live the life of the New World in an atmosphere of rejection and hate.

You see now why I feel that one ought to use the same concepts in discussing Negro life that one uses in discussing white life? It is the same life lifted to the heights of pain and pathos, drama and tragedy. The history of the Negro in America is the history of America written in vivid and bloody terms; it is the history of Western Man writ small. It is the history of men who tried to adjust themselves to a world whose laws, customs, and instruments of force were leveled against them. The Negro is America's metaphor.

Let me sum up the meaning of my comparison, for what it means will form the foundation of what I'll have to say to you about Negro literature. Let us imagine an abstract line and at one end of this line let us imagine a simple, organic culture—call it Catholic, feudal, religious, tribal, or what you will. Here are some of the features of that culture: It is bigger than the individual and the individual finds his meaning for living in it. The individual does not help to make up the rules or laws of that culture.

At the opposite end of our imaginary line, let us imagine another culture, such as the one in which we live. In contrast to entity, in which the personality is swallowed up, we have a constant striving for identity. Instead of pre-individualism, we have a strident individualism. Whereas French Quebec has holy days, we have holidays. Church bells toll the time of day in French Quebec; we look at our watches to see the hour. Fetes become festivals.

The distance between these two cultures is the distance between feudal Europe and present-day, vibrant, nervous, industrial America. And it is the distance between the tribal African culture of the Negro and the place which he now occupies, against such great and constant odds, in American life.

It will be along this imaginary line—between these two culture

types—that I'll string the Negro writers I'll discuss. For the development of Negro expression—as well as the whole of Negro life in
America—hovers always somewhere between the rise of man from
his ancient, rural way of life to the complex, industrial life of our
time. Let me sum up these differences by contrast: entity vs. identity; pre-individualism vs. individualism; the determined vs. the
free.

Now, with this idea in mind, let me read you a short passage
from the work of a world-famous Negro writer, a writer whose
identity I shall withhold from you for a moment:

> *"Sire, I am sorry to tell your majesty a cruel fact; but the
> feeling in Dauphiné is far from resembling that of Provence.
> The mountaineers are all Bonapartists, Sire."*
>
> *"Then," murmured Louis XVIII, "he was well informed.
> And how many men had he with him?"*
>
> *"I do not know, Sire," answered the minister of police.*
>
> *"What! You do not know? Have you neglected to obtain
> information of this circumstance? It is true this is of small
> importance," the king added with a withering smile.*
>
> *"Sire, it was impossible to learn; the dispatch simply
> stated the fact of the landing and the route taken by the
> traitor."*
>
> *"And how did this dispatch reach you?" inquired the
> king.*
>
> *The minister bowed his head, and while a deep color over-
> spread his cheeks, he stammered, "By the telegraph, Sire."*
>
> *Louis XVIII advanced a step, folded his arms over his
> chest as Napoleon would have done. "So, then," he exclaimed,
> turning pale with anger, "seven allied armies overthrew that
> man. A miracle of Heaven replaced me on the throne after
> twenty-five years in exile . . ."*

Did a Negro write that? It does not sound Negroid. And were
Negroes ever in this world so intimately associated with any culture
that they could write of kings and ministers and battles involving
Louis XVIII?

Well, what I just quoted to you was a short passage from
Alexander Dumas' *The Count of Monte Cristo.* Yes, it's true that
Dumas was a Negro according to American racial codes, but his
being a Negro was the least important thing about him. Why? Because there were no laws or customs barring him from the society in
which he lived. He could attend any school he wanted to; he could
go to any church he wanted to; he could engage in any profession
he wanted to; he could live where he wanted to; he could marry

whom he wanted to; and if he had the mind and talent, he could win fame if he wanted to. He did win fame. He was at one with the culture in which he lived, and he wrote out of the commonly shared hopes and expectations of his age.

Let me recall to you the imaginary, entity culture that we placed at one end of our line: a religious, tribal, feudal culture, a culture like that of French Quebec. I don't mean that a culture of this sort is an ideal for which we must strive; I put that culture at the end of an imaginary line to serve us as a guide, as a yardstick against which we could measure how well or ill men adjusted themselves.

We can say that Dumas was integrated with the culture of France and was a Frenchman.

Let me read you yet another passage from another Negro writer, a world famous one too:

> *The dawn was breaking. I was standing at my appointed place with my three seconds. With inexplicable impatience I awaited my opportunity. The spring sun rose, and it was already growing hot. I saw my opponent coming on foot, accompanied by just one second. We advanced to meet him. He approached holding his cap filled with cherries. The seconds measured twelve paces for us. I had to fire first, but my agitation was so great, that I could not depend upon the steadiness of my hands; and in order to give myself time to become calm, I ceded to my opponent the first shot. My adversary would not agree to this. It was decided that we should cast lots. The first number fell to him. He took aim and his bullet went through my cap. . . .*

Is this Negro writing? It does not sound like the expressions of Negroes who live in America today. Did Negroes ever engage in duels? Well, what I have just read to you is a passage from a short story by Alexander Pushkin, a Russian Negro who was more a Russian than a Negro. Like Alexander Dumas, he had no cause to lament that he was a Negro; his writing does not carry any of the bitter and wild echoes of hate, frustration, and revolt found in the writings of American Negroes. Pushkin wrote out of the rich tradition of Russian realism, and he helped to further and enrich that tradition. He was one with his culture; he went to the schools of his choice; he served in an army that was not Jim Crow; he worked where he wanted to; he lived where he wanted to; and there was no sense of psychological distance between him and the culture of the land in which he lived.

Let me recall to you once again the concept we started with: Entity, men integrated with their culture; and identity, men who are at odds with their culture, striving for personal identification. The writings I've just read to you were the work of men who were emotionally integrated with their country's culture; no matter what the color of their skins, they were not really Negroes. One was a Russian, the other was a Frenchman.

Has any American Negro ever written like Dumas or Pushkin? Yes, one. Only one. As though in irony, history decided that the first Negro who was to express himself with any degree of competence on the soil of America should strike a universal note. Before the webs of slavery had so tightened as to snare nearly all Negroes in our land, one was freed by accident to give utterance in poetry to what she felt, to give in clear, bell-like, limpid cadences the hope of freedom in the New World.

One day, in 1761, a slave ship, having made the horrible voyage from Africa to America, dropped anchor in Boston harbor. As usual an auction was held, with the slaves stripped naked and made to stand in public upon blocks. Would-be purchasers probed their fingers about the bodies of the black men and women to determine if they were sound of limb. Finally, all the slaves, except a delicate twelve-year-old black girl, were sold. Because she seemed too frail to render a good day's hard work, no one wanted her. But a Boston tailor by the name of Wheatley bought her and took her home, where she was trained to be the personal servant of Mrs. Wheatley.

This nameless black child was given the name of Phillis and was accepted into the Wheatley home as one of the family, enjoying all the rights of the other Wheatley children. She displayed a remarkable talent for learning and she was taught to read and write. Need I point out that this African-born child possessed dim recollections of her mother pouring out water to the rising sun, no doubt a recollection of some kind of tribal, African ceremony? Slavery had not yet cast its black shadow completely over the American scene, and the minds of white people were not so warped at that time as they are now regarding the capacities of the Negro. Hence, the Wheatley family was quite free of inhibitions about educating Phillis; they proceeded to educate her in the so-called classical manner; that is, she got the kind of education that the white girls of her time received.

At an early age she was writing verse, influenced by the heroic couplets of Pope, the reigning English poet of that time. Closely bound to the Wheatley family, absorbing the impulses of the Christian community in which she lived, sharing the culture of her country in terms of home and school and church, her poetry showed almost no traces of her being a Negro or having been born in Africa. Indeed, so closely integrated was she with the passions and hopes of America that, in the War of 1776, she wrote a poem about George Washington. She was received by Washington at his military headquarters and the Father of Our Country complimented her upon her poetic utterances. In praise of Washington and in rebuke to imperialistic England, Phillis Wheatley wrote:

> *Ah! cruel blindness to Columbia's state!*
> *Lament thy thirst of boundless power too late.*
> *Proceed great chief, with virtue on thy side,*
> *Thy ev'ry action let the goddess guide.*
> *A crown, a mansion, and a throne that shine,*
> *With gold unfading, Washington, be thine.*

There is a note of irony embedded in the life of this girl who wrote revolutionary poetry though her skin was black and she was born in Africa; she made a trip to England where the Countess of Huntingdon wanted to present her to the Court of George III, and only ill health robbed her of that honor. (This was, of course, after the Revolutionary War.)

Again let me recall to you the concept I mentioned before. Phillis Wheatley was at one with her culture. What a far cry this is from the Negro Seabees who staged a sit-down strike a few years ago on the Pacific Coast when the war against Japan was at its hardest! What makes for this difference in loyalty? Are the three excerpts I've read to you the writing of Negroes? No, not by present day American standards. Then, what is a Negro? What is Negro writing?

Being a Negro has to do with the American scene, with race hate, rejection, ignorance, segregation, discrimination, slavery, murder, fiery crosses, and fear. But we will examine that when we come to it.

At last we have found on the American scene, in the writing of Phillis Wheatley, someone whom we can establish at the head of our imaginary line. Now we can use her as a guide, a yardstick to measure the degree of integration of other Negro writers.

Suppose the personalities of many Phillis Wheatleys of America had been allowed to develop? What a different nation we might have been! What a different literary utterance the American Negro might have given voice to! But, as we move on to other Negro literary figures, a queer spell at once comes over the scene. We cannot examine other Negro literary figures without taking into account something terrible that was happening to Negroes in the United States.

Even though we had won the War of Independence, there was a reaction against the ideals of Patrick Henry and Thomas Jefferson; the cotton gin was invented and vast new lands were opened up in the South. Slavery grew from a tentative gesture into the greatest single aggregate of political power in the nation. There followed decades of killings and burnings and lynchings and beatings and futile hope on the part of the Negroes. Stripped of his tribal African culture and not allowed to partake of the culture of the New World, the Negro was consistently brutalized, reduced to a creature of impulse who worked in the fields. Again and again he tried to revolt, hurling himself against his foes who outnumbered him, but in vain. It was but natural then that the nature of Negro literary utterance would change.

The next Negro literary figure I want to call to your attention is that of George Moses Horton, born in 1797 and died in 1883. The dates of his birth and death are important, for they span the bloodiest period of the history of the Negro in America. Born in North Carolina, he was a slave of the Horton family; but his relationship to that family differed greatly from that of the Phillis Wheatley relationship to the Boston family in which she was reared. Horton was passed around from one member of the Horton family to another; finally, in 1865, his master allowed him to hire himself out. While working around the home of a university president, he learned to read and write; for years he was a village character, regarded with amusement by the white students. He hired himself out as a writer of verse, charging twenty-five and fifty cents for a poetic job.

Finally some of his verse crept into print; not too much is known about this obscure wanderer's life, but we can guess at what he really felt from the following lines:

> *Alas! and am I born for this,*
>   *To wear this slavish chain?*
> *Deprived of all created bliss,*
>   *Through hardship, toil and pain!*

> *Oh, Heaven! and is there no relief*
> *This side the silent grave—*
> *To soothe the pain—to quell the grief*
> *And anguish of a slave?*

The poem runs on, lamenting, fighting, imploring. Something has happened since Phillis Wheatley wrote. Entity has turned into a kind of sullen, raging sense of rebellious identity. Horton certainly was not at one with his culture, but neither had he completely broken away. He writes in English and tries to express himself in the poetic traditions of his time, but there is now a sense of psychological distance between him and the land in which he lives. Horton was an emotionally trapped man; he lived in a culture of which he was not really a part; he was a split man, believing and feeling something which he could not live; he was an agonizingly self-conscious man, always longing to perform an act against which there existed a dreadful taboo!

We are now, it seems, approaching the literature of the American Negro and I think that you can readily see what it is that makes the difference between American Negro writing and just plain American writing. Horton's writing does not stem from racial feeling, but from a social situation; and Horton's cry for freedom was destined to become the tradition of Negro literature in the United States. Almost unbrokenly this tradition of lament was to roll down the decades, swelling, augmenting itself, becoming a vast reservoir of bitterness and despair and infrequent hope. This tradition of bitterness was to become so complex, was to assume such a tight, organic form, that most white people would think, upon examining it, that all Negroes had embedded in their flesh and bones some peculiar propensity toward lamenting and complaining.

From now on we plunge into a welter of crude patterns of surging hate and rebellion; from Horton's time on but few Negroes would even possess the opportunity to live in stable family units.

Another Negro poet, James M. Whitfield, born in 1830 and died in 1870, was a barber by trade. Whitfield was born in Boston, then moved to Buffalo, New York; and not too much is known about how he came to write. His first poetic utterances were so favorably received that he quit barbering and took to the public platform; and his poems continue the tradition of Horton:

> *America, it is to thee,*
> *Thou boasted land of liberty,—*
> *It is to thee that I raise my song,*

Thou land of blood, and crime, and wrong.
It is to thee my native land,
From which has issued many a band
To tear the black man from his soil
And force him here to delve and toil
Chained on your blood-bemoistened sod,
Cringing beneath a tyrant's rod . . .

As you see, the fact of separation from the culture of his native land has now sunk home into the Negro's heart; the Negro loves his land, but that land rejects him. Here we can witness the slow emergence of a new type of personality; here is the beginning of insecurity as a way of life; of violence as a daily companion.

The next Negro poet to attract attention in America was a woman, Frances Ellen Harper; living from 1825 to 1911, her life spanned slavery, war, emancipation, and freedom; and when she put her pen to paper her eyes were filled with more scenes of violence than perhaps many of our soldiers saw in the war just ended. In a poem entitled "Bury Me in a Free Land," she says:

Make me a grave where'er you will
In a lowly plain, or a lofty hill;
Make it among the earth's humblest graves,
But not in a land where men are slaves.
I could not rest if around my grave
I heard the steps of a trembling slave;
His shadow above my silent tomb
Would make it a place of fearful gloom.

Truly, you must now know that the word Negro in America means something not racial or biological, but something purely social, something made in the United States. Poems such as the above seem to imply that the eyes of the American Negro were fastened in horror upon something from which he could not turn away. The Negro could not take his eyes off the auction block: he never had a chance to; he could not stop thinking of lynching: he never had a chance to. The Negro writer had no choice in his subject matter; he could not select his experiences. Hence, the monotonous repetition of horror that rolls in verse from one generation to another.

Let us pursue this melancholy tale.

Albery A. Whitman, born 1851 and died 1902, spanning with his life slavery, war, freedom, also spoke a tongue that denied him, belonged to a culture that rejected him, walked upon a soil that mocked him, and lived and labored among men who hated him.

In his poem "The Rape of Florida," he says:

> *So fared the land where slaves were groaning yet—*
> *Where beauty's eyes must feed the lusts of men!*
> *'Tis as when horrid dreams we half forget,*
> *Would then relate, and still relate again—*
> *Ah! cold abhorrence hesitates my pen!*
> *The heavens were sad, and hearts of men were faint;*
> *Philanthropy implored and wept, but then*
> *The Wrong, unblushing trampled on Restraint,*
> *While feeble Law sat by and uttered no complaint.*

In the verse of Whitman we see the beginnings of complexity; he too wrote of wrong, but there was in his rhymes a desire to please. But the split in Negro personality deepened despite the fact that men like Whitman strove to weave color and drama and movement into their poems. A tradition of bitterness has set in; the basic theme is now set, and there is no escape from it. All black lips that now sing pay tribute to the power of oppression. It is true that there was an urge in some black singers to write so that the whites would buy their poems; but in them no less than in others this sense of distance could not be ignored. So, self-consciously, while hiding what they saw and knew to be true, knew to be the real meaning of their lives, some Negro poets deliberately put forth the lighter, the more lyrical, side for *white* consumption.

The most gifted, vivid, and popular black poet to pay tribute to this contradiction was Paul Laurence Dunbar. During his tragically brief career (1872–1906), no sweeter verse than his was written in America:

> *Ere sleep comes down to soothe the weary eyes,*
> *Which all the day with ceaseless care have sought*
> *The magic gold which from the seeker flies;*
> *Ere dreams put on the gown and cap of thought,*
> *And make the waking world of lies—*
> *Of lies most palpable, uncouth, forlorn,*
> *That say life's full of aches and tears and sighs,—*
> *Oh, how with more than dreams the soul is torn,*
> *Ere sleep comes down to soothe the weary eyes.*

Dunbar was the first Negro singer to be really helped by whites; he was fostered by William Dean Howells and his verse was published in the leading periodicals of his time. He labored hard to fill the many commissions that poured in upon him; but through his lyrical songs now and again there broke a sense of the paradox that was his life, as in the following poem:

> *I know why the caged bird sings, ah me,*
> *When his wing is bruised and his bosom sore,—*
> *When he beats his bars and would be free;*
> *It is not a carol of joy or glee,*
> *But a prayer that he sends from his heart's deep core,*
> *But a plea, that upward to Heaven he flings—*
> *I know why the caged bird sings!*

Then there were times when he spoke out what was in his heart:

> *We smile, but, Oh great Christ, our cries*
> *To thee from tortured souls arise.*
> *We sing, but oh the clay is vile*
> *Beneath our feet, and long the mile;*
> *But let the world dream otherwise,*
> *   We wear the mask.*

Dunbar wrote many novels and poems which had wide sales. But there was a fatal conflict in him; he drank heavily to drown it, to resolve it, and failed. He tells us but little of what he really felt, but we know that he tried to turn his eyes as much as possible from that vision of horror that had claimed the exclusive attention of so many Negro writers, tried to communicate with his country as a man. Perhaps no other Negro writer ever demanded more of himself than Dunbar did, and that he achieved so much, that he did manage to wring a little unity out of the blatant contradiction that was his life, is truly remarkable.

The black singers who followed Dunbar, however, cared less about what their *white* friends thought and more about what *they* felt, and they resumed the tradition, sensing that the greatest and deepest meaning of their lives lay in it, that all that was truly human in them had to be wrung from its dark and painful depths.

But let us catch up with ourselves. Expression springs out of an environment, and events modify what is written by molding consciousness. From 1761 to 1900, roughly speaking, a kind of unity knit Negro expression together. But, starting with emancipation, many kinds of stratification took place in Negro life; Negroes became separated from Negroes, the rich from the poor, the ignorant from the educated, the city Negro from the country Negro, and so on.

While this stratification was taking place among Negroes, white attitudes gradually hardened and a still further atomization of Negro life took place, creating personality types far below even those that existed in slavery. Around the turn of the century, two tendencies became evident in Negro expression. I'll call the first tendency: The Narcissistic Level, and the second tendency I'll call: The Forms of Things Unknown, which consists of folk utterances, spirituals, blues, work songs, and folklore.

These two main streams of Negro expression—The Narcissistic Level and The Forms of Things Unknown—remained almost distinctly apart until the depression struck our country in 1929, when once again there surged up a tendency toward unity in Negro thought and feeling, though the traditional sense of distance still prevailed. This division in Negro life can be described in psychological as well as in class terms. It can be said there were Negroes who naively accepted what their lives were, lived more or less unthinkingly in their environment, mean as they found it, and sought escape either in religion, migration, alcohol, or in what I've called a sensualization of their sufferings in the form of jazz and blues and folk and work songs.

Then there were those who hoped and felt that they would ultimately be accepted in their native land as free men, and they put forth their claims in a language that their nation had given them. These latter were more or less always middle class in their ideology. But it was among the migratory Negro workers that one found, rejected and ignorant though they were, strangely positive manifestations of expression, original contributions in terms of form and content.

Middle-class Negroes borrowed the forms of the culture which they strove to make their own, but the migratory Negro worker improvised his cultural forms and filled those forms with a content wrung from a bleak and barren environment, an environment that stung, crushed, all but killed him.

But, before I tell of these migratory voices, let me explain what I mean by the Narcissistic Level of expression that prevailed among middle-class Negro writers, say, from 1900 to 1925.

Remember Phillis Wheatley and how she was at one with her country? After her time that oneness was no longer possible with Negroes; race hate and Jim Crowism would not let them feel it.

But there were some few Negroes who, through luck, diligence, and courage, did rise and make the culture of their nation their own even though that nation still rejected them; and, having made the culture of their nation their own, they hurled pleading words against the deaf ears of white America until the very meaning of their lives came to be in telling how and what the rejection which their country leveled against them made them feel. You remember the Greek legend of Narcissus who was condemned by Nemesis to fall in love with his own reflection which he saw in the water of a fountain? Well, the middle-class Negro writers were condemned by America to stand before a Chinese Wall and wail that they were like other men, that they felt as others felt. It is this relatively static stance of emotion that I call The Narcissistic Level. These Negroes were in every respect the equal of whites; they were valid examples of personality types of Western culture; but they lived in a land where even insane white people were counted above them. They were men whom constant rejection had rendered impacted of feeling, choked of emotion. During the first quarter of this century, these men, Trotter, DuBois, Washington, etc., fought as the Negro had never fought before for equal rights, but they fought in vain. It is true that when their voices reached the ears of many philanthropic whites, they did win a few concessions which helped Negro institutions to exist. But the irony in the efforts of these Negroes was that the gains they won fastened ever tighter around their necks the shackles of Jim Crowism. For example, every new hospital, clinic, and school that was built was a *Negro* hospital, a *Negro* clinic, a *Negro* school! So, though Negroes were slowly rising out of their debased physical conditions, the black ghettos were growing ever larger; instead of racial segregation lessening, it grew, deepened, spread. Today, Jim Crow institutions have fastened themselves organically upon the free soil of the nation and the Black Belt is commonplace.

While this was happening in the upper levels of Negro life, a chronic and grinding poverty set in in the lower depths. Semi-literate black men and women drifted from city to city, ever seeking what was not to be found: jobs, homes, love—a chance to live as free men. . . . Millions swarmed from the plantations to the small towns and cities of the South; and then from the southern towns and cities they flooded the northern industrial centers. Bereft of family life, poverty-stricken, bewildered, they moved restlessly amidst the highest industrial civilization the world has ever known, in it but not of it, unable to respond to the vivid symbols of power of an alien culture that met their eyes at every turn.

Because I feel personally identified with the migrant Negro, his folk songs, his ditties, his wild tales of bad men; and because my own life was forged in the depths in which they live, I'll tell first of the Forms of Things Unknown. Numerically, this formless folk utterance accounts for the great majority of the Negro people in the United States, and it is my conviction that the subject matter of future novels and poems resides in the lives of these nameless millions. There are two pools of this black folk expression: The sacred and the secular. (Let me recall to you quickly that we are now far beyond the world of Phillis Wheatley; she was an integrated individual, at one with her culture; we are now dealing with people who have lost their individuality, whose reactions are fiercely elemental, whose shattered lives are burdened by impulses they cannot master or control.) It is from the sacred songs of the plantation that we get the pathos of:

Sometimes I feel like a motherless child
Sometimes I feel like a motherless child
Sometimes I feel like a motherless child
A long ways from home . . .
A long ways from home . . .

And then there is the nostalgia for another world, an unappeasable longing to escape a painful life:

Swing low, sweet chariot,
Coming for to carry me home . . .

And here is a paradoxical note of triumphant defeat:

Steal away, steal away, steal away to Jesus,
Steal away, steal away home,
I ain't got long to stay here . . .

And here is militancy disguised in religious imagery:

Joshua fit the battle of Jericho,
Jericho, Jericho,
Joshua fit the battle of Jericho,
And the walls came tumbling down . . .

And tender, timid despair:

Oh, they whipped him up the hill, up the hill, up the hill
Oh, they whipped him up the hill, up the hill, up the hill

> *Oh, they whipped him up the hill, and he never said a*
> *   mumbling word,*
> *He just hung down his head, and he cried . . .*

Outright rebellion is couched in Biblical symbols; is it not plain that the Negro is a Negro even in his religion, that his consciousness of being a rejected American seeps into his worship, his prayers . . . ?

> *If I had-a my way,*
> *I'd tear this building down.*
> *Great God, then, if I had-a my way*
> *If I had-a my way, little children,*
> *If I had-a my way,*
> *I'd tear this building down . . .*

These authorless utterances sprang spontaneously from the lips of slaves and they remain the single most significant contribution of folk and religious songs to our national culture. It was through the door of religion that the American Negro first walked into the house of Western culture, and it was through religious symbols that he has given voice to his most poignant yearnings. And yet, instead of his songs being mystical or metaphysical, they are simply and directly wish fulfillments, projections of his longings to escape his chains and blows.

And even when the Negro turns from the sacred to the secular, he seems unable to escape the burdens and consciousness of his racial plight that determines all, making him feel that he is a Negro before he is a man. Recognition of wrong comes even in lilting ditties:

> *We raise the wheat,*
> *They give us the corn;*
> *We bake the bread,*
> *They give us the crust;*
> *We sift the meal,*
> *They give us the husk;*
> *We peel the meat,*
> *They give us the skin;*
> *And that's the way*
> *We skin the pot,*
> *They give us the liquor,*
> *And they say that's good enough for nigger.*

We get hints of probable dirty work of slaves against their masters in this humorous ditty which tells of a master who promised freedom to a slave, and it brought about an attempt on the part of the slave to hasten his day of liberation:

> *Yes, my old master promise me;*
> *But his papers didn't leave me free.*
> *A dose of poison helped him along.*
> *May the Devil preach his funeral song.*

Even at the very bottom of Negro life there existed a knowledge of the dual existence they were forced to live; in this work song, a laborer states the problem:

> *Me and my captain don't agree*
> *But he don't know, 'cause he don't ask me*
> *He don't know, he don't know my mind*
> *When he sees me laughing*
> *Laughing to keep from crying*
> *Got one mind for white folks to see*
> *Another for what I know is me . . .*

The impulses that prodded so many millions of southern Negroes to leave the plantations for the cities of the South, and the dissatisfaction that drove so many other millions from the cities of the South to the industrial centers of the North are summed up in the "Backwater Blues" as sung by Bessie Smith:

> *Then I went an' stood up on some high ol' lonesome hill*
> *I went an' stood up on some high ol' lonesome hill*
> *An' looked down on the house where I used to live*
>
> *Backwater blues done cause me to pack mah things and go*
> *Backwater blues done cause me to pack mah things and go*
> *Cause mah house fell down an' I cain' live there no mo'*

Many of them knew that their hope was hopeless, and it was out of this that the blues was born, the apex of sensual despair. A strange and emotional joy is found in contemplating the blackest aspects of life:

> *I'm going down to the river, set down on the ground*
> *I'm going down to the river, set down on the ground*
> *If the blues overtake me, I'll jump overboard and drown*

And what the psychoanalysts call ambivalence is put forward by illiterate Negroes in terms that would have shocked Dr. Freud:

I'm going to buy me a shotgun long as I am tall
I'm going to buy me a shotgun just as long as I am tall
I'm going to shoot my woman just to see her fall . . .

In "Dink's Blues" we hear a death-wish vented against white people:

I wish to God that east-bound train would wreck
I wish to God that east-bound train would wreck
Kill the engineer, break the fireman's neck . . .

Lower-class Negroes cannot be accused of possessing repressions or inhibitions! Out of the folk songs of the migrant Negro there has come one form of Negro folklore that makes even Negroes blush a little among themselves when it is mentioned. These songs, sung by more adult Negroes than would willingly admit it, sum up the mood of despairing rebellion. They are called *The Dirty Dozens.* Their origin is obscure but their intent is plain and unmistakable. They jeer at life; they leer at what is decent, holy, just, wise, straight, right, and uplifting. I think that it is because, from the Negro's point of view, it is the right, the holy, the just, that crush him in America. I'm sure that we've reached that point in our public life where straight, documentary facts can be presented without someone saying that they are in bad taste. I insist upon presenting *The Dirty Dozens* because they possess a meaning far beyond that of the merely risqué.

But first, picture to yourselves a vast mass of semi-literate people living amidst the most complex, the most highly industrialized, nation on earth, and try to understand these contradictions: The Negro's shattered families lived amidst the most stable families of the land; his broken speech was uttered in the same neighborhoods where white people spoke flawlessly. The Negro had but to turn his eyes from his unpainted wooden shack and he saw the painted homes of whites. Out of this organic contradiction, the Negro hurled his hardest words against the white world in which he lived. He had no family life; well, why worry about that? Was it not the family life of whites above him that was crushing him? These Negroes seemed to have said to themselves: "Well, if what is happening to me is right, then, dammit, anything is right."

The Dirty Dozens extol incest, celebrate homosexuality; even

God's ability to create a rational world is naively but scornfully
doubted, as in the following ditty:

> *God made Him an elephant*
> *And He made him stout*
> *But He wasn't satisfied*
> *'Til He made him a snout*
> *And He made his snout*
> *Just as long as a rail*
> *But He wasn't satisfied*
> *'Til He made him a tail*
> *He made his tail*
> *Just to fan the flies*
> *But He wasn't satisfied*
> *'Til he made him some eyes*
> *He made his eyes*
> *Just to look on the grass*
> *But He wasn't satisfied*
> *'Til He made his yes yes yes*
> *He made his yes yes yes*
> *But He didn't get it fixed*
> *But He wasn't satisfied*
> *'Til he made him six*
> *He made him six, Lord,*
> *And He made them well*
> *So you know by that*
> *That the elephant caught hell . . .*

This is not atheism; this is beyond atheism; these people do
not walk and talk with God; they walk and talk about Him. The
seduction of virgins is celebrated with amoral delight:

> *Why your little sister*
> * Why she ask me to kiss her*
> *I told her to wait*
> * 'Til she got a little bigger*
> *When she got a little bigger*
> * She said I could kiss her*
> *You know by that, boys,*
> * That I didn't miss her*
> *Now she's a dirty mistreat*
> * A robber and a cheat*
> *Slip her in the dozens*

> *Her papa is her cousin*
> *And her mama do the Lordy Lord . . .*

That white men who claimed that they followed the precepts of Christ should have been guilty of so much cruelty forced some nameless black bard to utter:

> *Our Father, who art in heaven*
> *White man owe me 'leven, and pay me seven,*
> *Thy kingdom come, thy will be done*
> *And ef I hadn't tuck that, I wouldn't got none.*

Do you catch the echoes of Communism here? If you do, you are suffering from an auditory illusion; for that irreverent ditty was written long before Communism was conceived of, long before Karl Marx wrote *Das Kapital*. If there's any Communism in that verse, it is of a divine origin.

A Negro woman exults consciously and publicly in the disorganization of life which America forces her to live:

> *My floor is dirty and my house ain't never clean*
> *My floor is dirty and my house ain't never clean*
> *Ain't got no husband but I got a dozen married men . . .*

Still another woman's knowledge of the sexual prowess of all the men living in her neighborhood reveals a compulsive promiscuity which she unshamedly and lyrically advertises:

> *There's nineteen men livin' in mah neighborhood*
> *Nineteen men livin' in mah neighborhood*
> *Eighteen of them are fools, an' de other ain' no doggone*
>   *good*

Well, what do you want? What can you expect from men and women who have been driven out of life?

But there are times when these torrid moods of meanness are lifted by gifted writers to the level of social and political direction, as in the bitter, fighting lyrics of Warren Cuney, who sums up what Jim Crowism in wartime means to Negroes:

> *Well, airplanes flying across the land and the sea*
> *Everybody's flying but a Negro like me*
> *Uncle Sam says your place is on the ground*
> *When I fly my airplanes I want no Negroes around*
> *The same thing for the navy when ships go to sea*
> *All they got is a mess-boy's job for me . . .*

But what was happening, so to speak, upstairs, when the Negro migrants were venting their spleen against the world? If you remember, we left the Negro middle-class writers standing before the Chinese Wall of America, narcissistically preoccupied with their feelings, saying, "If you prick me, I bleed; if you put fire to me, I burn; I am like you who exclude me. . . ." Perhaps the most graphic and lyrical of these men was W. E. B. DuBois; indeed, one might say that it was with him that the Negro complaint reached almost religious heights of expression. DuBois prays to God in public:

> *Listen to us, Thy children: our faces dark with doubt are made a mockery in Thy sanctuary. With uplifted hands we front Thy heaven, O God, crying;*
> *We beseech Thee to hear us, good Lord!*

And then, vehemently, in Old Testament style:

> *Doth not this justice of hell stink in Thy nostrils, O God? How long shall the mounting flood of innocent blood roar in Thine ears and pound in our hearts for vengeance? Pile the pale frenzy of blood-crazed brutes who do such deeds high on Thine altar, Jehovah, and burn it in hell forever and forever.*
> *Forgive us, good Lord! we know not what we say!*

Moods such as these have suffused the many books of DuBois, and where the mood is absent *per se*, we find it projected in terms of history, fiction, verse. Here we see the outright curse of the Negro migrant lifted to a hymn of bitterness; here we see the long, drawn-out moan of the blues turned into a phrase of lament; here we see the brutal cynicism of illiterate Negroes converted into irony; here we watch the jerky lines of *The Dirty Dozens* transmute themselves into the surging rhythms of free verse; here indeed we see Pushkin and Dumas turned into raging, livid demons! Poor Phillis Wheatley would have burned to a cinder if such searing emotions had ever entered her frail body.

Following DuBois, James Weldon Johnson lifted his voice; listen to Johnson, as conservative a Negro as ever lived in America; but his eyes were riveted upon this:

> *Quick! Chain him to that oak! It will resist*
> *The fire much longer than this slender pine.*
> *Now bring the fuel! Pile it 'round him! Wait!*
> *Pile not so fast or high, or we shall lose*
> *The agony and terror in his face.*
> *And now the torch! Good fuel that! the flames*

Already leap head-high. Ha! hear that shriek!
And there's another! wilder than the first.
Fetch water! Water! Pour a little on
The fire, lest it should burn too fast. Hold so!
Now let it slowly blaze again. See there!
He squirms! He groans! His eyes bulge wildly out,
Searching around in vain appeal for help!

Was it otherwise with other writers? No. You've seen the images of horror that a conservative like James Weldon Johnson evoked. Yet, I, coming from an entirely different social stratum, wove the same vision of horror into another pattern in a poem called "Between the World and Me":

And one morning while in the woods I suddenly stumbled upon the thing,
Stumbled upon it in a grassy clearing guarded by scaly oaks and elms.
And the sooty details of the scene rose, thrusting themselves between the world and me . . .

There was a design of white bones slumbering forgottenly upon a cushion of gray ashes.
There was a charred stump of a sapling pointing a blunt finger accusingly at the sky.
There were torn tree limbs, tiny veins of burnt leaves, and a scorched coil of greasy hemp;
A vacant shoe, an empty tie, a ripped shirt, a lonely hat, and a pair of trousers stiff with black blood.
And upon the trampled grass were buttons, dead matches, butt-ends of cigars and cigarettes, peanut shells, a drained gin-flask, and a whore's lipstick;
Scattered traces of tar, restless arrays of feathers, and the lingering smell of gasoline.
And through the morning air the sun poured yellow surprise into the eye sockets of a stony skull . . .

And while I stood there my mind was frozen with a cold pity for the life that was gone.
The ground gripped my feet and my heart was circled with icy walls of fear—
The sun died in the sky; a night wind muttered in the grass and fumbled with leaves in the trees; the woods poured forth the hungry yelping of hounds; the darkness

screamed with thirsty voices; and the witnesses rose and lived:
The dry bones stirred, rattled, lifted, melting themselves into my bones.
The gray ashes formed flesh firm and black, entering into my flesh.
The gin-flask passed from mouth to mouth; cigars and cigarettes glowed, the whore smeared the lipstick red upon her lips.
And a thousand faces swirled around me, clamoring that my life be burned . . .

And then they had me, stripped me, battering my teeth into my throat till I swallowed my own blood.
My voice was drowned in the roar of their voices, and my black wet body slipped and rolled in their hands as they bound me to the sapling.
And my skin clung to the bubbling hot tar, falling from me in patches,
And the down and the quills of the white feathers sank into my raw flesh, and I moaned in my agony.
Then my blood was cooled mercifully, cooled by a baptism of gasoline.
And in a blaze of red I leaped to the sky as pain rose like water, boiling my limbs.
Panting, begging, I clutched childlike, clutched to the hot sides of death.
Now I am dry bones and my face a stony skull staring in yellow surprise at the sun . . .

Did ever in history a race of men have for so long a time the same horror before their eyes? I know that for short periods horrors like this have come to men, but they ended at last; I know that in war horror fills the minds of all, but even wars pass. The horrors that confront Negroes stay in peace and war, in winter and summer, night and day.

Futility now enters the heart of the urban Negro; from the teeming city of Chicago Fenton Johnson comes with his testimony:

I am tired of work; I am tired of building up somebody else's civilization.
Let us take a rest, M'Lissy Jane.
I will go down to the Last Chance Saloon, drink a gallon or two of gin, shoot a game or two of dice and sleep the rest of the night on one of Mike's barrels . . .

Then again racial bitterness enters:

> *Throw the children into the river; civilization has given us too many. It is better to die than grow up and find out that you are colored.*
> *Pluck the stars out of the heavens. The stars mark our destiny. The stars marked my destiny.*
> *I am tired of civilization.*

And then Claude McKay reaches a white-hot pitch of passion with:

> *Your door is shut against my tightened face,*
> *And I am sharp as steel with discontent;*
> *But I possess the courage and the grace*
> *To bear my anger proudly and unbent.*
> *The pavement slabs burn loose beneath my feet,*
> *A chafing savage, down the decent street;*
> *A passion rends my vitals as I pass*
> *Where boldly shines your shuttered door of glass.*
> *Oh, I must search for wisdom every hour,*
> *Deep in my wrathful bosom sore and raw,*
> *And find in it the superhuman power*
> *To hold me to the letter of your law!*
> *Oh, I must keep my heart inviolate*
> *Against the potent poison of your hate!*

Remember that white faces were hovering in the minds of black men when they wrote those lines; this is their judgment upon you and your world. Are we not a long, long way from the innocence of Phillis Wheatley? To say that Claude McKay is a rebel is to understate it; his rebellion is a way of life.

Even when Negro poets become sensually lyrical now, they cannot escape the horrible vision of their life in America, as we can see in these lines of Jean Toomer:

> *O Negro slaves, dark purple ripened plums,*
> *Squeezed, and bursting in the pine-wood air,*
> *Passing, before they strip the old tree bare*
> *One plum was saved for me, one seed becomes*
> *An everlasting song, a singing tree,*
> *Caroling softly souls of slavery*
> *What they were, and what they are to me,*
> *Caroling softly souls of slavery.*

Even at the apex of lyrical utterance, color and race form the core of meaning for Countee Cullen, as in "Heritage":

What is Africa to me:
Copper sun or scarlet sea,
Jungle star or jungle track,
Strong bronzed men, or regal black
Women from whose loins I sprang
When the birds of Eden sang?

The conflict between the human needs of the Negro and what is demanded of him by white America reaches a point that all but overwhelms the poet:

All day long and all night through,
One thing only must I do:
Quench my pride, and cool my blood,
Lest I perish in the flood. . . .

No less than a black clergyman, James D. Corrothers, likens the plight of the Negro to that of Christ:

To be a Negro in a day like this
    Demands forgiveness. Bruised with blow on blow,
Betrayed, like Him whose woe-dimmed eyes gave bliss
    Still must one succor those who brought one low,
To be a Negro in a day like this.

George Leonard Allen again stresses the Biblical theme in an attempt to awaken compassion by reminding America that she acts like Pilate toward her darker brother:

Lord, 'twas not I that slew my guiltless brother
    Without a cause, save that his skin was black!
Not my fierce hate, but that of many another
    Stole what man's puny strength cannot give back!

In a bitter, masochistic mood of self-laceration a black poet, Frank Horne, tries to see his people and himself through white American eyes:

Little Black Boy
Chased down the street—
"Nigger, nigger, never die
Black face and shiny eye,
Nigger . . . nigger . . . nigger."

A mood of poignant nostalgia makes Arna Bontemps evoke:

The golden days are gone. Why do we wait
So long upon the marble steps, blood
Falling from our open wounds? and why
Do our black faces search the sky?

But despair is not the entire picture. Each new generation of Negro writers lived in an environment that was almost the same until World War I; but that war provided the first real break in this continuity of hopelessness. Out of the restlessness left in the wake of World War I, Soviet Russia rose and sent out her calls to the oppressed. Until that time the American Negro had to depend upon white Americans for a definition of his problem, of his position, had to accept the friendship of white liberals. For three centuries white America told the Negro that nowhere on earth would he be as highly regarded as in America; and the Negro had to fight and plead within the frame of reference of that charitable advice. But suddenly that spell was broken forever. Alien ideologies gripped men's minds and the most receptive minds in our land were those of rejected Negroes. Color consciousness lost some of its edge and was replaced in a large measure by class consciousness; with the rise of an integral working-class movement, a new sense of identification came to the American Negro.

Then, for the first time since Phillis Wheatley, the Negro began to make a wholehearted commitment to a new world; after wandering for three hundred years, he found a new sense of oneness, a new integration; it was possible once more for him to write out of the shared hopes and aspirations of millions of people. Phillis Wheatley visited the headquarters of George Washington, the father of our republic; Langston Hughes visited the headquarters of Lenin, the father of the Soviet Republic!

In the work of poets like Davis, Tolson, Hughes, Brown, Walker, Brooks, and Bontemps this new vision was reflected. One of the first lyrical-sounding voices of this new period was that of Langston Hughes; here, in plain images, we get, not complaints and pleas, but statements and demands:

Let America be America again,
Let it be the dream it used to be,
Let it be the pioneer in the plain,
Seeking a home where he himself is free. . . .

Out of a mood of bitter, political anger, he says:

Good morning, Revolution,
You're the very best friend I ever had;
Come on; let's pal around together . . .

Poet Robert E. Hayden imagines the dying testimony of
Gabriel, an executed slave, in these lyrical but bitter terms:

I see a thousand
Thousand slaves
Rising up
From forgotten graves
And their wounds drip flame
On slavery's ground,
And their chains shake Dixie
With a thunder sound.

Gabriel, Gabriel
The end is nigh,
What do you wish
Before you die?
That rebellion suckle
The slave-mother's breast
And black men
Never, never rest
Till slavery's pillars
Lie splintered in dust
And slavery's chains
Lie eaten with rust.

Sterling Brown hints at what the Negro would do if the numerical odds were more nearly equal:

They don't come [at us] by ones
They don't come by twos
But they come by tens
They got the judges
They got the lawyers
They got the law
  They don't come by ones
They got the sheriffs
They got the deputies
  They don't come by twos

> *They got the shotguns*
> *They got the rope*
>   *We get the justice*
>   *In the end*
> *And they come by tens. . . .*

Out of the Deep South, out of Texas, Melvin Tolson lifts his voice higher than that of Martin Dies and says:

> *Out of the dead-ends of poverty,*
> *Through the wilderness of Superstition,*
> *Across the barricades of Jim Crowism . . .*
> *We advance!*
> *With the peoples of the world . . .*
> *We advance!*

Margaret Walker, a Negro girl who started writing at about the age when Phillis Wheatley began writing, says in images that Phillis Wheatley could not imagine:

> *Let a new earth rise. Let another world be born. Let a bloody peace be written in the sky. Let a second generation full of courage issue forth, let a people loving freedom come to growth, let a beauty full of healing and a strength of final clenching be the pulsing in our spirits and our blood. Let the martial songs be written, let dirges disappear. Let a race of men now rise and take control!*

Out of this sense of identification with the workers of other lands, I too wrote:

> *I am black and I have seen black hands*
> *Raised in fists of revolt, side by side with the white fists of*
>   *white workers.*
> *And some day—and it is only this which sustains me—*
> *Some day there shall be millions of them,*
> *On some red day in a burst of fists on a new horizon!*

Now, I'm not naive. I know that many of you are shaking your heads and wondering what value there is in writing like that; you may feel that we ought to write like Phillis Wheatley, Alexander Dumas, or Alexander Pushkin. Well, we simply cannot; our world is not their world. We write out of what life gives us in the form of experience. And there is a value in what we Negro writers say. Is it not clear to you that the American Negro is the only group in our nation that consistently and passionately raises the question of freedom? This is a service to America and to the world. More than this: The voice of the American Negro is rapidly becoming the most representative voice of America and of oppressed people anywhere in the world today.

Let me remind you that during the past twenty-five years the great majority of the human race has undergone *experiences comparable to those which Negroes in* America have undergone for three centuries! These people, Russians, Germans, French, Chinese, Indians, Danes, Spaniards, suddenly heard a voice speaking of their wrongs. From the Argentine, Brazil, Sweden, Norway, England, France, and India have come questions about the American Negro; they want to know how we live; they want our testimony since we live here amidst the greatest pretense of democracy on earth. And we Negroes are answering, straight, honestly.

So, the voice that America rejected is finding a home at last, a home such as was never dreamed of.

But our hope is steeped in a sense of sober tragedy. In the final pages of a book I wrote called *12 Million Black Voices,* I tried to indicate the quality of that hope when I said:

"We black folk, our history and our present being, are a mirror of all the manifold experiences of America. What we want, what we represent, what we endure, is what America *is.* If we black folk perish, America will perish. If America has forgotten her past, then let her look into the mirror of our consciousness and she will see the *living* past living in the present, for our memories go back, through our black folk of today, through the recollections of our black parents, and through tales of slavery told by our black grandparents, to the time when none of us, black or white, lived in this fertile land.

"The differences between black folk and white folk are not blood or color, and the ties that bind us are deeper than those that separate us. The common road of hope which we have all traveled has brought us into a stronger kinship than any words, laws, or legal claims.

"Look at us and know us and you will know yourselves, for *we* are *you,* looking back at you from the dark mirror of our lives!

"What do we black folk want?

"We want what others have, the right to share in the upward march of American life, the only life we remember or have ever known.

"The Lords of the Land say: 'We will not grant this!'

"We answer: 'We ask you to grant us nothing. We are winning our heritage, though our toll in suffering is great!'

"The Bosses of the Buildings say: 'Your problem is beyond solution!'

"We answer: 'Our problem is being solved. We are crossing the line you dared us to cross, though we pay in the coin of death!'

"The seasons of the plantation no longer dictate the lives of many of us; hundreds of thousands of us are moving into the sphere of conscious history.

"We are with the new tide. We stand at the crossroads. We watch each new procession. The hot wires carry urgent appeals. Print compels us. Voices are speaking. Men are moving! And we shall be with them. . . ."

I am leaving off my interpretation of the literature of the American Negro at a point which antedates the present by some years. After World War II a list of new names and new themes entered the body of American Negro expression, but not enough time has elapsed for me to subject that new phase of expression to the same kind of analysis that I've used in the foregoing. Not enough perspective exists for me to feel the new trends. Yet the sheer absence of some of the old qualities is enough to allow one to draw some inferences. For example, in the work of Chester Himes, Ralph Ellison, James Baldwin, Ann Petry, Frank Yerby, Gwendolyn Brooks, etc., one finds a sharp loss of lyricism, a drastic reduction of the racial content, a rise in preoccupation with urban themes and subject matter both in the novel and the poem. Why is this?

Again I remind you that an understanding of Negro expression cannot be arrived at without a constant reference to the environment which cradles it. Directly after World War II, the United States and Soviet Russia emerged as the two dominant world powers. This meant a lessening of the influence of the ideology of Marxism in America and a frantic attempt on the part of white Americans to set their racial house somewhat in order in the face of world criticism. America's assumption of world leadership brought her racial problem to the fore in the mind of the world and the resulting shame and self-consciousness on the part of white Americans have resulted in several dramatic alterations in the Negro's relationship to the American scene. The recent decision of the United States Supreme Court to integrate the schools of America on a basis of racial equality is one, but by no means the chief, change that has come over the American outlook. Naturally this effort on the part of the American nation to assimilate the Negro has had its effect upon Negro literary expression.

I've heard some people express the view that they do not like the new literary expression of the Negro as much as they admired the old. This is a sentimental approach. What I've discussed with you in this lecture certainly should have proved that the mode and pitch of Negro literary expression would alter as soon as the attitude of the nation toward the Negro changed.

At the present moment there is no one dominant note in Negro literary expression. As the Negro merges into the main stream of American life, there might result actually a disappearance of Negro literature as such. If that happens, it will mean that those conditions of life that formerly defined what was "Negro" have ceased to exist, and it implies that Negroes are Negroes because they are treated as Negroes. Indeed, I'd say to you here who listen to my words that I could convert any of you into Negroes, in a psychological sense, in a period of six months. That is, I could, by subjecting you to certain restrictions, hatreds, hostilities, etc., make you express yourselves as the American Negro formerly did.

One last thought. . . . As Negro literary expression changes, one feels that American liberal thought has sustained a loss. What, then, was the relation of Negro expression to liberal thought in the United States? The Negro was a kind of conscience to that body of liberal opinion. The liberals were ridden with a sense of guilt, and the Negro's wailing served as something that enabled the liberal to define his relationship to the American scene. Today the relationship between liberals and Negroes is hard to define. Indeed, one feels that the liberals kind of resent the new trend of independence which the Negro exhibits. But this is inevitable; the Negro, as he learns to stand on his own feet and express himself not in purely racial, but human terms, will launch criticism upon his native land which made him feel a sense of estrangement that he never wanted. This new attitude could have a healthy effect upon the culture of the United States. At long last, maybe a merging of Negro expression with American expression will take place. As that process develops and continues, you may watch it, using the few concepts that I've discussed with you. In that case I feel that its human drama will have, perhaps, some meaning for you.

If the expression of the American Negro should take a sharp turn toward strictly racial themes, then you will know by that token that we are suffering our old and ancient agonies at the hands of our white American neighbors. If, however, our expression broadens, assumes the common themes and burdens of literary expression which are the heritage of all men, then by that token you will know that a humane attitude prevails in America towards us. And a gain in humaneness in America is a gain in humaneness for us all. When that day comes, there will exist one more proof of the oneness of man, of the basic unity of human life on this earth.

> *American Negro Literature*
> J. SAUNDERS REDDING

THERE IS this about literature by American Negroes—it has uncommon resilience. Three times within this century it has been done nearly to death: once by indifference, once by opposition, and once by the unbounded enthusiasm of its well-meaning friends.

By 1906, Charles W. Chesnutt, the best writer of prose fiction the race had produced, was silent; Paul Laurence Dunbar, the most popular poet, was dead. After these two, at least in the general opinion, there were no other Negro writers. Booker Washington had published *Up from Slavery*, but Washington was no writer—he was the orator and the organizer of the march to a questionable new Canaan. The poetic prose of Du Bois, throbbing in *The Souls of Black Folk*, had not yet found its audience. Polemicists like Monroe Trotter, Kelly, Miller and George Forbes were faint whispers in a lonesome wood. Indifference had stopped the ears of all but the most enlightened who, as often as not, were derisively labeled "nigger lovers."

But this indifference had threatened even before the turn of the century. Dunbar felt it, and the purest stream of his lyricism was made bitter and all but choked by it. Yearning for the recognition of his talent as it expressed itself in the pure English medium, he had to content himself with a kindly, but condescending praise of his dialect pieces. Time and again he voiced the sense of frustration brought on by the neglect of what he undoubtedly considered his best work. Writing dialect, he told James Weldon Johnson, was "the only way he could get them to listen to him." His literary friend and sponsor, William D. Howells, at that time probably the most influential critic in America, passing over Dunbar's verse in pure English with only a glance, urged him to write "of his own race in its own accents of our English."

During Dunbar's lifetime, his pieces in pure English appeared

more or less on sufferance. The very fo...   1901 edition of
Lyrics of the Hearthside, the book in ...   of his non-dialect
poetry was published, suggests this. No fancy binding on this book,
no handsome paper, no charming, illustrative photographs. *Lyrics
of the Hearthside* was the least publicized of all his books of poetry,
and four lines from his "The Poet" may tell why.

> He sang of love when earth was young,
>   And love itself was in his lays,
>   But, ah, the world it turned to praise
> A jingle in a broken tongue.

Enough has been said about the false concepts, the stereotypes
which were effective—and to some extent are still effective—in
white America's thinking about the Negro for the point not to be
labored here. History first, and then years of insidious labor to perpetuate what history had wrought, created these stereotypes. According to them, the Negro was a buffoon, a harmless child of nature, a dangerous despoiler (the concepts were contradictory), an
irresponsible beast of devilish cunning—soulless, ambitionless and
depraved. The Negro, in short, was a higher species of some creature that was not quite man.

What this has done to writing by American Negroes could
easily be imagined, even without the documentation, which is
abundant. No important critic of writing by American Negroes
has failed to note the influence of the concept upon it. Sterling
Brown, one of the more searching scholars in the field, gives it
scathing comment in "The Negro Author and His Publisher."
James Weldon Johnson touches upon it in his preface to the 1931
edition of his anthology, but he does so even more cogently in
"The Negro Author's Dilemma." The introduction to Countee Cullen's *Caroling Dusk* is a wry lament over it. In *The New Negro*,
Alain Locke expresses the well-founded opinion that the Negro
"has been a stock figure perpetuated as an historical fiction partly
in innocent sentimentalism, partly in deliberate reactionism."

There can be no question as to the power of the traditional
concepts. The Negro writer reacted to them in one of two ways.
Either he bowed down to them, writing such stories as would do
them no violence; or he went to the opposite extreme and wrote
for the purpose of invalidating, or at least denying, the tradition.
Dunbar did the former. Excepting only a few, his short stories
depict Negro characters as whimsical, simple, folksy, not-too-

bright souls, all of whose social problems are little ones, and all of whose emotional cares can be solved by the intellectual or spiritual equivalent of a stick of red peppermint candy. It is of course significant that three of his four novels are not about Negroes at all, and the irony of depicting himself as a white youth in his spiritual autobiography, *The Uncalled*, needs no comment.

Charles Chesnutt's experience is also to the point. When his stories began appearing in the *Atlantic Monthly* in 1887, it was not generally known that their author was a Negro. Stories like "The Gray Wolf's Ha'nt" and "The Goophered Grapevine" were so detached and objective that the author's race could not have been detected from a reading of them. The editor of the *Atlantic Monthly*, Walter H. Page, fearing that public acknowledgment of it would do the author's work harm, was reluctant to admit that Chesnutt was a Negro, and the fact of his race was kept a closely guarded secret for a decade.

It was this same fear that led to the rejection of Chesnutt's first novel, *The House behind the Cedars*, for "a literary work by an American of acknowledged color was a doubtful experiment . . . entirely apart from its intrinsic merit." The reception of Chesnutt's later books—those that came after 1900—was to prove that literary works by an "American of color" were more than doubtful experiments. *The Colonel's Dream* and *The Marrow of Tradition* did not pay the cost of the paper and the printing. They were honest probings at the heart of a devilish problem; they were, quite frankly, propaganda. But the thing that made the audience of the day indifferent to them was their attempt to override the concepts that were the props of the dialect tradition. Had Chesnutt not had a reputation as a writer of short stories (which are, anyway, his best work), it is likely that his novels would not have been published at all.

The poetry of Dunbar and the prose of Chesnutt proved that even with the arbitrary limitations imposed upon them by historical convention, Negro writers could rise to heights of artistic expression. They could even circumvent the convention, albeit self-consciously, and create credible white characters in a credible white milieu.

After about 1902, indifference began to crystallize into opposition to the culture-conscious, race-conscious Negro seeking honest answers to honest questions. It was opposition to the Negro's democratic ambitions which were just then beginning to burgeon. It was opposition to the Negro who was weary of his role of clown, scapegoat, doormat. And it was, of course, opposition to the Negro writer who was honest and sincere and anxious beyond the bounds of superimposed racial polity.

There is danger here of over-simplifying a long and complex story. Even with the advantage of hindsight, it is hard to tell what is cause and what effect. But let us have a look at some of the more revealing circumstances. In 1902 came Thomas Dixon's *The Leopard's Spots*, and three years later *The Clansman*. They were both tremendously popular. In 1906 there were race riots in Georgia and Texas, in 1908 in Illinois. . . . By this later year, too, practically all of the Southern states had disfranchised the Negro and made color caste legal. . . . The Negro's talent for monkeyshines had been exploited on the stage, and coon songs (some by James Weldon Johnson and his brother!) had attained wide popularity. Meantime, in 1904, Thomas Nelson Page had published the bible of reactionism, *The Negro, the Southerner's Problem*. And, probably most cogent fact of all, Booker Washington had reached the position of undisputed leader of American Negroes by advocating a racial policy strictly in line with the traditional concept.

There had been a time when the old concept of the Negro had served to ease his burden. He had been laughed at, tolerated, and genially despaired of as hopeless in a modern, dynamic society. White Americans had become used to a myth—had, indeed, convinced themselves that myth was reality. All the instruments of social betterment—schools, churches, lodges—adopted by colored people were the subjects of ribald jokes and derisive laughter. Even the fact that the speeches which Booker Washington was making up and down the country could have been made only by a really intelligent and educated man did not strike them as a contradiction of the concept. And anyway, there was this about Washington: he was at least half-white, and white blood in that proportion excused and accounted for many a thing, including being intelligent, lunching with President Theodore Roosevelt, and getting an honorary degree from Harvard.

Today any objective judgment of Booker Washington's basic notion must be that it was an extension of the old tradition framed in new terms. He preached a message of compromise, of humility, of patience. Under the impact of social change the concept was modified to include the stereotype of the Negro as satisfied peasant, a docile servitor under the stern but kindly eye of the white boss; a creature who had a place, knew it, and would keep it unless he got *bad* notions from somewhere. The merely laughable coon had become also the cheap laborer who could be righteously exploited for his own good and to the greater glory of God. By this addition to the concept, the Negro-white status quo—the condition of inferior-superior caste—could be maintained in the face of profound changes in the general society.

What this meant to the Negro artist and writer was that he must, if he wished an audience, adhere to the old forms and the acceptable patterns. It meant that he must work within the limitations of the concept, or ignore his racial kinship altogether and leave unsounded the profoundest depths of the peculiar experiences which were his by reason of his race. But fewer and fewer Negro writers were content with the limitations. The number of dialect pieces (the term includes the whole tradition) written after 1907 is very small indeed. Among Negro writers the tradition had lost its force and its validity. White writers like Julia Peterkin and Gilmore Millen, and, in a different way, Carl Van Vechten and DuBose Heyward, were to lend it a spurious strength down through the 1920's.

Negro writers of unmistakable talent chose the second course, and some of them won high critical praise for their work in non-racial themes. Their leader was William Stanley Braithwaite. Save only a few essays written at the behest of his friend, W. E. B. Du Bois, nothing that came from his pen had anything about it to mark it as Negro. His leading essays in the Boston *Transcript*, his anthologies of magazine verse, and his own poetry, might just as well have been written by someone with no background in the provocative experience of being colored in America.

Though the other Negro poets of this genre (which was not entirely a genre) developed a kind of dilettantist virtuosity, none carried it to Braithwaite's amazing lengths of self-conscious contrivance. They were simpler and more conventional in their apostasy. Alice Dunbar, the widow of Paul, wrote sonnets of uncommon skill and beauty. Georgia Johnson and Anne Spenser were at home in the formal lyric, and James Weldon Johnson in "The White Witch" and "My City" set a very high standard for his fellow contributors to the *Century Magazine*.

But given the whole web of circumstance—empirical, historic, racial, psychological—these poets must have realized that they could not go on in this fashion. With a full tide of race-consciousness bearing in upon them individually and as a group, they could not go on forever denying their racehood. To try to do this at all was symptomatic of neurotic strain. They could not go on, and they did not. The hardiest of them turned to expression of another kind the moment the pressure was off.

The pressure was not off for another decade and a half. As a matter of fact, it mounted steadily. For all of Booker Washington's popularity and ideological appeal among whites, who had set him up as *the* leader of the Negro race, and for all of his power, there was rebellion against him in the forward ranks of Negroes. Rebellion against Washington meant dissatisfaction with the social and economic goals which he had persuaded white Americans were the proper goals for the Negro race. The whites had not counted on this disaffection, and their reaction to it was willful, blind opposition.

What had happened was that Booker Washington, with the help of the historic situation and the old concept, had so thoroughly captured the minds of most of those white people who were kindly disposed to Negroes that not another Negro had a chance to be heard. Negro schools needing help could get it from rich and powerful whites only through Booker Washington. Negro social thought wanting a sounding board could have it only with the sanction of the Principal of Tuskegee. Negro politicians were helpless without his endorsement. Negro seekers after jobs of any consequence in either public or private capacities begged recommendations from Booker Washington.

This despotic power—and there is scarcely another term for it—was stultifying to many intelligent Negroes, especially in the North. White editors, who would have published anything under the signature of Booker Washington, consistently rejected all but the most innocuous work of other Negroes. Publishers were not interested in the ideas of Negroes unless those ideas conformed to Washington's, or in creative work by and about Negroes unless they fell into the old pattern.

So intelligent, articulate Negroes grew insurgent, and the leader of this insurgence was W. E. B. Du Bois. Nor was his the only voice raised in protest. Charles Chesnutt spoke out, and so did John Hope and Kelly Miller. In 1900 the *Chicago Defender* had been founded, and in 1901 Monroe Trotter's *Boston Guardian.* Courageous as these polemical organs were, they had not yet grown into full effectiveness. Neither had Du Bois, but he was growing fast. By 1903 the Atlanta University Studies of the Negro were coming out regularly under his editorship. In that year he published *The Souls of Black Folk*, which contained the essay "Of Mr. Booker T. Washington and Others," sharply critical of the Tuskegee leader. Du Bois was in on the founding of the National Association for the Advancement of Colored People, and in 1910 he became editor of the new monthly, the *Crisis*.

From the very first the *Crisis* was much more than the official organ of the N.A.A.C.P. It was a platform for the expression of all sorts of ideas that ran counter to the notion of Negro inferiority. Excepting such liberal and nonpopular journals as the *Atlantic Monthly* and *World's Work* and the two or three Negro newspapers that had not been bought or throttled by the "Tuskegee Machine," the *Crisis* was the only voice the Negro had. The opposition to that voice was organized around the person and the philosophy of Booker Washington, and there were times when this opposition all but drowned out the voice.

Nevertheless protestation and revolt were becoming bit by bit more powerful reagents in the social chemistry that produced the New Negro. Year by year more Negroes were transformed—and a lot of them needed transforming. Once James Weldon Johnson himself had written "coon songs" and been content to carol with sweet humility "Lift Every Voice and Sing." When Johnson wrote it in 1900, it had the approval of Booker Washington and became the "Negro National Anthem." Then followed Johnson's period of apostasy and such jejune pieces as "The Glory of the Day Was in Her Face," among others. But in 1912, when he was already forty-one, he wrote the novel *The Autobiography of an Ex-Colored Man*, and in 1917 he cried out bitterly that Negroes must cease speaking "servile words" and must "stand erect and without fear."

Other factors than simple protest contributed to the generation of the New Negro. In the first place, the notions regarding the Old Negro were based on pure myth. The changes occurring at the onset of war in Europe sloughed off some of the emotional and intellectual accretions, and the Negro stood partially revealed for what he was—a fellow whose opportunities had been narrowed by historical fallacies, "a creature of moral debate," but a man pretty much as other men. The war, which made him an inter-sectional migrant, proved that he, too, sought more economic opportunities, the protection of laws even-handedly administered, the enlargement of democracy. He, too, was a seeker for the realities in the American dream.

But when in 1917 the Negro was called upon to protect that

dream with his blood, he revealed himself more fully. He asked questions and demanded answers. Whose democracy? he wanted to know; and why, and wherefore? There followed the promises, which were certainly sincerely meant in the stress of the times. Then came the fighting and dying—and, finally, came a thing called Peace. But in 1919 and after, there were the race riots in the nation's capital, in Chicago, in Chester, Pennsylvania, and in East St. Louis.

By this time the New Negro movement was already stirring massively along many fronts. In the 1920's Negroes cracked through the prejudices that had largely confined them to super-numerary roles on Broadway. *Shuffle Along* was praised as "a sparkling, all-Negro musical of unusual zest and talent." Charles Gilpin's portrayal of the Emperor Jones was the dramatic triumph of 1921. The Garvey Movement, fast getting out of bounds, swept the country like a wildfire. James Weldon Johnson published an anthology of Negro verse. The monumental historical studies of the Negro were begun by Carter Woodson. *The Gift of Black Folk, Color, Fire In the Flint, Weary Blues, God's Trombones, Walls of Jericho,* and *Home to Harlem* had all been published, read, dis-cussed, praised or damned by 1928.

Fortunately some of the talents that produced these works were genuine. Had this not been so, the New Negro movement in art and literature would surely have come to nothing. The best of Johnson, Hughes, Cullen, McKay, Fisher and Du Bois would have lived without the movement, but the movement without them would have gone the way of mah-jongg. Their work considerably furthered the interest of white writers and critics in Negro mate-rial and Negro art expression. Whatever else Eugene O'Neill, Paul Rosenfeld and DuBose Heyward did, they gave validity to the new concept of the Negro as material for serious artistic treatment.

Writing by Negroes beginning with this period and continu-ing into the early thirties had two distinct aspects. The first of these was extremely arty, self-conscious and experimental. Jean Toomer's *Cane* and the "racial-rhythm" and jazz-rhythm poetry of Hughes represent it most notably, while the magazines *Harlem* and *Fire,* which published a quantity of nonsense by writers unheard of since, were its special organs. But the times were themselves arty and experimental. That Negro writers could afford to be touched by these influences was a good sign. It was healthy for them to be blown upon by the winds of literary freedom—even of license—

that blew upon e. e. cummings, Dos Passos and Hemingway. If their self-conscious experimentation proved nothing lasting, it at least worked no harm.

One searches in vain for a phrase to characterize the exact impulses behind the second aspect, which is the one best remembered. It was chock-full of many contradictory things. It showed itself naïve and sophisticated, hysterical and placid, frivolous and sober, free and enslaved. It is simple enough to attribute this contrariety to the effects of the war; but the atavistic release of certain aberrant tendencies in writing by Negroes in this period cannot be matched in all the rest of contemporary writing. The period produced the poignant beauty of Johnson's *God's Trombones* and the depressing futility of Thurman's *The Blacker the Berry*. Within a span of five years McKay wrote the wholesome *Banjo* and the pointlessly filthy *Banana Bottom*. The Hughes who wrote "I've Known Rivers" and "Mother to Son" could also find creative satisfaction in the bizarre "The Cat and the Saxophone."

The mass mind of white America fastened upon the exotic and the atavistic elements and fashioned them into a fad, the commercialized products of which were manufactured in Harlem. That that Harlem itself was largely synthetic did not seem to matter. It was "nigger heaven." There, the advertised belief was, Dullness was dethroned: Gaiety was king! The rebels from Sauk Center and Winesburg, Main Street and Park Avenue, sought carnival in Harlem. "Life," the burden of the dithyrambics ran, "had surge and sweep there, and blood-pounding savagery."

Commercialism was the bane of the Negro renaissance of the twenties. Jazz music became no longer the uninhibited expression of unlearned music-makers, but a highly sophisticated pattern of musical sounds. The "Charleston" and the "Black Bottom" went down to Broadway and Park Avenue. Losing much of its folk value, the blues became the "torch song" eloquently sung by Ruth Etting and Helen Morgan. Negro material passed into the less sincere hands of white artists, and Negro writers themselves, from a high pitch of creation, fell relatively and pathetically silent.

When Richard Wright's *Uncle Tom's Children* was published in 1938, only the least aware did not realize that a powerful new pen was employing itself in stern and terrible material; when *Native Son* appeared in 1940, even the least aware realized it. The first book is a clinical study of human minds under the stress of violence; the second is a clinical study of the social being under the

cumulative effects of organized repression. The two books comple-
ment each other. The theme of both is prejudice, conceptual pre-
judgment—the effects of this upon the human personality. For
Wright deals only incidentally—and for dramatic purposes, and
because of the authenticity of empiricism—with *Negro* and *white*.
"Bigger Thomas was not black all the time," Wright wrote in
"How Bigger Was Born." "He was white, too, and there were
literally millions of him, *everywhere*. . . . Certain modern experiences were creating types of personalities whose existence ignored racial and national lines. . . ."

Some critics have said that the wide appeal of Wright's work
(it has been translated into a dozen languages) is due to the
sensationalism in it, but one can have serious doubts that the
sensationalism comes off well in translation. What does come off
well is the concept of the primary evil of prejudice. This all peoples would understand, and a delineation of its effects, particular
though it be, interests them in the same way and for the same
reason that love interests them. *Black Boy*, which does not prove
the point, does not deny it either. Even here it may be argued that
Wright delineates and skewers home the point that "to live habitually as a superior among inferiors . . . is a temptation and a
hubris, inevitably deteriorating."

So Wright is a new kind of writer in the ranks of Negroes. He
has extricated himself from the dilemma of writing exclusively for
a Negro audience and limiting himself to a glorified and race-
proud picture of Negro life, and of writing exclusively for a white
audience and being trapped in the old stereotypes and fixed opinions that are bulwarks against honest creation. Negro writers traditionally have been impaled upon one or the other horn of this
dilemma, sometimes in spite of their efforts to avoid it. Langston
Hughes was sincere when he declared, back in the twenties, that
Negro writers cared nothing for the pleasure or displeasure of
either a white or a colored audience—he was sincere, but mistaken.

A writer writes for an audience. Until recently Negro writers
have not believed that the white audience and the colored audience
were essentially alike, because, in fact, they have not been essentially alike. They have been kept apart by a wide socio-cultural
gulf, by differences of concept, by cultivated fears, ignorance, race-
and caste-consciousness. Now that gulf is closing, and Negro
writers are finding it easier to appeal to the two audiences without
being either false to the one or subservient to the other. Thus

Margaret Walker, writing for the two audiences now becoming one, can carry away an important poetry prize with her book *For My People*. No longer fearing the ancient interdiction, Chester Himes in *If He Hollers Let Him Go* and *Lonely Crusade* writes of the sexual attraction a white woman feels for a Negro man. In *Knock on Any Door* Willard Motley can concern himself almost entirely with white characters. On the purely romantic and escapist side, Frank Yerby's *The Foxes of Harrow* sells over a million copies, and *The Vixens* and *The Golden Hawk* over a half-million each. Anthologists no longer think it risky to collect, edit and issue the works of Negro writers.

Facing up to the tremendous challenge of appealing to two audiences, Negro writers are extricating themselves from what has sometimes seemed a terrifying dilemma. Working honestly in the material they know best, they are creating for themselves a new freedom. Though what is happening seems very like a miracle, it has been a long, long time preparing. Writing by American Negroes has never before been in such a splendid state of health, nor had so bright and shining a future before it.

[
    ERNEST KAISER
    The Literature of Harlem
]

ONE WAY of getting at the diverse and myriad writings about the tremendous community of Harlem in New York City is the chronological approach. In this way, the literary and sociological materials can be correlated, to some extent, with the social and economic changes over the decades of this Negro city within a city.

Harlem as a Negro community began around 1900. As early as 1912, the Negro sociologist, scholar and a founder of the Urban League, George Edmund Haynes, did a doctoral dissertation, *The Negro at Work in New York City; a Study of Economic Progress*, published by Columbia University, which included Harlem. James Weldon Johnson's early novel *The Autobiography of an Ex-Coloured Man*, also published in 1912, embraced New York City but did not touch the Negro community. A rather early publication of the National Urban League, founded in 1911, was a pamphlet report *Housing Conditions Among Negroes in Harlem, New York City* in January 1915. Another early piece specifically on the new and growing Harlem community was Rev. Charles Martin's article *The Harlem Negro* in *The A.M.E. Zion Quarterly Review* (Fourth Quarter, 1916).

But Harlem really got its first sizeable population influx and growth from the first great migrations of southern Negroes north during and after World War I. Between 1915 and 1925, over a million Negroes moved north. Rural Negroes flocked to Harlem in the twenties, says Margaret Just Butcher in her book *The Negro in American Culture* (1956) based on materials left by the late Dr. Alain Locke. Several things important to Negro culture generally and to Harlem culture in particular occurred around this period. The pioneering and prolific Negro cultural and social chronicler, Benjamin Brawley, brought out his *The Negro in Literature and Art in the United States* in 1910 with another edition following in 1918. The NAACP magazine *Crisis*, founded in 1910 in New York City and edited by Dr. W. E. B. Du Bois (who earlier, in 1903, had brought out his literary classic, *The Souls of Black Folk*), was publishing poetry, fiction and essays by Negro writers. Charles S. Johnson of the National Urban League began editing in 1923 that organization's new magazine *Opportunity: Journal of Negro Life* which was also a literary as well as a sociological organ for Negroes. *Crisis* and *Opportunity* prizes for creative expression were announced in 1924 and continued for several years. In these two New York magazines a literary movement had gathered momentum.

Literature of early nineteen hundreds

James Weldon Johnson's book of poems *Fifty Years and Other Poems* containing *O Black and Unknown Bards* appeared in 1917 and his pioneering anthology *The Book of American Negro Poetry* appeared in 1922. The first edition of the Negro historian Carter G. Woodson's *The Negro in Our History* was published in 1922. He had already founded the *Journal of Negro History* in 1916. Claude McKay, a young poet who had come from Jamaica in the West Indies to America to study at Tuskegee Institute in 1912 and whose great poem *If We Must Die* appeared in the magazine *The Liberator* in 1919 about the time of the murderous Chicago and Washington (D.C.) race riots, published his powerful book of poetry about social and economic injustice, *Harlem Shadows*, also in 1922. Jean Toomer, that wonderfully talented, poetic Negro

writer, startled literary America with his book *Cane,* a collection
of sketches, short stories and poems in 1923. Jessie Fauset, a
Negro woman novelist concerned with the Negro middle class,
published her first book *There Is Confusion* in 1924. W. E. B. Du
Bois, whose book *Darkwater,* published in 1919, contained his
passionate poem *A Litany of Atlanta* about the terrible Atlanta
(Ga.) riot of 1906, brought out *The Gift of Black Folk,* a book of
historical and cultural essays, in 1924. (John Henrik Clarke's
essay *Transition in the American Negro Short Story* [*Phylon,* 4th
quarter, 1960] should be mentioned here as quite good in giving
the literary backdrop as well as a vivid description of the Harlem
Renaissance.)

This was the background for the assorted anthology of Negro
creative and historical writing, *The New Negro,* edited by Alain
Locke and published in 1925. With the publication of this book, as
all of the voluminous writings on the Harlem Renaissance period
of the 1920's have pointed out, Harlem as a cultural and pulsating
community really came into its own. *The New Negro* used the
special number of *Survey Graphic* titled *Harlem: Mecca of the
New Negro* (also edited by Alain Locke in 1925) as its nucleus
and enlarged the Negro Renaissance to its national and international scope. A large portion of the poetry, fiction and essays of
The New Negro was either about Harlem or written by Harlem
authors. Harlem was the cultural capital where the New Negro,
whom this volume documented socially and culturally, lived. This
interpretation of the Harlem Renaissance became a landmark of
the movement. The largest Negro community in the world became
a subject and theme for poets, novelists, essayists, painters, sculptors and musicians, Negro and white. Harlem began to have an
impact upon the national American culture.

Many other books either about Harlem or by Harlem writers
were published in 1925 and after as the New Negro movement
burgeoned to full flower. Countee Cullen, the lyrical and technically dazzling Harlem poet, published *Color* which won great
critical acclaim in 1925. Other Cullen books of poetry were *The
Ballad of the Brown Girl* and *Copper Sun* in 1927 and *The Black
Christ* in 1929. His novel about Harlem, *One Way to Heaven,*
appeared in 1932. Cullen served as assistant editor of the magazine *Opportunity* and in 1927 edited *Caroling Dusk,* an anthology
of verse by Negroes. Charles S. Johnson, the editor of *Opportunity,* brought out *Ebony and Topaz* (1927), an anthology of writings by about twenty young unknown Negro writers: poets, social

scientists and journalists (also Negro artists) such as Langston Hughes, Sterling Brown, Arna Bontemps, Abram Harris, Zora Neale Hurston, Frank Horne, E. Franklin Frazier, Ira De A. Reid and George Schuyler. In this same year, 1927, the New York Urban League issued a short study and interpretation of the living conditions of small Harlem wage earners titled *Twenty-Four Hundred Negro Families in Harlem*, and Ira De A. Reid published his article *Mirrors of Harlem—Investigations and Problems of America's Largest Colored Community (Social Forces*, June 1927) dealing with the growth of Harlem, its employment, health and housing problems.

The Long Island University English professor Eugene Arden's article *The Early Harlem Novel (Phylon*, 1st quarter, 1959) points to Paul Laurence Dunbar's naturalistic novel *The Sport of the Gods* (1902), about Negro migrants in urban New York, as the first novel to treat Negro life in New York seriously and at length. But, as Arden says, Dunbar's novel borrowed from the despicable white plantation-school writers in whose novels the north destroyed the Negro migrants who yearned for the south. The Negroes Dunbar wrote about were not in Harlem then, but down near the Pennsylvania Station, on San Juan Hill (West 64th Street) or on West 53rd Street. The Negroes in these Manhattan areas were written about in Mary White Ovington's article *The Negro Home in New York*. This piece, by a social worker and a founder of the NAACP, appeared in a special number (Oct. 7, 1905) of the early magazine *Charities* (later to become *Survey Midmonthly*, the twin publication of *Survey Graphic*) titled *The Negro in the Cities of the North*. Mary Ovington's book, *Half a Man: The Status of the Negro in New York*, was published in 1911.

The white writer Carl Van Vechten, Prof. Arden says further, expressed the indebtedness of his novel *Nigger Heaven* (1926, paperbacked in 1951) to Dunbar's *The Sport of the Gods* in the Introduction Van Vechten wrote to the 1927 edition of James Weldon Johnson's novel *The Autobiography of an Ex-Coloured Man* (paperbacked in 1948). Van Vechten, says Arden, as well as Claude McKay, Rudolph Fisher, Wallace Thurman and Countee Cullen were all following Dunbar. *Nigger Heaven* attempted to describe the Harlem urban Negro in human, realistic terms rather than as a stereotype. But its unfortunate title, its emphasis on the flamboyant and exotic, and the dissolute Negro life and characters it depicted led to severe Negro criticism of the book. Nevertheless, several Negro writers did imitate Van Vechten's novel in one way or another.

Claude McKay's naturalistic, primitive novel *Home to Harlem*, published in 1928 (paperbacked in 1951), and six of his twelve sexy, exotic short stories in the book *Gingertown* (1932) that were about Harlem, show Van Vechten's influence. The Negro writer Rudolph Fisher's novels *The Walls of Jericho* (1928) and *The Conjure-Man Dies* (1932) and his short stories give the lighter side of Harlem also in the realistic, satiric tradition. Another satiric Negro author who wrote about Harlem was Wallace Thurman whose article *Negro Life in New York's Harlem* appeared originally in the *Haldeman-Julius Quarterly* (Oct.-Nov.-Dec. 1924) and was published in 1928 as a 64-page Little Blue Book (No. 494) edited by E. Haldeman-Julius. In this booklet, the author describes the 200,000 Negro population of Harlem at that time, the social life, the Negro church, the Negro journalism and the New Negro in Harlem. Thurman wrote the novels *The Blacker the Berry* (1929) and *Infants of the Spring* (1932) and a highly sensational play *Harlem* (written in collaboration with W. J. Rapp) which had a successful run on Broadway also in 1929. He also helped found the short-lived Harlem magazines of this period *Fire* and *Harlem*.

The winner of the first prize in the *Opportunity* poetry contest of 1925 was Langston Hughes. His poetry books of this period, *The Weary Blues* (1926), *Fine Clothes to the Jew* (1927) and other books, dealt in part with Harlem, celebrated Negro beauty, and expressed race pride, a romantic interest in Africa and Negro history—all important ideas in the New Negro movement. The Negro woman novelist Nella Larsen's two books *Quicksand* (1928) and *Passing* (1930) describe upper-class Negro life in Harlem especially passing for white. The novels of Jessie Fauset, *Plum Bun* (1928), *The Chinaberry Tree* (1931) and *Comedy, American Style* (1933), and those of Walter White, *Fire in the Flint* (1925) and *Flight* (1928), though not specifically about Harlem, were authored by Negro writers who spent some time in New York City and therefore belong to the New Negro movement. T. B. Campbell's novel *Black Sadie* (1928) was a terribly stereotyped white southerner's attempt to debunk the Harlem of the twenties. Maxwell Bodenheim's naturalistic novel *Naked on Roller Skates* (1931), on the other hand, shows the harsher aspects of Harlem night life.

James Weldon Johnson's book *Black Manhattan*, published in

1930, was a long-awaited, popular history of Negroes in New York City as well as a history of Negroes on the stage in New York. It was also around 1930 that the great Spanish poet Garcia Lorca's book *Poet in New York* came out with these perceptive lines about Harlem:

> *Ay Harlem, Harlem, Harlem!*
> *There is no sorrow like your oppressed eyes,*
> *like your blood shuddering in the dark eclipse,*
> *like your great king, prisoner in a janitor's uniform.*

The white American poet William Rose Benét brought out a small book *Harlem and Other Poems* in 1935.

Clyde V. Kiser's doctoral dissertation, *Sea Island to City*, was published by Columbia University in 1932. It was a study of St. Helena islanders of South Carolina in Harlem and other urban centers.

Literature of the depression years

The unemployment, dispossession, suffering and rioting of Harlem Negroes during the Great Depression led to pamphlets like James W. Ford's *Hunger and Terror in Harlem* (1935) about the causes and remedies of the March 19, 1935, Harlem riot, and prepared for the Mayor's Commission to Investigate Conditions in Harlem. E. Franklin Frazier's article *Negro Harlem: An Ecological Study* (*American Journal of Sociology*, July 1937) traced Harlem's physical expansion and demographic growth from its beginning around 1900 and particularly from 1910 through 1934. This article was based on the materials Frazier collected when making a survey of Harlem also for the Mayor's Commission to Investigate Conditions in Harlem (1936) following the March 1935 riot.

About this time, two master's theses were done about Harlem by Negro graduate students at Columbia University and C.C.N.Y. respectively: Barrington Dunbar's *Factors in Cultural Backgrounds of the British West Indian Negro and the American Southern Negro that Condition their Adjustment in Harlem* (1936) and Myrtle E. Pollard's big, two-volume *Harlem As Is* (1936–37), a sociological study with emphasis on Negro business and the economic community.

Alain Locke's article *Harlem: Dark Weather Vane* (*Survey Graphic*, Aug. 1936), eleven years after the 1925 special issue of this magazine on Harlem and over a year after the Harlem riot of 1935, stated that the New Negro hopes of the twenties then seemed like illusions and mirages in the depth of the depression and social unrest. For no cultural advance is safe, said Locke, without some sound economic underpinning, that is, without the foundation of a decent standard of living.

The *Harlem Digest* was a magazine published from 1937 to 1939 by A. Merral Willis's Colonel Young Memorial Foundation. The outstanding Negro playwright Theodore Ward's play *Big White Fog* (1938) about the problems of poverty, unemployment, prejudice, Garveyism and Communism, was equally applicable to Negroes in Chicago or New York. It was produced in both places. In 1940 Claude McKay's third book about Harlem appeared, titled *Harlem: Negro Metropolis*. This book was exotic, bizarre and rather superficial; it dealt with Father Divine, the cultists, the occultists, number-playing, Marcus Garvey and the other early Harlem nationalist Sufi Abdul Hamid. The American Negro Theatre created a hit in Harlem with the Negro writer Abram Hill's play *On Strivers Row: A Comedy of Sophisticated Harlem* in the early 1940's. This play was a satirical, social comedy of Negro middle class life in Harlem.

Literature of the nineteen forties

Harlem As Seen by Hirschfeld, a book of caricatured drawings with text by the American novelist and playwright William Saroyan, was published in 1941.

Langston Hughes, rapidly becoming the poet laureate of Harlem, brought out *Shakespeare in Harlem* in 1942 which contained this poem *Evenin' Air Blues* about the frustrations of the southern Negro when he migrates north:

> *Folks, I come up North*
> *Cause they told me de North was fine.*
> *I come up North*
> *Cause they told me de North was fine.*
> *Been up here six months—*
> *I'm about to lose my mind.*
>
> *This mornin' for breakfast*
> *I chawed de mornin' air.*
> *This mornin' for breakfast*
> *Chawed de mornin' air.*
> *But this evenin' for supper,*
> *I got evenin' air to spare.*

The Negro novelist and short story writer Carl Offord's book *The White Face*, about a Georgia Negro family's woes in Harlem during World War II, came out in 1943. Bucklin Moon, a sensitive, progressive white writer and book editor, brought out his first book *The Darker Brother*, a novel about a Florida Negro migrant fighting for life in Harlem, in 1943 (paperbacked in 1949). Moon later published another novel about Negroes *Without Magnolias* (1949), which also touched on Harlem, and edited a very didactic and perceptive book of writings on the Negro titled *Primer for White Folks* (1945). Also published in 1943 was the white American novelist Ira Wolfert's *Tucker's People* about the underworld rackets in Harlem. This novel was issued in paperback in 1950 with the title *The Underworld*. The Right Rev. John H. Johnson, a long-time Harlem minister, brought out his book *Harlem, The War and Other Addresses* in 1942.

The Negro Quarterly, a review of Negro life and culture, was published during 1942–43 with offices at 125th Street and Lenox Avenue in Harlem. This magazine was edited by two Harlemites, Angelo Herndon and Ralph Ellison, who later became famous as a novelist and short story writer. It was national and international in scope and published only a few things about Harlem such as the poems *Lenox Avenue* and *Pawnbrokers* and the article *Anti-Semitism Among Negroes*. But many of the Negro writers who contributed to *The Negro Quarterly*, such as Langston Hughes, Harcourt Tynes, Carl G. Hill and L. D. Reddick, either resided in Harlem or were known Harlem figures.

The late Negro journalist and author Roi Ottley, who lived and worked in Harlem for many years, published his first book *New World A-Coming; Inside Black America* in 1943. This book, as its bibliography clearly showed, was a sort of jazzed up, condensed version of the massive boxes of unpublished material written and collected by the scores of Negro writers who worked on the Federal Writers' Project's book *Negroes in New York* which was never published because Congress killed all appropriations for the federal cultural projects. This material on the history, development, institutions, organizations, culture and personalities of Harlem is now catalogued and available at the Schomburg Collection of Negro Literature and History of the New York Public Library in Harlem. Ottley merely skimmed over this material (probably under his publisher's pressure) and he gave no credit to the many Negro writers who had compiled and written the unpublished papers. However, his eternally sanguine, optimistic book, coming during World War II and pointing to a new world for Negroes after the War, enjoyed a tremendous success especially among white Americans whose uneasy, guilty consciences about Negroes and the defense of American democracy were somewhat assuaged by this sort of book by a Negro.

Literature of the war years

But the war and civilian issues were not so easily resolved by Negroes. The anti-Negro riots by whites in Bessemer, Alabama, Philadelphia, Pennsylvania, Detroit, Michigan, and other cities against the upgrading of Negroes on their jobs, plus the widespread discrimination against Negroes in war plants everywhere and the Negro press' constant reports of Negro soldiers being beaten, denied service and even killed on southern buses and in southern camps and restaurants led to the devastating Harlem riot of August 1 and 2, 1943. Two of the reports written about this Sunday night–Monday morning riot are Harold Orlansky's pamphlet *The Harlem Riot: A Study in Mass Frustration* (1943), a social anthropological analysis, and the then publishing progressive New York City newspaper *PM's* big 19-page picture and text coverage titled *The Whole Story of the Harlem Riot* (Aug. 3, 1943). Also around this time during World War II the NAACP published a pamphlet *Food Costs More in Harlem*, a comparative survey of retail food prices after the O.P.A. had frozen prices at very high levels. In the fall of 1943, spurred no doubt by the August 1943 Harlem riot, the City-Wide Citizens' Committee on Harlem got busy with its proposed projects for Harlem. The Committee had already issued in 1942 three good, critical reports of its subcommittees on employment, education and recreation and housing in Harlem. It followed these up with another report on health and hospitals in Harlem in 1945.

The late Dan Burley, a well-known Harlem figure, published in 1944 his *Original Handbook of Harlem Jive* illustrated by the *New York Amsterdam News* cartoonist Melvin Tapley with a learned Foreword by Earl Conrad. The talented Negro woman novelist Ann Petry brought out her first book *The Street* in 1946. While, like most novels about Harlem, *The Street* may be too naturalistic and slice-of-life in spots, it is nevertheless an honest attempt to sum up what the author saw and heard during the six years she lived in Harlem and worked as a reporter for a Harlem newspaper: the ancient, evil housing; the tragic, broken families; and the high death rate. This book, which won a Houghton Mifflin

Literary Fellowship award, has been through several hard and paperback editions and is still on the paperback stands.

The *Harlem Quarterly* was published in 1949–50 edited by the Negro writer and now militant Negro leader of Brooklyn CORE, Benjamin A. Brown. The magazine carried symposia, short stories, poetry, articles, features and book reviews. Among the editors and contributors were many Harlem writers such as John H. Clarke, Ricardo Weeks, Willard Moore, John Hudson Jones, Gene Holmes, Waring Cuney, Langston Hughes, William Attaway and Ernest Kaiser. A *Who's Who in Harlem* for 1949–50, the biographical register of a group of distinguished persons of New York's Harlem, was edited and published by B. S. B. Trottman. It contained many of the Harlem personalities alive at that time. Trottman also brought out *New York's Harlem Business Register* in 1951, a listing of virtually all Harlem businesses of that time. Also following up on the *New Harlem Blue Book* (1940), a directory of organizations, businesses and professionals, which was long out of print, Constance Curtis, Adele Glasgow and Carl Lawrence brought out *Harlem's Top Thousand*, a similar directory, in 1949 and *Harlem's Top People*, a larger, more classified directory, in 1953. Olivia P. Frost, who had done an analysis of the characteristics of the population in Central Harlem for the New York Urban League published in 1946, completed her master's thesis, *Some Sociological Aspects of the Realty Investment Market in New York's Harlem*, in 1951.

Every book written about New York City as a whole has a section or sections on Harlem. This holds for books like the Federal Writers' Project's *New York City Guide* (1939), Eleanor Early's *New York Holiday* (1950), Kate Simon's *New York, Places and Pleasures* (1959) and Gay Talese's *New York: A Serendipiter's Journey* (1962). Some of these sections on Harlem are pretty good and some are exotic in their approach to Harlem.

White writers on Harlem

Many white writers like Hal Ellson, Wenzell Brown, Evan Hunter, Jack Lait and John Henry Hewlett have maligned Harlem, its youth and adults with their derogatory novels and inside and confidential books. Robert Lowry's novel *The Violent Wedding* (1953), a very crude take-off on Harlem's Ray Robinson, John H. Hewlett's novel *Harlem Story* (1948), Jack Lait's *New York: Confidential* (1948), Wenzell Brown's terrible paperback *The Big Rumble* (1955) subtitled *Teen-age Gangs in the [East] Harlem*

Jungle, are some examples of this. Also William Arnold's *Harlem Woman* (1952) and Floyd Miller's *The Dream Peddlers* (1956) are paperback novels about Puerto Ricans, prostitution and dope in East Harlem; Earl Conrad's *Rock Bottom* (1952), a novel about a Negro woman's experiences from Mississippi to Harlem; William Krasner's *North of Welfare* (1954), playing up Harlem gangs and violence and Evan Hunter's sensational novel *The Blackboard Jungle* (1954) (later made into a motion picture) through which the author tried to get attention by exploiting the deprivations of Harlem's school children. This book was supposed to show a public school classroom of juvenile delinquents in a terrible Harlem neighborhood.

Hal Ellson's paperback novels *Duke* (1949), *Rock* (1955), *I'll Fix You* (1956) and *This Is It* (1956) have been particularly vicious in their treatment of Harlem youth as only juvenile delinquents. We must also include in this category of deleterious books about Harlem the works of several Negro writers. George W. Henderson's novel *Jule: Alabama Boy in Harlem* (1946), Philip B. Kaye's novel *Taffy* (1950) (both also paperbacked), Robert Lucas's paperback *Harlem Model* (1953), and Chester Himes's recent paperback novels written in France about Harlem—*The Real Cool Killers* (1959), *The Crazy Kill* (1959), *All Shot Up* (1960) and *The Big Gold Dream* (1960)—are all novels by Negro writers that denigrate and demean Harlem youth and adults.

The Harlem of Langston Hughes

Arthur P. Davis, one of the editors of that huge anthology of American Negro writing, *The Negro Caravan* (1941), wrote an article for the magazine *Phylon* (4th quarter, 1952) titled *The Harlem of Langston Hughes' Poetry.* Hughes has mirrored Harlem rather faithfully in his poetry through the years. One of these poems titled *Harlem* in his book of poems mostly about Harlem— *Montage of a Dream Deferred* (1951)—goes like this:

> *What happens to a dream deferred?*
> *Does it dry up*
> *Like a raisin in the sun?*
> *Or fester like a sore—*
> *And then run?*
> *Does it stink like rotten meat?*
> *Or crust and sugar over—*
> *Like a syrupy sweet?*

Maybe it just sags
Like a heavy load.

Or does it explode?

Hughes's book about the now famous Harlem character Jesse Semple began as a series in *The Chicago Defender*, a Negro newspaper. These articles were collected and published as the book *Simple Speaks His Mind* in 1950 followed by two other collections: *Simple Takes a Wife* in 1953 and *Simple Stakes a Claim* in 1957. Hughes has selected his favorite Simple stories from these three volumes in *The Best of Simple* (1961). The book *Simple Takes a Wife* became the basis for the Langston Hughes and David Martin musical comedy *Simply Heavenly* of 1957. The text of this musical was published in 1959. Alice Childress, the outstanding Negro woman playwright and Harlemite, adapted the text of the Harlem-produced, Committee for the Negro in the Arts musical *Just a Little Simple* (1950) from Hughes's *Simple Speaks His Mind*. Her book *Like One of the Family* (1956), conversations from a Harlem domestic's life, is really the female Harlem counterpart of Hughes's "Simple" sketches. Hughes did the text for a book of Harlem photographs, *The Sweet Flypaper of Life* (1955), by that gifted Harlem photographer and Guggenheim Fellowship winner Roy de Carava. Hughes also brought out a novel *Tambourines to Glory* (1958) about pentecostal religion in Harlem. Often called the O. Henry of Harlem, he has written several of his short stories in *The Ways of White Folks* (1934), *Laughing to Keep from Crying* (1952) and in magazines, about Harlem. He has chosen 37 of these stories and vignettes with various locales for *Something in Common and Other Stories* (1963).

Other writers about Harlem
Around the World with the Harlem Globetrotters, a book about those zany clowns of basketball, appeared in 1953 and *I Always Wanted to Be Somebody*, Althea Gibson's autobiography of her tremendous rise from the slums of Harlem to the women's tennis championship of the world, was published in 1958. Samuel B. Charters and Leonard Kunstadt's recent book *Jazz: A History of the New York Scene* (1962) has material, historical and current, on Harlem jazz music and musicians. Bruce Kenrick's book *Come Out the Wilderness* (1962) is the dramatic story of the interracial East Harlem Protestant Parish.

There are some novels by Negro and white writers about

Harlem which, while not of the worst type, are so naturalistic, slice-of-life or distorted that Harlem could have done very well without them. In fact, the paperback reprints of these books show that they lend themselves to the usual damaging stereotypes of life in Harlem. In this category fall National Book Award winner Ralph Ellison's *Invisible Man* (1953) (about distorted Negro nationalism and nightmarish riot in Harlem); Julian Mayfield's two books *The Hit* (1957) and *The Long Night* (1958); Warren Miller's *The Cool World* (1959) (about youth gangs) that later had a very short run as a Broadway play; William Fisher's *The Waiters* (1953) (about the numbers racket); Arthur Joseph's *Volcano in Our Midst* (1952); Sheila S. Klass's *Come Back on Monday* (1960) (a novel written by a white teacher in Harlem about public schools there with an anti-Harlem Negro press slant); and Eugene Brown's *Trespass* (1952) (about interracial love).

The magazine and newspaper articles and series on Harlem have been many in number. We shall run through some of them along with some longer studies of Harlem. The now defunct magazine *Collier's* carried a terrible article *Harlem—Dense and Dangerous* in its September 23, 1944, number. Ann Petry's piece *Harlem* with beautiful pictures in rich color (*Holiday*, April 1949) was a kind of Cook's tour of Harlem with some interpretation. The famous liberal novelist Lillian Smith's article *Strange Fruit in Harlem* (*Ebony*, June 1950) gives impressions of her visit as a white southerner to the New York Negro community: of the children, the mothers and also the blighted areas of Harlem. The *New York Sunday News* ran a series of brief picture stories on Harlem from February to October 1953 which emphasized the way the community's Negroes study, train and work. The Negro free-lance journalist Alex Haley, who today, the Negro press says, is aiming for the top, published an article in 1954 titled *The Harlem Nobody Knows* (*Christian Science Monitor*, May 6, 1954). This article tells a dream-like, grossly exaggerated, everything-is-rosy story of what it calls the community's great progress over a fifty year period from about 1900 to about 1954. The piece was, naturally, immediately reprinted (if not planted originally in the *Monitor*) by *The Reader's Digest* (June 1954) and also by the *New York Amsterdam News*. In 1955, the research department of the Welfare and Health Council of New York City brought out studies of population characteristics and social and educational services in Central Harlem and East Harlem and in other Negro areas of the borough of Manhattan.

The veteran Negro reporter Ted Poston's long *New York Post* series *Prejudice and Progress: The Negro in New York* (April 1956) deals in part with Harlem. One article of the series is titled *How Harlem Got That Way*. The *New York Post* carried another long series of articles this time on Harlem by the white reporter and writer Stan Opotowsky, in March 1958. These articles maligned and denigrated Harlem and its people past and present. Mrs. Anna A. Hedgeman wrote a long reply to this series in which she tried to describe the positive, dignified, hard-working, "struggle" side of the Harlem Negroes' story left out by the *Post* reporter. She discussed the Harlem community with Opotowsky on a television program. But Opotowsky insisted to the end that he would write the series a second time exactly as he had already written it, and Mrs. Hedgeman's reply to his Harlem slander was never published in the *Post*. However, the *Post's* next series, *Inside Bedford-Stuyvesant* (May 1958), on Negroes in Brooklyn, was much better than its Harlem series by Opotowsky; and the newspaper later apparently tried to make amends for the earlier series with the short series on *Harlem and Beyond*, about the new Negro middle class, in April 1962.

Peter Abrahams, the South African colored journalist and writer now living in Jamaica in the West Indies, contributed an article *The Meaning of Harlem* to *Holiday* (June 1960) after having his original piece on Harlem written for *Holiday's* New York number (October 1959) rejected as too sociological. The Abrahams piece, as revised to meet *Holiday's* demands, still had more depth and interpretation than most *Holiday* pieces. About the same time the famous Negro novelist and essayist, James Baldwin, contributed an article *Fifth Avenue Uptown* to *Esquire's* special New York number (July 1960). This was an angry piece which told of the Harlem people's silent contempt for and hatred of their oppression. Baldwin, a native son of Harlem, has written extensively on Harlem from his early essay *The Harlem Ghetto* reprinted from *Commentary* (February 1948) in his book *Notes of a Native Son* (1955), through his largely autobiographical novel *Go Tell It on the Mountain* (1953) which delves deeply and with much insight into the religion and life of the people of Harlem's store front churches, to his popular novel *Another Country* (1962) about Harlem and Greenwich Village, although here he has been charged with creating stereotyped Negro characters such as white and Negro writers create when pandering to the public's distorted conception of Negro life.

Harlem of the sixties

The liberal southern journalist and writer Harry S. Ashmore's book *The Other Side of Jordan* (1960), which stemmed from a series of articles in the *New York Herald Tribune*, describes Negro life in the northern communities with a section on Harlem. The Harvard historian and sociologist Oscar Handlin's book *The Newcomers: Negroes and Puerto Ricans in a Changing Metropolis* (1959, paperbacked in 1962) also deals in great part with the housing, employment, education and welfare problems of Harlem. The Urban League of Greater New York brought out in 1960 a survey of *Gaps in Services to Children and Parents in Harlem: Your Agency's Role* when so many social agencies had either moved out of Harlem or closed down. The Teamsters Joint Council 16 released in June 1962 a report on New York City family income whose statistics on non-white income in the borough of Manhattan relate largely to Harlem. The Protestant Council of the City of New York published in September 1962 a two-part report, *Harlem—Upper Manhattan*, the most exhaustive study that has been made of Harlem in many years.

Finally, we have the *Ebony* (April 1963) article *Harlem's Antique Collector* about Mrs. W. D. Finkley, who collects antique furniture, china, silver and glassware; the Negro novelist Chester Himes' long essay *Harlem or the Cancer of America* written after his visit to New York City from France (during the latter part of 1962) and translated into French for the magazine *Presence Africaine* (1st quarter 1963); Conrad Kent Rivers' book of poems in preparation *The Still Voice of Harlem* whose title poem has already been published in Paul Bremen's second volume *Sixes and Sevens* (1963) of his projected four-volume Heritage (London) series of poetry by American Negroes; and Gay Talese's article *Harlem for Fun* (*Esquire*, September 1962).

In April 1955, almost a year after Dr. Alain Locke's death in June 1954, the Howard University Graduate School published *The New Negro: Thirty Years Afterward*. This book, coming exactly thirty years after Locke's book *The New Negro* (1925), consisted of papers read at the 16th annual spring conference of the University's Social Sciences Division. These papers were eulogies of Dr. Locke with a pretty good bibliography of his diverse writings and discussions of the historical setting, the political ideologies, the middle class, the modern art, the literature and the New Deal period of the New Negro by Rayford W. Logan, E. Franklin

Frazier, Charles S. Johnson, Emmett E. Dorsey, James A. Porter, Sterling A. Brown, Eugene C. Holmes and John Hope Franklin sweeping back in some instances to 1877 and forward three decades after 1925.

Present parallels with earlier writers

Arna Bontemps, the versatile Negro novelist, poet, historian and anthologist, in an article *The New Black Renaissance* (*Negro Digest*, November 1961) which is similar to some of the papers in *The New Negro Thirty Years Afterward*, says that the current Negro writers (Baldwin, Hansberry, Ellison, etc.) resemble the Harlem Renaissance writers more than they do the Negro writers of the late thirties and forties, their immediate forerunners (Willard Motley, the late Richard Wright, Margaret Walker, Gwendolyn Brooks, etc.). With the possible exception of Lorraine Hansberry (*Raisin in the Sun*) (and I would add John O. Killens, author of the novels *Youngblood* and *And Then We Heard the Thunder*) as descendants of Richard Wright, Bontemps sees some parallels between Ralph Ellison and Jean Toomer, James Baldwin and Wallace Thurman, Louis E. Lomax (*The Reluctant African, The Negro Revolt*) and the late Walter White (*Rope and Faggot* [1929]), Alston Anderson, author of *Lover Man* (1959), a book of short stories, and Eric D. Waldron whose book of short stories, *Tropic Death,* pleased the critics in the Harlem Renaissance period. Both Alston and Waldron have the West Indies and Panama in their backgrounds. Bontemps also brackets the Harlem flavor of Julian Mayfield's novels with that of Rudolph Fisher's short stories and novels; and novelist Paule Marshall, author of *Brown Girl, Brownstones* (1959) and *Soul Clap Hands and Sing* (1961) with the late Zora Neale Hurston who wrote *Mules and Men* (1935), *Their Eyes Were Watching God* (1937) and other works. (And I would bracket the novelist John A. Williams [*Night Song, Sissie*] and novelist Arna Bontemps [*God Sends Sunday, Black Thunder*].)

And if the Harlem Renaissance group had no Lorraine Hansberry (I would also add no John O. Killens) and no journalist like Carl T. Rowan (author of *South of Freedom, Go South to Sorrow* and other works), says Bontemps, neither have the present group of Negro writers any poets comparable to Claude McKay, Countee Cullen and Langston Hughes. The Harlem Renaissance group, he says, also included Helen Johnson, Dorothy West, Frank Horne, Sterling Brown, Nella Larsen, Jessie Fauset and Arthur Huff

Fauset. Our current crop of Negro writers, Bontemps says further, also includes the late Frank London Brown, LeRoi Jones, Gloria Oden, Herbert Simmons and William Melvin Kelley. (I would add the poet Conrad Kent Rivers, author of *Perchance to Dream, Othello* [1959] and *These Black Bodies and This Sunburnt Face* [1962].) But, says Bontemps probably correctly, it will take the best of all of these to fill the firmament as did the literary stars that brightened the Harlem sky in the twenties.

But if, as Locke has pointed out, no Negro cultural advance is safe without a sound foundation of a decent standard of living for Negroes generally, it is also true that a powerful Negro culture of novels, poetry, plays and the like can develop out of and also give direction to the current great struggles and protests of Negroes everywhere in our country against the injustices and denials of their rights. This is the tradition of Richard Wright in which John O. Killens with his novels, Lorraine Hansberry with her plays, and other Negro writers are working.

[
    HUGH M. GLOSTER
  Race and the Negro Writer
]

FROM THE beginnings of his active authorship in this country the Negro writer has been preoccupied with racial issues and materials. This obsession with race is not hard to explain, because the tragic plight of the colored population of the United States has forced the Negro writer to stand with his people and to voice their sufferings, reverses, triumphs, and aspirations. The inhumanities of slavery, the restrictions of segregation, the frustrations of prejudice and injustice, the debasements of concubinage and bastardy, the ravages of persecution and lynching—these have constituted the bitter experience of American black folk; and it is only natural that the Negro writer has focused upon the themes of racial defense, protest, and glorification.

While propaganda from inside sources has frequently assisted colored people in their struggle toward equality and freedom, the preponderating use of racial subject matter has handicapped the Negro writer in at least four important ways. In the first place, it has retarded his attainment of a cosmic grasp of the varied experiences, humorous as well as tragic, through which individuals pass in this life. Second, it has diminished his philosophical perspective to the extent that he has made only meager contributions to national and world ideologies. Third, it has usually limited his literary range to the moods and substance of race in the United States. Fourth and finally, it has helped certain critics and publishers to lure him into the deadly trap of cultural segregation by advising him that the black ghetto is his proper milieu and that he will write best when he is most Negroid. Incidentally, this insidious counsel, repeated many times in an attempt to stabilize cultural separation, has been propagated so effectively that the abandonment of black stereotypes by the Negro writer is traditionally viewed by many Americans as an artistic desertion of the race.

In spite of the limiting and crippling effects of racial hypersensitivity and Jim-Crow esthetics, the Negro writer has gradually loosened the shackles that have held him in mental bondage for the past two centuries. In recent years the emancipatory process has been accelerated through the efforts of such authors as Richard Wright, Ann Petry, Gwendolyn Brooks, Willard Motley, Frank Yerby, and Zora Neale Hurston. In *Native Son* (1940) Wright treats the old subject of Negro degradation and persecution but transcends the color line by identifying his downtrodden protagonist with underprivileged youth of other lands and races:

> More than anything else, as a writer, I was fascinated by the similarity of the emotional tensions of Bigger in America and Bigger in Nazi Germany and Bigger in old Russia. All Bigger Thomases, white and black, felt tense, afraid, nervous, hysterical, and restless.

This successful blending of class and race experience suggests that Wright's sympathies are comprehensive enough to include all exploited people; and *Native Son* illustrates, perhaps more effectively than any other novel by an American Negro, that it is possible to attack racial oppression and at the same time provide truthful implications for all mankind. In *The Street* (1946), a stirring record of delinquency in Harlem, and in *Annie Allen* (1949), a Pulitzer Prize-winning account of human fortunes in South Chicago, Ann Petry and Gwendolyn Brooks, respectively, disclose the common human denominators of passion, marriage, motherhood, and disillusionment in the lives of contemporary Negro women. Also lifting his work to the universal plane by representing humanity through an individual, Willard Motley reports the downfall and death of Nick Romano in *Knock on Any Door* (1947). In this important contribution to world literature the symbolic victim of organized society is an Italian boy who rapidly degenerates after his impoverished family moves to the slums of Chicago's West Side. With his motto of "Live fast, die young, and have a good-looking corpse," Nick could be any dissolute youth in any corrupt metropolis. Writing entertaining romances for big-money profits, Frank Yerby has produced in rapid succession five novels that are ideologically and esthetically unimportant but nevertheless noteworthy as the first series of best-seller triumphs by an American Negro writer in the field of general fiction. Following Yerby into the mainstream but not approaching his financial success have come Ann Petry with *Country Place* (1947), an account of clandestine love in a small New England town, and Zora Neale Hurston with *Seraph on the Suwanee* (1948), a local-color tale of romance and marriage among Florida Crackers. Wright, Mrs. Petry, Miss Brooks, Motley, Yerby, and Miss Hurston are tillers of broader fields than the circumscribed areas of racial life.

The gradual emancipation of the Negro writer from the fetters of racial chauvinism and cultural isolation has recently been facilitated by the rapid extension of democratic ideas and attitudes in this country and abroad. Despite the persistence of the plantation tradition with its apotheosis of slavery as a felicitous existence for the irresponsible "darky," the publishing and writing professions have exhibited an increasingly liberal attitude toward the Negro as author and as subject. During the past five years, for example, such firms as D. Appleton-Century Company, the Dial Press, Houghton Mifflin Company, and Charles Scribner's Sons have published Negro-authored books in the field of general fiction; and in advertisements of these works the practice has been to make no mention of the racial identity of the writers. Throughout the country, moreover, white authors are manifesting a growing disposition to describe frankly and understandingly the social and intellectual dilemmas of colored people. Even Southerners are treating Negro life with increasing honesty and objectivity, and Georgia-born Lillian Smith's *Killers of the Dream* (1949) may be regarded as a harbinger of an unbiased approach to racial subject matter by writers living below the Mason-Dixon Line. That the social conscience is disturbed not only in the United States but in other countries as well is convincingly demonstrated in Alan

Paton's *Cry, the Beloved Country* (1948), an epochal novel which records the interactions of South African natives and whites with the insight and courage that characterize the universal approach.

The main point of this essay is not that the Negro writer should suppress his ethnic individuality or relinquish racial subject matter. The chief emphasis is that he should consider all life as his proper milieu, treat race from the universal point of view, and shun the cultural insularity that results from racial preoccupation and Jim-Crow esthetics. If a liberal English clergyman can deal realistically and understandingly with the experience of South Africans in *Cry, the Beloved Country*, the broad-minded Negro artist can similarly handle the comedy and tragedy of his own racial group and of other folk as well. The Negro writer is also an American writer, a man of letters as free as any of his national confreres to tap the rich literary resources of our land and its people. To accept the principle that racial experience is the only natural province of the Negro writer is to approve an artistic double standard that is just as confining and demoralizing in American literature as is segregation in American life.

[
    LANGSTON HUGHES
    The Negro Artist and the
    Racial Mountain
]

ONE OF the most promising of the young Negro poets said to me once, "I want to be a poet—not a Negro poet," meaning, I believe, "I want to write like a white poet"; meaning subconsciously, "I would like to be a white poet"; meaning behind that, "I would like to be white." And I was sorry the young man said that, for no great poet has ever been afraid of being himself. And I doubted then that, with his desire to run away spiritually from his race, this boy would ever be a great poet. But this is the mountain standing in the way of any true Negro art in America—this urge within the race toward whiteness, the desire to pour racial individuality into the mold of American standardization, and to be as little Negro and as much American as possible.

But let us look at the immediate background of this young poet. His family is of what I suppose one would call the Negro middle class: people who are by no means rich yet never uncomfortable nor hungry—smug, contented, respectable folk, members of the Baptist church. The father goes to work every morning. He is a chief steward at a large white club. The mother sometimes does fancy sewing or supervises parties for the rich families of the town. The children go to a mixed school. In the home they read white papers and magazines. And the mother often says "Don't be like niggers" when the children are bad. A frequent phrase from the father is, "Look how well a white man does things." And so the word white comes to be unconsciously a symbol of all the virtues. It holds for the children beauty, morality, and money. The whisper of "I want to be white" runs silently through their minds. This young poet's home is, I believe, a fairly typical home of the colored middle class. One sees immediately how difficult it would be for an artist born in such a home to interest himself in interpreting the beauty of his own people. He is never taught to see that beauty. He is taught rather not to see it, or if he does, to be ashamed of it when it is not according to Caucasian patterns.

For racial culture the home of a self-styled "high-class" Negro has nothing better to offer. Instead there will perhaps be more aping of things white than in a less cultured or less wealthy home. The father is perhaps a doctor, lawyer, landowner, or politician. The mother may be a social worker, or a teacher, or she may do nothing and have a maid. Father is often dark but he has usually married the lightest woman he could find. The family attend a fashionable church where few really colored faces are to be found. And they themselves draw a color line. In the North they go to white theaters and white movies. And in the South they have at least two cars and a house "like white folks." Nordic manners, Nordic faces, Nordic hair, Nordic art (if any), and an Episcopal heaven. A very high mountain indeed for the would-be racial artist to climb in order to discover himself and his people.

But then there are the low-down folks, the so-called common element, and they are the majority—may the Lord be praised! The people who have their nip of gin on Saturday nights and are not too important to themselves or the community, or too well fed, or too learned to watch the lazy world go round. They live on Seventh Street in Washington or State Street in Chicago and they do not particularly care whether they are like white folks or anybody else. Their joy runs, bang! into ecstasy. Their religion soars to a shout. Work maybe a little today, rest a little tomorrow. Play awhile. Sing awhile. O, let's dance! These common people are not afraid of spirituals, as for a long time their more intellectual brethren were, and jazz is their child. They furnish a wealth of colorful, distinctive material for any artist because they still hold their own individuality in the face of American standardizations. And perhaps these common people will give to the world its truly great Negro artist, the one who is not afraid to be himself. Whereas the better-class Negro would tell the artist what to do, the people at least let him alone when he does appear. And they are not ashamed of him—if they know he exists at all. And they accept what beauty is their own without question.

Certainly there is, for the American Negro artist who can escape the restrictions the more advanced among his own group would put upon him, a great field of unused material ready for his art. Without going outside his race, and even among the better classes with their "white" culture and conscious American manners, but still Negro enough to be different, there is sufficient matter to furnish a black artist with a lifetime of creative work. And when he chooses to touch on the relations between Negroes and whites in this country with their innumerable overtones and undertones, surely, and especially for literature and the drama, there is an inexhaustible supply of themes at hand. To these the Negro artist can give his racial individuality, his heritage of rhythm and warmth, and his incongruous humor that so often, as in the Blues, becomes ironic laughter mixed with tears. But let us look again at the mountain.

A prominent Negro clubwoman in Philadelphia paid eleven dollars to hear Raquel Meller sing Andalusian popular songs. But she told me a few weeks before she would not think of going to hear "that woman," Clara Smith, a great black artist, sing Negro folksongs. And many an upper-class Negro church, even now, would not dream of employing a spiritual in its services. The drab melodies in white folks' hymnbooks are much to be preferred. "We want to worship the Lord correctly and quietly. We don't believe in 'shouting.' Let's be dull like the Nordics," they say, in effect.

The road for the serious black artist, then, who would produce a racial art is most certainly rocky and the mountain is high. Until recently he received almost no encouragement for his work from either white or colored people. The fine novels of Chesnutt go out of print with neither race noticing their passing. The quaint charm and humor of Dunbar's dialect verse brought to him, in his day, largely the same kind of encouragement one would give a sideshow freak (A colored man writing poetry! How odd!) or a clown (How amusing!).

The present vogue in things Negro, although it may do as much harm as good for the budding colored artist, has at least done this: it has brought him forcibly to the attention of his own people among whom for so long, unless the other race had noticed him beforehand, he was a prophet with little honor. I understand that Charles Gilpin acted for years in Negro theaters without any special acclaim from his own, but when Broadway gave him eight curtain calls, Negroes, too, began to beat a tin pan in his honor. I know a young colored writer, a manual worker by day, who had been writing well for the colored magazines for some years, but it was not until he recently broke into the white publications and his first book was accepted by a prominent New York publisher that the "best" Negroes in his city took the trouble to discover that he lived there. Then almost immediately they decided to give a grand dinner for him. But the society ladies were careful to whisper to his mother that perhaps she'd better not come. They were not sure she would have an evening gown.

The Negro artist works against an undertow of sharp criticism and misunderstanding from his own group and unintentional bribes from the whites. "Oh, be respectable, write about nice people, show how good we are," say the Negroes. "Be stereotyped, don't go too far, don't shatter our illusions about you, don't amuse us too seriously. We will pay you," say the whites. Both would have told Jean Toomer not to write *Cane*. The colored people did not praise it. The white people did not buy it. Most of the colored people who did read *Cane* hate it. They are afraid of it. Although the critics gave it good reviews the public remained indifferent. Yet (excepting the work of DuBois) *Cane* contains the finest prose written by a Negro in America. And like the singing of Robeson, it is truly racial.

But in spite of the Nordicized Negro intelligentsia and the desires of some white editors we have an honest American Negro literature already with us. Now I await the rise of the Negro theater. Our folk music, having achieved world-wide fame, offers itself to the genius of the great individual American Negro composer who is to come. And within the next decade I expect to see the work of a growing school of colored artists who paint and model the beauty of dark faces and create with new technique the expressions of their own soul-world. And the Negro dancers who

will dance like flame and the singers who will continue to carry
our songs to all who listen—they will be with us in even greater
numbers tomorrow.

Most of my own poems are racial in theme and treatment,
derived from the life I know. In many of them I try to grasp and
hold some of the meanings and rhythms of jazz. I am as sincere as I
know how to be in these poems and yet after every reading I
answer questions like these from my own people: Do you think
Negroes should always write about Negroes? I wish you wouldn't
read some of your poems to white folks. How do you find anything
interesting in a place like a cabaret? Why do you write about
black people? You aren't black. What makes you do so many jazz
poems?

But jazz to me is one of the inherent expressions of Negro life
in America: the eternal tom-tom beating in the Negro soul—the
tom-tom of revolt against weariness in a white world, a world of
subway trains, and work, work, work; the tom-tom of joy and
laughter, and pain swallowed in a smile. Yet the Philadelphia
clubwoman is ashamed to say that her race created it and she does
not like me to write about it. The old subconscious "white is best"
runs through her mind. Years of study under white teachers, a
lifetime of white books, pictures, and papers, and white manners,
morals, and Puritan standards made her dislike the spirituals. And
now she turns up her nose at jazz and all its manifestations—
likewise almost everything else distinctly racial. She doesn't care
for the Winold Reiss portraits of Negroes because they are "too
Negro." She does not want a true picture of herself from anybody.
She wants the artist to flatter her, to make the white world believe
that all Negroes are as smug and as near white in soul as she
wants to be. But, to my mind, it is the duty of the younger Negro
artist, if he accepts any duties at all from outsiders, to change
through the force of his art that old whispering "I want to be
white," hidden in the aspirations of his people, to "Why should I
want to be white? I am a Negro—and beautiful!"

So I am ashamed for the black poet who says, "I want to be a
poet, not a Negro poet," as though his own racial world were not
as interesting as any other world. I am ashamed, too, for the colored artist who runs from the painting of Negro faces to the
painting of sunsets after the manner of the academicians because
he fears the strange un-whiteness of his own features. An artist
must be free to choose what he does, certainly, but he must also
never be afraid to do what he might choose.

Let the blare of Negro jazz bands and the bellowing voice of Bessie Smith singing Blues penetrate the closed ears of the colored near-intellectuals until they listen and perhaps understand. Let Paul Robeson singing "Water Boy," and Rudolph Fisher writing about the streets of Harlem, and Jean Toomer holding the heart of Georgia in his hands, and Aaron Douglas drawing strange black fantasies cause the smug Negro middle class to turn from their white, respectable, ordinary books and papers to catch a glimmer of their own beauty. We younger Negro artists who create now intend to express our individual dark-skinned selves without fear or shame. If white people are pleased we are glad. If they are not, it doesn't matter. We know we are beautiful. And ugly too. The tom-tom cries and the tom-tom laughs. If colored people are pleased we are glad. If they are not, their displeasure doesn't matter either. We build our temples for tomorrow, strong as we know how, and we stand on top of the mountain, free within ourselves.

HOYT W. FULLER
Towards a Black Aesthetic

THE BLACK revolt is as palpable in letters as it is in the streets, and if it has not yet made its impact upon the Literary Establishment, then the nature of the revolt itself is the reason. For the break between the revolutionary black writers and the "literary main-stream" is, perhaps of necessity, cleaner and more decisive than the noisier and more dramatic break between the black militants and traditional political and institutional structures. Just as black intellectuals have rejected the NAACP, on the one hand, and the two major political parties, on the other, and gone off in search of new and more effective means and methods of seizing power, so revolutionary black writers have turned their backs on the old "certainties" and struck out in new, if uncharted, directions. They have begun the journey toward a black aesthetic.

The road to that place—if it exists at all—cannot, by defini-tion, lead through the literary mainstream. Which is to say that few critics will look upon the new movement with sympathy, even if a number of publishers might be daring enough to publish the works which its adherents produce. The movement will be reviled as "racism-in-reverse," and its writers labeled "racists," opprobrious terms which are flung lightly at black people now that the piper is being paid for all the long years of rejection and abuse which black people have experienced at the hands of white people —with few voices raised in objection.

Is this too harsh and sweeping a generalization? White people might think so; black people will not; which is a way of stating the problem and the prospect before us. Black people are being called "violent" these days, as if violence is a new invention out of the ghetto. But violence against the black minority is in-built in the established American society. There is no need for the white majority to take to the streets to clobber the blacks, although there certainly is *enough* of that; brutalization is inherent in all the customs and practices which bestow privileges on the whites and relegate the blacks to the status of pariahs.

These are old and well-worn truths which hardly need repeating. What is new is the reaction to them. Rapidly now, black people are turning onto that uncertain road, and they are doing so with the approval of all kinds of fellow-travellers who ordinarily are considered "safe" for the other side. In the fall 1967 issue of the *Journal of the National Medical Association* (all-black), for example, Dr. Charles A. De Leon of Cleveland, Ohio, explained why the new turn is necessary: "If young Negroes are to avoid the unnecessary burden of self-hatred (via identification with the aggressor) they will have to develop a keen faculty for identifying, fractionating out, and rejecting the absurdities of the conscious as well as the unconscious white racism in American society from what is worthwhile in it."

Conscious and unconscious white racism is everywhere, infecting all the vital areas of national life. But the revolutionary black writer, like the new breed of militant activist, has decided that white racism will no longer exercise its insidious control over his work. If the tag of "racist" is one the white critic will hang on him in dismissing him, then he is more than willing to bear that. He is not going to separate literature from life.

But just how widespread is white racism—conscious and unconscious—in the realm of letters? In a review of Gwendolyn Brooks's *Selected Poems* in the old *New York Herald Tribune Book Week* back in October 1963, poet Louis Simpson began by writing that the Chicago poet's book of poems "contains some lively pictures of Negro life," an ambiguous enough opener which did not necessarily suggest a literary putdown. But Mr. Simpson's next sentence dispelled all ambiguity. "I am not sure it is possible for a Negro to write well without making us aware he is a Negro," he wrote. "On the other hand, if being a Negro is the only subject, the writing is not important."

All the history of American race relations is contained in that appraisal, despite its disingenuousness. It is civilized, urbane, gentle and elegant; and it is arrogant, condescending, presumptuous and racist. To most white readers, no doubt, Mr. Simpson's words, if not his assessment, seemed eminently sensible; but it is all but impossible to imagine a black reader not reacting to the words with unalloyed fury.

Both black and white readers are likely to go to the core of Mr. Simpson's statement, which is: "if being a Negro is the only subject, the writing is not important." The white reader will, in all probability, find that clear and acceptable enough; indeed, he is used to hearing it. "Certainly," the argument might proceed, "to be important, writing must have *universal values, universal implications;* it cannot deal exclusively with Negro problems." The plain but unstated assumption being, of course, that there are no "universal values" and no "universal implications" in Negro life.

Mr. Simpson is a greatly respected American poet, a winner of the Pulitzer Prize for poetry, as is Miss Brooks, and it will be considered the depth of irresponsibility to accuse him of the viciousness of racism. He is probably the gentlest and most compassionate of men. Miss Brooks, who met Mr. Simpson at the University of California not many months after the review was published, reported that the gentleman was most kind and courteous to her. There is no reason to doubt it. The essential point here is not the presence of overt hostility; it is the absence of clarity of vision. The glass through which black life is viewed by white Americans is, inescapably (it is a matter of extent), befogged by the hot breath of history. True "objectivity" where race is concerned is as rare as a necklace of Hope diamonds.

In October 1967, a young man named Jonathan Kozol published a book called *Death at an Early Age,* which is an account of his experiences as a teacher in a predominantly Negro elementary school in Boston. Mr. Kozol broke with convention in his approach to teaching and incurred the displeasure of a great many people, including the vigilant policeman father of one of his few white pupils. The issue around which the young teacher's opponents seemed to rally was his use of a Langston Hughes poem in his classroom. Now the late Langston Hughes was a favorite target of some of the more aggressive right-wing pressure groups during his lifetime, but it remained for an official of the Boston School Committee to come to the heart of the argument against the poet. Explaining the opposition to the poem used by Mr. Kozol, the school official said that "no poem by any Negro author can be considered permissible if it involves suffering."

There is a direct connecting line between the school official's rejection of Negro poetry which deals with suffering and Mr. Simpson's facile dismissal of writing about Negroes "only." Negro life, which is characterized by suffering imposed by the maintenance of white privilege in America, must be denied validity and banished beyond the pale. The facts of Negro life accuse white people. In order to look at Negro life unflinchingly, the white viewer either must relegate it to the realm of the subhuman, thereby justifying an attitude of indifference, or else the white viewer must confront the imputation of guilt against him. And no man who considers himself humane wishes to admit complicity in crimes against the human spirit.

There is a myth abroad in American literary criticism that Negro writing has been favored by a "double standard" which judges it less stringently. The opposite is true. No one will seriously dispute that, on occasions, critics have been generous to Negro writers, for a variety of reasons; but there is no evidence that generosity has been the rule. Indeed, why should it be assumed that literary critics are more sympathetic to blacks than are other white people? During any year, hundreds of mediocre volumes of prose and poetry by white writers are published, little noted, and forgotten. At the same time, the few creative works by black writers are seized and dissected and, if not deemed of the "highest" literary quality, condemned as still more examples of the failure of black writers to scale the rare heights of literature. And the condemnation is especially strong for those black works which have not screened their themes of suffering, redemption and triumph behind frail facades of obscurity and conscious "universality."

Central to the problem of the irreconcilable conflict between the black writer and the white critic is the failure of recognition of a fundamental and obvious truth of American life—that the two races are residents of two separate and naturally antagonistic worlds. No manner of well-meaning rhetoric about "one country" and "one people," and even about the two races' long joint-occupancy of this troubled land, can obliterate the high, thick dividing walls which hate and history have erected—and maintain—between them. The breaking down of those barriers might be a goal, worthy or unworthy (depending on viewpoint), but the reality remains. The world of the black outsider, however much it approximates and parallels and imitates the world of the white insider, by its very nature is inheritor and generator of values and viewpoints which threaten the insiders. The outsiders' world, feeding on its own sources, fecundates and vibrates, stamping its progeny with its very special ethos, its insuperably logical bias.

The black writer, like the black artist generally, has wasted much time and talent denying a propensity every rule of human dignity demands that he possess, seeking an identity that can only do violence to his sense of self. Black Americans are, for all practical purposes, colonized in their native land, and it can be argued that those who would submit to subjection without struggle deserve to be enslaved. It is one thing to accept the guiding principles on which the American republic ostensibly was founded; it is quite another thing to accept the prevailing practices which violate those principles.

The rebellion in the streets is the black ghetto's response to the vast distance between the nation's principles and its practices. But that rebellion has roots which are deeper than most white people know; it is many-veined, and its blood has been sent pulsating to the very heart of black life. Across this country, young black men and women have been infected with a fever of affirmation. They are saying, "We are black and beautiful," and the ghetto is reacting with a liberating shock of realization which transcends mere chauvinism. They are rediscovering their heritage and their history, seeing it with newly focused eyes, struck with the wonder of that strength which has enabled them to endure and, in spirit, to defeat the power of prolonged and calculated oppression. After centuries of being told, in a million different ways, that they were not beautiful, and that whiteness of skin, straightness of hair, and aquilineness of features constituted the only measures of beauty, black people have revolted. The trend has not yet reached the point of avalanche, but the future can be clearly seen in the growing number of black people who are snapping off the shackles of imitation and are wearing their skin, their hair, and their features "natural" and with pride. In a poem called "Nittygritty,"

which is dedicated to poet LeRoi Jones, Joseph Bevans Bush put
the new credo this way:

> . . . *We all gonna come from behind*
>   *those*
> *Wigs and start to stop using those*
> *Standards of beauty which can never*
> *Be a frame for our reference; wash*
> *That excess grease out of our hair,*
> *Come out of that bleach bag and get*
> *Into something meaningful to us as*
> *Nonwhite people—Black people* . . .

If the poem lacks the resonances of William Shakespeare, that
is intentional. The "great bard of Avon" has only limited relevance to the revolutionary spirit raging in the ghetto. Which is not
to say that the black revolutionaries reject the "universal" statements inherent in Shakespeare's works; what they do reject, however, is the literary assumption that the style and language and the
concerns of Shakespeare establish the appropriate limits and
"frame of reference" for black poetry and people. This is above
and beyond the doctrine of revolution to which so many of the
brighter black intellectuals are committed, that philosophy articulated by the late Frantz Fanon which holds that, in the time of
revolutionary struggle, the traditional Western liberal ideals are
not merely irrelevant but they must be assiduously opposed. The
young writers of the black ghetto have set out in search of a black
aesthetic, a system of isolating and evaluating the artistic works of
black people which reflect the special character and imperatives of
black experience.

That was the meaning and intent of poet-playwright LeRoi
Jones' aborted Black Arts Theater in Harlem in 1965, and it is
the generative idea behind such later groups and institutions as
Spirit House in Newark, the Black House in San Francisco, the
New School of Afro-American Thought in Washington, D.C., the
Institute for Black Studies in Los Angeles, Forum '66 in Detroit,
and the Organization of Black American Culture in Chicago. It is
a serious quest, and the black writers themselves are well aware of
the possibility that what they seek is, after all, beyond codifying.
They are fully aware of the dual nature of their heritage, and of
the subtleties and complexities; but they are even more aware of
the terrible reality of their outsideness, of their political and economic powerlessness, and of the desperate racial need for unity.

And they have been convinced, over and over again, by the ir-
refutable facts of history and by the cold intransigence of the
privileged white majority that the road to solidarity and strength
leads inevitably through reclamation and indoctrination of black
art and culture.

In Chicago, the Organization of Black American Culture has
moved boldly toward a definition of a black aesthetic. In the
writers' workshop sponsored by the group, the writers are deliberately striving to invest their work with the distinctive styles and
rhythms and colors of the ghetto, with those peculiar qualities
which, for example, characterize the music of a John Coltrane or a
Charlie Parker or a Ray Charles. Aiming toward the publication
of an anthology which will manifest this aesthetic, they have established criteria by which they measure their own work and eliminate from consideration those poems, short stories, plays, essays
and sketches which do not adequately reflect the black experience.
What the sponsors of the workshop most hope for in this delicate
and dangerous experiment is the emergence of new black critics
who will be able to articulate and expound the new aesthetic and
eventually set in motion the long overdue assault against the re-
strictive assumptions of the white critics.

It is not that the writers of OBAC have nothing to start with.
That there exists already a mystique of blackness even some white
critics will agree. In the November 1967 issue of *Esquire* magazine, for instance, George Frazier, a white writer who is not in the
least sympathetic with the likes of LeRoi Jones, nevertheless did a
commendable job of identifying elements of the black mystique.
Discussing "the Negro's immense style, a style so seductive that
it's little wonder that black men are, as Shakespeare put it in *The
Two Gentlemen of Verona*, 'pearls in beauteous ladies' eyes,' " Mr.
Frazier singled out the following examples;

"The formal daytime attire (black sack coats and striped
trousers) the Modern Jazz Quartet wore when appearing in concert; the lazy amble with which Jimmy Brown used to return to
the huddle; the delight the late "Big Daddy" Lipscomb took in
making sideline tackles in full view of the crowd and the way, after
crushing a ball carrier to the ground, he would chivalrously assist
him to his feet; the constant cool of 'Satchel' Paige; the chic of
Bobby Short; the incomparable grace of John Bubbles—things like
that are style and they have nothing whatsoever to do with ability
(although the ability, God wot, is there, too). It is not that there

are no white men with style, for there is Fred Astaire, for one, and Cary Grant, for another, but that there are so very, very few of them. Even in the dock, the black man has an air about him—Adam Clayton Powell, so blithe, so self-possessed, so casual, as contrasted with Tom Dodd, sanctimonious, whining, an absolute disgrace. What is it that made Miles Davis and Cassius Clay, Sugar Ray Robinson and Archie Moore and Ralph Ellison and Sammy Davis, Jr. seem so special was their style. . . .

"And then, of course, there is our speech.

"For what nuances, what plays of light and shade, what little sharpnesses our speech has are almost all of them, out of the black world—the talk of Negro musicians and whores and hoodlums and whatnot. 'Cool' and all the other words in common currency came out of the mouths of Negroes.

" 'We love you madly,' said Duke Ellington, and now the phrase is almost a cliché. But it is a quality of the Negro's style—that he is forever creative, forever more stylish. There was a night when, as I stood with Duke Ellington outside the Hickory House, I looked up at the sky and said, 'I hope it's a good day tomorrow. I want to wake up early.'

" 'Any day I wake up,' said Ellington, 'is a good day.'

"And that was style."

Well, yes. . . .

Black critics have the responsibility of approaching the works of black writers assuming these qualities to be present, and with the knowledge that white readers—and white critics—cannot be expected to recognize and to empathize with the subtleties and significance of black style and technique. They have the responsibility of rebutting the white critics and of putting things in the proper perspective. Within the past few years, for example, Chicago's white critics have given the backs of their hands to worthy works by black playwrights, part of their criticism directly attributable to their ignorance of the intricacies of black style and black life. Oscar Brown, Jr.'s rockingly soulful *Kicks and Company* was panned for many of the wrong reasons; and Douglas Turner Ward's two plays, *Day of Absence* and *Happy Ending*, were tolerated as labored and a bit tasteless. Both Brown and Ward had dealt satirically with race relations, and there were not many black people in the audiences who found themselves in agreement with the critics. It is the way things are—but not the way things will continue to be if the OBAC writers and those similarly concerned elsewhere in America have anything to say about it.

[JULIAN MAYFIELD
      *Into the Mainstream
         and Oblivion*   ]

RECENTLY AN African student, long resident in this country, con-
fessed to a group of his intimates that he did not trust the American Negro. "What will you do," he asked them, "in the unlikely
event that the United States becomes involved in a colonial war in
Africa?" The immediate answer was: "Man, we will shoot you
down like dogs." The remark prompted general laughter, but, on
reflection, it is not amusing.

The visiting student had sensed what his friends already took
for granted: that the contemporary American Negro is faced with
a most perplexing dilemma. He does not know who he is or where
his loyalties belong. Moreover, he has every right to his confusion
for he exists on a moving plateau that is rapidly shifting away
from the candid oppression of the past toward—what? The future
of the American Negro is most often depicted as an increasingly
accelerated absorption into the mainstream of American life
where, presumably, he will find happiness as a first-class citizen.
This is perhaps the rosy view, but it already has validity insofar as
it represents the attitude and aspiration of a majority of Negroes,
especially those who are called leaders.

Unfortunately—and one cannot see how it could have been
otherwise—the Negro writer has been unable to escape this confusion. The AMSAC writers' conference demonstrated that the Negro writer is having trouble squaring his art and his sense of
reality with the American dream. He, too, finds himself wondering
who he is, an American or what? And if finally the scholars convince him that he is indeed an American, he asks if this condition
must be the extent of his vision. He is all too aware that in recent
years a myth that was once accepted without question has shown
signs of being discredited. This myth implied that if one could
become a real American, he had achieved the best that world could
offer.

The conference panel on social protest was especially interesting in regard to the advisability of the Negro's embracing the

white American's literary values in exchange for those of his own that he now finds outmoded. Many of the speakers felt that social protest, as we have known it, had outlived its usefulness. They knew, of course, that racial injustice still flourishes in our national life, but they felt that the moral climate has been established for the eventual breakdown of racism, and that they need not therefore employ their literary tools to attack it in the same old way, that is to say, directly and violently. To this participant it seemed that the younger writer was seeking a new way of defining himself. Grudgingly he admitted that his work in the past may have suffered artistically because of his preoccupation with the problem of being a Negro in the United States. Yet he seemed reluctant to leap head first into the nation's literary mainstream (a word that was heard repeatedly throughout the conference).

In this I believe the writers were being wiser than most of our church, civic, and political leaders, who are pushing with singular concentration toward one objective: integration. This is to be applauded and actively encouraged so long as integration is interpreted to mean the attainment of full citizenship rights in such areas as voting, housing, education, employment, and the like. But if, as the writers have reason to suspect, integration means completely identifying the Negro with the American image—that great-power face that the world knows and the Negro knows better—then the writer must not be judged too harshly for balking at the prospect.

Perhaps some of them had seen a recent film called *The Defiant Ones*, which attracted world-wide attention because of its graphic, symbolic depiction of American Negro-white relations. In the film a black convict and a white convict are chained to one another in a desperate bid for freedom. Each hates the other intensely, but both soon realize that if they are to find freedom they must cooperate for their mutual good. By the time their actual chains are removed, they have come to believe that they are bound together in a larger way—that their fates, their destinies, are intertwined—so much so that in the end, most remarkably (and, one hopes, not prophetically), the Negro foregoes his chance for freedom because his white comrade is too weak to escape.

The symbolism is obvious and, to one observer at least, disturbing in its implications. For it is not uncommon to hear nowadays that the American Negro and the white are forever bound together and must, perforce, pursue a common destiny. On the face of it this approach seems soundly based on common sense. Throughout his long, cruel history in this land, the Negro has been the most avid seeker of the American dream—most avid because for him its realization was often a matter of life and death. If he could but grasp the dream, he could walk in dignity without fear of the abuse heaped on him by a scornful white majority. So fervid has been his pursuit of the dream that in every war and regardless of the nature of the war, his leaders have offered up his sons, the strength of any race, saying, "Take our youth—take our youth and they will prove their worth as Americans."

But the dream has proved elusive, and there is reason to believe that for the Negro it never had a chance of realization. Now, because of a combination of international and domestic pressures, a social climate is being created wherein, at least in theory, he may win the trappings of freedom that other citizens already take for granted. One may suggest that during this period of transition the Negro would do well to consider if the best use of these trappings will be to align himself totally to the objectives of the dominant sections of the American nation. Just as an insurance company will not issue a policy without determining the life expectancy of the buyer, neither should the Negro—in this case the buyer—accept the policy before he determines if the company is solvent. If the dream he has chased for three centuries is now dying even for white Americans, he would be wise to consider alternative objectives. The urgency of our times demands a deeper and more critical approach from Negro leadership. This new approach is suggested by the Negro mother who, having lost one of her sons in the Korean adventures, was heard to remark: "I don't care if the army is integrated; next time I want to know what kind of war my boy is being taken to."

In the same sense the Negro writer is being gently nudged toward a rather vague thing called "the mainstream of American literature." This trend also would seem to be based on common sense. But before plunging into it he owes it to the future of his art to analyze the contents of the American mainstream to determine the full significance of his commitment to it. He may decide that, though the music is sweet, he would rather play in another orchestra. Or, to place himself in the position of the black convict in *The Defiant Ones*, he may decide that he need not necessarily share the fate of his white companion who, after all, proffers the hand of friendship a little late. The Negro writer may conclude that his best salvation lies in escaping the narrow national orbit—artistic, cultural and political—and soaring into the space of more universal experience.

What are the principal characteristics of the mainstream of American literature? To this observer they are apathy and either a reluctance or a fear of writing about anything that matters. William Barrett in *The New York Times* (May 10, 1959) asserts that power, vitality and energy have been abundant in recent American writing, but concedes that "the writers have lacked a center somewhere, they have been without great and central themes."

The phenomenon of our era is the seeming lack of concern shown by American creative writers for the great questions facing the peoples of the world. The most important of these, and the most obvious, is the madness of war. There are other great issues that challenge us, but the American writer has turned his back on them. He deals with the foibles of suburban living, the junior executive, dope addiction, homosexuality, incest and divorce.

I am not suggesting that anyone (least of all the present writer) should sit down with the grand purpose of writing a novel against war. But I do mean to imply that writers of the mainstream, reflecting the attitude of the American people generally seem determined not to become involved in any of the genuine fury, turmoil, and passion of life; and it is only such involvement that makes life worth living. Where, for instance, is the humor that once characterized our national literature, and what has happened to the American's ability, indeed his proclivity, to laugh at himself? A stultifying respectability hangs over the land, and that is always a sign of decline, for it inhibits the flowering of new ideas that lead to progress and cultural regeneration. In short, the literary mainstream seems to be running dangerously shallow.

It would be pleasant to report that Negro writers have been unaffected by the current literary atmosphere, but it would not be candid. If the AMSAC conference demonstrated any one thing, it was that Negro writers generally are uncertain about the path they should explore in seeking to illuminate the life of man. I say "generally," for the individual writer charts his own course and follows or changes it at will. But it is interesting that there was evident so little unity of approach. One would have thought that Negro writers, representing a tragic and unique experience in our national history, would be bound together by a dominant theme in their work. But if this is the case, it was not obvious at the conference, and such a theme is difficult to detect in recent novels and plays.

The advantage of the Negro writer, the factor that may keep his work above the vacuity of the American mainstream, is that for him the facade of the American way of life is always transparent. He sings the national anthem *sotto voce* and has trouble reconciling the "dream" to the reality he knows. If he feels American at all, it is only when he is on foreign soil and, peculiarly enough, often finds himself defending that which he hated at home. He walks the streets of his nation an alien, and yet he feels no bond to the continent of his ancestors. He is indeed the man without a country. And yet this very detachment may give him the insight of the stranger in the house, placing him in a better position to illuminate contemporary American life as few writers of the mainstream can. This alienation should serve also to make him more sensitive to philosophical and artistic influences that originate beyond our national cultural boundaries.

Finally, if the situation I have described is real, a tragic future is indicated for the American Negro people. Unlike most of the colored peoples of the earth, he has no land and cannot realistically aspire to supremacy in the environment that has been his home for three centuries. In his most optimistic moods—and this period is one of them—the best he can hope for is submersion in what is euphemistically called the American melting pot. Despite the vigorous efforts of Negro leaders and the international pressures on the United States, it seems unlikely that this submersion will occur to any large degree within the foreseeable future. The likelihood is that the Negro people will continue for several decades to occupy, to a diminishing degree, the position of the unwanted child who, having been brought for a visit, must remain for the rest of his life. This is a hard conclusion to draw, but if it has validity, it is better recognized than ignored.

IF THE NEGRO author's past achievements have not been great, at least they have been motivated by great intentions. He has created the kind of literature that Walt Whitman had in mind when he said, "Literature is big only in one way—when used as an aid in the growth of the humanities—a furthering of the cause of the masses—a means whereby men may be revealed to each other as brothers."

But as we face the second half of the twentieth century, there is a babel of voices seeking to direct the harassed author. There is widespread dissatisfaction not only with the failure of these authors to achieve a maturity in artistic technique, but also with the limited goals some of them seemingly have set for themselves. In this welter of confusion I dare suggest a blueprint for writers who wish to accept the glorious opportunities and grave reponsibilities of the next half century.

The first of my requirements is a mastery of craftsmanship. The past record in this respect is dismal. Despite one hundred and ninety years of effort, no American Negro poet has achieved a status comparable to such first-rate white poets as Robert Frost or Edwin Arlington Robinson. In the field of drama the record is almost nil. Only in fiction, and that within the last decade, has the Negro author achieved first-rate distinction.

The chief weakness of these writers has been in the area of craftsmanship and design rather than theme. No Negro author before the advent of Richard Wright's *Native Son* (1940) had deserved a listing among first-rate American novelists. Only Frank Yerby and Willard Motley have earned such a place since. Other authors have treated equally potent themes, but mastery of the art of fiction has been lacking. For the most part, the style is heavy and laborious, more suitable to a sociological treatise than to a novel. They fail in the three major essentials of good craftsmanship—namely, the ability to invent interesting and natural conversation, the ability to create memorable characters, and the ability to construct unforgettable scenes through the creation of pity and terror.

In addition to Wright, Yerby, and Motley, there are five other novelists who possess one or more of these qualities to a considerable degree, and who, if they continue to improve, will achieve first rank in the near future: they are William Attaway, Ann Petry, Arna Bontemps, William Gardner Smith, and J. Saunders Redding.

My second requirement for the Negro author is the continued use of racial themes. In certain quarters a great clamor has arisen for Negro authors to abandon racial material and launch out in the "universal depths." It is the belief of this school of thought that a writer's preoccupation with materials dealing with his own race is an admission that he is incapable of dealing with any other. It further maintains that such a writer is adding fuel to the fires of race consciousness, segregation, and racial proscription. To counteract these sinister forces, the writer must treat universal themes, and leave to white authors the exploitation of subject matter dealing with Negro life.

In my opinion such perverted reasoning is pure sophistry. In all ages and climates of man's civilization, one of the major purposes of literature has been to represent the thought and actions of men with as much truth to life as is possible. Naturally a writer can portray life that he feels deeply and understands minutely with a greater degree of genuineness and truth than he can life which is more foreign to his experience. I cannot believe that a Negro, sensitive, as all artists must be, can feel and understand anything in America as minutely and as truthfully as he can the effects of race. Then, why should he not write about that which he knows best? No white man or woman can understand the tragedy, the pathos, and the humor of being a Negro in America as well as a talented Negro. Sir Philip Sidney's advice to the young poet, "Look in thy heart, and write," has not yet been proved either invalid or unwise.

Furthermore, the record shows that up to this point, at least, the most powerful and most significant poetry, drama, and fiction by Negro authors have been based on racial themes. Ann Petry's second novel, which logically should have been better than the first, is greatly inferior to *The Street* both in design and execution. She had to be so concerned with conjuring up vicarious experiences of a white society with which she was not minutely familiar that she lost the naturalness of expression necessary to good art.

Zora Neale Hurston's *Seraph on the Suwanne,* which portrays life
among white Floridians, is almost unbelievably inferior to her two
novels of Negro life. Even Frank Yerby achieved greater artistic
perfection in *The Foxes of Harrow* and *The Vixens,* both of which
have a background of Negro life and action, than he did in *The
Golden Hawk* and *Pride's Castle,* which completely ignore the
racial angle.

Professor Harry A. Overstreet of New York City College was
right when he said, "The whites need to know the Negro and like
him. A special obligation, therefore, is upon the Negro writer to
turn to the story as a means whereby he may make his people
known."

My third requirement for the Negro author is the use of
social propaganda subordinated so skillfully to the purposes of art
that it will not insult the average intelligent reader. I do not think
it is sufficient for the Negro author to treat racial themes with no
regard to their deeper social implications as was done by Countee
Cullen in *One Way to Heaven* and Zora Neale Hurston in *Jonah's
Gourd Vine* and *Their Eyes Were Watching God.*

Is propaganda a legitimate ingredient of literature? Albert
Guerard, in *Art for Art's Sake,* says, "An artist does not suffer
from being identified with a cause; if the cause is himself, a vital
part of himself, it is also a fit element of his art. He suffers most
from not being identified with his cause, from adopting and serv-
ing a purpose which remains alien to his personality."

In *The Great Tradition* Granville Hicks maintains, "In the
whole history of American literature one can scarcely think of a
writer, commonly recognized as great, who did not immerse himself in the life of the times, who did not concern himself with the
problems of his age."

Tolstoi, in *What Is Art?,* declares, "We know that the well
being of man lies in union with his fellowmen. . . . Art should
transform this perception into feeling."

If one accepts the conclusions of the three critics quoted
above, as I certainly do, he must also accept propaganda as a
legitimate ingredient of serious literature. But I do not advocate
art for the sake of propaganda. I demand a proper subordination
and the observance of good taste. An example of the violation of
the limitations I place upon this requirement may be seen in the
poetry of Frank Marshall Davis. His propaganda, though based on
sound critical analysis, is so blunt and militant that it has little
chance of winning sympathetic consideration. In addition, much

of it offends good taste. Such bitter iconoclasm as the following quotation from "Christ Is a Dixie Nigger" goes beyond the bounds which I have prescribed:

> *Your pink priests who whine about Pilate and Judas and Gethsemane I'd like to hog-tie and dump into the stinking cells to write a New Testament around the Scottsboro Boys.*
> *Subdivide your million dollar temples into liquor taverns and high class whore-houses. . . . My nigger Christ can't get past the door anyway.*
> *Remember this, you wise guys.*
> *Your tales about Jesus of Nazareth are no go with me. . . . I've got a dozen Christs in Dixie all bloody and black.*

With his extraordinary imagination and his marvelous skill in the use of words, Davis could make a favorable impression in the world of poetry, provided he curb his bitterness and temper his cynicism with reasonable restraint.

My fourth requirement grows out of the third. One of the best methods of subordinating propaganda to art is the skillful use of symbolism. By this means the Negro author can fight the battles of his race with subtlety and popularity. Willard Motley, in presenting the story of an Italian minority in *Knock on Any Door*, has symbolized the problems of all minorities, including his own race.

But the chief symbolist among Negro authors is Frank Yerby. Starting his literary career in 1944 with "Health Card," a bitter story of America's rejection of the Negro as a dignified human being, which won for him an O. Henry Memorial Prize, he has steadily progressed from complete absorption in a racial theme to complete abandonment of racial material. But in all of his non-racial writings he has substituted a racial symbol, the symbol of rejection.

He finds in the social rebels of the white race, in men and women who because of birth, or manner of livelihood, or disregard of social and moral proprieties have become pariahs among their own people, an archetype of racial rejection. But these white rejectees fight back. They build industrial empires, or pile up huge mountains of illicit wealth, or become swashbuckling pirates who defy the laws of the smug and the respectable. Thus, symbolically the white rejectees get their revenge on a proud and haughty society, and through them the rejected Negro can feel a sense of vicarious triumph.

I conclude with the challenging words of J. Donald Adams: "Sometimes I think the wheel has turned full circle, and that writers must be the fighters now. They really stand at Armageddon, and must battle for the Lord. They, more than anyone else, perhaps, can be effective in preserving the values that are threatened."

> ADDISON GAYLE, JR.
> *Perhaps Not So Soon One Morning*

IN THE INTRODUCTION to *Soon One Morning*, editor Herbert Hill observes: "Negro authors in dealing with the reality of American life, have, of course, been unable to escape an awareness of the racial situation, especially one that fundamentally changes so very little. *Now*, however, this awareness is transmuted brilliantly and powerfully into literature. . . . *today the Negro artist is asserting his vision and his creative imagination."* (*Italics mine.*)

If one pushes Hill's thesis to its logical conclusion, the Negro writer is now, at long last, capable of entering the "mainstream of American Literature." The prodigal son has returned home, been scrubbed clean of the dirt and grime of protest, been baptized in the crystal-clear waters of universality and, like Ralph Ellison, "transcend[ed] the traditional preoccupations of the Negro writer; [and] ultimately . . . is concerned not with race but with man."

One is reminded of John Bunyan's *Pilgrim's Progress*, wherein the character, Christian, moves from one continuum to another; from sin and avarice to redemption and salvation, at which point he is welcomed into the councils of the heavenly host. Likewise, if one believes Hill, soon one morning the society will become cognizant of the fact that the Negro writer has come down from "The Hill Difficulty," journeyed through "By Pass Meadow," and around "Doubting Castle," on through "The Sea of Despond," travesting "the limits of racial parochialism into the whole range of the modern writer's preoccupations."

Presumably, therefore, the Negro writer will at long last be welcomed into the company of the literary host; shown his rightful seat in the academic circles; and annointed with the oils of fame, posterity, and wealth. In other words, the New Canaan lies across the road, and soon one great getting up morning, "in sandal schoon and scallop shells," the Negro writer will waltz through the gilded doors which lead to American literary immortality.

The purpose of this paper is not to argue with Herbert Hill's observations or assumptions. Suffice it to say that his claims that the Negro writer is finally being assimilated into the American literary community is negated by the two writers whom he chooses to support his claims: "In the work of both Ellison and Baldwin, the Negro's color, his identity, or rather, his 'invisibility,' are used poetically and symbolically to communicate the dilemma of all men who are denied dignity and purpose in the contemporary world. Their work demonstrates a new literary sensibility that distinguishes their writing from the work of most Negro authors of the past."

A cursory examination of Baldwin's novels and plays, how-ever, will reveal that Baldwin's major characters, despite his pro-nounced literary creed, differ little from the characters of Chester Himes, William Gardner Smith, Ann Petry, and, of course, Rich-ard Wright. In fact, Richard Henry of *Blues for Mr. Charlie* and Rufus Scott of *Another Country* are poor imitations of Wright's Bigger Thomas, lacking the grandeur, force, and magnetism of their predecessor. Baldwin's Ida Scott, likewise, had been drawn before, with much more artistic competence by Ann Petry in *The Street*. As Irving Howe observes: "Baldwin has not yet succeeded in composing the kind of novel he counterposed to the work of Richard Wright."

But neither has Ralph Ellison. Despite Ellison's claims to the contrary, *Invisible Man* is saturated throughout with protest: the protagonist's reaction to the credo of his grandfather; the treat-ment of the "white liberal," Mr. Norton; the realistic portraiture of Dr. Bledsoe (a character whom Saunders Redding has also drawn in *Stranger and Alone*); the protagonist's reaction to the seduction attempt of a communist official's white wife; the power-ful, evocative scene of the race riot; and overall, the major conflict of the novel, a poetic rendition of the race-rending conflict between the philosophy of W. E. B. DuBois and that of Booker T. Washing-ton, which has played so important a part in modern Negro his-tory. It is because of the protest that *Invisible Man*, to quote Hill, "evokes a world which perhaps only an American Negro can fully apprehend."

But, too, Hill's thesis is based upon an untenable premise.

The argument is that the Negro writer is denied entrance into Canaan because he has not met the artistic rules for entrance. Nothing, however, could be further from the truth. To my knowledge, no critic has accused William Dean Howells of overwhelming artistic ability; none has suggested that artistically, Harriet Beecher Stowe measures up to Marcel Proust or Henry James. And one discusses Upton Sinclair's *The Jungle*, Dreiser's *Sister Carrie*, and Fitzgerald's *The Great Gatsby* in sociological, not aesthetic, terminology. It would appear, therefore, that the Negro writer has been excluded from contemporary American literature not because of artistic deficiencies, but primarily because of race.

Nothing better illustrates this point than my experiences at the City College of New York. In the spring of 1965, the City College initiated a Pre-Baccalaureate Program designed to offer youngsters, economically deprived, and unable to meet the rigid admissions criteria of the college, the opportunity to progress from a nonmatriculated status to full membership, within a few years, in the college community. To aid in this pursuit, remedial courses were established to meet the needs of students who came with special problems. The English Department participated in this endeavor.

Though an integral part of the Department of English, the Pre-Baccalaureate staff functioned as a unit, under the directorship of a member appointed by the chairman. I joined the staff in the fall of 1966, and was assigned to teach three courses: two grammar courses and one composition course. In the spring semester of 1967, my assignment was reversed: two composition courses and one grammar course. My text for the spring semester, *The Essayist*, a collection of essays edited by Sheridan Baker, was chosen for me by the director. Though not a bad text, I believed that for this experience *The Essayist* was lacking in material which held more than superficial interest for our students. Certainly, the essays had not been collected with Negro and Puerto Rican students in mind.

To remedy this defect, I proposed, at a staff meeting, to supplement *The Essayist* with two other texts: Cervantes' *Don Quixote* and Hill's *Soon One Morning*. Only a satirist of the wit and skill of a Jonathan Swift could accurately portray the ensuing battle of the books. When I announced the text, *Soon One Morning*, the director began, hastily, to scribble the title in his notebook. However, after hearing my subsequent description of the text (an anthology of Negro writing) the moving hand ceased to move on, other staff members shuffled uneasily in their seats, and the battle commenced. A blow by blow account of our comic, but heated, debate over the usage of a text which none of the staff except myself had read, would require too much space to record here; suffice it to say that Odysseus' battle with the Cyclops pales in comparison.

The major arguments of the opposition may be condensed to three: 1. The anthology was not in the "mainstream of American literature," 2. Puerto Rican, Chinese, and Caucasian students would be insulted if forced to use a text with Negro writers, and 3. Negro students, themselves, would be embarrassed if forced to study from such a text. The debate ended in a stalemate. I was asked to choose some writer who had inspired me, whereat I boldly announced, James Baldwin, a completely unsuspected choice, leaving the conflict still pending.

Subsequently, due to the pressure of two Negro staff members, more diplomatic than I, negotiations were carried on, resulting in permission to use the text for the following semester. Therefore, during the spring semester of 1967, I used as a supplementary text, Herbert Hill's anthology, *Soon One Morning*. Yet the arguments raised by the opposition continued to annoy me. Only the charge that the anthology was not in the "American literary mainstream" could be dismissed outright. The mainstream of American literature is what the instructors, publishers, and critics say it is, and the fact that few Negro writers are included reflects more on the intellectual bias of the academicians than on the shortcomings of the Negro writer.

The other arguments, however, were cause for concern. Would students, other than Negro, who had been nursed on curricula which systematically excluded Negro writers, be insulted by having now, as one of their texts, a Negro anthology? Further, had Negroes degenerated to that condition of Baldwin's Rufus Scott wherein, in despair, hopelessness, and futility, they turned their anger inward in self hate, trepidation, and shame?

In an attempt to answer these questions, I implored a colleague, Betty Rawls, a counselor on the Pre-Baccalaureate staff of wide experience and competence, to draw up a questionnaire which I administered to each of my classes at the end of the spring semester.

The "Attitudinal Questionnaire" was composed of ten questions, each followed by four statements of which the student was to choose the most plausible to him. The students were instructed not to put their names on the questionnaire, and the only additional information sought was age, sex, and family background. Students were encouraged to write whatever comments they wished about either the text or the course. The questionnaire was submitted to forty-one students, of whom eleven were Puerto Rican, two, Caucasian, one, Chinese, and twenty-seven, Negro. Examples of the questions are as follows: The choice of *Soon One Morning* as a classroom textbook

> a. was a good one providing interesting reading material.
> b. was not good; the writing tended to be boring and unstimulating.
> c. was all right but another text including Negro writers as well as writers from other races would have been better.
> d. was objectionable because it did not really relate to what we should be learning in literature.

Again:

> Having this anthology as a textbook made me feel
>
> a. very embarrassed throughout the course.
> b. somewhat embarrassed only when we read certain stories.
> c. somewhat embarrassed throughout the course.
> d. totally at ease, having no feelings of embarrassment or uncomfortableness.

In response to the second example, thirty-six students checked answer d, two b, and three did not respond. Of the Negro students, all checked d, with the exception of three students who did not respond.

Another question sought a direct response based on attitudes:

> Circle the comment that best explains your feelings about the use of *Soon One Morning*.
>
> a. I felt resentful about having a text with just Negro authors.
> b. I had a feeling of pride knowing that Negro authors were finally being read for study in major university English classes.
> c. I really didn't think about the issue of whether the authors were Negro or not; it didn't matter to me one way or the other.
> d. I felt proud that Negro writers were finally being studied in a college English class; but I felt the scope was limited inasmuch as we did not study, in this anthology, other than Negro authors.

Of the forty-one students, twenty-one checked answer c, fifteen, answer b, and five, answer d. None checked answer a.

Another question dealt with overall evaluation:

My overall evaluation for the choice of *Soon One Morning* as
a text for this English course is

      a. excellent   c. fair
      b. good   d. poor

Twenty-four students thought that the text was excellent; thirteen
that the text was good, and two thought that the text was fair.
None rated the text below fair.

The statistics, however, reveal only part of the story.
Throughout the semester, the majority of the students drew parallels between the writings in the anthology and writings assigned in
the library, using Negro writers as their "touchstones." Further,
in an experience, perhaps, without precedent in a predominantly
white university, fourteen students, in one semester, wrote research papers on Negro writers. One such paper, written by a
Puerto Rican after discussion of an essay by Saunders Redding,
was a critical analysis of Redding's *On Being Negro in America.*
Another paper dealt with DuBois' *The Souls of Black Folk,* and
still another was an extensive study of the poetry of Langston
Hughes.

The results of the experience were favorable, evidencing the
fact that if the keys to the gates of Canaan were held by students,
the Negro writer would be welcomed with little trepidation. Such,
however, is not the case and, though the Negro writer may have
undergone the Odyssean experience, still, at this late hour of the
twentieth century, he wanders in pursuit of that promised morning
of acknowledgement and acceptance.

Yet, it remains doubtful that such a morning will ever come.
In colleges and universities throughout America, Negro literature,
when taught at all, is taught as an elective course, never as an
integral part of the American experience. As critic James Emanuel
has observed, the Negro writer is the invisible man of American
literature and, despite attempts at assimilation, remains invisible,
primarily because those who could do most to give him corporeal
form, are mired within the narrow walls of tradition, ignorance,
and bias.

With few exceptions, the Pre-Baccalaureate staff was opposed
to an anthology which none had read; and the protestations, thun-
dered forth in heated exchange, were but echoes of those voiced or
otherwise indicated in the academic communities of this country.
For far more important than the merit of the anthology, was the
tradition which had operated—one can only say purposefully—to
exclude the Negro writer.

This exclusion, however, holds only in the case of Negroes writing about Negroes. An anthology, *Essays of Our Times*, edited by the chairman of the English Department and a colleague, containing the essays, "What the Negro Needs Most" and "The White Negro," both written by white men, was assigned, with no opposition, to the students. Among the first books to be ordered as part of a standing library, was a collection of writings by William Faulkner.

At this point the consensus of the college and the society are the same. Presumably, those most capable of writing objectively about Negroes are whites. Presumably, Norman Mailer knows more about Negro aspirations, desires, and needs than Saunders Redding, W. E. B. DuBois, John Killens, or James Baldwin. Presumably, Faulkner's stereotyped portrayal of Negroes is more acceptable than the realistic ones of Richard Wright, William Gardner Smith, or Ronald Fair.

This, of course, is to say something very insidious. The same factors operating to restrict the Negro in the society at large, are operative too, in the ivoried halls of those institutions where knowledge, tolerance, and justice are most often debated. Expunged from the history books, denied admission in the sociological texts, and banned from the archives of the English departments, the Negro is a non-being here, in this place where men of all races, creeds, and persuasions should be given visibility.

Such facts, therefore, negate the assumptions of Herbert Hill. If one takes Hill seriously, the sun-bathed morning of Negro literature begins with James Baldwin and Ralph Ellison, everything before is ensconced in darkening, oppressive clouds, an empty, black void of pessimism, despair, and "unrelieved protest." Thus out of the whirlwind, riding the tremors of the apocalypse, came Baldwin and Ellison, twin redeemers, pilots who would ferry Negro literature toward the promised shore of academic acceptance.

Hill fails to see, however, that the strictures leveled against the Negro writer have never been based on aesthetic criterion alone. For long before Baldwin and Ellison, Negro writers were exhibiting a mastery of the mechanics of their art. Jean Toomer's *Cane* is one such example; James Weldon Johnson's *Autobiography of an Ex-Coloured Man* is another; DuBois' *The Souls of Black Folk*, still another; and most of all, the *Native Son* of Richard Wright. And these writers are not studied in English classes in America, primarily, because they, unlike some of the present crop, have never cried out in anguish—to paraphrase Samuel Taylor

Coleridge—Shrieve me, shrieve me, and make me white as snow.

And yet this appeal has not been answered. In one of the most prestigious universities in the West, the novels of Ellison and Baldwin are catalogued in both of the libraries under the heading "Negro Literature." And, despite the admonitions of both Robert Bone and Ralph Ellison, instructors and critics still regard *Invisible Man* as a Negro novel. Surely then, the walls of Canaan have not been breached by attempts at assimilation in which the Negro writer, to achieve visibility, is washed clean of his blackness.

Students, however, demand no such purgation. Those in the Pre-Bacc class of City College debated the merits of the works they read, irrespective of the race of the writer. They found in Saunders Redding's "The Alienated Land of Richard Wright," themes of expatriation which have plagued writers as far back as Spencer; they found in Baldwin and Wright themes of alienation, of man's estrangement from other men, which have their genesis in Biblical history; and they found in a poem by Langston Hughes, the theme of dashed dreams and the concomitant despair thereof —a theme so applicable to their own experiences.

Moreover, they withheld judgment until the material upon which judgment would be based had been carefully perused. They thought, with no exceptions, that Negro literature should be included in college syllabi; and, yet, their eager, inquisitive minds took them far beyond this plateau: A Puerto Rican male writes: "The text is a good one and I think should be read not only in classes like this one, but all English classes because I think it is a worthwhile experience." Another student writes: "I did not think that having Negro authors as contributors was a bad idea. I'm glad it [the anthology] was given because it gave the students a chance to read other than literature by just white authors. I enjoyed every single thing I read and I learned much." Another student, tossing a hint to future anthologists, writes: "I would recommend the use of *Soon One Morning* for future English classes, and would like to see a book like this with other authors in it also."

It would appear, therefore, that the Negro writer remains outside the walls of Canaan—irrespective of the wishes of students, unable to penetrate the solid enclosure before him, because those who hold the key have not recognized in all these years, that his presence within the walls would add to the grandeur, brilliance, and greatness of Canaan.

The tales that he tells, the songs that he sings, derive from those experiences, that life of turmoil, sorrow, joy, and confusion, so akin to Canaan's other inhabitants. That Canaan would be enriched by his presence, few of my students would deny; yet their elders share neither their wishes nor their enthusiasms. Critics, publishers, and instructors continue to thunder forth their "everlasting nay" to the legitimate cries of the Negro writer to be heard. Such a response has been given in the past, is repeated in the present, and, unless something radical happens to America's educational system, will continue to be heard in the future.

Canaan, therefore, despite its apparent nearness, lies many miles distant; and the argument that the Negro writer will gain admittance soon any morning is open to serious questioning. For few in the universities of this country are endowed with that clearness of vision, that unbiased perception, that dedication to scholarship and understanding, which would enable them to believe with a nineteen-year-old freshman: "Negro literature should be brought to the attention of all English classes, no matter what the culture or background of the students."

WILLIAM GARDNER SMITH
*The Negro Writer: Pitfalls
and Compensations*

THIS IS, as everyone recognizes by now, a world of relativity. We measure the rights of individuals against the rights of the society; the rights of the artist against the rights of his public; the right of free speech against the right of the individual to protection from slander. Degrees of good and evil are measured against other degrees of good and evil.

This apprehension of infinite relativity is, I think, instructive in considering the position of the Negro writer—I speak particularly of the novelist—in American society. For a moment, disregard the mechanical pros and cons, debits and credits—whether it is easier, or more difficult, for a Negro writer to have his work published; consider the purely esthetic question: What handicaps, and what advantages, does the American writer possess by virtue of being a Negro?

Because the handicaps are better known, and perhaps easier

to understand, I will consider them first. The Negro writer is, first of all, invariably bitter. There are degrees of this bitterness, ranging from the anger of Richard Wright and the undercurrent of contempt for the white world in Chester Himes to the cruel satire exhibited by George Schuyler in his semi-classic *Black No More.* A writer is a man of sensitivity; otherwise, he would not be a writer. The sensitivities of the Negro writer react, therefore, more strongly against the ignorance, prejudice and discrimination of American society than do those of the average Negro in America.

There are all forms and varieties of this inevitable strain of bitterness in the Negro writer. Sometimes it results in militancy; sometimes in contempt for race and self; sometimes in hatred for the whole of American society, with blindness for the good things contained therein. It is often hard for the Negro writer to resist polemicizing. He is driven often to write a tract, rather than a work of art. So conscious is he of the pervading evil of race prejudice that he feels duty-bound to assault it at every turn, injecting opinion into alleged narration and inserting his philosophy into the mouths of his characters.

Writing of Negroes, the novelist has difficulty with his characterizations. His people usually become walking, talking propaganda, rather than completely rounded individuals. The Negro writer hesitates, perhaps unconsciously, to temper the goodness of his Negro characters with the dialectical "evil." Fearful of reenforcing stereotypes in the white reader's mind, he often goes to the other extreme, idealizing his characters, making them flat rather than many-sided. Or, conscious of the pitfalls listed above, and anxious to prove that he is not idealizing his Negro characters, the writer goes to the other extreme—in the name of naturalism—and paints the American Negro as an exaggerated Bigger Thomas, with all the stereotyped characteristics emphasized three times over. To strike a compromise—and, incidentally, the truth—is possibly the most difficult feat for a Negro writer. Proof of this is the fact that I have not read one Negro novel which has truthfully represented the many-sided character of the Negro in American society today. Chester Himes, perhaps, has come closer than any other Negro author to such a representation.

It seems that it is difficult for the Negro writer to add to his weighty diatribes the leaven of humor. Writing is an art; the writer works upon the emotions of his reader. Every sentence, every cadence, every description, every scene, produces an emotional response in this reader. Consciously did Shakespeare lead

his audiences through one powerful emotion after another to
achieve the final, powerful effect of the death of Desdemona at the
hands of Othello; consciously did Marlowe lead to the final descent
into hell of Faust. In each of these journeys through dramatic
experience there were rises and falls; there were moments of stern
conflict and moments of relative relaxation; there were moments
of tears and moments of relieving laughter.

Too often, however, in Negro novels do we witness the dull
procession of crime after crime against the Negro, without relief
in humor or otherwise. These monotonous repetitions of offenses
against the Negro serve only to bore the reader in time; and in so
doing, they defeat the very purpose of the writer, for they become
ineffective. One might even say that the chronicles of offenses
constitute truth; however, they do not constitute art. And art is the
concern of any novelist.

Novels which last through all time are concerned with universal themes. Dostoievski's great Raskolnikov is all of us in the
aftermath of great crime; Tolstoi describes the universal ruling
class in time of national crisis. The Negro writer is under tremendous pressure to write about the topical and the transient—the
plight of the Negro in American society today. It may be that the
greatest of such novels will last because of their historical interest.
It may even be that one or two will last because the writer has
managed to infuse into his work some universal elements—as
Dickens did, even when writing about the social conditions in the
England of his day. But most Negro writers do not inject the
universal element. They write only about the here and the now.
Thus, their novels come and they go: in ten years, they are forgotten.

At this point, let me emphasize that the drive of the Negro
writer to write about purely topical themes is of fantastic strength,
and difficult for the non-Negro to appreciate. Starving and land-
hungry Chinese want food and land: they are not much concerned
about such abstractions as the rights of free speech, habeas corpus,
the ballot, etc. When day to day problems press upon the individual, they become, in his mind, paramount. This sense of the immediate problem confronts the Negro writer. But it is significant to
note that we do not today consider highly that literature which
arose in protest against, say, the system of Feudalism, or even, in
the United States, slavery.

But there are compensations for these difficulties confronting
the Negro writer. They are great compensations.

Writing is concerned with people, with society and with ethics. Great writing is concerned with the individual in the group or tribe; obedience to or deviation from the laws of that tribe, and the consequences. Usually, by the very process of selection, omission and arrangement of his material, the author implies a judgment—approval or rejection of the laws of the society, be they in legal, ethical or religious form. Basic to such writing, obviously, is some understanding of both the society and the people in it.

To grasp social and individual truth, it is my opinion that the novelist must maintain emotional contact with the basic people of his society. At first glance, this appears a simple thing; but, in reality, it is difficult. Consider the material circumstances of the "successful" writer. He becomes a celebrity. He makes money. Usually, he begins to move in the sphere of people like himself— authors, artists, critics, etc. He purchases a home on Long Island. He no longer uses the subway; for now he has an automobile. He lectures; he speaks at luncheons; he autographs books; he attends cocktail parties; he discusses style, form, and problems of psychology with friends in a rather esoteric circle; and he writes. In a word, he moves, to some degree, into an ivory tower; he becomes, in a fashion, detached from the mainstream of American life.

In times of stability this detachment is often not too harmful: for the moral code remains what it was at the moment of the writer's detachment and, despite its rarification in his new environment, still may serve as the wellspring for vital work. In moments of social crisis, however, the established moral code comes into violent conflict with the desires of the people of society. Thus, immediately prior to the French Revolution, the ethics of Feudalism, though still officially recognized, actually were outdated and in conflict with the democratic tendencies of the people; and thus, today, the individualistic and basically selfish ethic of Capitalism, while still officially proclaimed, is in reality contrary to the socialist tendency which has spread over the world, and even made itself felt in America through Roosevelt's New Deal and Truman's election on a Fair Deal program.

The writer who is detached from society does not perceive this contradiction; and thus is missing from his writing some element of social truth. He is behind the times; he is holding onto a shell. Part of the greatness of Tolstoi is that he perceived the ethical, i.e., social, conflict, and accurately recorded it.

The Negro writer cannot achieve—at least, not as easily as the white American writer—this social detachment, however much he might desire it. The very national prejudice he so despises compels him to remember his social roots, perceive the social reality; in a word, compels him to keep his feet on the ground. He cannot register at the Mayflower Hotel. He cannot loll on the Miami Beach. He cannot ignore disfranchisement, epithets, educational and employment discrimination, mob violence. He is bound by unbreakable cords to the Negro social group. And so his writing, however poor artistically, must almost invariably contain some elements of social truth.

The Negro writer is endowed by his environment with relative emotional depth. What does a writer write about? We have said: people, and their problems, conflicts, etc. But—what problems, what conflicts? Pick up any popular American magazine or book and you will find out—the problem of whether John D., a thoroughly empty individual, should leave his wife Mary C., a thoroughly empty individual, to marry Jane B., a thoroughly empty individual. To this problem are devoted hundreds of pages; hundreds of thousands of words. And in the end the reader of intelligence must ask the question: So what?

Emotional depth, perception of real problems and real conflicts, is extremely rare in American literature—as it is in American society generally. Instead of issues of significance, our fiction (our serious fiction) is overladen with such trite themes as that of Tennessee Williams' *The Roman Spring of Mrs. Stone*. America's is a superficial civilization: it is soda-pop land, the civilization of television sets and silk stockings and murder mysteries and contempt for art and poetry. It is difficult, out of such environment, to bring forth works with the emotional force of, say, *Crime and Punishment*.

Here again the Negro writer's social experience is, despite its bitterness, also an artistic boon. To live continually with prejudice based on the accident of skin color is no superficial experience; and neither is the reaction produced by such constant exposure superficial. There is a depth and intensity to the emotions of Negroes—as demonstrated in "Negro music"—which is largely lacking in white Americans. How often has the Negro maid or housecleaner come home to laugh at her white mistress' great concern about the color of a hat, the shape of a shoe, keeping up with the next-door Joneses? How often have Negroes, on the job, laughed in amazement at the inane trivialities which occupy the thoughts of their white fellow workers. And this laughter is logical. The Europeans would understand it. For, what man or woman who has seen a lynching, or been close to the furnaces of Dachau, or been rebuffed and rejected because of his skin color, can really seriously concern himself with the insipid and shallow love affair between Susie Bell and Jerry?

Thus, the Negro writer, if he does not make the tragic error of trying to imitate his white counterparts, has in his possession the priceless "gift" of thematic intuition. Provided he permits his writing to swell truthfully from his deepest emotional reaches, he will treat problems of real significance, which can strike a cord in the heart of basic humanity. He will be able to convey suffering without romanticizing; he will be able to describe happiness which is not merely on the surface; he will be able to search out and concretize the hopes and ambitions which are the basic stuff of human existence. And he will, in Hemingway's words, be able to do this "without cheating." For the basic fact about humanity in our age is that it suffers; and only he who suffers with it can truthfully convey its aches and pains, and thwarted desires.

And now, speaking only of this period in which we live, I should like to point out one last advantage which I feel accrues to the writer by virtue of being a Negro. It concerns the international power struggle.

We live, it appears, in an age of struggle between the American brand of Capitalism and the Russian brand of Communism. This is the obvious struggle; and most of the individuals in the world seem to feel that one must choose between one or the other. But is this, really, the root struggle? Or is mankind, the great majority of it, not actually groping for a rational social order, free from the tensions of economic and political crisis, free from war and from dictatorship, in which the individual will be permitted to live according to an ethic all sensible and truly just men can subscribe to?

For a moment, leave the last question. Consider the writer in the American scene, in this day and age. Picture him as being young and filled with ideals; consider him intelligent, sensitive and understanding. Ask the question: Can he approve of American society as it exists today?

I say, on the basis of experience and of individual reaction, no! The young writer will notice many good things, worthy of retention, in the America of today. He will approve of free speech (now being seriously curtailed); he will approve the idea of a free press (even though becoming a monopoly because of the economics involved); he will believe in free artistic expression, realizing that only through freedom can real art survive. But can he approve of the dog-eat-dog existence we glorify by the name of Free Enterprise?—an existence which distorts the personality, turns avarice into virtue and permits the strong to run roughshod over the weak, profiteering on human misery? Can he approve chronic depressions and endless wars? Can he approve racial and religious prejudice?

The young writer of ideas and ideals, I say, must instantly be repelled by the ugly aspects of American society. The history of our literature will bear this out—at a swift glance, I think of Emily Dickinson, Thoreau, Emerson, Hawthorne, Dos Passos, Faulkner, Henry James, Melville and, recently, Norman Mailer. And, being repelled, the writer seeks a substitute, something which offers hope of cure. Today, at first glance, the only alternative seems to be Russian Communism.

To list the important American writers who have turned from American Capitalism to Communism since the latter part of the nineteenth century would take up more space than this article is permitted. Suffice it to say that nearly every naturalistic writer in America has made this turn. Our young writer of intelligence and ideals, then, makes this turn. He embraces Communism of the Russian brand. And, immediately, he begins to feel uncomfortable.

For he discovers, in the folds of Russian Communism, the evils of dictatorship. He learns about purge trials; and is handed fantastic lies, which insult his intelligence, to justify them. He learns of the stifling of literature, art and music in the Soviet Union. He learns that Hitler is one day evil, the next day (following a pact with the Soviet Union) good, and the next day evil again. He discovers that Roosevelt is today a warmonger, tomorrow a true democrat and peoples' friend, whose "grand design" the Communist Party, U. S. A., seeks only to imitate. He learns that Tito, only yesterday a Communist hero only a little lower than Stalin, has in reality been a spy and a Fascist since 1936. He learns that a book which is "good" today becomes "bad," "bourgeois" and "decadent" tomorrow when the Party Line changes.

In panic does our idealistic and intelligent writer flee from alliance with the Communist Party. And at this point, the advantage of the Negro writer is discovered. For, having become disillusioned with the Soviet dictatorship, where does the white writer turn for political truth? Back to Capitalism, in ninety-nine out of a hundred cases; back to the very decaying system which lately he had left, a system he now calls "Democracy," "Freedom" and "Western Culture." He repeats the performance of John Dos

Passos and, more recently and more strikingly (though in another field) Henry Wallace. The things he formerly found unbearable in Capitalism—he now ignores. Prejudice, depressions, imperialism, political chicanery, support of dictators, dog-eat-dog, strong-kill-the-weak philosophy—these things no longer exist. Black becomes white again. And the creative artist is dead! For he is blind.

The Negro writer, too, makes this retreat from Communism —for he, too, is opposed to lies, deceit, dictatorship and the other evils of the Soviet regime. But—and this is the significant point— the Negro writer does not, in most cases, come back to bow at the feet of Capitalism. He cannot, as can the white writer, close his eyes to the evils of the system under which he lives. Seeing the Negro ghetto, feeling the prejudice, his relatives and friends experiencing unemployment, injustice, police brutality, segregation in the South, white supremacy—seeing these things, the Negro writer cannot suddenly kiss the hand which slaps him. Looking at China, at Indochina, and at Africa, he cannot avoid the realization that these are people of color, struggling, as he is struggling, for dignity. Again, prejudice has forced him to perceive the real, the ticking world.

Denied many freedoms, robbed of many rights, the Negro— and the Negro writer—rejects those aspects of both American Capitalism and Russian Communism which trample on freedoms and rights. Repelled now by both contending systems, the Negro writer of strength and courage stands firmly as a champion of the basic human issues—dignity, relative security, freedom and the end of savagery between one human being and another. And in this stand he is supported by the mass of human beings the world over.

So add it up. The handicaps are great. Many Negro writers— the majority, I should say, so far—have been unable to overcome them. The work of others is impaired by them. But if the handicaps can be overcome, the advantages remain. And, as I said before, they are great advantages. Because I believe that an increasing number of Negro writers will be able to overcome the disadvantages inherent in their social situation, I predict that a disproportionate percentage of the outstanding writers of the next decade will be Negroes.

NATHAN A. SCOTT, JR.
*The Dark and Haunted Tower
of Richard Wright*

THE EXISTENTIALIST overtones and the explicit allusions to Nietzsche and Heidegger in *The Outsider* led some of the reviewers of
his book of 1953 to conclude that Richard Wright was misguid-
edly experimenting with intellectual traditions outside his actual
experience and that he had taken a wrong turning. This was a
judgment, however, which surely had to require as its basic
premise something like the rather incomprehensible *mystique*
about the Negro intellectual which is occasionally invoked by fools
and professional obscurantists, that he is somehow ancestrally
fated to exclusion from the general Atlantic community of cultural
exchange simply because his racial identity does itself, in some
ineffable way, consign him to a permanent ghetto of the mind. But,
if this *mystique* is abandoned as the nonsense that it really is,
there should have been no occasion for surprise at the expression
which *The Outsider* provided of the extent to which Mr. Wright,
after several years of residence in France, had been influenced by
the secular modes of European existentialism. For here is a philosophical movement which has found its basic subject matter not so
much in the history of philosophy as in the crises and distempers
of human existence in the twentieth century. The fundamental
reality about which it has very often wanted to speak is that of
"the extreme situation"—the situation, that is, in which man's
essential dignity is radically challenged by an unconscionable sub-
version of justice and an intolerable distance between master and
slave. And this is precisely the reality that stirred Mr. Wright's
imagination into life—from the time of his first forays into the
literary life, under the sponsorship of the Communist Party, while
still a Chicago postal employee in the 'thirties, up to the time of
his sudden death in Paris in November of 1960.

So there was nothing at all unnatural in this American Negro
writer having responded affirmatively to the *Angst*-ridden accents
and idioms of Jean-Paul Sartre and Georges Bataille and Maurice
Blanchot. For, among those Negro intellectuals of his time whose

gift of expression enabled them to have a "voice," it may well be that there was none for whom the reality of their "extreme situation" constituted so great a burden. The social statisticians today are busy, of course, in their notations of the steadily increasing improvement in what they call "race relations," and it is probably the case that the moral quality of our life is, in this dimension, something less of an embarrassment than it was a decade or so ago. But the tokens of acceptance that the Negro has won here and there are not yet so great as to make it impossible for others to imagine that he, when he is sensitive and discerning, still feels his status to be precarious and undecided. He has only to contemplate the bitter intransigence of the South and the subtle but firmly maintained exclusions of the North to be reminded of how meagre and insubstantial is the new ground that he has recently gained. Though it is only in the occasional pockets of Southern depravity that he is still exposed to the nakeder forms of violence and intimidation, he knows that the actuality of the American experience continues to involve for him that most unhinging kind of frustration which is a result of the glitter and promise of life in a great country being near enough for the mind to be dazzled by the sense of their availability, and yet far enough away to exact a sense of defeat more exacerbating than anything a slave could possibly feel. When this bitter irony is explored by a radical imagination, the nature of the human material is surely such as will permit its being seized by way of the image of Tantalus: for all of the bland notations of achieved progress that may be offered by the social scientist, there is still an *agonia* here whose gall partakes of the "extreme situation"—and this was the perspective by which Richard Wright was consistently guided in all his efforts to shape the story of the American Negro into something whose tragic sorrow might quicken the conscience of our time.

Though he had numerous minor predecessors, Mr. Wright was the first American Negro writer of large ambitions to win a major reputation in our literary life. *Uncle Tom's Children,* his first collection of stories, achieved a limited currency in the late 'thirties among readers of leftist social sympathies, but it was not until *Native Son* burst upon the scene in 1940 that he won access to the kind of forum that Sunday Supplement reviewers and a national book club could give. Within a month after its publication tens of thousands of copies were moving across book dealers' counters all over the land; it frequently was being said that nothing so comparable to the great tragic fictions of Dostoievski had yet appeared in our literature; and hordes of Mr. Wright's readers were enjoying that great thrilling shiver of delight that the intellectual middle class in this country during the 'thirties had come to find in what Eric Bentley has called "the fun-world of proletarian legend," particularly when the fun involved the tabooed exoticism of the Negro. The very simplicity and violence of the novel's didacticism did, in a way, permit many people to envisage themselves as in league with Mr. Wright and with Christ in the harrowing of a Hell full of all the forces of reaction and illiberality; and, in this way perhaps, the illusion grew that *Native Son*, by itself and quite suddenly, had very greatly enlarged and deepened our imaginative understanding of a whole dimension of American experience.

This was, however, an illusion, and when one reads today the story of Bigger Thomas, one cannot but be struck by how little the novel gives us of the bite and flavor either of social actuality or of the particular kind of human individual of whom Bigger is offered as an *exemplum*. To read such a book, for example, as Ralph Ellison's brilliant novel of 1953, *Invisible Man*, is to find, among one's richest satisfactions, the sense of immersion in all the concrete materialities of Negro life. One hears the very buzz and hum of Harlem in the racy, pungent speech of his West Indians and his native hipsters, and all the *grotesquerie* in his opening account of the dreary little backwater of a remote Southern Negro college has in it a certain kind of empirically absolute rightness. Indeed, the book is packed full of the acutest observations of the manners and idioms and human styles that comprise the ethos of Negro life in the American metropolis; and it gives us such a sense of social fact as can be come by nowhere in the stiffly pedantic manuals of academic sociology.

But, at its center, *Native Son* exhibits nothing other than a socially discarnate and demoniac wrath. In the moments before her "little death," the Negrophile Joanna Burden in *Light in August* cries out to her Negro lover Joe Christmas, "Negro, Negro," as if, in the instant of sexual transport, his human particularity were of no account; and, in the same novel, a lynch mob, Faulkner tells us, "believed aloud that it was an anonymous Negro crime committed not by a Negro but by Negro. . . ." And this is the character whom we find to be the protagonist of Richard Wright's novel of 1940—called, yes, for the sake of the novelistic convention, Bigger Thomas, but really Negro, *Negro*. Thus it is that, for all of the anger the novel directs at the moral imagination that has been poisoned by racism, its own pathos is, finally, a consequence of the degree to which it is overwhelmed by the cancer it wants to cauterize. From the moment, on its first page, when Bigger is awakened by the *Brrriiiinnng!* of his alarm clock, until his "faint, wry, bitter smile" of farewell at Mr. Max on the final page, the novel is controlled by precisely those hopeless assumptions about Negro life which elicited its rage, and its protagonist's sense of his own identity is formed by just that image of himself which, as it lives in the larger culture, has caused his despair. So, in its entirety, the novel moves wholly within the envenomed abstractions of racial myth.

In one of the stories in *Uncle Tom's Children*, "Long Black Song," the husband of a Negro woman who has been seduced by a white salesman says: "The white folks ain never gimme a chance! They ain never give no black man a chance! There ain nothing in yo whole life yuh kin keep from em! . . . Ahm gonna be hard like they is! So hep me Gawd, Ahm gonna be *hard!* When they come fer me Ahm gonna *be* here!" Not only is this the posture of all but one of his protagonists in the stories that make up his first collection, it is also the posture of the young Chicago Negro whose story Mr. Wright tells in *Native Son*. He, too, is one who intends to "be hard"; indeed, as he says, "Every time I think about it I feel like somebody's poking a red-hot iron down my throat." So it is with a sullen suspiciousness that he faces the Chicago philanthropist who takes him off the relief rolls by hiring him as a chauffeur. And it is with an even greater scepticism that he views his employer's daughter and her Communist sweetheart who make gestures of fraternity toward him by inviting him to join them in a café as an equal. But this is a relation that never becomes genuinely complicated, for, at the end of their first evening together, the girl is so intoxicated that Bigger, having been entrusted with seeing her home, has to carry her bodily from the family automobile to her bedroom—into which her blind mother comes suddenly, just in the moment when he is contemplating taking Mary sexually. And, in order to prevent the mother's knowing that he and Mary are in the room, he smothers the girl and then, in his panic, stuffs her body into the furnace. This, in turn, leads eventually to his second crime, against his mistress Bessie, to whom he confesses the first deed and whom he must finally remove to prevent her betraying him to the police. But he cannot ultimately avoid his nemesis and is at last captured on a South Side tenement rooftop, as a raging mob clamors for his life in the street below.

Now the engine that Mr. Wright desperately relied upon to whip this lurid fairy-tale into some semblance of probability was the courtroom defense of Bigger by his Jewish lawyer, Mr. Max. And here is what we are told, that Bigger

> . . . murdered Mary Dalton accidentally, without thinking, without plan, without conscious motive. But, after he murdered, he accepted the crime. And that's the important thing. It was the first full act of his life; it was the most meaningful, exciting and stirring thing that had ever happened to him. He accepted it because it made him free, gave him the possibility of choice, of action, the opportunity to act and to feel that his actions carried weight. . . .
>
> Let me tell you more. Before this trial the newspapers and the prosecution said that this boy had committed other crimes. It is true. He is guilty of numerous crimes. But search until the day of judgment, and you will find not one shred of evidence of them. He has murdered many times, but there are no corpses. Let me explain. This Negro boy's entire attitude toward life is a *crime!* The hate and fear which we have inspired in him, woven by our civilization into the very structure of his consciousness, into his blood and bones, into the hourly functioning of his personality, have become the justification of his existence.
>
> Every time he comes in contact with us, he kills! It is a physiological and psychological reaction, embedded in his being. Every thought he thinks is potential murder. . . . Every desire, every dream, no matter how intimate or personal, is a plot or a conspiracy. Every hope is a plan for insurrection. Every glance of the eye is a threat. *His very existence is a crime.* . . .

And, what is more, we are told that we have only to "multiply Bigger Thomas twelve million times, allowing for environmental and temperamental variations, and for those Negroes who are completely under the influence of the church, and you have the psychology of the Negro people."

Thus it is, I say, that the novel is, paradoxically, controlled by precisely the assumptions about Negro life that elicited its rage, for the astonishing thing that it finally does is to offer a depraved and inhuman beast as the comprehensive archetypal image of the American Negro.

The imagination that we meet here, in other words, is extremist and melodramatic, feeding on the horrific themes of alienation and violence and abysmal fear, and its single occupation is with the racial tragedy. But all the great ones have had what was two hundred years ago called a "ruling passion," and it does indeed seem to be very much a part of the kind of brilliance and assertiveness that we associate with major art. That Mr. Wright should have had his ruling passion is not, therefore, something that we shall hold against him; what was unfortunate in him was his utter defenselessness before it. And here I mean that, despite his cursory tutelage under European existentialism in the late 'forties and 'fifties and despite the attention which he gave to the literature of modern psychology and social science, he never won such a point of purchase in the realm of systematic ideas as might have afforded his mind some protection against the deracinative force of the tragic encounters which it had had with the world. After reading, for example, the heartrendingly poignant story that is told in *Black Boy*, his autobiography of 1945—which is one of the great human testaments in modern American literature—it would surely take an exceedingly sluggish moral imagination for one not to perceive how inevitable it was that this man should bear to his grave the scars of the scalding humiliations that, as a Negro, he was subjected to in his youth in the state of Mississippi. Here, indeed, was a man who knew the insidious day-by-day intimidation, the fear that is in the air, and the atrocious brutality that make up the moral stench of the concentration camp; and, unlike the German Jew under Hitler, he lived this infernal life of the damned and the rejected not just for a few nightmarish years that were known to be absurdly discontinuous with the normal state of things, but he lived it as the historic inheritance of his people; this was all that he knew, from infancy until he was old enough to risk the journey of flight from Memphis to Chicago. So we accept the authenticity of the rage and the anger which were the emotions with which he impulsively faced the world. But, when some such extremity as this constitutes his basic situation, whatever the needs of the existing human being, the artist needs to be equipped with some defense against the intensity of his own experience, for, unless he has some means of supporting or controlling it, the great likelihood is that his work will then express not a coherent ordering of human experience in objective form but only the emotional tics of his own incipient hysteria. And it was just some such vantage point as this that might have enabled him to distance himself from his *agonia* and to be released to the sheer labor of composition itself—it was just this that Mr. Wright never managed. In his famous essay on "Technique as Discovery," Professor

Mark Schorer has, of course, proposed that it is in the dynamism of the creative process itself, and through his wrestling with the medium of his language, that the artist comes by those major insights into the meaning of his experience that enable him to take control of it. But the logic whereby *technique* is assigned so decisive a role in the formation of *vision* is something that still escapes me. So mine, therefore, is the older axiom, that an artist needs to know a very great deal *before* he puts pen to paper; and, if he does not, he may then, I take it, be expected to provide us with some variety of what the late R. P. Blackmur called "the fallacy of expressive form."

Now this was, I believe, at bottom, Mr. Wright's crucial failure: he simply did not *know* enough about the labyrinthine interiorities of the human soul. His own life-experience conditioned him, of course, to keep a lively awareness that (as W. H. Auden says) "Ubiquitous within the bond/Of one impoverishing sky,/Vast spiritual disorders lie." Yet these were not really *spiritual* disorders, since he made no allowance for human existence having anything other than a purely social-historical dimension. In the *New Year Letter* Mr. Auden suggests that

> *There are two atlases: the one*
> *The public space where acts are done,*
> *In theory common to us all. . . .*
> *The other is the inner space*
> *Of private ownership, the place*
> *That each of us is forced to own,*
> *Like his own life from which it's grown,*
> *The landscape of his will and need. . . .*

But so obsessed was Mr. Wright with the demonic aberrations that disfigure "the public space" that he lost any deep sense of what wretchedness there is within "the inner space," within what Mr. Auden calls "our parish of immediacy." T. S. Eliot once said of Ezra Pound's *Cantos* that they posit a Hell for other people, not for Mr. Pound or his readers. It might also be said of the books of Richard Wright that, though theirs is a Hell for most of Mr. Wright's readers (who are white), it is not a Hell for Mr. Wright himself and his racial kinsmen; both he and they bear upon themselves the stigmata of its fury, but both he and they are exempted from that which is generally problematic in the human soul, and from which the fury proceeds. The complex relations between the "two atlases" are not explored. And, in this way, it was possible for Mr. Wright to envisage the human community as though it were split into two opposed camps, the one black and the other white. But, in this way, it was never possible for him even to approximate the Baudelairean astringency—"*Hypocrite lecteur,— mon semblable,—mon frère!*"

And it is also this exclusive and simplistic concentration upon the one atlas, "the public space," which enabled Mr. Wright so disastrously to insist upon racial humiliation as the ultimate suffering, the ultimate indignity. And I speak of the disastrousness of it, because, however thumpingly tautologous it may be to assert that evil is evil, whatever its aspect, this is, nevertheless, the fact of the matter; and to assert that some special evil is the ultimate evil, simply because this is that by which one has oneself been most hurtfully victimized, is merely to indulge in a desperate kind of sentimentality. This was, however, the unpromising position that consistently controlled Mr. Wright's way of performing the act of self-definition as an artist, and, for all of the ardor, it is this sentimentality which makes so humanly impertinent a body of writing than which there is none in our time that ought to have greater pertinence to those like ourselves, who are drenched in the particular American experience that gave to Mr. Wright his ruling passion.

In his review of *Native Son* in March of 1940, Malcolm Cowley, having in mind the consistency with which Mr. Wright's executive design, both in the stories of *Uncle Tom's Children* and in his novel, had been a design of violence, suggested that his "sense of the indignities heaped on his race" might well go so deep as to make it his unconscious tendency in his fiction to revenge himself "by a whole series of symbolic murders." And though Mr. Cowley may at this point have been somewhat overstating things, the propensity for violence cannot, it is true, be gainsaid: Mr. Wright may not have been bent on symbolic murder, but at least it can be asserted that he was eager to sound a hue and a cry and had something of a penchant for "holding a loaded pistol at the head of the white world while he [muttered] between clenched teeth: 'Either you grant us equal rights as human beings or else this is what will happen.' " * But, of course, the unfortunate consequence of his taking this kind of position was that, inevitably, it compelled him to practice a terrible brutalization upon his characters: he had, as in the wronged husband of "Long Black Song," to

* Glicksberg, Charles I.: "Negro Fiction in America," *The South Atlantic Quarterly* 45:482 (Oct.) 1946.

make them "hard," in order to give dramatic substance to the threat he wanted to utter; and, in thus sweeping them into the raging abysses of violent criminality, he forged an image of *la présence noire* that is in no great way removed from the wild and lickerish nigger who inhabits the demented imagination of the racial paranoiac. For all of the new sophistications that appeared in *The Outsider*, this is as true of his novel of 1953 as it is of his early work of the 'thirties.

Cross Damon is a half-educated intellectual who bears the Negro's ancestral burden of rejection and marginality, but his concern with what is socially problematic in his situation is but one phase of a deeper concern with what is metaphysically problematic in human life. He is a man whose sense of the world has been formed by that tradition of philosophic radicalism that runs from Nietzsche to contemporary existentialists like Heidegger and Sartre, and so he is particularly alert to the religious vacuum which this tradition has asserted to be at the heart of modern experience. He regards the old "myths" as a mischievous and archaistic legacy bequeathed us by the primitive ages of human history in which man,

> naked and afraid, found that only one thing could really quiet his terrors: that is *Untruth*. He . . . was afraid of the clamoring world of storms, volcanoes, and heaving waves, and he wanted to change the world. His myths sought to recast that world, tame it, make it more humanly meaningful and endurable. The more abjectly frightened the nation or race of men, the more their myths and religions projected out upon the world another world in *front* of the real world, or, in another way of speaking, they projected another world *behind* the real world they saw, lived, suffered, and died in. Until today almost all of man's worlds have been either preworlds or backworlds, *never* the real world. . . .

But in this "real world" in which modern man must live today the non-existence of God is not to be argued; it is simply to be taken for granted, and the theistic hypothesis is simply to be understood as "something projected compulsively from men's minds in answer to their chronic need to be rid of fear, something to meet the obscure needs of daily lives lived amidst strange and threatening facts." And this means, in Cross Damon's analysis of the modern predicament, that the dreadful burden which man must bear today is the burden of freedom, the burden, as he says, of being "nothing in particular," except what man chooses through his actions to become. This is why panic sometimes drapes the world which Cross looks out upon, for what he knows himself to confront is "the empty possibility of action," the necessity of actually making something of himself, and the knowledge that he can do what he damn well pleases on this earth, that everything is permitted, and that he must discover

> good or evil through his own actions, which were more exacting than the edicts of any God because it was he alone who had to bear the brunt of their consequences with a sense of absoluteness made intolerable by knowing that this life was all he had and would ever have. For him there was no grace or mercy if he failed.

He has, in other words, undergone the most expensive denudation that a man can suffer, for to Cross Damon God is dead. And, being thus stripped of that which might alone furnish some objective warrant for the human enterprise, there is nothing else to which he owes any loyalty; he is on his own, a pure *isolé*, and he gives his suffrage to neither family nor tradition nor church nor state; nor does he give it to race. "My hero," said Mr. Wright, "could have been of any race."

When we first meet Cross he is a clerk in a Chicago post office, and his personal life, like that of Sartre's Mathieu in the initial phase of his drama, is in a state of messy disorder. As a result of an early and unsuccessful marriage, he is having to support a wife with whom he no longer lives and three children. And then there is little Dot, his mistress, whom he had supposed to be seventeen years of age but whom he discovers, after the onset of her pregnancy, to be not quite sixteen. Gladys refuses to give him a divorce so that he may marry the girl, and Dot, desperately hoping somehow to trap him into a marriage, intends to seek legal counsel. When Gladys learns of this, she begins to be fearful that Cross may be jailed and that she and the children may be robbed of his support: so she demands that he sign over the house and the car to her. She further demands that he borrow eight hundred dollars from the Postal Union on his salary, so that the titles on both the house and the car may be cleared, and she tells him that, if he refuses, she will go to the police with Dot and assist her in filing charges of rape against him. So Cross has no alternative but to accede to her requests.

But, then, on that fateful night when he is returning home after having just received from the Postal Union the eight hundred dollars which he is to deliver to Gladys on the following morning, he is involved in a subway accident in which it is supposed that he has lost his life, the smashed body of another man being identified as his. This is, of course, Cross' great chance, and he is quick to seize it, for it means an opportunity to gain release from the inauthenticity of his existence, an opportunity to escape all those pledges and promises to his wife and his mother and his mistress "which he had not intended to make and whose implied obligations had been slowly smothering his spirit." By this "stroke of freakish good luck" he is able to "rip the viscous strands" of that "vast web of pledges and promises . . . and fling them behind him." Now, for the first time, this young man feels that his life is determined by a really valid project—namely, that of making something of himself and of giving some vital definition to his human identity.

So he takes a train out of Chicago for New York City, where he quickly becomes involved in a phantasmagoric drama of the Communist underworld which culminates in his committing murder three times and in the suicide of Eva Blount, the widow of one of his victims, who, after falling in love with him, cannot bear the truth, when she finally learns of the terrible deeds that he has performed. And Cross at last is destroyed by the Party's assassins.

Now, when the novel is thus summarized, it may appear to be only a rather lurid sort of potboiler; and, to be sure, there is no minimizing the harshness of its violence. Yet, for all of its melodramatic sensationalism, it is an impressive book. Indeed, it is one of the very few American novels of our time that, in admitting into itself a large body of systematic ideas, makes us think that it wants seriously to compete with the major philosophic intelligence of the contemporary period. And it may well be that the strange kind of indifference or even outright denigration that the book elicited at the time of its appearance demands to be understood in terms of the easy assumption which is habitually made in our literary life, that the difference in method and intention between poetry and philosophy ordains the impropriety of a work of fiction being complicated by the dialectical tensions of systematic thought. But this is a kind of finickiness notably unsupported by the European tradition exemplified by such books as Mann's *Doktor Faustus* and Malraux's *La Condition Humaine* and Camus' *La Peste*. And it was toward this tradition that Mr. Wright was reaching in *The Outsider*, which, though it is a very imperfect work, is yet (after *Black Boy*) his finest achievement and, as the one emphatically existentialist novel in contemporary American literature, a book that deserves to have commanded a great deal more attention than it has.

Though Mr. Wright insisted that his hero "could have been of any race" and that his primary quality was the metaphysical horror he felt before the yawning emptiness in things created by the demise of the old "myths," the fact remains, however, that Cross is a Negro. And, as such, he is dubiously privileged to have what the prosecutor Ely Houston calls "a dreadful objectivity," the kind of "double vision," that is, which belongs to one who is "both inside and outside of our culture." But, given the ardency of his commitment to atheistic premises, the actual content of this "double vision" proves to be the conviction of Ivan Karamazov, that therefore "everything is permitted," not even murder being debarred. And so that night when he walked into the room where the Fascist nigger-hater Herndon and the Communist Blount were fighting and bludgeoned them both to death, he was "not taking sides . . . not preferring the lesser evil," for, in the world as it was apprehended by Cross, there were no sides to be taken; he no longer slept in the old myths of the Greeks and the Jews, and he knew that nothing was to be preferred to anything else. So his act was simply "a sweeping and supreme gesture of disdain and disgust with both of them!" The logic, in other words, is this, that to be a Negro is to be an outsider, not only in a sociological sense but also, and more decisively, in a moral sense as well. And the mission of the outsider, like that of Camus' Caligula, is to reveal to mankind that the human City is really a jungle and that all the disciplines and restraints of civilization are "just screens which men have used" to throw a kind of "veneer of order" over the disorder that still seethes beneath the surface. But since, as it appears, this is a mission that cannot be accomplished apart from terrorism, Mr. Wright's conclusion of 1953 entailed essentially the same mischievousness that had been implicit thirteen years earlier in *Native Son*, the notion that the natural life-movement of the Negro who bears the full burden of his situation is toward a great blasting moment of supreme destruction. Bigger Thomas is an inarticulate proletarian who enacts his role unthinkingly, whereas Cross Damon, having read his Nietzschean primers, accepts his mission with deliberation and in the spirit of a kind of inverted messianism—but this is the only significant difference between them, for both aim, as it were, at getting outside of history altogether, through an act of consummate violence. Like Conrad's

Kurtz, Cross does, to be sure, behold at last "the horror," as he
gaspingly admits to Houston a moment before his death; but he
has, nevertheless, tasted the terrible joy of his murderous orgasm:
he has burst the belt and been "hard" and won through at least to
the unhistorical realm of the dream—which is of revenge.

Mr. Wright was always too impatient with what Henry James
called the "proving disciplines" of art to win the kind of genuine
distinction as a writer for which his talents qualified him. And,
like George Orwell, for him the greatest uses of art were not those
by which we distance ourselves from the world in order to contemplate more strenuously its pattern and meaning. They were, rather,
those by which we seek a more direct entry into the world for the
sake of redeeming it from the brutality and the indecencies by
which it must otherwise be overwhelmed. So it is rather a sad
irony that his own art did in point of fact so often drift toward a
definition of man, and particularly of the American Negro, that
deeply undercut his conscious intention to make it serve a genuinely humane vision. As James Baldwin has said, the real tragedy
of Bigger Thomas "is not that he is cold or black or hungry, not
even that he is American, black, but that he has accepted a theology that denies him life, that he admits the possibility of his being
subhuman and feels constrained, therefore, to battle for his humanity according to those brutal criteria bequeathed him at his
birth." * And this is precisely what it is that renders so ambiguous
many of the other chief protagonists in Mr. Wright's fiction.

His last years, unhappily, were not, it seems, a period of rich
fulfillment and harvest. Mr. Baldwin has reported † on some of the
asperities that increasingly isolated him from friends and ac-
quaintances and young American Negro and African intellectuals
who were living in Paris. And I suspect that his crotchetiness was
not unconnected with the fortunes of his reputation in the literary
life. Though *The Outsider* won a respectful reception in some
quarters, it by no means achieved any large *succès d'estime* in the
critical forum; and the novel of 1958, *The Long Dream*, met little
more than polite indifference. So it was the publication in 1956 of
Black Boy which had brought him to the zenith of his success.
Thereafter his fiction and his political criticism, though no different in tone and emphasis from his earlier work, seemed to be

* Baldwin, James: *Notes of a Native Son*, p. 23. Boston: The Beacon Press,
1961.
† Baldwin, James: *Nobody Knows My Name*, pp. 200–215. New York: The
Dial Press, 1961.

nettling in their effect, and the reputation of the early 'forties has today become merely a minor datum of that earlier time. This is, of course, in part, I suspect, but a particular case of the more general demise of the naturalism of the American nineteen-thirties. At the beginning of the decade Edmund Wilson had suggested in *Axel's Castle* that this was an idiom which could survive only by consenting to be complicated by disciplines of intelligence and imagination that he somewhat clumsily denominated as "Symbolism," but this was a challenge that did not begin to be responded to until the early 'fifties, by the generation of Ralph Ellison and Saul Bellow and William Styron. And, however robust our respect may still be for the Dos Passos of the *U.S.A.* trilogy or the Steinbeck of *The Grapes of Wrath* or the Wright of *Native Son*, we find them today to be writers with whom it is virtually impossible any longer to have a genuinely reciprocal relation, for the simple fact is that the rhetoric of what once used to be called "reportage" proves itself, with the passage of time, to be a language lacking in the kind of amplitude and resonance that *lasts*. This may not be the precise judgment which the cunning of history, in its ultimate justice, will sustain, but it is, at any rate, *ours*.

It may, of course, be that this is a kind of verdict on our fiction of twenty-five or thirty years ago that has sometimes been applied with too alacritous a facility by the high priests of our present dispensation, and I am prepared even now to confess to the irritation that I recently felt when I came again upon the patrician hauteur of a sentence of the late R. P. Blackmur's in which it is asserted that "*Native Son* is one of those books in which everything is undertaken with seriousness except the writing." But whatever may in turn be history's ultimate verdict on our present way of dealing with the American naturalism of the recent past, there is, quite apart from the line that in this respect we want now to take, a more specific and more cogent reason for the revision that we may want to practice on the accolades of the early 'forties for Mr. Wright's work (the enthusiastic equations of the author of *Native Son* with Dostoevski, etc.), and it is a reason which is clarified by the collection of stories entitled *Eight Men* that appeared a few weeks after his death.

At least three of the stories of which this book is composed were written before 1945, but, since the collection was supervised by the author himself, we are justified in assuming that they do all reflect his final sense of life—and what is most remarkable about the book is the summation that it provides of the consistencies which, throughout his career, formed Richard Wright's personal signature. In each of the eight stories which comprise this volume the central figure is a black *isolé* whose crucifixion by a hostile world is offered as type and example of a collective suffering and a collective fate. And all these various statements are marked by an immoderate and melodramatic imagination of the world as "split in two, a white world and a black one, the white one being separated from the black by a million psychological miles." The last of the eight pieces, "The Man Who Went to Chicago"—which is, I take it, autobiographical—ingeniously interweaves narrative and essay, and, at one point, in recounting his experience in the early 'thirties "as an orderly to a medical research institute in one of the largest and wealthiest hospitals in Chicago," Mr. Wright says:

> Each Saturday morning I assisted a young Jewish doctor in slitting the vocal cords of a fresh batch of dogs from the city pound. The object was to devocalize the dogs so that their howls would not disturb the patients in the other parts of the hospital. I held each dog as the doctor injected Nembutal into its veins to make it unconscious; then I held the dog's jaws open as the doctor inserted the scalpel and severed the vocal cords. Later, when the dogs came to, they would lift their heads to the ceiling and gape in a soundless wail. The sight became lodged in my imagination as a symbol of silent suffering.

And though the image comes toward the close of this collection, once it is encountered it seems then to resonate backward across the entire book, indeed across the entire *oeuvre*, and we feel that the human presence at the center of Mr. Wright's dramatic world has itself somehow been converted into a howling dog whose wails are soundless. In one instance, the long story called "The Man Who Lived Underground," this is an extremism which makes for a wonderfully scarifying and improbable piece of Gothicism which is absolutely self-contained and brilliant. And the piece called "Man of All Work" is a beautifully constructed account of a man who, not being able to find any employment, disguises himself as a woman and, in his wife's clothes, hires himself out as a domestic, being certain that, since Negroes are never really looked at anyway, he'll be able to carry the stunt off—a situation which enables Mr. Wright, with a remarkable deftness and irony, to probe the kind of demasculinization of the male and the kind of resulting rupture of the primitive bonds of the family which have often occurred in Negro life; nor does he also fail, with a savage funniness, to suggest what is outrageous in the sexual panic of American whites. But in every other case, as we move through the stories in *Eight Men,* though we are kept going from page to page and though the writing has the minor virtues of a professionally skillful naturalism, we are dealing with a body of work which totters and collapses under the pressure of a radical imagination unequipped with any defense against its own radicalism; and nowhere else is there a fully achieved work of art.

But, when we have done, it may be that we ought to remember that there are in human experience issues weightier and more exacting than the issues of aesthetics and literary criticism. And it may also be that, in whatever kingdom of the spirit Richard Wright now dwells, as he broods over this uncongenial world of earth, he finds it sufficient merely to say, "I am the man, I suffer'd, I was there." Of this I am reminded, as I glance now at the Dedication of *The Outsider*—"For Rachel, my daughter who was born on alien soil."

$$\Big[\quad \begin{array}{c} \text{RALPH ELLISON} \\ \textit{Richard Wright's Blues} \end{array} \quad\Big]$$

> *If anybody ask you*
> *who sing this song,*
> *Say it was ole [Black Boy]*
> *done been here and gone.**

As A WRITER, Richard Wright has outlined for himself a dual role: to discover and depict the meaning of Negro experience; and to reveal to both Negroes and whites those problems of a psychological and emotional nature which arise between them when they strive for mutual understanding.

Now, in *Black Boy,* he has used his own life to probe what qualities of will, imagination and intellect are required of a Southern Negro in order to possess the meaning of his life in the United States. Wright is an important writer, perhaps the most articulate

---

* Signature formula used by blues singers at conclusion of song.

Negro American, and what he has to say is highly perceptive. Imagine Bigger Thomas projecting his own life in lucid prose, guided, say, by the insights of Marx and Freud, and you have an idea of this autobiography.

Published at a time when any sharply critical approach to Negro life has been dropped as a wartime expendable, it should do much to redefine the problem of the Negro and American Democracy. Its power can be observed in the shrill manner with which some professional "friends of the Negro people" have attempted to strangle the work in a noose of newsprint.

What in the tradition of literary autobiography is it like, this work described as a "great American autobiography"? As a nonwhite intellectual's statement of his relationship to Western culture, *Black Boy* recalls the conflicting pattern of identification and rejection found in Nehru's *Toward Freedom*. In its use of fictional techniques, its concern with criminality (sin) and the artistic sensibility, and in its author's judgment and rejection of the narrow world of his origin, it recalls Joyce's rejection of Dublin in *A Portrait of the Artist*. And as a psychological document of life under oppressive conditions, it recalls *The House of the Dead*, Dostoievsky's profound study of the humanity of Russian criminals.

Such works were perhaps Wright's literary guides, aiding him to endow his life's incidents with communicable significance; providing him with ways of seeing, feeling and describing his environment. These influences, however, were encountered only after these first years of Wright's life were past and were not part of the immediate folk culture into which he was born. In that culture the specific folk-art form which helped shape the writer's attitude toward his life and which embodied the impulse that contributes much to the quality and tone of his autobiography was the Negro blues. This would bear a word of explanation.

The blues is an impulse to keep the painful details and episodes of a brutal experience alive in one's aching consciousness, to finger its jagged grain, and to transcend it, not by the consolation of philosophy but by squeezing from it a near-tragic, near-comic lyricism. As a form, the blues is an autobiographical chronicle of personal catastrophe expressed lyrically. And certainly Wright's early childhood was crammed with catastrophic incidents. In a few short years his father deserted his mother, he knew intense hunger, he became a drunkard begging drinks from black stevedores in Memphis saloons; he had to flee Arkansas, where an uncle was

lynched; he was forced to live with a fanatically religious grandmother in an atmosphere of constant bickering; he was lodged in
an orphan asylum; he observed the suffering of his mother, who
became a permanent invalid, while fighting off the blows of the
poverty-stricken relatives with whom he had to live; he was
cheated, beaten and kicked off jobs by white employees who dis-
liked his eagerness to learn a trade; and to these objective circumstances must be added the subjective fact that Wright, with his
sensitivity, extreme shyness and intelligence, was a problem child
who rejected his family and was by them rejected.

Thus along with the themes, equivalent descriptions of milieu
and the perspectives to be found in Joyce, Nehru, Dostoievsky,
George Moore and Rousseau, *Black Boy* is filled with blues-
tempered echoes of railroad trains, the names of Southern towns
and cities, estrangements, fights and flights, deaths and disap-
pointments, charged with physical and spiritual hungers and pain.
And like a blues sung by such an artist as Bessie Smith, its lyrical
prose evokes the paradoxical, almost surreal image of a black boy
singing lustily as he probes his own grievous wound.

In *Black Boy*, two worlds have fused, two cultures merged,
two impulses of Western man become coalesced. By discussing
some of its cultural sources I hope to answer those critics who
would make of the book a miracle and of its author a mystery. And
while making no attempt to probe the mystery of the artist (who
Hemingway says is "forged in injustice as a sword is forged"), I
do hold that basically the prerequisites to the writing of *Black Boy*
were, on the one hand, the microscopic degree of cultural freedom
which Wright found in the South's stony injustice, and, on the other,
the existence of a personality agitated to a state of almost manic
restlessness. There were, of course, other factors, chiefly ideological;
but these came later.

Wright speaks of his journey north as

> . . . taking a part of the South to transplant in alien soil to
> see if it could grow differently, if it could drink of new and
> cool rains, bend in strange winds, respond to the warmth of
> other suns, and perhaps, to bloom. . . .

And just as Wright, the man, represents the blooming of the delin-
quent child of the autobiography, just so does *Black Boy* represent
the flowering—cross-fertilized by pollen blown by the winds of
strange cultures—of the humble blues lyric. There is, as in all acts
of creation, a world of mystery in this, but there is also enough

that is comprehensible for Americans to create the social atmosphere in which other black boys might freely bloom.

For certainly, in the historical sense, Wright is no exception. Born on a Mississippi plantation, he was subjected to all those blasting pressures which in a scant eighty years have sent the Negro people hurtling, without clearly defined trajectory, from slavery to emancipation, from log cabin to city tenement, from the white folks' fields and kitchens to factory assembly lines; and which, between two wars, have shattered the wholeness of its folk consciousness into a thousand writhing pieces.

Black Boy describes this process in the personal terms of *one* Negro childhood. Nevertheless, several critics have complained that it does not "explain" Richard Wright. Which, aside from the notion of art involved, serves to remind us that the prevailing mood of American criticism has so thoroughly excluded the Negro that it fails to recognize some of the most basic tenets of Western democratic thought when encountering them in a black skin. They forget that human life possesses an innate dignity and mankind an innate sense of nobility, that all men possess the tendency to dream and the compulsion to make their dreams reality, that the need to be ever dissatisfied and the urge ever to seek satisfaction is implicit in the human organism, and that all men are the victims and the beneficiaries of the goading, tormenting, commanding and informing activity of that imperious process known as the Mind— the Mind, as Valéry describes it, "armed with its inexhaustible questions."

Perhaps all this (in which lies the very essence of the human, and which Wright takes for granted) has been forgotten because the critics recognize neither Negro humanity nor the full extent to which the Southern community renders the fulfillment of human destiny impossible. And while it is true that *Black Boy* presents an almost unrelieved picture of a personality corrupted by brutal environment, it also presents those fresh, human responses brought to its world by the sensitive child:

> There was the *wonder* I felt when I first saw a brace˙ of mountainlike, spotted, black-and-white horses clopping down a dusty road . . . the *delight* I caught in seeing long straight rows of red and green vegetables stretching away in the sun . . . the faint, cool kiss of *sensuality* when dew came on to my cheeks . . . the vague *sense of the infinite* as I looked down upon the yellow, dreaming waters of the Mississippi . . . the echoes of *nostalgia* I heard in the crying strings of wild geese . . . the

> *love* I had for the mute regality of tall, moss-clad oaks . . . the
> hint of *cosmic cruelty* that I *felt* when I saw the curved timbers
> of a wooden shack that had been warped in the summer sun
> . . . and there was the *quiet terror* that suffused my senses
> when vast hazes of gold washed earthward from star-heavy
> skies on silent nights. . . .*

And a bit later, his reactions to religion:

> Many of the religious symbols appealed to my sensibilities and
> I responded to the dramatic vision of life held by the church,
> feeling that to live day by day with death as one's sole thought
> was to be so compassionately sensitive toward all life as to
> view all men as slowly dying, and the trembling sense of fate
> that welled up, sweet and melancholy, from the hymns blended
> with the sense of fate that I had already caught from life.

There was also the influence of his mother—so closely linked
to his hysteria and sense of suffering—who (though he only implies it here) taught him, in the words of the dedication prefacing
Native Son, "to revere the fanciful and the imaginative." There
were also those white men—the one who allowed Wright to use his
library privileges and the other who advised him to leave the
South, and still others whose offers of friendship he was too
frightened to accept.

Wright assumed that the nucleus of plastic sensibility is a
human heritage, the right and the opportunity to dilate, deepen
and enrich sensibility—democracy. Thus the drama of *Black Boy*
lies in its depiction of what occurs when Negro sensibility attempts
to fulfill itself in the undemocratic South. Here it is not the individual that is the immediate focus, as in Joyce's *Stephen Hero*, but
that upon which his sensibility was nourished.

Those critics who complain that Wright has omitted the development of his own sensibility hold that the work thus fails as
art. Others, because it presents too little of what they consider
attractive in Negro life, charge that it distorts reality. Both groups
miss a very obvious point: That whatever else the environment
contained, it had as little chance of prevailing against the overwhelming weight of the child's unpleasant experiences as Beethoven's Quartets would have of destroying the stench of a Nazi
prison.

We come, then, to the question of art. The function, the psychology, of artistic selectivity is to eliminate from art form all

---

* Italics mine.

those elements of experience which contain no compelling significance. Life is as the sea, art a ship in which man conquers life's
crushing formlessness, reducing it to a course, a series of swells,
tides and wind currents inscribed on a chart. Though drawn from
the world, "the organized significance of art," writes Malraux, "is
stronger than all the multiplicity of the world; . . . that significance alone enables man to conquer chaos and to master destiny."

Wright saw his destiny—that combination of forces before
which man feels powerless—in terms of a quick and casual violence inflicted upon him by both family and community. His response was likewise violent, and it has been his need to give that
violence significance which has shaped his writings.

What were the ways by which other Negroes confronted their
destiny?

In the South of Wright's childhood there were three general
ways: They could accept the role created for them by the whites
and perpetually resolve the resulting conflicts through the hope
and emotional catharsis of Negro religion; they could repress
their dislike of Jim Crow social relations while striving for a
middle way of respectability, becoming—consciously or unconsciously—the accomplices of the whites in oppressing their brothers;
or they could reject the situation, adopt a criminal attitude, and
carry on an unceasing psychological scrimmage with the whites,
which often flared forth into physical violence.

Wright's attitude was nearest the last. Yet in it there was an
all-important qualitative difference: it represented a groping for
individual values, in a black community whose values were what
the young Negro critic, Edward Bland, has defined as "pre-
individual." And herein lay the setting for the extreme conflict set
off, both within his family and in the community, by Wright's
assertion of individuality. The clash was sharpest on the psychological level, for, to quote Bland:

> In the pre-individualistic thinking of the Negro the stress is
> on the group. Instead of seeing in terms of the individual, the
> Negro sees in terms of "races," masses of peoples separated
> from other masses according to color. Hence, an act rarely
> bares intent against him as a Negro individual. He is singled
> out not as a person but as a specimen of an ostracized group.
> He knows that he never exists in his own right but only to the
> extent that others hope to make the race suffer vicariously
> through him.

This pre-individual state is induced artificially—like the regression to primitive states noted among cultured inmates of Nazi prisons. The primary technique in its enforcement is to impress the Negro child with the omniscience and omnipotence of the whites to the point that whites appear as ahuman as Jehovah, and as relentless as a Mississippi flood. Socially it is effected through an elaborate scheme of taboos supported by a ruthless physical violence, which strikes not only the offender but the entire black community. To wander from the paths of behavior laid down for the group is to become the agent of communal disaster.

In such a society the development of individuality depends upon a series of accidents, which often arise, as in Wright's case, from conditions within the Negro family. In Wright's life there was the accident that as a small child he could not distinguish between his fair-skinned grandmother and the white women of the town, thus developing skepticism as to their special status. To this was linked the accident of his having no close contacts with whites until after the child's normal formative period.

But these objective accidents not only link forward to these qualities of rebellion, criminality and intellectual questioning expressed in Wright's work today. They also link backward into the shadow of infancy where environment and consciousness are so darkly intertwined as to require the skill of a psychoanalyst to define their point of juncture. Nevertheless, at the age of four, Wright set the house afire and was beaten near to death by his frightened mother. This beating, followed soon by his father's desertion of the family, seems to be the initial psychological motivation of his quest for a new identification. While delirious from this beating Wright was haunted "by huge wobbly white bags like the full udders of a cow, suspended from the ceiling above me and I was gripped by the fear that they were going to fall and drench me with some horrible liquid . . ."

It was as though the mother's milk had turned acid, and with it the whole pattern of life that had produced the ignorance, cruelty and fear that had fused with mother-love and exploded in the beating. It is significant that the bags were of the hostile color white, and the female symbol that of the cow, the most stupid (and, to the small child, the most frightening) of domestic animals. Here in dream symbolism is expressed an attitude worthy of an Orestes. And the significance of the crisis is increased by virtue of the historical fact that the lower-class Negro family is matriarchal, the child turns not to the father to compensate if he feels mother-rejection, but to the grandmother, or to an aunt—and Wright rejected both of these. Such rejection leaves the child open to psychological insecurity, distrust and all of those hostile environmental forces from which the family functions to protect it.

One of the Southern Negro family's methods of protecting the child is the severe beating—a homeopathic dose of the violence generated by black and white relationships. Such beatings as Wright's were administered for the child's own good; a good which the child resisted, thus giving family relationships an undercurrent of fear and hostility, which differs qualitatively from that found in partriarchal middle-class families, because here the severe beating is administered by the mother, leaving the child no parental sanctuary. He must ever embrace violence along with maternal tenderness, or else reject, in his helpless way, the mother.

The division between the Negro parents of Wright's mother's generation, whose sensibilities were often bound by their proximity to the slave experience, and their children, who historically and through the rapidity of American change stand emotionally and psychologically much farther away, is quite deep. Indeed, sometimes as deep as the cultural distances between Yeats' *Autobiographies* and a Bessie Smith blues. This is the historical background to those incidents of family strife in *Black Boy* which have caused reviewers to question Wright's judgment of Negro emotional relationships.

We have here a problem in the sociology of sensibility that is obscured by certain psychological attitudes brought to Negro life by whites.

The first is the attitude which compels whites to impute to Negroes sentiments, attitudes and insights which, as a group living under certain definite social conditions, Negroes could not humanly possess. It is the identical mechanism which William Empson identifies in literature as "pastoral." It implies that since Negroes possess the richly human virtues credited to them, then their social position is advantageous and should not be bettered, and, continuing syllogistically, the white individual need feel no guilt over his participation in Negro oppression.

The second attitude is that which leads whites to misjudge Negro passion, looking upon it as they do, out of the turgidity of their own frustrated yearning for emotional warmth, their capacity for sensation having been constricted by the impersonal mechanized relationships typical of bourgeois society. The Negro is idealized into a symbol of sensation, of unhampered social and sexual relationships. And when *Black Boy* questions their illusion they are thwarted much in the manner of the occidental who, after observing the erotic character of a primitive dance, "shacks up" with a native woman—only to discover that far from possessing the hair-trigger sexual responses of a Stork Club "babe," she is relatively phlegmatic.

The point is not that American Negroes are primitives, but that as a group their social situation does not provide for the type of emotional relationships attributed them. For how could the South, recognized as a major part of the backward third of the nation, nurture in the black, most brutalized section of its population, those forms of human relationships achievable only in the most highly developed areas of civilization?

Champions of this "Aren't-Negroes-Wonderful?" school of thinking often bring Paul Robeson and Marian Anderson forward as examples of highly developed sensibility, but actually they are only its *promise*. Both received their development from an extensive personal contact with European culture, free from the influences which shape Southern Negro personality. In the United States, Wright, who is the only Negro literary artist of equal caliber, had to wait years and escape to another environment before discovering the moral and ideological equivalents of his childhood attitudes.

Man cannot express that which does not exist—either in the form of dreams, ideas or realities—in his environment. Neither his thoughts nor his feelings, his sensibility nor his intellect are fixed, innate qualities. They are processes which arise out of the interpenetration of human instinct with environment, through the process called experience, each changing and being changed by the other. Negroes cannot possess many of the sentiments attributed to them because the same changes in environment which, through experience, enlarge man's intellect (and thus his capacity for still greater change) also modify his feelings, which in turn increase his sensibility, i.e., his sensitivity, to refinements of impression and subtleties of emotion. The extent of these changes depends upon the quality of political and cultural freedom in the environment.

Intelligence tests have measured the quick rise in intellect which takes place in Southern Negroes after moving north, but little attention has been paid to the mutations effected in their sensibilities. However, the two go hand in hand. Intellectual complexity is accompanied by emotional complexity; refinement of thought, by refinement of feeling. The movement north affects more than the Negro's wage scale, it affects his entire psychosomatic structure.

The rapidity of Negro intellectual growth in the North is due partially to objective factors present in the environment, to influences of the industrial city and to a greater political freedom. But there are also changes within the "inner world." In the North energies are released and given *intellectual* channelization— energies which in most Negroes in the South have been forced to take either a *physical* form or, as with potentially intellectual types like Wright, to be expressed as nervous tension, anxiety and hysteria. Which is nothing mysterious. The human organism responds to environmental stimuli by converting them into either physical and/or intellectual energy. And what is called hysteria is suppressed intellectual energy expressed physically.

The "physical" character of their expression makes for much of the difficulty in understanding American Negroes. Negro music and dances are frenziedly erotic; Negro religious ceremonies violently ecstatic; Negro speech strongly rhythmical and weighted with image and gesture. But there is more in this sensuousness than the unrestraint and insensitivity found in primitive cultures, nor is it simply the relatively spontaneous and undifferentiated responses of a people living in close contact with the soil. For despite Jim Crow, Negro life does not exist in a vacuum, but in the seething vortex of those tensions generated by the most highly industrialized of Western nations. The welfare of the most humble black Mississippi sharecropper is affected less by the flow of the seasons and the rhythm of natural events than by the fluctuations of the stock market; even though, as Wright states of his father, the sharecropper's memories, actions and emotions are shaped by his immediate contact with nature and the crude social relations of the South.

All of this makes the American Negro far different from the "simple" specimen for which he is taken. And the "physical" quality offered as evidence of his primitive simplicity is actually the form of his complexity. The American Negro is a Western type whose social condition creates a state which is almost the reverse of the cataleptic trance: Instead of his consciousness being lucid to the reality around it while the body is rigid, here it is the body which is alert, reacting to pressures which the constricting forces of Jim Crow block off from the transforming, concept-creating activity of the brain. The "eroticism" of Negro expression springs from much the same conflict as that displayed in the violent gesturing of a man who attempts to express a complicated concept with a limited vocabulary; thwarted ideational energy is converted into unsatisfactory pantomime, and his words are burdened with meanings they cannot convey. Here lies the source of the basic ambiguity of *Native Son*, wherein in order to translate Bigger's complicated feelings into universal ideas, Wright had to force into Bigger's consciousness concepts and ideas which his intellect could not formulate. Between Wright's skill and knowledge and the potentials of Bigger's mute feelings lay a thousand years of conscious culture.

In the South the sensibilities of both blacks and whites are inhibited by the rigidly defined environment. For the Negro there is relative safety as long as the impulse toward individuality is suppressed. (Lynchings have occurred because Negroes painted their homes.) And it is the task of the Negro family to adjust the child to the Southern milieu; through it the currents, tensions and impulses generated within the human organism by the flux and flow of events are given their distribution. This also gives the group its distinctive character. Which, because of Negroes' suppressed minority position, is very much in the nature of an elaborate but limited defense mechanism. Its function is dual: to protect the Negro from whirling away from the undifferentiated mass of his people into the unknown, symbolized in its most abstract form by insanity, and most concretely by lynching; and to protect him from those unknown forces *within* himself which might urge him to reach out for that social and human equality which the white South says he cannot have. Rather than throw himself against the charged wires of his prison he annihilates the impulses within him.

The pre-individualistic black community discourages individuality out of self-defense. Having learned through experience that the whole group is punished for the actions of the single member, it has worked out efficient techniques of behavior control. For in many Southern communities everyone knows everyone else and is vulnerable to his opinions. In some communities everyone is "related" regardless of blood-ties. The regard shown by the group for its members, its general communal character and its cohesion are often mentioned. For by comparison with the coldly impersonal relationships of the urban industrial community, its relationships are personal and warm.

Black Boy, however, illustrates that this personal quality, shaped by outer violence and inner fear, is ambivalent. Personal warmth is accompanied by an equally personal coldness, kindliness by cruelty, regard by malice. And these opposites are as quickly set off against the member who gestures toward individuality as a lynch mob forms at the cry of rape. Negro leaders have often been exasperated by this phenomenon, and Booker T. Washington (who demanded far less of Negro humanity than Richard Wright) described the Negro community as a basket of crabs, wherein should one attempt to climb out, the others immediately pull him back.

The member who breaks away is apt to be more impressed by its negative than by its positive character. He becomes a stranger even to his relatives and he interprets gestures of protection as blows of oppression—from which there is no hiding place, because every area of Negro life is affected. Even parental love is given a qualitative balance akin to "sadism." And the extent of beatings and psychological maimings meted out by Southern Negro parents rivals those described by the nineteenth-century Russian writers as characteristic of peasant life under the Czars. The horrible thing is that the cruelty is also an expression of concern, of love.

In discussing the inadequacies for democratic living typical of the education provided Negroes by the South, a Negro educator has coined the term *mis-education.* Within the ambit of the black family this takes the form of training the child away from curiosity and adventure, against reaching out for those activities lying beyond the borders of the black community. And when the child resists, the parent discourages him; first with the formula, "That there's for white folks. Colored can't have it," and finally with a beating.

It is not, then, the family and communal violence described by *Black Boy* that is unusual, but that Wright *recognized* and made no peace with its essential cruelty—even when, like a babe freshly emerged from the womb, he could not discern where his own personality ended and it began. Ordinarily both parent and child are protected against this cruelty—seeing it as love and finding subjective sanction for it in the spiritual authority of the Fifth Commandment, and on the secular level in the legal and extralegal structure of the Jim Crow system. The child who did not rebel, or who was unsuccessful in his rebellion, learned a masochistic submissiveness and a denial of the impulse toward Western culture when it stirred within him.

Why then have Southern whites, who claim to "know" the Negro, missed all this? Simply because they, too, are armored against the horror and the cruelty. Either they deny the Negro's humanity and feel no cause to measure his actions against civilized norms; or they protect themselves from their guilt in the Negro's condition and from their fear that their cooks might poison them, or that their nursemaids might strangle their infant charges, or that their field hands might do them violence, by attributing to them a superhuman capacity for love, kindliness and forgiveness. Nor does this in any way contradict their stereotyped conviction that all Negroes (meaning those with whom they have no contact) are given to the most animal behavior.

It is only when the individual, whether white or black, *rejects* the pattern that he awakens to the nightmare of his life. Perhaps much of the South's regressive character springs from the fact that many, jarred by some casual crisis into wakefulness, flee hysterically into the sleep of violence or the coma of apathy again. For the penalty of wakefulness is to encounter ever more violence and horror than the sensibilities can sustain unless translated into some form of social action. Perhaps the impassioned character so noticeable among those white Southern liberals so active in the Negro's cause is due to their sense of accumulated horror; their passion—like the violence in Faulkner's novels—is evidence of a profound spiritual vomiting.

This compulsion is even more active in Wright and the increasing number of Negroes who have said an irrevocable "no" to the Southern pattern. Wright learned that it is not enough merely to reject the white South, but that he had also to reject that part of the South which lay within. As a rebel he formulated that rejection negatively, because it was the negative face of the Negro community upon which he looked most often as a child. It is this he is contemplating when he writes:

> Whenever I thought of the essential bleakness of black life in America, I knew that Negroes had never been allowed to catch the full spirit of Western civilization, that they lived somehow in it but not of it. And when I brooded upon the cultural barrenness of black life, I wondered if clean, positive tenderness, love, honor, loyalty and the capacity to remember were native to man. I asked myself if these human qualities were not fostered, won, struggled and suffered for, preserved in ritual from one generation to another.

But far from implying that Negroes have no capacity for
culture, as one critic interprets it, this is the strongest affirmation
that they have. Wright is pointing out what should be obvious
(especially to his Marxist critics) that Negro sensibility is socially
and historically conditioned; that Western culture must be won,
confronted like the animal in a Spanish bullfight, dominated by
the red shawl of codified experience and brought heaving to its
knees.

Wright knows perfectly well that Negro life is a byproduct of
Western civilization, and that in it, if only one possesses the humanity and humility to see, are to be discovered all those impulses,
tendencies, life and cultural forms to be found elsewhere in Western society.

The problem arises because the special condition of Negroes
in the United States, including the defensive character of Negro
life itself (the "will toward organization" noted in the Western
capitalist appears in the Negro as a will to camouflage, to dissimu-
late), so distorts these forms as to render their recognition as
difficult as finding a wounded quail against the brown and yellow
leaves of a Mississippi thicket—even the spilled blood blends with
the background. Having himself been in the position of the quail
—to expand the metaphor—Wright's wounds have told him both
the question and the answer which every successful hunter must
discover for himself: "Where would I hide if *I* were a wounded
quail?" But perhaps that requires more sympathy with one's
quarry than most hunters possess. Certainly it requires such a
sensitivity to the shifting guises of humanity under pressure as to
allow them to identify themselves with the human content, whatever its outer form; and even with those Southern Negroes to
whom Paul Robeson's name is only a rolling sound in the fear-
charged air.

Let us close with one final word about the blues: Their attraction lies in this, that they at once express both the agony of life
and the possibility of conquering it through sheer toughness of
spirit. They fall short of tragedy only in that they provide no
solution, offer no scapegoat but the self. Nowhere in America
today is there social or political action based upon the solid realities of Negro life depicted in *Black Boy*; perhaps that is why, with
its refusal to offer solutions, it is like the blues. Yet in it thousands
of Negroes will for the first time see their destiny in public print.
Freed here of fear and the threat of violence, their lives have at
last been organized, scaled down to possessable proportions. And

in this lies Wright's most important achievement: He has converted the American Negro impulse toward self-annihilation and
"going-underground" into a will to confront the world, to evaluate
his experience honestly and throw his findings unashamedly into
the guilty conscience of America.

[
JAMES BALDWIN
Many Thousands Gone
]

IT IS ONLY in his music, which Americans are able to admire
because a protective sentimentality limits their understanding of it,
that the Negro in America has been able to tell his story. It is a
story which otherwise has yet to be told and which no American is
prepared to hear. As is the inevitable result of things unsaid, we
find ourselves until today oppressed with a dangerous and rever-
berating silence; and the story is told, compulsively, in symbols
and signs, in hieroglyphics; it is revealed in Negro speech and in
that of the white majority and in their different frames of reference. The ways in which the Negro has affected the American
psychology are betrayed in our popular culture and in our morality; in our estrangement from him is the depth of our estrangement from ourselves. We cannot ask: what do we *really* feel about
him—such a question merely opens the gates on chaos. What we
really feel about him is involved with all that we feel about everything, about everyone, about ourselves.

The story of the Negro in America is the story of America—
or, more precisely, it is the story of Americans. It is not a very
pretty story: the story of a people is never very pretty. The Negro
in America, gloomily referred to as that shadow which lies athwart
our national life, is far more than that. He is a series of shadows,
self-created, intertwining, which now we helplessly battle. One may
say that the Negro in America does not really exist except in the
darkness of our minds.

This is why his history and his progress, his relationship to
all other Americans, has been kept in the social arena. He is a
social and not a personal or a human problem; to think of him is

to think of statistics, slums, rapes, injustices, remote violence; it is to be confronted with an endless cataloguing of losses, gains, skirmishes; it is to feel virtuous, outraged, helpless, as though his continuing status among us were somehow analogous to disease—cancer, perhaps, or tuberculosis—which must be checked, even though it cannot be cured. In this arena the black man acquires quite another aspect from that which he has in life. We do not know what to do with him in life; if he breaks our sociological and sentimental image of him we are panic-stricken and we feel ourselves betrayed. When he violates this image, therefore, he stands in the greatest danger (sensing which, we uneasily suspect that he is very often playing a part for our benefit) ; and, what is not always so apparent but is equally true, we are then in some danger ourselves—hence our retreat or our blind and immediate retaliation.

Our dehumanization of the Negro then is indivisible from our dehumanization of ourselves: the loss of our own identity is the price we pay for our annulment of his. Time and our own force act as our allies, creating an impossible, a fruitless tension between the traditional master and slave. Impossible and fruitless because, literal and visible as this tension has become, it has nothing to do with reality.

Time has made some changes in the Negro face. Nothing has succeeded in making it exactly like our own, though the general desire seems to be to make it blank if one cannot make it white. When it has become blank, the past as thoroughly washed from the black face as it has been from ours, our guilt will be finished—at least it will have ceased to be visible, which we imagine to be much the same thing. But, paradoxically, it is we who prevent this from happening, since it is we, who, every hour that we live, reinvest the black face with our guilt; and we do this—by a further paradox, no less ferocious—helplessly, passionately, out of an unrealized need to suffer absolution.

Today, to be sure, we know that the Negro is not biologically or mentally inferior; there is no truth in those rumors of his body odor or his incorrigible sexuality; or no more truth than can be easily explained or even defended by the social sciences. Yet, in our most recent war, his blood was segregated as was, for the most part, his person. Up to today we are set at a division, so that he may not marry our daughters or our sisters, nor may he—for the most part—eat at our tables or live in our houses. Moreover, those who do, do so at the grave expense of a double alienation: from their own people, whose fabled attributes they must either deny or, worse, cheapen and bring to market; from us, for we require of them, when we accept them, that they at once cease to be Negroes and yet not fail to remember what being a Negro means—to remember, that is, what it means to us. The threshold of insult is higher or lower, according to the people involved, from the boot-black in Atlanta to the celebrity in New York. One must travel very far, among saints with nothing to gain or outcasts with noth-ing to lose, to find a place where it does not matter—and perhaps a word or a gesture or simply a silence will testify that it matters even there.

For it means something to be a Negro, after all, as it means something to have been born in Ireland or in China, to live where one sees space and sky or to live where one sees nothing but rubble or nothing but high buildings. We cannot escape our origins, however hard we try, those origins which contain the key—could we but find it—to all that we later become. What it means to be a Negro is a good deal more than this essay can discover; what it means to be a Negro in America can perhaps be suggested by an examination of the myths we perpetuate about him.

Aunt Jemima and Uncle Tom are dead, their places taken by a group of amazingly well-adjusted young men and women, almost as dark, but ferociously literate, well-dressed and scrubbed, who are never laughed at, who are not likely ever to set foot in a cotton or tobacco field or in any but the most modern of kitchens. There are others who remain, in our odd idiom, "underprivileged"; some are bitter and these come to grief; some are unhappy, but, continually presented with the evidence of a better day soon to come, are speedily becoming less so. Most of them care nothing whatever about race. They want only their proper place in the sun and the right to be left alone, like any other citizen of the republic. We may all breathe more easily. Before, however, our joy at the demise of Aunt Jemima and Uncle Tom approaches the indecent, we had better ask whence they sprang, how they lived? Into what limbo have they vanished?

However inaccurate our portraits of them were, these por-traits do suggest, not only the conditions, but the quality of their lives and the impact of this spectacle on our consciences. There was no one more forbearing than Aunt Jemima, no one stronger or more pious or more loyal or more wise; there was, at the same time, no one weaker or more faithless or more vicious and cer-tainly no one more immoral. Uncle Tom, trustworthy and sexless, needed only to drop the title "Uncle" to become violent, crafty, and sullen, a menace to any white woman who passed by. They prepared our feast tables and our burial clothes; and, if we could boast that we understood them, it was far more to the point and far more true that they understood us. They were, moreover, the only people in the world who did; and not only did they know us better than we knew ourselves, but they knew us better than we knew them. This was the piquant flavoring to the national joke, it lay behind our uneasiness as it lay behind our benevolence: Aunt Jemima and Uncle Tom, our creations, at the last evaded us; they had a life—their own, perhaps a better life than ours—and they would never tell us what it was. At the point where we were driven most privately and painfully to conjecture what depths of contempt, what heights of indifference, what prodigies of resilience, what untamable superiority allowed them so vividly to endure, neither perishing nor rising up in a body to wipe us from the earth, the image perpetually shattered and the word failed. The black man in our midst carried murder in his heart, he wanted vengeance. We carried murder too, we wanted peace.

In our image of the Negro breathes the past we deny, not dead but living yet and powerful, the beast in our jungle of statistics. It is this which defeats us, which continues to defeat us, which lends to interracial cocktail parties their rattling, genteel, nervously smiling air: in any drawing room at such a gathering the beast may spring, filling the air with flying things and an unenlightened wailing. Wherever the problem touches there is confusion, there is danger. Wherever the Negro face appears a tension is created, the tension of a silence filled with things unutterable. It is a sentimental error, therefore, to believe that the past is dead; it means nothing to say that it is all forgotten, that the Negro himself has forgotten it. It is not a question of memory. Oedipus did not remember the thongs that bound his feet; nevertheless the marks they left testified to that doom toward which his feet were leading him. The man does not remember the hand that struck him, the darkness that frightened him, as a child; nevertheless, the hand and the darkness remain with him, indivisible from himself forever, part of the passion that drives him wherever he thinks to take flight.

The making of an American begins at that point where he himself rejects all other ties, any other history, and himself adopts the vesture of his adopted land. This problem has been faced by all

Americans throughout our history—in a way it *is* our history—
and it baffles the immigrant and sets on edge the second generation
until today. In the case of the Negro the past was taken from him
whether he would or no; yet to forswear it was meaningless and
availed him nothing, since his shameful history was carried, quite
literally, on his brow. Shameful; for he was heathen as well as
black and would never have discovered the healing blood of Christ
had not we braved the jungles to bring him these glad tidings.
Shameful; for, since our role as missionary had not been wholly
disinterested, it was necessary to recall the shame from which we
had delivered him in order more easily to escape our own. As he
accepted the alabaster Christ and the bloody cross—in the bearing
of which he would find his redemption, as, indeed, to our outraged
astonishment, he sometimes did—he must, henceforth, accept that
image we then gave him of himself: having no other and standing,
moreover, in danger of death should he fail to accept the dazzling
light thus brought into such darkness. It is this quite simple dilemma that must be borne in mind if we wish to comprehend his
psychology.

However we shift the light which beats so fiercely on his
head, or *prove*, by victorious social analysis, how his lot has
changed, how we have both improved, our uneasiness refuses to be
exorcized. And nowhere is this more apparent than in our literature on the subject—"problem" literature when written by whites,
"protest" literature when written by Negroes—and nothing is
more striking than the tremendous disparity of tone between the
two creations. *Kingsblood Royal* bears, for example, almost no
kinship to *If He Hollers Let Him Go*, though the same reviewers
praised them both for what were, at bottom, very much the same
reasons. These reasons may be suggested, far too briefly but not at
all unjustly, by observing that the presupposition is in both novels
exactly the same: black is a terrible color with which to be born
into the world.

Now the most powerful and celebrated statement we have yet
had of what it means to be a Negro in America is unquestionably
Richard Wright's *Native Son*. The feeling which prevailed at the
time of its publication was that such a novel, bitter, uncompromis-
ing, shocking, gave proof, by its very existence, of what strides
might be taken in a free democracy; and its indisputable success,
proof that Americans were now able to look full in the face without flinching the dreadful facts. Americans, unhappily, have the
most remarkable ability to alchemize all bitter truths into an

innocuous but piquant confection and to transform their moral contradictions, or public discussion of such contradictions, into a proud decoration, such as is given for heroism on the field of battle. Such a book, we felt with pride, could never have been written before—which was true. Nor could it be written today. It bears already the aspect of a landmark; for Bigger and his brothers have undergone yet another metamorphosis: they have been accepted in baseball leagues and by colleges hitherto exclusive; and they have made a most favorable appearance on the national screen. We have yet to encounter, nevertheless, a report so indisputably authentic, or one that can begin to challenge this most significant novel.

It is, in a certain American tradition, the story of an unremarkable youth in battle with the force of circumstance; that force of circumstance which plays and which has played so important a part in the national fables of success or failure. In this case the force of circumstance is not poverty merely but color, a circumstance which cannot be overcome, against which the protagonist battles for his life and loses. It is, on the surface, remarkable that this book should have enjoyed among Americans the favor it did enjoy; no more remarkable, however, than that it should have been compared, exuberantly, to Dostoevsky, though placed a shade below Dos Passos, Dreiser, and Steinbeck; and when the book is examined, its impact does not seem remarkable at all, but becomes, on the contrary, perfectly logical and inevitable.

We cannot, to begin with, divorce this book from the specific social climate of that time: it was one of the last of those angry productions, encountered in the late twenties and all through the thirties, dealing with the inequities of the social structure of America. It was published one year before our entry into the last world war—which is to say, very few years after the dissolution of the WPA and the end of the New Deal and at a time when bread lines and soup kitchens and bloody industrial battles were bright in everyone's memory. The rigors of that unexpected time filled us not only with a genuinely bewildered and despairing idealism—so that, because there at least was *something* to fight for, young men went off to die in Spain—but also with a genuinely bewildered self-consciousness. The Negro, who had been during the magnificent twenties a passionate and delightful primitive, now became, as one of the things we were most self-conscious about, our most oppressed minority. In the thirties, swallowing Marx whole, we discovered the Worker and realized—I should think with some relief—that the aims of the Worker and the aims of the Negro

were one. This theorem—to which we shall return—seems now to
leave rather too much out of account; it became, nevertheless, one
of the slogans of the "class struggle" and the gospel of the New
Negro.

As for this New Negro, it was Wright who became his most
eloquent spokesman; and his work, from its beginning, is most
clearly committed to the social struggle. Leaving aside the considerable question of what relationship precisely the artist bears to
the revolutionary, the reality of man as a social being is not his
only reality and that artist is strangled who is forced to deal with
human beings solely in social terms; and who has, moreover, as
Wright had, the necessity thrust on him of being the representative
of some thirteen million people. It is a false responsibility (since
writers are not congressmen) and impossible, by its nature, of
fulfillment. The unlucky shepherd soon finds that, so far from
being able to feed the hungry sheep, he has lost the wherewithal
for his own nourishment: having not been allowed—so fearful was
his burden, so present his audience!—to recreate his own experience. Further, the militant men and women of the thirties were
not, upon examination, significantly emancipated from their ante-
cedents, however bitterly they might consider themselves estranged
or however gallantly they struggled to build a better world. However they might extol Russia, their concept of a better world was
quite helplessly American and betrayed a certain thinness of imagination, a suspect reliance on suspect and badly digested formulae,
and a positively fretful romantic haste. Finally, the relationship of
the Negro to the Worker cannot be summed up, nor even greatly
illuminated, by saying that their aims are one. It is true only
insofar as they both desire better working conditions and useful
only insofar as they unite their strength as workers to achieve
these ends. Further than this we cannot in honesty go.

In this climate Wright's voice first was heard and the struggle
which promised for a time to shape his work and give it purpose
also fixed it in an ever more unrewarding rage. Recording his days
of anger he has also nevertheless recorded, as no Negro before him
had ever done, that fantasy Americans hold in their minds when
they speak of the Negro: that fantastic and fearful image which we
have lived with since the first slave fell beneath the lash. This is
the significance of *Native Son* and also, unhappily, its overwhelming limitation.

Native Son begins with the *Brring!* of an alarm clock in the
squalid Chicago tenement where Bigger and his family live. Rats

live there too, feeding off the garbage, and we first encounter
Bigger in the act of killing one. One may consider that the entire
book, from that harsh *Brring!* to Bigger's weak "Good-by" as the
lawyer, Max, leaves him in the death cell, is an extension, with the
roles inverted, of this chilling metaphor. Bigger's situation and
Bigger himself exert on the mind the same sort of fascination. The
premise of the book is, as I take it, clearly conveyed in these first
pages: we are confronting a monster created by the American
republic and we are, through being made to share his experience,
to receive illumination as regards the manner of his life and to feel
both pity and horror at his awful and inevitable doom. This is an
arresting and potentially rich idea and we would be discussing a
very different novel if Wright's execution had been more perceptive and if he had not attempted to redeem a symbolical monster in
social terms.

One may object that it was precisely Wright's intention to
create in Bigger a social symbol, revelatory of social disease and
prophetic of disaster. I think, however, that it is this assumption
which we ought to examine more carefully. Bigger has no dis-
cernible relationship to himself, to his own life, to his own people,
nor to any other people—in this respect, perhaps, he is most
American—and his force comes, not from his significance as a
social (or anti-social) unit, but from his significance as the incar-
nation of a myth. It is remarkable that, though we follow him step
by step from the tenement room to the death cell, we know as little
about him when this journey is ended as we did when it began;
and, what is even more remarkable, we know almost as little about
the social dynamic which we are to believe created him. Despite
the details of slum life which we are given, I doubt that anyone
who has thought about it, disengaging himself from sentimentality, can accept this most essential premise of the novel for a
moment. Those Negroes who surround him, on the other hand, his
hard-working mother, his ambitious sister, his poolroom cronies,
Bessie, might be considered as far richer and far more subtle and
accurate illustrations of the ways in which Negroes are controlled
in our society and the complex techniques they have evolved for
their survival. We are limited, however, to Bigger's view of them,
part of a deliberate plan which might not have been disastrous if
we were not also limited to Bigger's perceptions. What this means
for the novel is that a necessary dimension has been cut away; this
dimension being the relationship that Negroes bear to one another,
that depth of involvement and unspoken recognition of shared

experience which creates a way of life. What the novel reflects—
and at no point interprets—is the isolation of the Negro within his
own group and the resulting fury of impatient scorn. It is this
which creates its climate of anarchy and unmotivated and unap-
prehended disaster; and it is this climate, common to most Negro
protest novels, which has led us all to believe that in Negro life
there exists no tradition, no field of manners, no possibility of
ritual or intercourse, such as may, for example, sustain the Jew
even after he has left his father's house. But the fact is not that the
Negro has no tradition but that there has as yet arrived no sensibility sufficiently profound and tough to make this tradition articulate. For a tradition expresses, after all, nothing more than the
long and painful experience of a people; it comes out of the battle
waged to maintain their integrity or, to put it more simply, out of
their struggle to survive. When we speak of the Jewish tradition
we are speaking of centuries of exile and persecution, of the
strength which endured and the sensibility which discovered in it
the high possibility of the moral victory.

This sense of how Negroes live and how they have so long
endured is hidden from us in part by the very speed of the Negro's
public progress, a progress so heavy with complexity, so bewildering and kaleidoscopic, that he dare not pause to conjecture on the
darkness which lies behind him; and by the nature of the American psychology which, in order to apprehend or be made able to
accept it, must undergo a metamorphosis so profound as to be
literally unthinkable and which there is no doubt we will resist
until we are compelled to achieve our own identity by the rigors of
a time that has yet to come. Bigger, in the meanwhile, and all his
furious kin, serve only to whet the notorious national taste for the
sensational and to reinforce all that we now find it necessary to
believe. It is not Bigger whom we fear, since his appearance
among us makes our victory certain. It is the others, who smile,
who go to church, who give no cause for complaint, whom we
sometimes consider with amusement, with pity, even with affection
—and in whose faces we sometimes surprise the merest arrogant
hint of hatred, the faintest, withdrawn, speculative shadow of
contempt—who make us uneasy; whom we cajole, threaten, flatter,
fear; who to us remain unknown, though we are not (we feel with
both relief and hostility and with bottomless confusion) unknown
to them. It is out of our reaction to these hewers of wood and
drawers of water that our image of Bigger was created.

It is this image, living yet, which we perpetually seek to evade with good works; and this image which makes of all our good works an intolerable mockery. The "nigger," black, benighted, brutal, consumed with hatred as we are consumed with guilt, cannot be thus blotted out. He stands at our shoulders when we give our maid her wages, it is his hand which we fear we are taking when struggling to communicate with the current "intelligent" Negro, his stench, as it were, which fills our mouths with salt as the monument is unveiled in honor of the latest Negro leader. Each generation has shouted behind him, *Nigger!* as he walked our streets; it is he whom we would rather our sisters did not marry; he is banished into the vast and wailing outer darkness whenever we speak of the "purity" of our women, of the "sanctity" of our homes, of "American" ideals. What is more, he knows it. He is indeed the "native son": he is the "nigger." Let us refrain from inquiring at the moment whether or not he actually exists; for we *believe* that he exists. Whenever we encounter him amongst us in the flesh, our faith is made perfect and his necessary and bloody end is executed with a mystical ferocity of joy.

But there is a complementary faith among the damned which involves their gathering of the stones with which those who walk in the light shall stone them; or there exists among the intolerably degraded the perverse and powerful desire to force into the arena of the actual those fantastic crimes of which they have been accused, achieving their vengeance and their own destruction through making the nightmare real. The American image of the Negro lives also in the Negro's heart; and when he has surrendered to this image life has no other possible reality. Then he, like the white enemy with whom he will be locked one day in mortal struggle, has no means save this of asserting his identity. This is why Bigger's murder of Mary can be referred to as an "act of creation" and why, once this murder has been committed, he can feel for the first time that he is living fully and deeply as a man was meant to live. And there is, I should think, no Negro living in America who has not felt, briefly or for long periods, with anguish sharp or dull, in varying degrees and to varying effect, simple, naked and unanswerable hatred; who has not wanted to smash any white face he may encounter in a day, to violate, out of motives of the cruelest vengeance, their women, to break the bodies of all white people and bring them low, as low as that dust into which he himself has been and is being trampled; no Negro, finally, who has not had to make his own precarious adjustment to the "nigger" who surrounds him and to the "nigger" in himself.

Yet the adjustment must be made—rather, it must be attempted, the tension perpetually sustained—for without this he has surrendered his birthright as a man no less than his birthright as a black man. The entire universe is then peopled only with his enemies, who are not only white men armed with rope and rifle, but his own far-flung and contemptible kinsmen. Their blackness is his degradation and it is their stupid and passive endurance which makes his end inevitable.

Bigger dreams of some black man who will weld all blacks together into a mighty fist, and feels, in relation to his family, that perhaps they had to live as they did precisely because none of them had ever done anything, right or wrong, which mattered very much. It is only he who, by an act of murder, has burst the dungeon cell. He has made it manifest that *he* lives and that his despised blood nourishes the passions of a man. He has forced his oppressors to see the fruit of that oppression; and he feels, when his family and his friends come to visit him in the death cell, that they should not be weeping or frightened, that they should be happy, *proud* that he has dared, through murder and now through his own imminent destruction, to redeem their anger and humiliation, that he has hurled into the spiritless obscurity of their lives the lamp of his passionate life and death. Henceforth, they may remember Bigger—who has died, as we may conclude, for them. But they do not feel this; they only know that he has murdered two women and precipitated a reign of terror; and that now he is to die in the electric chair. They therefore weep and are honestly frightened—for which Bigger despises them and wishes to "blot" them out. What is missing in his situation and in the representation of his psychology—which makes his situation false and his psychology incapable of development—is any revelatory apprehension of Bigger as one of the Negro's realities or as one of the Negro's roles. This failure is part of the previously noted failure to convey any sense of Negro life as a continuing and complex group reality. Bigger, who cannot function therefore as a reflection of the social illness, having, as it were, no society to reflect, likewise refuses to function on the loftier level of the Christ-symbol. His kinsmen are quite right to weep and be frightened, even to be appalled: for it is not his love for them or for himself which causes him to die, but his hatred and his self-hatred; he does not

redeem the pains of a despised people, but reveals, on the contrary, nothing more than his own fierce bitterness at having been
born one of them. In this also he is the "native son," his progress
determinable by the speed with which the distance increases between himself and the auction-block and all that the auction-block
implies. To have penetrated this phenomenon, this inward conten-
tion of love and hatred, blackness and whiteness, would have given
him a stature more nearly human and an end more nearly tragic;
and would have given us a document more profoundly and genuinely bitter and less harsh with an anger which is, on the one
hand, exhibited and, on the other hand, denied.

Native Son finds itself at length so trapped by the American
image of Negro life and by the American necessity to find the ray
of hope that it cannot pursue its own implications. This is why
Bigger must be at the last redeemed, to be received, if only by
rhetoric, into that community of phantoms which is our tena-
ciously held ideal of the happy social life. It is the socially conscious whites who receive him—the Negroes being capable of no
such objectivity—and we have, by way of illustration, that
lamentable scene in which Jan, Mary's lover, forgives him for her
murder; and, carrying the explicit burden of the novel, Max's long
speech to the jury. This speech, which really ends the book, is one
of the most desperate performances in American fiction. It is the
question of Bigger's humanity which is at stake, the relationship in
which he stands to all other Americans—and, by implication, to
all people—and it is precisely this question which it cannot clarify,
with which it cannot, in fact, come to any coherent terms. He is
the monster created by the American republic, the present awful
sum of generations of oppression; but to say that he is a monster
is to fall into the trap of making him subhuman and he must,
therefore, be made representative of a way of life which is real and
human in precise ratio to the degree to which it seems to us
monstrous and strange. It seems to me that this idea carries,
implicitly, a most remarkable confession: that is, that Negro life is
in fact as debased and impoverished as our theology claims; and,
further, that the use to which Wright puts this idea can only
proceed from the assumption—not entirely unsound—that Americans, who evade, so far as possible, all genuine experience, have
therefore no way of assessing the experience of others and no way
of establishing themselves in relation to any way of life which is
not their own. The privacy or obscurity of Negro life makes that
life capable, in our imaginations, of producing anything at all;

and thus the idea of Bigger's monstrosity can be presented without fear of contradiction, since no American has the knowledge or authority to contest it and no Negro has the voice. It is an idea, which, in the framework of the novel, is dignified by the possibility it promptly affords of presenting Bigger as the herald of disaster, the danger signal of a more bitter time to come when not Bigger alone but all his kindred will rise, in the name of the many thousands who have perished in fire and flood and by rope and torture, to demand their rightful vengeance.

But it is not quite fair, it seems to me, to exploit the national innocence in this way. The idea of Bigger as a warning boomerangs not only because it is quite beyond the limit of probability that Negroes in America will ever achieve the means of wreaking vengeance upon the state but also because it cannot be said that they have any desire to do so. *Native Son* does not convey the altogether savage paradox of the American Negro's situation, of which the social reality which we prefer with such hopeful superficiality to study is but, as it were, the shadow. It is not simply the relationship of oppressed to oppressor, of master to slave, nor is it motivated merely by hatred; it is also, literally and morally, a *blood* relationship, perhaps the most profound reality of the American experience, and we cannot begin to unlock it until we accept how very much it contains of the force and anguish and terror of love.

Negroes are Americans and their destiny is the country's destiny. They have no other experience besides their experience on this continent and it is an experience which cannot be rejected, which yet remains to be embraced. If, as I believe, no American Negro exists who does not have his private Bigger Thomas living in the skull, then what most significantly fails to be illuminated here is the paradoxical adjustment which is perpetually made, the Negro being compelled to accept the fact that this dark and dangerous and unloved stranger is part of himself forever. Only this recognition sets him in any wise free and it is this, this necessary ability to contain and even, in the most honorable sense of the word, to *exploit* the "nigger," which lends to Negro life its high element of the ironic and which causes the most well-meaning of their American critics to make such exhilarating errors when attempting to understand them. To present Bigger as a warning is simply to reinforce the American guilt and fear concerning him, it is most forcefully to limit him to that previously mentioned social arena in which he has no human validity, it is simply to condemn

him to death. For he has always been a warning, he represents the
evil, the sin and suffering which we are compelled to reject. It is
useless to say to the courtroom in which this heathen sits on trial
that he is their responsibility, their creation, and his crimes are
theirs; and that they ought, therefore, to allow him to live, to make
articulate to himself behind the walls of prison the meaning of his
existence. The meaning of his existence has already been most
adequately expressed, nor does anyone wish, particularly not in
the name of democracy, to think of it any more; as for the possibility of articulation, it is this possibility which above all others
we most dread. Moreover, the courtroom, judge, jury, witnesses
and spectators, recognize immediately that Bigger is their creation
and they recognize this not only with hatred and fear and guilt
and the resulting fury of self-righteousness but also with that
morbid fullness of pride mixed with horror with which one regards the extent and power of one's wickedness. They know that
death is his portion, that he runs to death; coming from darkness
and dwelling in darkness, he must be, as often as he rises, banished, lest the entire planet be engulfed. And they know, finally,
that they do not wish to forgive him and that he does not wish to
be forgiven; that he dies, hating them, scorning that appeal which
they cannot make to that irrecoverable humanity of his which
cannot hear it; and that he *wants* to die because he glories in his
hatred and prefers, like Lucifer, rather to rule in hell than serve in
heaven.

For, bearing in mind the premise on which the life of such a
man is based, *i.e.*, that black is the color of damnation, this is his
only possible end. It is the only death which will allow him a kind
of dignity or even, however horribly, a kind of beauty. To tell this
story, no more than a single aspect of the story of the "nigger," is
inevitably and richly to become involved with the force of life and
legend, how each perpetually assumes the guise of the other, creating that dense, many-sided and shifting reality which is the world
we live in and the world we make. To tell his story is to begin to
liberate us from his image and it is, for the first time, to clothe this
phantom with flesh and blood, to deepen, by our understanding of
him and his relationship to us, our understanding of ourselves and
of all men.

But this is not the story which *Native Son* tells, for we find
here merely, repeated in anger, the story which we have told in
pride. Nor, since the implications of this anger are evaded, are we
ever confronted with the actual or potential significance of our

pride; which is why we fall, with such a positive glow of recognition, upon Max's long and bitter summing up. It is addressed to
those among us of good will and it seems to say that, though there
are whites and blacks among us who hate each other, we will not;
there are those who are betrayed by greed, by guilt, by blood-lust,
but not we; we will set our faces against them and join hands and
walk together into that dazzling future when there will be no white
or black. This is the dream of all liberal men, a dream not at all
dishonorable, but, nevertheless, a dream. For, let us join hands on
this mountain as we may, the battle is elsewhere. It proceeds far
from us in the heat and horror and pain of life itself where all men
are betrayed by greed and guilt and blood-lust and where no one's
hands are clean. Our good will, from which we yet expect such
power to transform us, is thin, passionless, strident: its roots,
examined, lead us back to our forbears, whose assumption it was
that the black man, to become truly human and acceptable, must
first become like us. This assumption once accepted, the Negro in
America can only acquiesce in the obliteration of his own personality, the distortion and debasement of his own experience,
surrendering to those forces which reduce the person to anonymity
and which make themselves manifest daily all over the darkening
world.

[
    ELDRIDGE CLEAVER
    Notes on a Native Son
]

AFTER READING a couple of James Baldwin's books, I began experiencing that continuous delight one feels upon discovering a
fascinating, brilliant talent on the scene, a talent capable of penetrating so profoundly into one's own little world that one knows
oneself to have been unalterably changed and *liberated*, liberated
from the frustrating grasp of whatever devils happen to possess
one. Being a Negro, I have found this to be a rare and infrequent
experience, for few of my black brothers and sisters here in America have achieved the power, which James Baldwin calls his revenge, which outlasts kingdoms: the power of doing whatever cats
like Baldwin do when combining the alphabet with the volatile

elements of his soul. (And, like it or not, a black man, unless he has become irretrievably "white-minded," responds with an additional dimension of his being to the articulated experience of another black—in spite of the universality of human experience.)

I, as I imagine many others did and still do, lusted for anything that Baldwin had written. It would have been a gas for me to sit on a pillow beneath the womb of Baldwin's typewriter and catch each newborn page as it entered this world of ours. I was delighted that Baldwin, with those great big eyes of his, which one thought to be fixedly focused on the macrocosm, could also pierce the microcosm. And although he was so full of sound, he was not a noisy writer like Ralph Ellison. He placed so much of my own experience, which I thought I had understood, into new perspective.

Gradually, however, I began to feel uncomfortable about something in Baldwin. I was disturbed upon becoming aware of an aversion in my heart to part of the song he sang. Why this was so, I was unable at first to say. Then I read *Another Country,* and I knew why my love for Baldwin's vision had become ambivalent.

Long before, I had become a student of Norman Mailer's *The White Negro,* which seemed to me to be prophetic and penetrating in its understanding of the psychology involved in the accelerating confrontation of black and white in America. I was therefore personally insulted by Baldwin's flippant, schoolmarmish dismissal of *The White Negro.* Baldwin committed a literary crime by his arrogant repudiation of one of the few gravely important expressions of our time. *The White Negro* may contain an excess of esoteric verbal husk, but one can forgive Mailer for that because of the solid kernel of truth he gave us. After all, it is the baby we want and not the blood of afterbirth. Mailer described, in that incisive essay, the first important chinks in the "mountain of white supremacy"—important because it shows the depth of ferment, on a personal level, in the white world. People are feverishly, and at great psychic and social expense, seeking *fundamental and irrevocable liberation*—and, what is more important, *are succeeding in escaping*—from the big white lies that compose the monolithic myth of White Supremacy/Black Inferiority, in a desperate attempt on the part of a new generation of white Americans to enter into the cosmopolitan egalitarian spirit of the twentieth century. But let us examine the reasoning that lies behind Baldwin's attack on Mailer.

There is in James Baldwin's work the most grueling, agonizing, total hatred of the blacks, particularly of himself, and the most shameful, fanatical, fawning, sycophantic love of the whites that one can find in the writings of any black American writer of note in our time. This is an appalling contradiction and the implications of it are vast.

A rereading of *Nobody Knows My Name* cannot help but convince the most avid of Baldwin's admirers of the hatred for blacks permeating his writings. In the essay "Princes and Powers," Baldwin's antipathy toward the black race is shockingly clear. The essay is Baldwin's interpretation of the Conference of Black Writers and Artists which met in Paris in September 1956. The portrait of Baldwin that comes through his words is that of a mind in unrelenting opposition to the efforts of solemn, dedicated black men who have undertaken the enormous task of rejuvenating and reclaiming the shattered psyches and culture of the black people, a people scattered over the continents of the world and the islands of the seas, where they exist in the mud of the floor of the foul dungeon into which the world has been transformed by the whites.

In his report of the conference, Baldwin, the reluctant black, dragging his feet at every step, could only ridicule the vision and efforts of these great men and heap scorn upon them, reserving his compliments—all of them lefthanded—for the speakers at the conference who were themselves rejected and booed by the other conferees because of their reactionary, sycophantic views. Baldwin felt called upon to pop his cap pistol in a duel with Aimé Césaire, the big gun from Martinique. Indirectly, Baldwin was defending his first love—the white man. But the revulsion which Baldwin felt for the blacks at this conference, who were glorying in their blackness, seeking and showing their pride in Negritude and the African Personality, drives him to self-revealing sortie after sortie, so obvious in "Princes and Powers." Each successive sortie, however, becomes more expensive than the last one, because to score each time he has to go a little farther out on the limb, and it takes him a little longer each time to hustle back to the cover and camouflage of the perfumed smoke screen of his prose. Now and then we catch a glimpse of his little jive ass—his big eyes peering back over his shoulder in the mischievous retreat of a child sneak-thief from a cookie jar.

In the autobiographical notes of *Notes of a Native Son*, Baldwin is frank to confess that, in growing into his version of manhood in Harlem, he discovered that, since his African heritage had

been wiped out and was not accessible to him, he would appropriate the white man's heritage and make it his own. This terrible
reality, central to the psychic stance of all American Negroes,
revealed to Baldwin that he hated and feared white people. Then
he says: "This did not mean that I loved black people; on the
contrary, I despised them, possibly because they failed to produce
Rembrandt." The psychic distance between love and hate could be
the mechanical difference between a smile and a sneer, or it could
be the journey of a nervous impulse from the depths of one's brain
to the tip of one's toe. But this impulse in its path through North
American nerves may, if it is honest, find the passage disputed:
may find the leap from the fiber of hate to that of love too taxing
on its meager store of energy—and so the long trip back may
never be completed, may end in a reconnaissance, a compromise,
and then a lie.

Self-hatred takes many forms; sometimes it can be detected
by no one, not by the keenest observer, not by the self-hater himself, not by his most intimate friends. Ethnic self-hate is even more
difficult to detect. But in American Negroes, this ethnic self-hatred
often takes the bizarre form of a racial death-wish, with many and
elusive manifestations. Ironically, it provides much of the impetus
behind the motivations of integration. And the attempt to suppress
or deny such drives in one's psyche leads many American Negroes
to become ostentatious separationists, Black Muslims, and back-to-
Africa advocates. It is no wonder that Elijah Muhammad could
conceive of the process of controlling evolution whereby the white
race was brought into being. According to Elijah, about 6300
years ago all the people of the earth were Original Blacks. Se-
cluded on the island of Patmos, a mad black scientist by the name
of Yacub set up the machinery for grafting whites out of blacks
through the operation of a birth-control system. The population on
this island of Patmos was 59,999 and whenever a couple on this
island wanted to get married they were only allowed to do so if
there was a difference in their color, so that by mating black with
those in the population of a brownish color and brown with brown
—but never black with black—all traces of the black were eventually eliminated; the process was repeated until all the brown was
eliminated, leaving only men of the red race; the red was
bleached out, leaving only yellow; then the yellow was bleached
out, and only white was left. Thus Yacub, who was long since
dead, because this whole process took hundreds of years, had

finally succeeded in creating the white devil with the blue eyes of death.

This myth of the creation of the white race, called "Yacub's history," is an inversion of the racial death-wish of American Negroes. Yacub's plan is still being followed by many negroes today. Quite simply, many Negroes believe, as the principle of assimilation into white America implies, that the race problem in America cannot be settled until all traces of the black race are eliminated. Toward this end, many Negroes loathe the very idea of two very dark Negroes mating. The children, they say, will come out ugly. What they mean is that the children are sure to be black, and this is not desirable. From the widespread use of cosmetics to bleach the black out of one's skin and other concoctions to take Africa out of one's hair, to the extreme, resorted to by more Negroes than one might wish to believe, of undergoing nose-thinning and lip-clipping operations, the racial death-wish of American Negroes—Yacub's goal—takes its terrible toll. What has been happening for the past four hundred years is that the white man, through his access to black women, has been pumping his blood and genes into the blacks, has been diluting the blood and genes of the blacks—i.e., has been fulfilling Yacub's plan and accelerating the Negroes' racial death-wish.

The case of James Baldwin aside for a moment, it seems that many Negro homosexuals, acquiescing in this racial death-wish, are outraged and frustrated because in their sickness they are unable to have a baby by a white man. The cross they have to bear is that, already bending over and touching their toes for the white man, the fruit of their miscegenation is not the little half-white offspring of their dreams but an increase in the unwinding of their nerves—though they redouble their efforts and intake of the white man's sperm.

In this land of dichotomies and disunited opposites, those truly concerned with the resurrection of black Americans have had eternally to deal with black intellectuals who have become their own opposites, taking on all of the behavior patterns of their enemy, vices and virtues, in an effort to aspire to alien standards in all respects. The gulf between an audacious, bootlicking Uncle Tom and an intellectual buckdancer is filled only with sophistication and style. On second thought, Uncle Tom comes off much cleaner here because usually he is just trying to survive, choosing to pretend to be something other than his true self in order to please the white man and thus receive favors. Whereas the intellectual sycophant does not pretend to be other than he actually is, but hates what he is and seeks to redefine himself in the image of his white idols. He becomes a white man in a black body. A self-willed, automated slave, he becomes the white man's most valuable tool in oppressing other blacks.

The black homosexual, when his twist has a racial nexus, is an extreme embodiment of this contradiction. The white man has deprived him of his masculinity, castrated him in the center of his burning skull, and when he submits to this change and takes the white man for his lover as well as Big Daddy, he focuses on "whiteness" all the love in his pent up soul and turns the razor edge of hatred against "blackness"—upon himself, what he is, and all those who look like him, remind him of himself. He may even hate the darkness of night.

The racial death-wish is manifested as the driving force in James Baldwin. His hatred for blacks, even as he pleads what he conceives as their cause, makes him the apotheosis of the dilemma in the ethos of the black bourgeoisie who have completely rejected their African heritage, consider the loss irrevocable, and refuse to look again in that direction. This is the root of Baldwin's violent repudiation of Mailer's *The White Negro*.

To understand what is at stake here, and to understand it in terms of the life of this nation, is to know the central fact that the relationship between black and white in America is a power equation, a power struggle, and that this power struggle is not only manifested in the aggregate (civil rights, black nationalism, etc.) but also in the interpersonal realtionships, actions, and reactions between blacks and whites where taken into account. When those "two lean cats," Baldwin and Mailer, met in a French living room, it was precisely this power equation that was at work.

It is fascinating to read (in *Nobody Knows My Name*) in what terms this power equation was manifested in Baldwin's immediate reaction to that meeting: "And here we were, suddenly, circling around each other. We liked each other at once, but each was frightened that the other would pull rank. He could have pulled rank on me beacuse he was more famous and *had more money* and also *because he was white;* but I could have pulled rank on him precisely because I was black and knew more about that periphery he so helplessly maligns in *The White Negro* than he could ever hope to know." [Italics added.]

Pulling rank, it would seem, is a very dangerous business, especially when the troops have mutinied and the basis of one's authority, or rank, is devoid of that interdictive power and has become suspect. One would think that for Baldwin, of all people, these hues of black and white were no longer armed with the power to intimidate—and if one thought this, one would be exceedingly wrong: for behind the structure of the thought of Baldwin's quoted above, there lurks the imp of Baldwin's unwinding, of his tension between love and hate—love of the white and hate of the black. And when we dig into this tension we will find that when those "two lean cats" crossed tracks in that French living room, one was a Pussy Cat, the other a Tiger. Baldwin's purr was transmitted magnificently in *The Fire Next Time.* But his work is the fruit of a tree with a poison root. Such succulent fruit, such a painful tree, what a malignant root!

It is ironic, but fascinating for what it reveals about the ferment in the North American soul in our time, that Norman Mailer, the white boy, and James Baldwin, the black boy, encountered each other in the eye of a social storm, traveling in opposite directions; the white boy, with knowledge of white Negroes, was traveling toward a confrontation with the black, with Africa; while the black boy, with a white mind, was on his way to Europe. Baldwin's nose, like the North-seeking needle on a compass, is forever pointed toward his adopted fatherland, Europe, his by intellectual osmosis and in Africa's stead. What he says of Aimé Césaire, one of the greatest black writers of the twentieth century, and intending it as an ironic rebuke, that "he had penetrated into the heart of the great wilderness which was Europe and stolen the sacred fire . . . which . . . was . . . the assurance of his power," seems only too clearly to speak more about Peter than it does about Paul. What Baldwin seems to forget is that Césaire explains that fire, whether sacred or profane, burns. In Baldwin's case, though the fire could not burn the black off his face, it certainly did burn it out of his heart.

I am not interested in denying anything to Baldwin. I, like the entire nation, owe a great debt to him. But throughout the range of his work, from *Go Tell It on the Mountain,* through *Notes of a Native Son, Nobody knows My Name, Another Country,* to *The Fire Next Time,* all of which I treasure, there is a decisive quirk in Baldwin's vision which corresponds to his relationship to black people and to masculinity. It was this same quirk, in my opinion, that compelled Baldwin to slander Rufus Scott in *Another Coun-*

try, venerate André Gide, repudiate *The White Negro*, and drive
the blade of Brutus into the corpse of Richard Wright. As Baldwin
has said in *Nobody Knows My Name*, "I think that I know something about the American masculinity which most men of my
generation do not know because they have not been menaced by it
in the way I have been." O.K., Sugar, but isn't it true that Rufus
Scott, the weak, craven-hearted ghost of *Another Country*, bears
the same relation to Bigger Thomas of *Native Son*, the black rebel
of the ghetto and a man, as you yourself bore to the fallen giant,
Richard Wright, a rebel and a man?

Somewhere in one of his books, Richard Wright describes an
encounter between a ghost and several young Negroes. The young
Negroes rejected the homosexual, and this was Wright alluding to
a classic, if cruel, example of a ubiquitous phenomenon in the
black ghettos of America: the practice by Negro youths of going
"punk-hunting." This practice of seeking out homosexuals on the
prowl, rolling them, beating them up, seemingly just to satisfy
some savage impulse to inflict pain on the specific target selected,
the "social outcast," seems to me to be not unrelated, in terms of
the psychological mechanisms involved, to the ritualistic lynchings
and castrations inflicted on Southern blacks by Southern whites.
This was, as I recall, one of Wright's few comments on the subject
of homosexuality.

I think it can safely be said that the men in Wright's books,
albeit shackled with a form of impotence, were strongly heterosexual. Their heterosexuality was implied rather than laboriously
stated or emphasized; it was taken for granted, as we all take men
until something occurs to make us know otherwise. And Bigger
Thomas, Wright's greatest creation, was a man in violent, though
inept, rebellion against the stifling, murderous, totalitarian white
world. There was no trace in Bigger of a Martin Luther King-type
self-effacing love for his oppressors. For example, Bigger would
have been completely baffled, as most Negroes are today, at Baldwin's advice to his nephew (*The Fire Next Time*), concerning
white people: "You must accept them *and accept them with love.*
For these innocent people have no other hope." [Italics added.]

Rufus Scott, a pathetic wretch who indulged in the white
man's pastime of committing suicide, who let a white bisexual
homosexual fuck him in his ass, and who took a Southern Jezebel
for his woman, with all that these tortured relationships imply,
was the epitome of a black eunuch who has completely submitted

to the white man. Yes, Rufus was a psychological freedom rider,
turning the ultimate cheek, murmuring like a ghost, *"You took the
best so why not take the rest,"* which has absolutely nothing to do
with the way Negroes have managed to survive here in the hells of
North America! This all becomes very clear from what we learn of
Erich, the arch-ghost of *Another Country,* of the depths of his
alienation from his body and the source of his need: "And it had
taken him almost until this very moment, on the eve of his departure, to begin to recognize that part of Rufus' great power over
him had to do with the past which Erich had buried in some deep,
dark place; was connected with himself, in Alabama, *when I wasn't
nothing but a child;* with the cold white people and the warm black
people, warm at least for him. . . ."

So, too, who cannot wonder at the source of such audacious
madness as moved Baldwin to make this startling remark about
Richard Wright, in his ignoble essay "Alas, Poor Richard": "In
my own relations with him, I was always exasperated by his notions of society, politics, and history, for they seemed to me utterly
fanciful. I never believed that he had any real sense of how a
society is put together."

Richard Wright is dead and Baldwin is alive with us. Baldwin says that Richard Wright held notions that were utterly fanciful, and Baldwin is an honorable man.

> *O judgment; thou art fled to*
> *brutish beasts,*
> *And men have lost their reason!*

Wright has no need, as Caesar did, of an outraged Antony to plead
his cause: his life and his work are his shield against the mellow
thrust of Brutus' blade. The good that he did, unlike Caesar's, will
not be interred with his bones. It is, on the contrary, only the
living who can be harmed by Brutus.

Baldwin says that in Wright's writings violence sits enthroned
where sex should be. If this is so, then it is only because in the
North American reality hate holds sway in love's true province.
And it is only through a rank perversion that the artist, whose
duty is to tell us the truth, can turn the two-dollar trick of wedding
violence to love and sex to hate—if, to achieve this end, one has
basely to transmute rebellion into lamblike submission—*"You
took the best,"* sniveled Rufus, *"so why not take the rest?"*
Richard Wright was not ghost enough to achieve his cruel distortion. With him, sex, being not a spectator sport or a panacea but

the sacred vehicle of life and love, is itself sacred. And the America which Wright knew and which *is*, is not the Garden of Eden but its opposite. Baldwin, embodying in his art the self-flagellating policy of Martin Luther King, and giving out falsely the news that the Day of the Ghost has arrived, pulled it off in *Another Country*.

Of all black American novelists, and indeed of all American novelists of any hue, Richard Wright reigns supreme for his profound political, economic, and social reference. Wright had the ability, like Dreiser, of harnessing the gigantic, overwhelming environmental forces and focusing them, with pinpoint sharpness, on individuals and their acts as they are caught up in the whirlwind of the savage, anarchistic sweep of life, love, death, and hate, pain, hope, pleasure, and despair across the face of a nation and the world. But, ah! "O masters," it is Baldwin's work which is so void of a political, economic, or even a social reference. His characters all seem to be fucking and sucking in a vacuum. Baldwin has a superb touch when he speaks of human beings, when he is inside of them—especially his homosexuals—but he flounders when he looks beyond the skin; whereas Wright's forte, it seems to me, was in reflecting the intricate mechanisms of a social organization, its functioning as a unit.

Baldwin's essay on Richard Wright reveals that he despised—not Richard Wright, but his masculinity. He cannot confront the stud in others—except that he must either submit to it or destroy it. And he was not about to bow to a *black* man. Wright understood and lived the truth of what Norman Mailer meant when he said ". . . for being a man is the continuing battle of one's life, and one loses a bit of manhood with every stale compromise to the authority of any power in which one does not believe." Baldwin, compromised beyond getting back by the white man's *power*, which is real and which has nothing to do with *authority*, but to which Baldwin has ultimately succumbed psychologically, is totally unable to extricate himself from that horrible pain. It is the scourge of his art, because the only way out for him is psychologically to embrace Africa, the land of his fathers, which he utterly refuses to do. He has instead resorted to a despicable underground guerrilla war, waged on paper, against black masculinity, playing out the racial death-wish of Yacub, reaching, I think, a point where Mailer hits the spot: "Driven into defiance, it is natural if regrettable, that many homosexuals go to the direction of assuming that there is something intrinsically superior in homosexuality, and carried far enough it is a viewpoint which is as stultifying, as ridiculous, and as anti-human as the heterosexual's prejudice."

I, for one, do not think homosexuality is the latest advance over heterosexuality on the scale of human evolution. Homosexuality is a sickness, just as are baby-rape or wanting to become the head of General Motors.

A grave danger faces this nation, of which we are as yet unaware. And it is precisely this danger which Baldwin's work conceals; indeed, leads us away from. We are engaged in the deepest, the most fundamental revolution and reconstruction which men have ever been called upon to make in their lives, and which they absolutely cannot escape or avoid except at the peril of the very continued existence of human life on this planet. The time of the sham is over, and the cheek of the suffering saint must no longer be turned twice to the brute. The titillation of the guilt complexes of bored white liberals leads to doom. The grotesque hideousness of what is happening to us is reflected in this remark by Murray Kempton, quoted in *The Realist:* "When I was a boy Stepin Fetchit was the only Negro actor who worked regularly in the movies. . . . The fashion changes, but I sometimes think that Malcolm X and, to a degree, even James Baldwin are *our* Stepin Fetchits."

Yes, the fashion does change. "Will the machinegunners please step forward," said LeRoi Jones in a poem "The machine gun on the corner," wrote Richard Wright, "is the symbol of the twentieth century." The embryonic spirit of kamikaze, real and alive, grows each day in the black man's heart and there are dreams of Nat Turner's legacy. The ghost of John Brown is creeping through suburbia. And I wonder if James Chaney said, as Andrew Goodman and Michael Schwerner stood helplessly watching, as the grizzly dogs crushed his bones with savage blows of chains—did poor James say, after Rufus Scott—"*You took the best, so why not take the rest?*" Or did he turn to his white brothers, seeing their plight, and say, after Baldwin, "That's your problem, baby!"

I say, after Mailer, "There's a shit-storm coming."

[JOHN HENRIK CLARKE
  *The Alienation of
   James Baldwin*]

THE NOW flourishing literary talent of James Baldwin had no easy
birth, and he did not emerge overnight, as some of his new discov-
erers would have you believe. For years this talent was in incuba-
tion in the ghetto of Harlem, before he went to Europe nearly a
decade ago in an attempt to discover the United States and how he
and his people relate to it. The book in which that discovery is
portrayed, *The Fire Next Time*, is a continuation of his search for
place and definition.*

The hardships of that search were recently described by Sterling Stuckey, Chairman of the Committee on Negro Culture and
History:

> The tragedy of the American Negro is born of the twin
> evils of the slave experience and varying patterns of segrega-
> tion, supported by law and custom, that have been nation-wide
> in dimension for a century. The consequences of the Negro's
> quasi freedom, unfolded against a grim backdrop of two and
> a half centuries of slavery, have been no less destructive to his
> spiritual world—his hierarchy of values and his image of him-
> self—than to his every day world of work.

This quasi freedom of the Negro is often more humiliating
than slavery and more difficult to fight, because it gives the Negro
the illusion of freedom while denying him the fact. Thus the Negro
continues his alien status in a country where his people have lived
for more than three hundred years. *The Fire Next Time*, like most
of Baldwin's writings, is about this alienation.

Two essays, one long and one short, make up the book. The
short essay, "My Dungeon Shook," originally appeared in the
Progressive magazine. The long essay, "Down at the Cross," originally appeared in the *New Yorker* under the title, "Letter From a
Region in My Mind," and the issue in which it came out is now a
collector's item.

* James Baldwin, *The Fire Next Time* (New York: Dial Press, 1963).

Baldwin, more than any other writer of our times, has succeeded in restoring the personal essay to its place as a form of
creative literature. From his narrow vantage point of personal
grievance, he has opened a "window on the world." He plays the
role traditionally assigned to thinkers concerned with the improvement of human conditions—that of alarmist. He calls our attention
to things in our society that need to be corrected and things that
need to be celebrated. The narrowness of his vantage point is no
assurance that he is right or wrong; nor does it negate the importance of what he is saying. The oppressed person is the best authority on his oppression.

Racism in the United States has forced every Negro into a
prolonged and pathetic war. He is either at war against his oppression or against the weakness within himself that frustrates his
ability to participate in this war effectively. The saddest partici-
pants in this war for mental and physical survival and basic
human dignity are those Negroes who think that they are removed
from it—those who live with the illusion that they have been
integrated. The limitation and uniqueness of Baldwin's vantage
point is that he is addressing his audience from the war zone.

The first essay, subtitled "Letter to My Nephew on the One
Hundredth Anniversary of the Emancipation," is Baldwin's advice
to a young relative entering the area of racial conflict on the
anniversary of the proclamation that is supposed to have set his
people free. The thrust of the author's eloquent anger is deep.

> This innocent country set you down in a ghetto in which,
> in fact, it intended that you should perish. Let me spell out
> precisely what I mean by that, for the heart of the matter is
> here, and the root of my dispute with my country. You were
> born where you were born and faced the future that you faced
> because you were black and for no other reason. The limits
> of your ambition were, thus, expected to be set forever. You
> were born into a society which spelled out with brutal clarity,
> and in as many ways as possible, that you were a worthless
> human being. You were not expected to aspire to excellence:
> you were expected to make peace with mediocrity.
>
> Wherever you have turned, James, in your short time on
> this earth, you have been told where you could go and what
> you could do (and how you could do it) and where you could
> live and whom you could marry. I know your countrymen do
> not agree with me about this, and I hear them saying, "You
> exaggerate." They do not know Harlem, and I do. So do you.
> Take no one's word for anything, including mine—but trust

your experience. Know whence you came. If you know whence you came, there is really no limit to where you can go.

This is close to the root of the matter. The Negro was not brought to the United States to be given democracy. When the promise of democracy was made, it was not made to him, and this is the main reason why the growth of democracy in this nation is retarded. Nonetheless, Baldwin advises his nephew not to despair:

> You came from sturdy, peasant stock, men who picked cotton and dammed rivers and built railroads, and in the teeth of the most terrifying odds, achieved an unassailable and monumental dignity. You came from a long line of poets, some of the greatest poets since Homer. One of them said: "The very time I thought I was lost, my dungeon shook and my chains fell off." You know, and I know that the country is celebrating one hundred years of freedom one hundred years too soon.

The long essay, "Down at the Cross," is brilliantly written, though much too long and involved for the meagerness of its message. In essence, it consists of Baldwin's reflections on growing up in Harlem and on how this ghetto upbringing influenced him. Baldwin's evaluation of the Black Muslims and their leader, Elijah Muhammad, tells us more about the author than about his subject. As a guest in the home of Muhammad, he seems to have vacillated between personal attraction and ideological estrangement. He speaks of his host as follows:

> I felt that I was back in my father's house—as indeed, in a way, I was—and I told Elijah that I did not care if white and black people married and that I had many white friends. I would have no choice, if it came to it, but to perish with them, for (I said to myself, but not to Elijah) "I love a few people and they love me and some of them are white, and isn't love more important than color?"

But the people in control of the power structure of the United States have already answered Baldwin's question in the negative. This answer is one of the main reasons for the existence of the Black Muslims, for in spite of all that can justifiably be said against them, they have found what most Negroes are still searching for—a way of reclaiming their dignity as human beings.

Baldwin is a highly regarded intellectual, the most honored Negro writer since Richard Wright. Yet the word struggle, inseparable from the existence of the Negro people, rarely appears in his work, nor as a novelist has he yet created a single Negro character who attains stature in a fight against his condition. Neither does he show any awareness of the economic base for oppression. These are serious limitations in a man hailed by many as the spokesman for his people.

There is a tangential aspect of Baldwin that requires brief comment. That is the cult of white followers that has grown up around him. These disciples flock to all his public appearances as to some masochistic ceremony of penance. It is as though they cry out: "Oh, Jimmy, punish us for the sins we have committed against your people." Tears yes, action never. For them Baldwin has become a sponge, soaking up the wastes of their conscience. In fairness to Baldwin, one must say that this cult is not of his making nor is it under his control.

A lot of people are hearing Baldwin's words but missing his message. What the Negro wants is justice, not sympathy; and if justice is not forthcoming, there may well be "the fire next time" —and sooner than we think.

BARBARA CHRISTIAN
Ralph Ellison:
A Critical Study *

IN 1952, reviewers across the country in both black and white periodicals hailed the then newly published book, *Invisible Man,* as a most impressive work of fiction. In that same year, Ralph Ellison's first novel was given collective critical acclaim for it was called the best novel of the last twenty years. There is no doubt that Ellison, although not very prolific (*Invisible Man* is his only completed creative work), is a skilled, impressive and lyrical writer. But he is not only a novelist; Ellison is also a critic with a particular point of view. His point of view can be seen in almost any paragraph in his collected essays, *Shadow and Act* (1966). Ellison's speech when he received the National Book Award reveals his particular slant:

> Thus to see America with an awareness of its rich diversity and its almost magical fluidity and freedom, I was forced to conceive of a novel unburdened by the narrow naturalism

* City College Lecture on Ralph Ellison's *Invisible Man*, May, 1967.

which has led, after so many triumphs, to the final and unrelieved despair which marks so much of our current fiction. I was to dream of a prose which was flexible and swift as American change is swift, confronting the inequalities, but yet thrusting forth its images of hope, human fraternity and individual self-realization. It would use the richness of our speech, the idiomatic expression and the rhetorical flourishes from past periods which are still alive among us. And despite my personal failures, there must be possible a fiction, which, leaving sociology to the scientists, can arrive at the truth about the human condition, here and now, with all the bright magic of a fairy tale.

The emphasis in this acceptance speech is without a doubt on the aesthetic problems of the artist. Unlike Wright and other notable black writers, Ellison is the spokesman for the "infinite possibilities" that he feels is inherent in the condition of being an artist rather than a Negro artist. He repeatedly states in his essays that his primary concern is not the social but rather the aesthetic responsibilities of the writer.

As we shall see, Ellison's positions in many of his essays do not always coincide with the ideas expressed in *Invisible Man*. Nonetheless, the essays, such as "Richard Wright's Blues," his interview with *Partisan Review*, and many of his essays on music are worth our attention for they reveal his interests and philosophy as they have developed and in this sense are a means of clarifying certain sections of *Invisible Man*.

There is one word that crops up repeatedly in both the essays and *Invisible Man* and which is at the base of Ellison's aesthetic beliefs. That word is *myth*, the magical transformer of life. Influenced by T. S. Eliot whom he calls his literary ancestor, Ellison combines the literary past and the memory and culture of the individual with the present, thus placing the contemporary writer alongside the other men who have written in the English language. Baldwin stresses the fact that the writer creates out of his own experience. Ellison would add that one writes out of one's experience as understood through one's knowledge of self, culture, and literature. Self, in Ellison's case, refers to his own past and background, culture to the American culture and more specifically to Negro American culture, and literature to the entire range of works in European literature that help to make up Western sensibility.

Even Ellison's name itself is steeped in myth as he points out in the essay, "Hidden Names and Complex Fate." His father had named him after Ralph Waldo Emerson and Ellison recalls that "much later after I began to write and work with words, I came to suspect that my father had been aware of the suggestive powers of names and the magic involved in naming." The name *Ralph Waldo* indeed had magic for it enabled Ellison to see the power of the myth and to envision the role that myth could play in achieving his aim which was, as he put it, "to add to literature the wonderful American speech and idiom and to bring into range as fully as possible the complex reality of American experience as it shaped and was shaped by the lives of my own people." Myths in order to be preserved and appreciated must be written down and Ellison, in his comments on Hemingway and Faulkner, is constantly aware that one element of the American past is sorely missing from most American literature. As Ralph Waldo Emerson could merge the myths and attitudes of New England into his philosophy of Transcendentalism, Ralph Waldo Ellison would merge that essential element, the nature of black folklore and life style, into American literature—and myth could be the carrier.

The past, especially the American past, is also a magical word for Ellison. Perhaps the impact of this concept on Ellison can be seen only when one looks at this writer's individual history. He was born and grew up in Oklahoma City in the 20's; he was raised in a virtual frontier town which had been a state only seven years when he was born. The newness of the state, the lack of a tradition of slavery allowed the boy to believe that nothing was hopelessly beyond the reach of the black world really, "because if you worked and you fought for your rights, and so on, you could finally achieve it." By early adolescence, Ellison remembers that "the idea of the Renaissance Man had drifted down to him and his friends and that they discussed mastering themselves and everything in sight as though no such thing as racial discrimination existed." No doubt, Ellison's background, with its illusion of personal freedom, is a strong determinant in his philosophy of "infinite possibilities."

In addition to the belief that he could be a Renaissance man, Ellison wanted to be a great musician. His youth and dreams were obsessed by his love of music both in the classical field which he studied at school and in the blues and jazz that he heard in the black community around him. The sense of timing, the flow of lyricism developed through this first love comes to fruition in

Invisible Man and is one of the most beautiful aspects of the book.
Music, too, gave Ellison an insight into the life around him. He
tells us:

> The blues speak to us simultaneously of the tragic and comic
> aspects of the human condition and they express a profound
> sense of life shared by many Negro Americans precisely be-
> cause their lives have combined these modes. This has been the
> heritage of a people who for hundreds of years could not cele-
> brate birth or dignify death and whose need to live despite the
> dehumanizing pressures of slavery developed an endless ca-
> pacity for laughter at their painful experience.

This analysis of the blues as a tragic-comic form was to contribute
a great deal to *Invisible Man*, for this is precisely the stance that
the hero takes when he explains his invisibility to us. But more
important for Ellison, the craftsman, music taught him that "technique was that which transforms the individual before he is able to
transform it. The artist discovers that he has taken on certain
obligations; that he must not embarrass his chosen form, and that
in order to avoid this he must develop taste." The meditation on
form led Ellison to one of his basic tenets:

> He (the artist) learns—and this is most discouraging—that
> he is involved with values which turn in their own way, and
> not in the way of politics, upon the central issues affecting his
> nation and his time.

The aesthetic, rather than the political, was to be Ellison's concern; his grand social gesture was to be his creative work.

After graduating from high school, Ellison's love of music
took him to Tuskegee where he planned to study under a famous
musician. But like the hero in *Invisible Man*, he left the shelter of
the dream-like college to work in New York for the summer, and
never came back. Unable to find work, and disappointed with the
sculpture he had come to study, the young man began to write. In
his travels through Harlem he met Richard Wright who was then
writing *Native Son* and who got Ellison's first piece, a book review, published. Wright encouraged the young musician in the art
of writing, stressing not so much a mystical process but emphasiz-
ing craft, hard work, and thought. He guided Ellison to such
writers as Henry James, and discussed the literary effects of Conrad, Joyce, and Dostoevsky with his new student. Although Ellison
was overwhelmed by the towering personality of Richard Wright
and though he learned a great deal about writing from him, he,

even at that time, found Wright's novels disturbing. His comment on *Native Son* was that "Bigger Thomas had none of the fine qualities of Richard Wright, none of the imagination, none of the sense of poetry, the sense of gaiety," and Ellison summarily preferred Wright to Bigger Thomas. The younger writer always thought of himself as an artist taken up with the magical quality of writing and the poetry of it, while Richard Wright, he felt, was overcommitted to ideology.

By 1945, Ellison had devised a plan for a book which would incorporate the myth and literature of the Western world into the experience of the American black man. This book would reveal the travelings of the mind as it escaped from the darkness of illusion into the light of reality. Just as Dante had summarized the whole of medieval myth in his passing from the dark circles of Hell to the light of the Paradiso, Ellison would use the literature and legends of American society, both black and white, as a means of clarifying and transforming the meaning of twentieth century existence. This was a grand aim and it took Ellison seven years, from 1945 to 1952, to create and revise the book.

Like Joyce's *Portrait of an Artist as a Young Man,* a book which has greatly influenced Ellison's work, *Invisible Man* has been called the story of a young man's search for his identity. Both heroes must escape from the illusions and limitations of their environments in order to find themselves. Joyce's Stephen has to confront his Irish, Catholic, and family traditions. Ellison's hero has to penetrate the illusions built around the fact that he is black, not only in others, but more importantly in himself. As he moves from darkness to light, a basic motif in the book, the hero must encounter variations of deception which attempt to blind him to his image, that as a black man in America, he does not in relation to the rest of his world really exist.

This is the substance of the book but actually the hero has found his identity before the book opens. His first statement is to assure us that he knows who he is. "I am an invisible man," he proclaims with mingled pride and fear. Rather than searching for his identity, he is more interested in clarifying for himself his reasons for descending into his hell-like hole, and possibly for rising out of it, if and when he decides to do so. His goal in telling us his story is to separate the pride from the fear to make sense out of his experience. He is forced to explain himself not because it is necessary in that hole of his, but because he needs to face the world outside: "What did I do to be so black and blue?" Just as hibernation could not work for Dostoevsky's hero in his underground, so it cannot work for Ellison's hero. It is impossible for both of these intellectuals to protest their situation silently (hibernation is nothing less than passive protest) because of the nature of their minds.

> So I took to the cellar; I hibernated, I got away from it all. But that wasn't enough. I couldn't be still in hibernation. Because, damn it, there's the mind, the mind. It wouldn't let me rest.

It is the mind that puts these heroes in hell and it is the pain of consciousness that forces them to murder an old self and create a new one.

Actually the invisible man's mind hadn't been at rest since his grandfather had uttered that loathsome curse on his deathbed. The old man, usually meek and gentle, turned violent on his deathbed and hissed out his last words of advice:

> Live with your head in the lion's mouth. I want you to overcome 'em with yeses, undermine 'em with grins, agree 'em to death and destruction, let them swoller you till they vomit or bust wide open.

The snake had crawled into the garden of Paradise. These words were to haunt the life and dreams of the hero throughout the book not so much because he does not understand them but because he senses the irony that lies beneath them.

It is with this mental assault, rather than with a physical attack, that Ellison begins the book (contrast this with the beginning of *Native Son*); it is with his first disturbance of a child's mind. The narrator's grandfather had simply accepted the fact that Negroes survived by lying to white people and he suggests that the lie is not only the tool for survival but a means of victory as well. But the narrator does not want to believe this and it is precisely by telling the truth, accidentally sometimes, as in the speech he makes at the Battle Royale, that he continues to get into trouble. His grandfather's warnings, though, held another meaning—that a person, a race, a people must not fool itself into believing its own lies. Our narrator does believe in his own deceptive speech at the Battle Royale, in his own behavior at the college; he believes the actions that are meant to fool white people. But in spite of his resistance to the truth, his grandfather's swan song is harsh enough to unsettle him for the rest of his life.

The power of the lie, the fact that it is at the base of the relations between whites and blacks in this country, is forced home traumatically to the hero in the junior year at his dream-world college which had been built on and had survived exactly by those very lies. And Ellison, anxious to show the complexity and attractiveness of the illusion, literally flushes this section with pseudo myth and ritual. The college is the hero's religion, its ceremonies, his act of worship. Presiding over this universe, untouchable and benevolent, are the great white fathers, like Mr. Norton who had created this world through the mediation of the Christ-like Negro teacher and leader of his people. Barbee, the blind minister, gives us the full impact of the Founder who could effectively mediate between the gods and the people, since he was brother racially to the people and understood mentally the wishes of the gods. The religious overtones in this section are heightened even more by the hero's encounter with one of these white gods, Mr. Norton. Such words as *destiny, fate, salvation* regularly flow out of Norton's lips just as sums of money for the benefit of the college flow out of his pocketbook. In exchange for creating this dream-world, Mr. Norton expects, kindly it is true, adoration and power.

In this setting, Ellison then introduces Jim Trueblood and the vet, two demoniac characters, companions no doubt of the hissing grandfather. Both are blasphemers, for Jim Trueblood (the pun is marvellous) commits the unforgivable sin and lives, despite the pronouncement of the gods, while the vet deliberately attacks the supremacy and benevolence of the gods who had supposedly given him so much. During Norton's talk with Trueblood and the vet, the narrator shows signs of increasing disturbance and fear, for these men were talking to white men as if they were simply other men, not gods. These men were speaking the truth. The vet, protected by his status as an insane man, says ironically:

> You don't have to be a complete fool to succeed. Play the game but don't believe in it.

Bledsoe, president of the college, tells the narrator the whole truth, puts his finger exactly on what was wrong with the Golden-Day episode, why it was actual treason, and why the hero must be expelled from the college:

> You're dangerous, boy, why the dumbest black bastard in the cotton patch knows that the only way to please a white man is to tell him a lie. What kind of education are you getting around here?

So much for the American Dream. The dream-world college is built on a lie, Bledsoe knows it, he assumes every Negro does; but our narrator naively believes that he is telling the truth when in fact he has not even found it. Bledsoe lives the doctrine of the grandfather. He is the first of the long line of yes-ers in the book, of people who are used by and use white people and who know exactly where it's at. He represents for the invisible man his first concrete glimpse into the real world and the narrator never forgives him for it.

The trip North, archetypal for the black man in this country, precipitates the hero's search for work and then for his own identity. Cast out from the dream-world college, both physically and spiritually, he descends into *Mister* Brockway's underground hole where Optic White paint is made. The irony of this scene is hilarious as Ellison juxtaposes the supreme lie of the Negro "white is right" with the slogan of the company, "If it's Optic White, it's the right white." Why not whitewash everything? Just as Negroes had conveniently told whites that they were right when in fact they knew they weren't, Lucius Brockway improves on the saying by turning it into a slogan which gives him prestige in the eyes of the man upstairs. The whole nightmarish experience, underlined by the hero's first attempt at violence and by the serious injury he receives, his first literal blow on the head, is a preparation for one of Ellison's most impressive pieces, the surrealistic hospital dream of castration and loss of identity that the narrator suffers. Dreams had been used before in the book. "Keep that nigger running," the dream caused by his grandfather's words, is a father to the horrifying dream sequence that the hero now experiences. Music, too, plays an essential part in dramatizing the trauma of the nightmare. Beethoven's Fifth becomes unbearable and is pitted against the hero's childhood songs now magnified in horrifying proportions in his dream. Although the Invisible Man knows who Brer Rabbit is, he hasn't learned what this cunning fellow, essential to Negro folklore, really represents. Brer Rabbit, the symbol of the yes-er who destroys through yessing, knows when he is conning and when he is not. The hero is still trapped by his wish to believe that in fact he can survive by deceiving himself.

The nightmare with all its grotesque images of the hero's past indicates that he does know unconsciously the truth but that the mind with its affinity for rationality cannot stand for the absurdity that is implied in the truth. How can his mind grasp the fact that he does not really exist? The dream does rid the narrator of one fear though. When he is released from the factory hospital he reflects:

> Leaving him and going out into the paint-fuming air I had the feeling that I had been talking beyond myself, had used words and expressed attitudes not my own, that I was in the grip of some alien personality lodged deep within me. It was as though I were acting out a scene from some crazy movie. Or perhaps I was catching up with myself and had put into words feelings which I had hitherto suppressed. Or was it I thought that I was no longer afraid? I was no longer afraid. Not of important men, not of trustees and such; for knowing now that there was nothing which I could expect from them, there was no reason to be afraid.

At this point in the story, the intensity of the action subsides; the narrator becomes "cool" as he withdraws from society for the first time. This time it is not into the hole but into the warm generous arms of Mary, Mary Rambo, whom he does not think of as a friend but as a force, familiar and stabilizing. And during this hibernation with Mary, we see the hero wrestle with his benefactor. Mary belongs to his past for she insists that he do something, that he be one of those men who will save his people. But he becomes more and more convinced that anything he could do would only be futile.

This time the feeling of futility lasts only for a little while. The voice of the past wins out. The hero returns to sociey as he is reminded by those hot juicy yams as to who he is and that he had tried to suppress his past in his dream-world college. It is no accident, I think, that Ellison follows up the eating of yams with the eviction scene in which the hero speaks his mind. But this time he speaks an accepted lie, "We are a law-abiding people," in order to provoke and arouse the crowd to action. For the first time in the book he feels potent and alive. Just as Bigger Thomas becomes aware of his own life through the murder he had unintentionally committed, so too Ellison's hero comes to life as he destroys the false myth that Negroes can and will suffer anything.

But another obstacle is placed in the hero's path before he can see it like it is. Intrigued by the power and stability which the brotherhood represents, he becomes a part of their group. Again, he feels, as he had at college, that he is engaged in discovering and promoting the truth, that he has gained recognition, that he is living a significant life. However, just as Barbee, the blind minister, had perpetuated the myth of the great Christlike Founder, so

Jack, the one-eyed leader of the Brotherhood, worships the myth of history. As patronizing as Norton, Jack leads the hero into another deception, that in history, there is salvation and that salvation can be attained through subordinating the individual to a cause bigger than himself. Thus, in dealing with Christianity and Communism, and in relating them to each other, Ellison presents two important paths by which black people have tried to find themselves.

That Ellison calls his organization the Brotherhood rather than the Communist Party, which it obviously is, is significant, I believe. For what he might be suggesting is that the essence of any such *ism* is an abstraction such as "history saves." And that when push comes to shove, this abstraction rules and controls the living entities within it. Harlem is only a political entity to Jack. He doesn't know nor want to know

> the gin mills, and the barber shops and the juke joints and the churches and the beauty parlors on Saturday when they're frying hair, the whole of unrecorded history called reality.

History, as Jack sees it, is a means of imposing order on chaos. It is not the reality itself; it is an ideal which is imposed on the real. Thus, the problem of scientific objectivity, the ritual of this organization, is the first obstacle that the hero now turned orator faces when he joins the Brotherhood. Many brothers protest that although his speeches are effective, they are not scientific. And when the narrator, angered by the fact that the organization will not avenge the death of Tod Clifton, accuses Brother Hambro of being mechanical, communication between him and the organization falls apart. The organization called for the sacrifice of Harlem, but the narrator sees that "for them it was simple, but hell, I was both sacrificer and victim. *That was reality.* They did not have to put the knives to their own throats."

Enraged by the brotherhood's betrayal, the hero looks for another alternative. Ras and Rinehart, the two powerful figures who dominate the rest of the book, represent other means of existence. The narrator's introduction to Ras is worth looking at closely since Ras represents a complete departure from the other characters in the book. He is definitely visible (perhaps the only completely visible person in the book) in the most dangerous fashion imaginable. Tod Clifton acknowledges after his street brawl with Ras: "But it's on the inside that Ras is strong. On the inside he's dangerous." The narrator misreads Clifton's comment as he believes the inside that Tod is talking about to be the inside

of the Brotherhood. Tod's tragic end itself, though, is a testimony
to the truth of Ras's philosophy. The narrator, helpless, looks on
as Tod, months later, goes nuts, peddling Sambo dolls on Times
Square, and is finally gunned down by the police. "I don't know,"
Tod had said, "I suppose sometimes a man has to plunge outside
history . . . otherwise he might kill somebody, go nuts." And
Ras is nuts to those who do not understand his logic, his existence,
his visibility. The narrator obviously does not understand that the
militant Ras is an alternative to his present existence, as can be
seen in their encounter during the riots.

Rinehart, however, is an alternative to our nameless hero—
Rinehart, numbers runner, preacher, lover, conman, whose invisibility gives him the potential to live more than one life at the same
time—who indulges in the infinite possibilities of life. Rinehart is
an urban Brer Rabbit; he yesses everybody. This multiple personality knows that the people around him recognize him only by his
outer trappings, that the people are blind and that he can take
advantage of their blindness. Rinehart is a boldface liar, but he
has flair and is effective precisely because he knows that he does
not really exist. The hero's one night transformation into Rinehart
brings him to the realization that "the people who define him are
blind, bat blind, hearing only the echoes of their own voices. And
because they were blind, they would destroy themselves and he
would help them." In a Rinehart fashion, the hero sees that "it
was a joke, an absurd joke." Once the narrator's mind accepts the
absurdity of his world, he is able to see himself as he really is:

> And now I looked around a corner in my mind and saw Jack
> and Norton and Emerson merge into one single white figure.
> They were very much the same, each attempting to force his
> picture of reality upon me and neither giving a hoot in hell for
> how things looked to me. I was simply a material, a natural
> resource to be used. I had switched from the arrogant absurdity
> of Norton and Emerson to that of Jack and the Brotherhood,
> and it all came out the same—except that now I recognize my
> invisibility.

Now that he knows he is invisible, what should he do? Well, he
could be a Rinehart, "he could overcome them with yesses, under-
mine them with grins, he could agree them to death and destruction."

But it is too late to become Brer Rabbit. The truth will out
and it bursts out violently in the riots, a scene which is packed full

of the swift American idiom that Ellison delights in. Rinehartism
eventually is bound to fail for the acrobatics that one has to
perform to keep it up tries the nerves. As the hero says at the
beginning of the book:

> You often doubt if you really exist. You wonder whether you
> aren't simply a phantom in other people's minds. Shy, a figure
> in a nightmare which the sleeper tries with all his strength to
> destroy. It's when you feel like this that out of resentment,
> you begin to bump people back. And let me confess, you feel
> that way most of the time. You ache with the need to convince
> yourself that you do exist in the real world, that you're a part
> of all the sound and anguish, and you strike out with your fists,
> you curse and you swear to make them recognize you. And
> alas, it' s seldom successful.

Alas it is seldom successful. The hero, buried alive in his hole at
the end of the riots, is most painfully aware of that fact. The
horror of that realization calls up the maddening, powerful, and
tortuous dream that keeps him in his hole. Accosted by the grotesque figures of Jack, Norton, Bledsoe, and the rest, tortured by
their question: "How does it feel to be free of illusions?", the
crushed invisible man can only scream with intense ferocity,
"Painful and empty, painful and empty." What is an invisible man
but a man who doesn't exist?

If Ellison's novel had ended with that dream, it would fall
into the well-known category of the absurd along with the French
existentialists of the '40's and the American playwrights of today.
But that mind won't leave the hero be. He has progressed from
being blind to being invisible. He has traveled a long way. Nonetheless he must deal with invisibility as a concept which is still an
unknown quality to him, a concept that eludes even his imagination, far less his rational mind.

The epilogue reasserts his need to make his past rational. By
reliving his experience he sees that many false ideas have been
cleared away. Still, he is left with his will to transcend invisibility.
Pushed by his instinct for survival, the narrator stumbles into the
efficacy of diversity, the inevitability of necessity. "Life," he says,
"is to be lived not controlled and humanity is won by continuing
to play in the face of certain defeat." A worthy and noble ideal but
not very convincing. As the invisible man prepares (perhaps) to
leave his hole, he gives us a more credible reason for doing so.
Could it be that we're all invisible men? That white men could
blind themselves to their own invisibility, but black men could not?

And he settles on this point with a howl, a sense of triumph as well
as a sense of terror,

> *Who knows that on the lower frequencies*
> *I speak for you.*

> DAVID HENDERSON
> *The Man Who Cried*
> *I Am: A Critique*

SINCE WE all are acquainted with the elaborate plans that the
United States government has to destroy Russia and/or China in
the event of an emergency vis-à-vis such "cold war" suppositions
as *Fail-Safe, Doctor Strangelove* or most recently *The President's
Plane Is Missing*, it should not surprise us if our government also
has a plan to exterminate or detentionize black persons in America
in the event that the yearly racial riots all over America (would)
suddenly burst into a race war.

Since a strafing or napalm or atomic bomb has never fallen
on an American city, nor a strafing and napalm mission ever
performed, it would be difficult for us to imagine such a scene.
Only Japan was A-bombed. But we do not speak the language. We
have only the science-fiction movie monster fantasies to prepare
us, and Japan is the exporter and Joseph E. Levine, the impres-
sario of a great many of them such as *Godzilla, Rodan,* and *The
Monster That Devoured Cleveland.* Whereas, the horror the Jews
experienced in Nazi Germany is closer to the imagination and
dream psyche of Americans.

It is not difficult for black people to recall how they were
brought to America. Nor can they easily forget the usurpation of
black civil rights during the post-Reconstruction era, and most
recently the special treatment Adam Clayton Powell was afforded
by the House of Representatives. The so-called conscience of the
nation was aroused when TV showed the police of Birmingham
Alabama, brutally suppressing black civil rights marchers. The
gargantuan police use of "fire-power" (bullets) in the Harlem
riots of 1964, the Newark and Detroit riots of 1967, shows that the
law enforcement authorities of the land will go to great lengths to

protect the stores and properties. A plan for the extermination of American Blacks would not be contrary to American History.

Such a plan, as the climax of the twenty-year saga of a black writer, which spans three continents in interracial jet-set romances and is chock full of black existential artists, spies, and counter-spies, makes *The Man Who Cried I Am* picaresque best-seller material.

The Man Who Cried I Am is the dying vision of a black writer, Max Reddick. As the book opens, we meet Max in a Dutch cafe waiting for his former Dutch wife. He is "without chick or child," forty-three, and dying from progressed cancer of the anus. Frequent doses of morphine are necessary to quell the pain. Frequent shots of liquor are also necessary to quell a different sort of pain—the pain that began twenty years ago, when he decided to be a serious writer.

America has never been kind to her writers, least of all the ones who happen to be black. Max began to die, in a way, when he became a writer. As a young writer in the early forty's, Max met and became fast friends with Harry Ames (the most vivid por-trayal of Richard Wright to date) who in turn was not so kind to America either. Max regarded Ames as his mentor, as Ames was indeed "The Father of the Black writers." From the twenty-year starting line Max and Harry Ames dash through life: through women and books, parties, joy, and misery; Ames to self-exile in France where he was sure he would be treated as a man and an artist; Max Reddick from novelist to top-notch journalist, who is awarded the African desk of *Events* (a *Newsweek*-type magazine) and who becomes as well a speech writer and advisor to the Presi-dent of the United States. Max, too, had wanted to be treated as an artist. Somewhere along the way he becomes aware of the fact that the publishing houses thought it sufficient to have only one black writer in the house, one boy. By the same token the monotheism that caps the spirituality of America carries over to the treatment of black writers. Therefore Ames could be the only god, the Father, and hence, his death was eagerly awaited by the younger black writers. As Marion Dawes (James Baldwin) put it to Ames: "It is the duty of the son to destroy the father." This flabbergasted Ames, but Max who was with him noticed that he was secretly pleased. The scenes depicting the black artists' expatriate scene in Europe and America are the best in the book. There is little known or written about the black artist underground and Williams in his role as novelist-documentarian has provided us with some well chosen insights. Many of Williams' characters and events parallel real-life figures and occurrences. Williams has been known to do this before. His second novel, *Nightsong*, for all its shortcomings, provided a powerful characterization of another famous black artist: Charlie "Yardbird" Parker, the master jazz saxophonist.

"Yardbird" is a "live" character in *Nightsong*, but ironically it is the death of Harry Ames that causes the story of *The Man Who Cried I Am* to be told. Max has traveled from his African desk to Europe to attend the surprise funeral of Harry Ames. His legal dope addiction and the alcohol combine with the funeral to swing him into a heightened state of reverie about this man who has had such a profound impact upon his life and about whom he has ambivalent feelings. Soon his reveries are fueled by the strange legacy Harry Ames has left him, in the form of a prefacing letter and a briefcase containing a top-secret United States government document called "The King Alfred Plan."

In the letter, written as it seems from the grave, Harry Ames gives a history of the international politics behind The King Alfred Plan and also tells how it got into his hands. Harry Ames starts off with the chilling remark: "knowing may kill you, just as knowing killed me and a few other people you'll meet in this letter." Ames goes on to say that in the late fifties Africa threw a scare into its European masters when it seemed to be heading toward a United States of Africa. "Couldn't Africa become another giant, like China, with even more hatred for the white West?" The West acted quickly. "Representatives from France, Great Britain, Belgium, Portugal, Australia, Spain, Brazil, South Africa and the United States of America met along with white observers from most of the African countries that appeared to be on their way to independence." The meetings, called The Alliance Blanc, were held in absolute secrecy and moved from country to country. Meetings in America were held "around Saranac Lake—Dreiser's setting for *An American Tragedy*. . . ." The disclosure of America's membership in The Alliance Blanc would have touched off a racial cataclysm—but America went far beyond the evils the Alliance was perpetuating. The Europeans had recovered from their initial panic when they realized that they could control Africa's destiny economically. But "America sitting on a bubbling black cauldron felt that it had to map its own contingency plans for handling 22 million black Americans in case they became unruly . . . ," thus King Alfred:

In the event of widespread and continuing and coordinated racial disturbances in the United States, King Alfred, at the discretion of the President, is to be put into action immediately.

Participating Federal Agencies in the plan include the FBI, CIA, National Security Council, Departments of Defense, Justice, and Interior.

In case of emergency, minority members will be evacuated from the cities by federalized national guard units, local and state police and, if necessary, by units of the Regular Armed Forces, using public and military transportation, and detained in nearby military installations until a further course of action has been decided.

The areas having the largest populations of black people are designated on a map by numbered priority areas. Leaders of all "minority rights" organizations are to be rounded up at once and detained. "Minority members of Congress will be unseated at once. This move is not without precedent in American History." (As indeed it is not from the post-Reconstruction era up to the unseating of Adam Clayton Powell.)

Harry Ames received the King Alfred Plan from an African ambassador named Jaja Enzkwu who had stumbled upon an Alliance Blanc meeting while vacationing in Spain, and had subsequently gathered the rest of the material. Inasmuch as the plan was top secret, concealing the report was the priority assignment of the National Security Council and the Central Intelligence Agency. They naturally came after Enzkwu when they learned he had the report. As Ames says: "Then Jaja started to deal. He'd give over the papers and keep his mouth shut, if the Americans gave him Nigeria." Nevertheless Jaja was killed, but he made sure another brother—Harry Ames—got King Alfred.

Harry Ames' letter continues:

The material fascinated me. I'd spent so much of my life writing about the evil machinations of Mr. Charlie without really *knowing* the truth, as this material made me know it. It was spread out before me, people, places and things. I became mired in them, and I *knew* now that the way black men live on this earth was no accident. . . . I gripped the material, I hugged it to my chest, for now I would know; if they killed me, I would know that this great evil did exist, indeed thrive. And Dr. Faustus came to my mind.

Max had always wanted to provide America with a vision of her existence. He wanted black people to know the ugly truth, the ugly plot, behind their existence. He wanted white people to know that the black people "would tear up the country" rather than absorb any more lies. He spent most of his life trying—perhaps only as an artist would—to change or at least to alter the destiny of America. He rose about as high as a journalist could rise: an advisor to the President, a top man with *Events*, an important magazine. But he discovered he had no power, no say. He screamed long and hard trying to direct the President's (a carica- ture of Kennedy) attention away from the Russian-American space competition and the problems of Cuba to the duress of the black man in America. Max thought his bitter words warning the administration that the black man "would tear up this country," went unheeded. But indeed they could well have been taken to heart and might have contributed handsomely to the gloomy anticipa- tion of race war that brought about the King Alfred Plan. A high- ranking civil rights activist once said that much of the data com- piled by war-on-poverty agencies and other progressive govern- ment agencies for the ostensible betterment of the black race, have been classified by the government as counterinsurgency informa- tion.

The death of Harry Ames strikes a strange chord in the swan song of Max's existence. The legacy Ames left him gives Max his last chance for redemption. But *Events* magazine would never print it. They would call it a hoax. Max also begins to see from the closing lines of the letter that Ames had found out that Max had once slept with his blond wife, Charlotte. It all becomes clear. This is the *coup de grâce*, the legacy of death that the "father of the black writers" has passed on to his heir. It is nullified, though, by the fact that Max is dying anyway. But what does one do with a portable Pandora's box? Max calls up Minister Q in New York (Malcolm X?) to read off King Alfred into the minister's perpetu- ally running tape recorder. He prefaces his reading with the re- mark: "Hello, you are a dead man. Maybe?"

Having passed on the truth to another brother, Max prepares to meet his fate. He loads his pistol and holds it in his lap as he drives back to Holland. As the sergeant in an all-black company during World War II leading poorly trained men who were the objects of intense hatred from both the German soldiers and the American bigoted military men, Max saw his platoon suffer great casualties. Max instructs a new platoon on survival: "You want to live, you shoot first and ask questions later. All you got to tell me is that you saw a white face. Don't tell me what the white face was wearing because I don't want to know."

But Max is in for a surprise. Death, for him, shows up in the guise of two black CIA agents (Coffin Ed Johnson and Grave Digger Jones). To boot, they had both hung around the black artist expatriate scene, posing as writers. Max's prior preoccupation with guns comes in handy. He shoots Roger "the lover" in the groin, before he dies by way of a pellet that has only to contact his skin to cause a heart eruption. So Max dies from a more modern American disease than cancer. And a hero as well, in the James Bond tradition of Her Majesty's Secret Service.

It seems one cannot rely on shooting only white faces anymore. The only black men on TV to hold down full-time jobs are law enforcement officers or military men. The medium is the message. And Bill Cosby is the swingingest spy you would ever want to meet.

Max Reddick had participated in the American power structure more than most black men, most men, get to. Perhaps the fruit of his participation is the cancer that eats away at his anus. (Even while the pain wracks away at him, he remembers that he had never had a red head.) There are those who believe that because the black mass has not participated in the mainstream of American life, due to segregation, enforced poverty and ghetto substandard living, the black man has remained free from many of the syndromes (luxury emphasis, competitiveness, impercise) that poison much of the American way of life. But young black men such as Stokely and Rap are calling for black power, a share of the spoils—since black people are in it too, even by default, whether they want it or not. Black Power is a piece of the action. And a piece of the action will be, by agreement, not only of the good parts of society but the bad as well.

Harry Ames thought that he had found the truth in King Alfred. That truth was death. Perhaps the truth of the black masses' existence in America is destined to be death. Doctor Faustus wanted to know everything. He made a deal with the devil (Elijah-jargon for the white man) and then tried to get out of it.

In the United States six sites have already been chosen for the detention of Americans who would contribute or might contribute to what would appear to be a sabotage or insurrection. Although part one of the McCarran Act of 1950, dealing with communist registration, has been declared unconstitutional by the Supreme Court, part 2 of the National Security Act is still on the books as a protection against an emergency in the eyes of the President, involving internal security. Part 2 calls for the detention camps which are located in Florida, Tulip Lake, California, Reno, Oklahoma, Allenwood, Pa., and one other site. These camps are set up ready and waiting.

[SUGGESTED]
[READINGS]

Folklore

Brewer, J. Mason. "Introduction," *Worse Days and Better Times.* Chicago: Quadrangle Press, 1965.

Brooks, Stella Brewer. "Introduction," *Joel Chandler Harris: Folklorist.* Atlanta: Georgia Press, 1950.

Brown, Sterling. "The Spirituals," *Book of Negro Folklore,* eds. Langston Hughes and Arna Bontemps. New York: Dodd, Mead and Company, 1966.

————. "The Blues as Folk Poetry," *Book of Negro Folklore,* eds. Langston Hughes and Arna Bontemps. New York: Dodd, Mead and Company, 1966.

Butcher, Margaret Just. Chapters IV and V, *The Negro in American Culture.* New York: Knopf, 1957.

Dett, R. Nathaniel. *Religious Folk Songs of the Negro.* G. Schirmer, 1925.

————. "American Negro Music," *Musical America* (August, 1918 and May, 1919).

Ellison, Ralph. "As the Spirit Moves Mahalia," *Shadow and Act.* New York: New American Library, 1966.

————. "Change the Joke and Slip the Yoke," *Shadow and Act.* New York: New American Library, 1966.

————. "The Charlie Christian Story," *Shadow and Act.* New York: New American Library, 1966.

Fauset, Arthur H. *Black Gods of the Metropolis: Negro Religious Cults of the Urban North.* Philadelphia: University of Pennsylvania Press, 1944.

Gloster, Hugh M. "Zora Neale Hurston, Novelist and Folklorist," *Phylon,* IV (Second Quarter, 1943).

Hobson, Charles. "Black Bourgeoisie and Gospel Music," *Liberator,* V (January, 1965).

Johnson, James Weldon and Rosamond. *The Book of American Negro Spirituals.* New York: The Viking Press, 1925.

Jones, LeRoi. *Blues People.* New York: William Morrow and Company, 1967.

Locke, Alain. "Apropos of Africa," *Opportunity,* (February, 1924).

————. *The Negro and His Music.* Washington: Associates in Negro Education, 1936.

————. "The Negro's Contribution to American Culture," *The Journal of Negro Education,* VIII (July, 1939).

Neal, Lawrence P. "Black Musicians in White America," *Negro Digest,* XVI (March, 1967).

Patterson, Cecil L. "A Different Drum: The Image of the Negro in the Nineteenth Century Songster," *C. L. A. Journal*, VII, (1964).

Puckett, N. N. "Introduction," *Folk Beliefs of the Southern Negro*. Chapel Hill: University of North Carolina Press, 1926.

Smith, Robert A. "A Note on the Folktales of Charles W. Chesnutt," *C. L. A. Journal* V, (1962).

Thurman, Wallace. "Nephew of Uncle Remus," *Independent*, CXLX (1927).

Woodson, Carter, G. *Negro Orators and their Orations*. Washington: Associated Publishers, 1925.

Poetry

Brathwaite, William Stanley. *The Poetic Year for 1916: A Critical Anthology*. Boston: Small, Maynard, 1917.

Brawley, Bejamin G. *Paul Lawrence Dunbar, Poet of his People*. Chapel Hill: University of North Carolina Press, 1936.

Brooks, Gwendolyn. "Foreword," *New Negro Poets: U. S. A.*, ed. Langston Hughes. Bloomington: Indiana University Press, 1964.

Brown, Sterling. *Negro Poetry and Drama*. Washington: The Association in Negro Folk Education, 1937.

Bontemps, Arna. "Introduction," *American Negro Poetry*. New York: Hill and Wang, 1963.

———. "The Negro Renaissance: Jean Toomer and the Harlem Writers of the 1920's," *Anger and Beyond*, ed. Herbert Hill. New York: Harper and Row, 1966.

Butcher, Margaret Just. Chapters V and VI, *The Negro in American Culture*. New York: Knopf, 1957.

Davis, Arthur P. "The Black and Tan Motif in the Poetry of Gwendolyn Brooks," *CLA Journal*, VI (1962).

———. "Gwendolyn Brooks: A Poet of the Unheroic," *CLA Journal*, VIII (1963).

———. "The Harlem of Langston Hughes' Poetry," *Phylon*, XIII (1952).

Emanuel, James A. *Langston Hughes*. New York: Twayne Publishers, Inc., 1967.

———. and Theodore L. Gross, eds. *Dark Symphony: The Development of Negro Literature in America*. New York: The Free Press, 1968.

Gregory, Montgomery. "The Spirit of Phillis Wheatley," *Opportunity*, VIII (June, 1924).

Hughes, Langston and Arna Bontemps, eds. *The Poetry of the Negro, 1746–1949.* Garden City: Doubleday, 1949.

Hughes, Langston. "My Adventures as a Social Poet," *Phylon,* VIII (1947).

Jackson, Blyden. "The Essential McKay," *Phylon,* XIV (1953).

Jackson, Miles M. "Documentary Sidelights: James Weldon Johnson and Claude McKay," *Negro Digest,* XVII (June, 1968).

Johnson, James Weldon. "Introduction," *The Book of American Negro Poetry.* New York: Harcourt, Brace Company, 2d edition, 1922.

———. *Black Manhattan.* New York: Knopf, 1930.

Lee, Don L. "On Kaleidoscope and Robert Hayden," *Negro Digest,* XVII (January, 1968).

Randall, Dudley. "Three Giants Gone," *Negro Digest,* XVI (November, 1967).

Smith Robert H. "Claude McKay, an Essay in Criticism," *Phylon,* IX (1948).

Tolson, Melvin B. "A Poets Odyssey," *Anger and Beyond,* ed. Herbert Hill. New York: Harper and Row, 1966.

Drama

Bailey, Peter. "Is the Negro Ensemble Company Really Black Theatre?" *Negro Digest,* LXVII (April, 1968).

Brown, Sterling. *Negro Poetry and Drama.* Washington: The Association in Negro Folk Education, 1937.

Campbell, Dick. "Is There a Conspiracy Against Black Playwrights?" *Negro Digest,* XVII (April, 1968).

Childress, Alice. "Why Talk About That?" *Negro Digest,* XVI (April, 1967).

Cruse, Harold. Chapter VI, *The Crisis of the Negro Intellectual.* New York: William Morrow and Company, 1967.

Dodson, Owen. "Playwrights in Dark Glasses," *Negro Digest,* XVII (April, 1968).

DuBois, W.E.B. "Criteria of Negro Art," *Crisis* (May, 1962).

Ford, Clebert. "Towards a Black Community Theatre," *Liberator,* IV (1964).

———. "Lorraine Hansberry's World," *Liberator,* IV (1964).

Fuller, Hoyt. "Black Theatre in America," *Negro Digest,* XVII (April, 1968).

Gaffney, Floyd. "The Black Actor in Central Park," *Negro Digest,* XVI (April, 1967).

Jones, LeRoi. "What the Arts Need Now," *Negro Digest*, XVI (April, 1967).

Killens, John Oliver. "Broadway in Black and White," *African Forum*, I (1966).

Lewis, C. L. "Black Knights of the Theatre, Ira Aldridge," *Negro Digest*, XVI (1967).

Milner, Ronald. "Black Theatre Go Home," *Negro Digest*, XVII (April, 1968).

Mitchell, Loften. *Black Drama*. New York: Hawthorn Books, 1967.

Neal, Lawrence P. "Development of LeRoi Jones," *Liberator*, VI (February, 1966).

Nicholas, Denise. "View From the Free Southern Theatre," *Liberator*, VI (July, 1966).

Riley, Clayton. "Song of the Lusitanian Bogey," *Liberator*, VIII (February, 1968).

———. "Dutchman," *Liberator*, VII (1967).

Turner, Darwin. "The Negro Dramatist's Image of the Universe," *CLA Journal*, (1961).

Fiction

Baldwin, James. "Everybody's Protest Novel," *Notes of a Native Son*. New York: Dial Press, 1963.

———. "Richard Wright," *Encounter*, XVI (1961).

Braithwaite, William Stanley. "The Novels of Jesse Fauset," *Opportunity*, XII (1934).

Brawley, Benjamin G. *The Negro Genius*. New York: Dodd, Mead and Company, 1937.

———. "The Promise of Negro Literature," *The Journal of Negro History*, XIX (January, 1934).

———. *The Negro in Literature and Art*. New York: Duffield and Company, 1929.

Brown, Sterling. "The Negro Author and his Publisher," *Quarterly Review of Higher Education Among Negroes*, IX (July, 1941).

DuBois, W. E. B. "The Negro in Literature and Art," *Annals of the American Academy of Political and Social Sciences*, XLIX (1913).

Ellison, Ralph. "Light on Invisible Man," *Crisis*, LX (1953).

———. "Recent Negro Fiction," *New Masses* (August 5, 1941).

Emanuel, James. "The Invisible Men of American Literature," *Books Abroad*, XXXVII (1963).

Ford, Nick Aaron. *The Contemporary Negro Novel*. Boston: Mesdor Publishing Company, 1936.

———. "The Negro Novel as a Vehicle of Propaganda," *Quarterly*

Review of Higher Education Among Negroes, IX (July, 1941).
Fuller, C. H., Jr. "Black Writing: Release from Object," *Liberator,* VII (September, 1967).
Fuller, Hoyt. "On the Death of Richard Wright," *Southwest Review,* VI–VII (1961).
Gayle, Addison Jr. "White Experts and Black Subjects," *Rights and Reviews,* III (Fall-Winter, 1967).
———. "A Defense of James Baldwin," *CLA Journal,* X (March, 1967).
Gloster, Hugh M. *Negro Voices in American Fiction.* Chapel Hill: University of North Carolina Press, 1948.
Jackson, Blyden. "Essay in Criticism," *Phylon* (Fourth Quarter, 1950).
Johnson, James Weldon. "Race Prejudice and the Negro Writer," *Harper's,* CLVII (1928).
———. "Negro Authors and White Publishers," *Crisis,* XXXVI (1929).
Kaiser, Ernest. "On Heightening the Social Muse," *Freedomways,* II (1962).
———. "Negro Images in American Writing," *Freedomways,* VII (1967).
———. "The Literature of Negro Revolt," *Freedomways,* III (Winter, 1963).
Leaks, Sylvester. "James Baldwin, I Know His Name," *Freedomways,* III (1963).
Mayfield, Julian. "And Then Came Baldwin," *Freedomways,* III (1963).
Neal, Lawrence P. "The Black Writer's Role," *Liberator,* VI (1966).
Phoenix, Timothy. "Black Writers Must be Free," *Liberator,* VII (1967).
Redding, Saunders. "Since Richard Wright," *Africa Forum,* I (1966).
———. "The Negro Writer, Shadow and Substance," *Phylon* (Fourth Quarter, 1950).
Schuyler, George. "What's Wrong with Negro Authors," *Negro Digest,* (May, 1950).
Wright, Richard. "Blueprint for Negro Writing," *New Challenge,* (Fall, 1937).
———. "How Bigger Was Born," *Saturday Review of Literature,* (June, 1940).

Magazine Bibliography

AFRICAN FORUM, founded in 1965 by The American Society of African Culture, is a quarterly journal of contemporary African and Afro-American affairs which has published several issues devoted entirely to literature. Edited by John A. Davis.

THE CRISIS, founded in 1910 as the official organ of the N.A.A.C.P., is published monthly from October to May. Edited by Henry Lee Moon.

FREEDOMWAYS, founded in 1961 by Shirley Graham, W. E. B. DuBois, and Esther Jackson, and published by Freedomways Associates, is a quarterly review of all phases of the Negro Freedom Movement. Edited by John Henrik Clarke.

THE JOURNAL OF HUMAN RELATIONS, founded in 1952 by Charles Wesley and Anna O'Hara Williamson and published by Central State University, is a quarterly dedicated to the improvement of human relations through an interdisciplinary approach. Edited by Ralph T. Templin for the past six years, its editorship will soon be taken over by Don Werkheiser.

JOURNAL OF NEGRO EDUCATION, founded by Charles H. Thompson and published by the Bureau of Educational Research at Howard University, although a quarterly review concerned mainly with problems incidental to the education of Negroes, also publishes articles on literary criticism. Edited by Walter G. Daniel.

THE JOURNAL OF NEGRO HISTORY, founded in 1916 by Carter G. Woodson and published by The Association for the Study of Negro Life and History, is a quarterly issued scholarly journal concerned with all phases of Negro life and history. Edited by William M. Brewer.

LIBERATOR MAGAZINE, founded in 1961 and published by the Afro-American Research Institute, is a monthly concerned with all phases of the lives of black people and is very receptive to the works of new, young writers. Edited by Daniel Watts.

NEGRO DIGEST, founded in 1942, was the first magazine published by the Johnson Publishing Company. *Negro Digest* is a valuable source of material on the black man and his art and is quite receptive to works of young, unpublished writers. Issued monthly and edited by Hoyt W. Fuller.

NEGRO HISTORY BULLETIN, founded in 1937 by Carter G. Woodson and published by The Association for the Study of Negro Life and History, is a monthly (October through May) which focuses on the role of the Negro in building history and civilization. Edited by Charles Walker Thomas.

ONYX MAGAZINE, scheduled to begin publication in the fall of 1968, will be a monthly dealing with all phases of black culture. Edited by Charles L. Russell.

PHYLON, founded in 1940 by W. E. B. DuBois and published by Atlanta University, is a scholarly quarterly review of all aspects of race and culture. Edited by Tilman C. Cothran.

RIGHTS AND REVIEWS, founded in 1964 as the ideological organ of The Congress of Racial Equality, is a quarterly which, while dedicated to the coverage of all aspects of the Movement, often publishes articles on the theatre and literary criticism as well. Edited by Doris Innis.

UMBRA, published three times a year by the Society of Umbra, is primarily a poetry magazine although articles on literary criticism, music, painting, and black culture are generally included in each issue. Edited by David Henderson.

[*Index*]

Abrahams, Peter, 252
Abyssinia, 130
Academy of Arts and Letters,
    99
Adams, E.C.L., 3
Adoff, Arnold
    I Am the Darker Brother, 111
African influence on black
        American culture
    drama, 127-28
    folk tales, 5, 6, 7, 8-9, 14, 16,
        18-19, 20, 30
    music, 40, 41, 191, 194
Aldridge, Ira, 129, 150
Alhamisi, Ahmed, 111, 112
    The Black Narrator, 113
    Black Spiritual Gods, 113
Allen, George Leonard, 222
Allen, Samuel, 149
    Ivory Tusks, 113
American Academy of Arts and
        Letters, 84
Anderson, Alston
    Lover Man, 254
Anderson, Garland
    Appearances, 153

Andrews, Regina, 154
Apollo Theatre, 156-57
Archer, Thomas
    Black Doctor, 129
Ashmore, Harry S., 253
Atkins, Russell, 111, 113
Attaway, William, 248, 277

Baldwin, James, 36, 134 192,
        227, 254, 283, 286, 287,
        339-353, 354, 366
    The Amen Corner, 193
    Another Country, 252, 281,
        340, 345, 346-48
    Blues for Mr. Charlie, 135-
        36, 281
    Eight Men, 309-11
    The Fire Next Time, 345,
        346, 350
    Go Tell It on the Mountain,
        252, 345
    Home, 138
    Nobody Knows My Name,
        308, 341, 344, 345
    Notes of a Native Son, 252,
        341, 345

Beckett, Samuel
  Krapp's Last Tape, 144-45
  Waiting for Godot, 144
Behn, Aphra
  Oronooko, 129
Belgrave, Cynthia, 136
Benét, William Rose, 244
Birth of a Nation, The. *See*
    Thomas Dixon
Black Arts School, 134
Black folk songs, "The Dirty
    Dozens," 215-17
Black folk tales
  animal, 5-10, 16, 18-19, 30-31
  Brer Rabbit, 3, 6, 8, 9, 10,
    12, 13, 15, 16, 19, 29, 31
Black   liberation   movement,
    263-270
Black music, 191-92, 194, 325
Black Panther Party, 141
  Black theater for, 140, 142
Black people, genocide of, 365-
    66, 370-71
Black people depicted in the
    short story (1906-1915),
    186-189
Black theater groups, 124-25,
    140-41
  African Company, 150
  American Place, 140, 141
  American   Negro   Theatre,
    154, 155, 156, 245
  Black Arts Theater, 268
  Black Patti's Troubadors, 152
  Committee for the Negro in
    the Arts, 156, 157
  Council on the Harlem Thea-
    ter, 156, 157
  Elks   Community   Theatre,
    156, 157
  The Ethiopian Art Theatre,
    124, 126, 132

Hapgood Players, 124
Harlem Experimental Play-
    ers, 154
Harlem Players, 154
Harlem Showcase, 156
Harlem Suitcase Theatre, 154
Horizon Guild, 124
Howard Players, 124, 132,
    193
The National Ethiopian Art
    Theatre, 124
Negro Ensemble Company,
    140
Negro People's Theatre, 154
Negro Playwrights Company,
    154, 155
New Lafayette, 140, 141
Rose McClendon Players, 154
The Shadows, 124
Williams and Walker Com-
    pany, 152
Bland, Edward, 316
Blues, The, 5, 35-36, 96, 192,
    214-15, 237, 312-13, 324,
    356
Bodenheim, Maxwell
  Naked on Roller Skates, 243
Bontemps, Arna, 76, 118, 222-
    23, 242, 277
  American Negro Poetry, 111
  Black Thunder, 254
  God Sends Sunday, 254
  *The Poetry of the Negro
    1746-1949*, 110
Boucicault, Dion
  Octoroon, The, 129, 130, 151
Bradford, Roark, 4, 12
  *Ol' Man Adam an' His Chil-
    lun*, 5, 12
Bradstreet, Ann, 175
Braithwaite, William Stanley,
    75, 233

*Anthologies of Magazine
    Verse*, 87
Lyrics of Life and Love, 87
Branch, William
    In Splendid Error, 157
    A Medal for Willie, 157
Brawley, Benjamin
    *The Negro in Literature and
        Art in the United States*,
        240
Brecht, Berthold, 144, 145
Breman, Paul
    I Saw How Black I Was, 111,
        112
    Sixes and sevens, 111, 253
Brewer, J. Mason, 8, 32
Briggs-Hall, Austin, 154
Broonzy, Big Bill, 4
Brooke, Peter, 144
Brooks, Gwendolyn, 36, 88, 93,
        96-97, 107, 110, 117,
        223, 227, 254, 264-65
    Annie Allen, 95, 96-97, 99,
        105-06, 256
    In the Mecca, 114
    A Street in Bronzeville, 84,
        93, 94, 97
Brooks, Jay, 158
Brooks, Stella Brewer, 8
Brown, Benjamin A., 248
Brown, Eugene
    Trespass, 251
Brown, Frank London, 255
Brown, Oscar, Jr.
    Kicks and Company, 270
Brown, Sterling, 36, 87, 88,
        110, 223, 224-25, 230,
        242, 254
    Southern Road, 91
Brown, Theodore
    Natural Man, 155
Bullins, Ed, 136, 140

Clara's Ole Man, 141-42
Electronic Nigger, 141
How Do You Do, 142
A Son Come Home, 141
Burgie, Irving, 148
Burley, Dan
    *Original Handbook of Har-
        lem Jive*, 247
Burrough, Margaret
    *For Malcolm: Poems on the
        Life and the Death of
        Malcolm X*, 111
Bush, Joseph Bevans, 268
Butcher, Margaret Just, 240

Cabin in the Sky, 154
Cable, George W., 171, 180
    The Grandissimes, 183-84
    Madame Delphine, 184
    Old Creole Days, 183
Cambridge, Ed, 148, 149, 156
Campbell, Dick, 154
Campbell, T. B.
    Black Sadie, 243
Cannon, David Wadsworth
    Black Labor Chant, 92
Cannon, J. D., 138
Charles, Ray, 116, 134, 196,
        269
Charters, Samuel B., 250
Chesnutt, Charles W., 8, 191,
        229, 234, 260
    The Colonel's Dream, 181,
        190, 231
    The Conjure Woman, 180
    *The House Behind the Ce-
        dars*, 180-81, 190, 231
    The Marrow of Tradition,
        180, 190, 231
    *The Wife of His Youth
        and Other Stories*, 180,
        190

Childress, Alice
    Just a Little Simple, 156, 250
    Like One of the Family, 250
    Trouble in Mind, 157
    Chocolate Dandies, 152
Christian, Marcus B., 23
    Common Peoples Manifesto,
        94
Clarke, John Henrik, 149, 241,
        248
Cohen, Octavus Roy, 172
Cole, Bob
    A Trip to Coontown, 151
Cole and Johnson, 130, 161, 165
Cooper, Opal, 131
Cook, Will Marion
    *Clorindy, the Origin of the
        Cakewalk*, 151
Corbie, Eugene, 132
Corrothers, James, 111, 222
Cotter, Joseph, Jr., 76, 177
Crane, Stephen, 172
Critics Circle Award, 158
Culbertson, Howard, 124
    Goat Alley, 126, 152, 174
    Jackey, 126
Cullen, Countee, 59, 76, 77, 78-
        79, 82, 83, 84, 85, 86,
        89, 96, 221-22, 230, 236,
        242, 254
    The Black Christ, 241
    Caroling Dusk, 110, 241
    Color, 90, 241
    Copper Sun, 90, 241
    One Way to Heaven, 241,
        278
Cuney, Waring, 84, 217, 248
Curtis, Constance, 248

Danner, Margaret, 110
    *Impressions of African Art
        Forms*, 114

Poem Counterpoem, 113
Davis, Arthur, 249
    The Negro Caravan, 110
Davis, Frank Marshall, 110,
        223, 278-79
    Black Man's Verse, 85, 92
    I Am the American Negro,
        92
Davis, Ossie
    Alice in Wonder, 156, 157
    Purlie Victorious, 158
de, Carava, Roy
    Sweet Flypaper of Life, 250
    Deep River, 153
    Defiant Ones, The, 272, 273
Delany, Clarissa Scott, 87
    Dixie to Broadway, 152
Dixon, Thomas, 183
    The Clansman, 151, 185, 232
    The Leopard's Spots, 172,
        173, 185, 232
Dodson, Owen, 85, 94, 110
    Garden of Time, 155
    Powerful Long Ladder, 86,
        93
Dorsey, Emmett E., 254
Douglass, Frederick, 175
Drama League, 131
Dreer, Herman
    *American Literature by
        Negro Authors*, 110
Drinkwater, John
    Abraham Lincoln, 152
Duberman, Martin
    In White America, 136, 137
DuBois, William
    Haiti, 154
DuBois, W. E. B., 33, 52, 133,
        211, 218, 233, 234, 235,
        236, 240, 281, 285
    Darkwater, 179, 241
    The Gift of Black Folk, 241

The Quest of the Silver Fleece, 179, 181, 190
The Souls of Black Folk, 48, 178-79, 229, 286
Dudley, S. H., 130, 151
Dumas, Alexander, 202
The Count of Monte Cristo, 201
Dunbar, Alice, 233
Dunbar, Barrington, 244
Dunbar, Paul Lawrence, 36, 72, 74-75, 80, 86, 88, 96, 110, 116, 117, 175, 176-77, 208-09, 229-30, 231, 260-61
Clorindy, the Origin of the Cakewalk, 151
Lyrics of Lowly Life, 74, 76, 176
Lyrics of the Hearthside, 230
Oak and Ivy, 72, 74
Sport of the Gods, 180, 242
The Uncalled, 180, 190
Durem, Ray, 111

Early, Eleanor, 248
Easton, Sidney, 153
Ellis, Helen, 136
Ellison, Ralph, 29, 35, 192, 227, 246, 254, 280, 281, 286, 340, 353-65
The Invisible Man, 251, 287, 298, 353, 357-65
Shadow and Act, 353
Emanuel, James A., 111
The Treehouse, 113
Evans, Mari, 111, 113

Fabio, Sarah Webster, 113
Fair, Ronald, 286
Fauset, Arthur Huff, 8, 31, 255

Fauset, Jessie Redmond, 88, 133, 254
The Chinaberry Tree, 243
The Marshalls, 181
There Is Confusion, 181, 241
Federal Writers' Project
New York City Guide, 248
Ferrell, Rick, 148
Fields, Julia, 111, 113
Fisher, Rudolph, 254, 263
Conjure Man Dies, 154, 242, 243
The Walls of Jericho, 243
Fisher, William
The Waiters, 251
Fiske Jubilee Singers, 38-39, 50
Fly Blackbirds, 158
Forbes, George, 229
Ford, James W., 244
Franklin, John Hope, 104, 254
Frazier, E. Franklin, 242, 244, 253
Frazier, George, 269
From Dixie to Broadway, 130
Frost, Olivia, 248
Fugard, Atholl
The Blood Knot, 138
Fuller, Hoyt, 102

Garcia Lorca, Federico, 244
Genet, Jean
The Blacks, 136, 137, 158
Gentry, Minnie, 140
Gershwin, George
Porgy and Bess, 153
Gibson, Althea
I Always Wanted to Be Somebody, 250
Gilpin, Charles, 131, 132, 133, 152, 164, 236, 261
Giovanni, Nikki
Black Feeling Black Talk, 113

Glanville, Maxwell, 158
Glasgow, Adele, 248
Glasgow, Ellen, 184
Goncalves, Joe, 112
Gossett, Lou, 136, 138, 148
Grave, Milford, 136
Green, Paul, 126
    Native Son (play), 154
    The No 'Count Boy, 124
Gregory, Montgomery, 132
Gribble, Harry Wagstaff
    Anna Lucasta, 155
Grimke, Angelina W., 87, 88,
    124, 178
    Rachel, 175
Guggenheim fellowships, 84,
    99, 250
Gunn, Moses, 136

Haley, Alex, 251
Hamilton, Bobb, 111, 113
Hamilton, Lynn, 148
Hammon, Jupiter, 59, 60-63, 66,
    70, 71, 109
    *An Address to the Negroes in
    the State of New York*,
    60, 62
Handlin, Oscar, 253
Hansberry, Lorraine, 254, 255
    A Raisin in the Sun, 158
Harlem Renaissance, 83, 87, 88,
    110, 241, 254-55
Harper, Frances Ellen, 73, 207
Harris, Abram, 242
Harris, Joel Chandler, 3, 6, 7-8,
    9, 14-17, 19, 31, 183
    Uncle Remus, 3, 7, 12, 14,
    17, 29, 30, 31, 172, 184,
    185, 189
Hawkins, Everett, 177
Hayden, Robert E., 84-85, 88,
    110, 224

A Ballad of Remembrance,
    113
Heart-Shape in the Dust, 85,
    92, 93, 95, 98
Kaleidoscope, 111
The Lion and the Archer, 86,
    95, 98
Selected Poems, 114
Hayes, Donald Jeffrey, 84, 87
Hedgeman, Anna Arnold, 252
Herndon, Angelo, 246
Hernton, Calvin C., 111
Hewlett, James, 150
Heyward, DuBose, 233, 236
    Porgy, 153
Hill, Abram
    Anna Lucasta, 155
    On Strivers Row, 154, 245
Hill, Carl G., 246
Hill, Herbert, 280, 281, 282,
    286
    Soon One Morning, 282-83,
    284-85, 287
Hill, Leslie Pinckney, 177
Himes, Chester, 227, 253, 281,
    289
    If He Hollers Let Him Go,
    239, 329
    Lonely Crusade, 239
Hogan, Ernest, 130, 151, 152,
    160, 165
Holiday, Billie, 196
Holifield, Harold
    Cow in the Apartment, 156
Holman, Moses Carl, 86, 88,
    100, 110
Holmes, Eugene C., 248, 254
Hooks, Robert, 137
Hope, John, 234
Hopwood Award, 84
Horne, Frank, 83, 87, 88, 222,
    242, 254

Horton, George, 65, 66-70, 73, 109-10, 205-06
Houghton Mifflin Literary Fellowship Award, 247-48
Houseman, John, 154
Howells, William Dean, 172, 176, 189, 208, 229, 282
Hughes, Langston, 30, 59, 76, 77, 78, 80-82, 86, 87, 88, 96, 105, 110, 116, 117, 118, 134, 223-24, 242, 245, 246, 248, 249-50, 254, 265, 285, 287
Don't You Want to Be Free, 154
Mulatto, 153
New Negro Poets: USA, 111
The Panther and the Lash, 114
La Poésie Négro Américaine, 111
The Poetry of the Negro 1746-1949, 110
Simply Heavenly, 158
Simple stories, 250
Something in Common and Other Stories, 250
Sweet Flypaper of Life, 250
Tambourines to Glory, 250
Thé Weary Blues, 89, 90, 236, 243
Hurston, Zora Neale, 3, 5, 8, 11, 12, 36, 242, 256
Mules and Men, 254
Seraph on the Suwanee, 257, 278
Their Eyes Were Watching God, 254, 278
Hyman, Earl, 157

In Abraham's Bosom, 153

In Dahomey, 130
Isham, John W., 130

Jack, Sam T.
The Creole Show, 151
Jackman, Harold, 154
Jackson, Mahalia, 4, 29, 116
James, Luther, 157
Jameson, Roscoe, 177
Jeanette, Gertrude, 148
Bolt from the Blue, 156
This Way Forward, 156
Joans, Ted, 113
John, Errol
The Moon on a Rainbow Shawl, 158
Johnson, Alicia, 113
Johnson, Charles B., 177
Johnson, Charles S., 133, 240, 254
Ebony and Topaz, 241
Johnson, Fenton, 76, 177, 220-21
Johnson, Georgia Douglas, 76, 84, 87-88, 107, 177, 178, 233
Johnson, Hall
Run, Little Children, 153
Johnson, Helene, 76, 83, 87, 88, 254
Johnson, J. Rosamond, 151
Johnson, Jack, 193-94
Johnson, James Weldon, 33, 36, 53, 56, 72, 75-76, 89, 117, 176, 177, 218-19, 229, 230, 232, 233, 236
The Autobiography of an Ex-Colored Man, 235, 239, 242, 286
Black and Unknown Bards, 29, 90, 101, 170-71
Black Manhattan, 243-44

The Book of American Negro Poetry, 110, 240
God's Trombones, 75, 76, 80, 90, 110, 236, 237
Johnson, Right Rev. John H., 246
Johnston, Greer
  Mrs. Patterson, 157
Johnston, Mary, 184
Jones, James Earl, 136, 137, 138
Jones, John Hudson, 248
Jones, LeRoi, 107, 111, 112, 134, 142, 145, 148, 255, 268, 349
  Black Mass, 146
  Blues People, 135, 138
  The Dutchman, 116, 137
  The Slave, 137-38
  The Toilet, 137
Jones, Robert Edmond, 152
Joseph, Arthur
  Volcano in Our Midst, 251

Kaiser, Ernest, 248
Kaufman, Bob
  Solitudes Full of Loneliness, 113
Kelley, William Melvin, 255
Kelly, George
  The Showoff, 154
Kenrick, Bruce
  Come Out the Wilderness, 250
Kester, Paul
  His Own Country, 173
Kgositsile, William K., 113
Killens, John O., 255
  And Then We Heard the Thunder, 254
  Youngblood, 254
King, Grace, 184

King, Martin Luther, 34, 346, 348
Kirkpatricks, 132
Klass, Sheila S.
  Come Back on Monday, 251
Knight, Etheridge
  Poems from Prison, 113
Kozol, Jonathan, 265-66
  Death at an Early Age, 265
Kunstadt, Leonard, 250

LaGrone, Oliver, 113
Larsen, Nella, 254
  Passing, 243
  Quicksand, 243
Latimer, Bette, 86, 88
Latimore, Jewel, 113
Lawrence, Carl, 248
Leacock, John, 150
  The Fall of British Tyranny, 150
Ledbetter, Huddie, 3
Lee, Canada, 154
Lee, Don L.
  Black Pride, 113
  Think Black, 113
Lee, Ulysses, 110
  The Negro Caravan
Lewis, Sinclair
  Kingsblood Royal, 329
Library of Congress Archives of Folk Music, 4
Lindsay, Powell, 154
Living Theater, The, 144
Liza, 163
Locke, Alain, 132, 240, 244
  The New Negro, 110, 230, 241, 253
Logan, Rayford, W., 253
Lomax, Louis E.
  The Negro Revolt, 254
  The Reluctant African, 254

Lorde, Audre, 111
  The Lost Cities, 113
Lucky Sambo, 153

McClendon, Rose, 154
McEntee, George
  The Case of Philip Lawrence,
    154
McKay, Claude, 74, 76, 77-78,
    82, 89, 106-09, 110, 117,
    150, 177, 178, 221, 236,
    237, 242, 254
  Gingertown, 243
  Harlem: Negro Metropolis,
    245
  Harlem Shadows, 83, 90, 240
  Home to Harlem, 243
  Songs of Jamaica, 86
McWright, Bruce, 86
  From the Shaken Tower, 95,
    98
Madgett, Naomi Long
  Star by Star, 113
Mailer, Norman
  "The White Negro," 139, 286,
    340, 344, 346, 348, 349
Malcolm X., birthday tribute,
    134, 140, 142, 349
Marshall, Paule
  Brown Girl, Brownstones,
    254
  Soul Clap Hands and Sing,
    254
Martin, David
  Simply Heavenly, 158
Marvin X.
  Black Man, Listen, 113
Mason, Mason Jordan, 86
Mayfield, Julian, 254
  The Hit, 251
  The Long Night, 251
  The Other Foot, 156

Meyers, Pauline, 134
Millen, Gilmore, 233
Miller, Kelly, 229, 234
Miller, Warren
  The Cool World, 251
Miller and Lyles, 130, 163
Mills, Florence, 130, 131, 163
Milner, Ron, 136
Minstrel shows, 29, 129-130,
    133, 151, 159-60
Mr. Johnson, 157
Mr. Lode of Coal, 130
Mitchell, Loften
  The Bancroft Dynasty, 156
  The Cellar, 156
  A Land Beyond the River,
    158
Moon, Bucklin
  The Darker Brother, 246
  Primer for White Folks, 246
  Without Magnolias, 246
Moore, Willard, 248
Moore-Forrest, Marie, 132
Morrell, Peter
  Turpentine, 154
Motley, Willard, 254, 256, 276
  Knock on Any Door, 239,
    257, 279
Muhammad, Elijah, 342, 352
Murphy, Beatrice
  Ebony Rhythm, 110
Murray, Albert, 142
Murray, Pauli, 88

National Association for the
    Advancement of Colored
    People, 235, 240, 247,
    263
National Book Award, 353
National Urban League, 239,
    240
  New York, 248, 253

Neal, Larry, 113
Negro American Exposition, 85
Newton, Huey, 134
Norford, George
    Joy Exceeding Glory, 154

Oden, Gloria C., 107, 113, 255
Offord, Carl
    The White Face, 246
O'Higgins, Myron, 86, 88, 95
    The Lion and the Archer, 97-
        98
O'Neill, Eugene, 125, 128, 133,
        236
    All God's Chillun Got Wings,
        124, 132, 152, 164, 174
    The Emperor Jones, 124, 129,
        131, 132, 152, 153, 164,
        174, 236
O'Neill, Frederick, 154
O'Neill, Raymond, 126, 132
Organization of Black Ameri-
        can Culture in Chicago,
        268, 269
Orlansky, Harold, 247
Ottley, Roi
    New World A-Coming, 246
Ovington, Mary White, 174,
        242

Page, Thomas Nelson, 171, 180
        183, 185, 232
Paton, Alan
    Cry the Beloved Country, 258
Patterson, Raymond, 111, 112-
        13
Periodicals
    Black Dialogue, 112
    Black Expression, 112
    Broadside Series, 112
    Crisis, 88, 133, 177, 235, 240
    Dasein, 112
    Ebony, 251, 253
    Fire, 236, 243
    Free Lance, 112
    Freedomways, 112
    Harlem, 236, 243
    Harlem Digest, 245
    Harlem Quarterly, 248
    Journal of Black Poetry, 111-
        12
    Journal of Negro History,
        112, 240
    Journal of the National Med-
        ical Association, 264
    Negro Digest, 111, 254
    Negro Quarterly, The, 246
    Opportunity, 133, 240, 241,
        243
    Phylon, 112, 241, 249
    Soulbook, 112
    Uhuru, 112
    Umbra, 112
Peterkin, Julia, 233
Peters, Paul
    Stevedore, 153
Peterson, Louis
    Take a Giant Step, 157, 158
Petry, Ann, 227, 251, 256, 277
    Country Place, 257
    The Street, 247-48, 256, 277,
        281
Piscator, 144, 145
Plantation Revue, The, 152
The Polish Lab, 144
Pollard, Myrtle, 244
Pomare, Elio, 134, 136
Pool, Rosey E., 110
    Black and Unknown Bards
    Beyond the Blues, 111
    I Saw How Black I Was, 111
Porter, James A., 254
Powell, Adam Clayton, 365,
        368

Preer, Evelyn, 132
Publishers
  Black Arts Publications, 112
  Broadside Press, 112
  Counterpoise Series, 112
  Heritage Series, 112
  Jihad Press, 112
  Journal of Black Poetry
    Press, 112
Pulitzer Prize, 84, 99, 265
Pullens, Don, 136
Pushkin, Alexander, 202

Rahn, Muriel, 154
Randall, Dudley, 111, 112
  Cities Burning, 113
  *For Malcolm: Poems on the
    Life and the Death of
    Malcolm X*, 111, 112
  Poem Counterpoem, 113
Rapp, W. J.
  Harlem, 243
Reddick, L. D., 246
Redding, J. Saunders, 277, 285,
    286, 287
  On Being Negro in America,
    285
Reid, Ira De A., 242
Richardson, Willis, 124, 152
  Chip Woman's Fortune, 126,
    132, 152
Rivers, Conrad Kent
  Perchance to Dream, Othello,
    255
  The Still Voice of Harlem,
    113, 253
  *These Black Bodies and This
    Sunburnt Face*, 255
Robeson, Paul, 54, 88, 132,
    153, 154, 164, 261, 263,
    319, 324
Rodgers, Carolyn, 113

Rogers, Alex, 151
Rolle, Esther, 148
Rosenfeld, Paul, 236
Rosenwald Fund, 85, 86, 99
Rowan, Carl T.
  Go South to Sorrow, 254
  South of Freedom, 254
Rowland, Margaret
  Son of Laughter, 130
Rufus Rastus, 130
Runnin' Wild, 130, 163
Russell, Irwin W., 171

Sanchez, Sonia, 113
  Homecoming
Saroyan, William, 245
Sartre, Jean Paul
  Black Orpheus, 139
Schomburg Collection, 246
Schuyler, George, 242
  Black No More, 289
Sebree, Charles
  Mrs. Patterson, 157
Shakespeare, William, 128,
    132, 150, 268
  Comedy of Errors, 132
  Macbeth, 154
  Othello, 129, 154
Shand
  White and Black, 174
Shaw, George Bernard
  Androcles and the Lion, 154
Sheldon, Edward
  Nigger, The, 124, 131, 173
Shepp, Archie, 134
  Junebug Graduates Tonight,
    139-40
Shipp, Jesse, 148, 149, 151
Shuffle Along, 130, 152, 163,
    236
Silvera, Frank, 154
Simmons, Herbert, 255

Simpson, Louis, 264-65, 266
Sissle and Blake, 130, 163
Sklar, George
  Stevedore, 153
Smith, Bessie, 3, 4, 116, 196, 263, 318
Smith, Clara, 260
Smith, J. Augustus
  Turpentine, 154
Smith, Lillian, 251
  Killers of the Dream, 257
Smith, Mamie, 4
Smith, Welton, 113
Smith, William Gardner, 277, 281
Snellings, Rolland. *See* Askia Muhammad Touré.
Society for American Folk Lore, 17
Soyinka, Wole
  Kongi's Harvest, 140
Spellman, A. B., 113
Spencer, Anne, 87, 88, 177, 178, 233
Spirituals, 37-56, 212-13, 262
Spriggs, Ed, 113
Star of the Morning, 148
Stone, Ronald, 111
Stowe, Harriet Beecher, 282
  Uncle Tom's Cabin, 129, 151, 170
Stribling, T. S.
  Birthright, 174
Strut Miss Lizzie, 152
Stuart, Ruth McEnery
  Uncle 'Riah's Christmas Eve, 184

Talley, Thomas, 8
Tapley, Melvin, 247

Terry, Blind Sonny, 4
Theatrical Owners and Bookers Association, 153
Thompson, James, 111, 113
Thornton, Willie Mae, 116
Throckmorton, Cleon, 132
Trottman, B. S. B.
  Who's Who in Harlem, 1949-50, 248
Thurman, Wallace, 242, 243, 254
  The Blacker the Berry, 237, 243
  Harlem, 153, 243
Till, Emmett, 135
Tolson, Melvin B., 88, 93-94, 107, 110, 115-16, 117, 118, 223, 225
  Harlem Gallery, 114, 115
  Rendezvous with America, 85, 93
Toomer, Jean, 36, 83, 89, 110, 126, 192, 221, 263
  Cane, 181, 236, 241, 261, 286
  Kabnis, 126
  Topsy and Eva, 152
Torrence, Ridgeley, 124, 131, 132, 133, 152
  Three Plays for a Negro Theater, 124, 131, 152, 173
Touré, Askia Muhammad, 111
Trotter, Monroe, 211, 229, 234
Trowbridge, J. T.
  Neighbor Jackwood, 151
Tynes, Harcourt, 246

U.S. Supreme Court Decision of May 17, 1954, 107, 227

Van Vechten, Carl, 163-64, 233
Nigger Heaven, 242-43
Voices, Inc., 134

Waldron, Eric D.
Black and Unknown Bards, 110
Tropic Death, 254
Walker, George, 151, 152, 160, 161, 165
Walker, Margaret, 36, 85-86, 93, 110, 223, 225, 239, 254
For My People, 93, 239
Ward, Douglas Turner, 136
Days of Absence, 140, 270
Happy Ending, 140, 270
Ward, Theodore
The Big White Fog, 154, 245
Our Lan', 155, 156
Washington, Booker T., 211, 229, 232-33, 234, 235, 281, 322
Up from Slavery, 175
Watkins, Gordon, 141
Watkins, Lucien, 177
Weeks, Ricardo, 248
Welles, Orson, 154
West, Dorothy, 254
West, Jennifer, 137
Wexley, John
They Shall Not Die, 153
Wheatley, Phyllis, 61, 62, 63-66, 68, 71-72, 109, 116, 175, 190, 191, 203-04, 210, 212, 223, 225
Memoirs of Phillis Wheatley, 66, 69
White, George L., 38, 50
White, Josh, 3, 4

White, Walter
The Fire in the Flint, 181, 243
Flight, 243
Rope and Faggot, 254
White theatrical productions featuring black actors, 153, 155-56, 164
White writers on Harlem, 248-49, 251-52, 253
Whitfield, James M., 206-07
Whitman, Albery A., 207-08
Wilde, Oscar, 132
Salome, 132
Williams, Bert, 29, 130, 131, 148, 151, 152, 160-62, 163, 165
Williams, John A.
The Man Who Cried I Am, 366-70
Night Song, 254, 367
Sissie, 254
Williams and Walker. *See* Bert Williams, George Walker.
Red Shawl
Wilson, Frank
Walk Together, Chillun, 154
Wolfert, Ira
Tucker's People, 246
Wolter, Anne, 132
Wood, Clement
Nigger
Woodson, Carter, 236
The Negro in Our History, 240
Works Progress Administration, 4, 91, 154, 246
World Conference of Negro Arts, Prize for Poetry in English, 113

Wright, Ellsworth, 153
Wright, Richard, 36, 88, 154,
        192, 219-20, 225, 237-
        38, 254, 255, 256, 281,
        287, 289, 296-325, 346,
        347-48, 349, 352, 354,
        356, 366
   Black Boy, 238, 301, 308,
        311-12, 313-15, 318,
        319, 322, 324
   Native Son, 256, 276, 286,
        297-301, 303, 308, 309,
        315, 321, 329-30, 346
   Native Son (play), 154, 331-
        33, 335-39, 358
   The Outsider, 296, 304-08

   Twelve Million Black Voices,
        226-27
   Uncle Tom's Children, 237,
        297, 299, 303

Yale University Younger Poets
        competition, 86, 99
Yerby, Frank, 87, 227, 256,
        257, 276, 279
   The Foxes of Harrow, 239
   The Golden Hawk, 239
   Health Card, 279
   Pride's Castle, 278
   The Vixens, 239

Ziegfeld Follies, 130, 152

Addison Gayle, Jr., was born in Newport News, Virginia, in 1932. He was educated at The City College of New York and The University of California at Los Angeles, and is presently a lecturer in English in the S.E.E.K. Program at City College. He has written articles, short stories, and reviews for *Negro Digest, Liberator Magazine, Rights and Reviews, Dimensions, Phylon, Journal of Human Relations,* and *C.L.A. Journal.*